THE INSIDERS' GUIDE® TO

Lexington

AND THE KENTUCKY BLUEGRASS

by
Jeff Walter
and
Susan Miller

The Insiders' Guide®
An imprint of Falcon® Publishing Inc.
A Landmark Communications company
P.O. Box 1718
Helena, MT 59624
(800) 582-2665
www.insiders.com

Sales and Marketing: Falcon Publishing, Inc.
P.O. Box 1718
Helena, MT 59624
(800) 582-2665
www.falconguide.com

•

FOURTH EDITION
1st printing

•

Copyright ©1999
by Falcon Publishing, Inc.

•

Printed in the United States
of America

•

Publications from *The Insiders' Guide*® series are available at special discounts for bulk
purchases for sales promotions, premiums or fundraisings. Special editions, including
personalized covers, can be created in large quantities for special needs.
For more information, please contact Falcon Publishing.

ISBN 1-57380-113-5

Preface

Between them, the authors have lived in the greater Lexington area for more than 50 years. In this time, they have dined in most of the restaurants; been members of various organizations; attended untold athletic and cultural events; participated in who knows how many activities; traveled the highways, city streets and back roads of this region; and interacted with thousands upon thousands of people.

In other words, we have basically done what most people do wherever they might live: We have lived here. And, as is the case with so many of us, we have often done these things without giving them a whole lot of thought. You might say we have tended to take it all for granted.

A project such as *The Insiders' Guide to Lexington* is designed to illuminate the reader, to present him or her with information, insight and perhaps a few words of wisdom. We hope that everyone who reads this book will gain a better understanding of the Lexington area and all it has to offer. The pleasant surprise is that this project has also illuminated its writers. We have learned even as we were making revisions for this, the third edition of this book — you see, Lexington is a dynamic city, constantly changing and bringing new surprises and discoveries. Forced to take stock of our own experiences and do a fair amount of research to supplement our acquired knowledge, we have, time after time, gained a new appreciation for this place we call home.

But a book, however well intentioned and however well researched, cannot do justice to a city such as this. Use it as a guide for further exploration, not as the sole source of your Lexington knowledge. Experience the city and the region for yourself. While we have made every attempt to provide you with accurate and useful information, we cannot pretend to be objective. As an Insiders' guide, this book is inherently subjective, filled with our personal observations, tastes and opinions. As a result, you may disagree with parts of it, and that is certainly your right. We welcome your feedback: If you think we've really missed the boat on something, let us know; on the other hand, we're open to fawning praise too.

Happy reading.

About the Authors

Jeff Walter

. . . co-author of three editions of *The Insiders' Guide to Lexington and the Kentucky Bluegrass*, has lived in Lexington since 1983. Since May 1996, he has also lived part time in Nashville, where he is pursuing a songwriting career. He is putting his rapidly expanding Music City knowledge to use as co-author of *The Insiders' Guide to Nashville*.

Walter, a University of Kentucky journalism graduate, has spent his entire professional career as a writer and editor. His restless energy and desire for new challenges have moved him from newspapers to freelancing to corporate advertising, marketing and public relations and back to freelancing.

His work has been honored by the International Association of Business Communicators and the Lexington Advertising Club. In addition, his song "Baby Ain't a Baby Anymore" captured first place in the country category of the Austin Songwriters' Group's 1996 competition.

In his limited amount of free time, Walter enjoys playing and watching sports (especially Kentucky Wildcat basketball), reading, writing, concerts, cooking and travel.

Walter and his artist/schoolteacher wife, Roberta, have one son, Reece, a budding artist and musician in his own right, and a husky/collie mix named Lyle.

Note: Before the fourth edition of Insiders' Guide to Lexington and the Kentucky Bluegrass went to press, Walter and his family moved to Nashville so that he could pursue his music career fulltime.

Susan Miller

. . . was born and raised — and is still growing up — in Lexington, leaving for only about ten of her 53 years to pursue "educational opportunities" with her husband.

She has a master's degree in health education from Eastern Kentucky University and has been a freelance writer for 20 years. Her articles have appeared in both national and regional magazines, and she was a contributing writer and restaurant critic for the *Lexington Herald-Leader* for nearly a decade. For the past two years she has been a partner in The Write Angle doing promotions for small businesses.

Miller lives on a rustic, wooded farm on historic Boone Creek "where we make sunrises and sunsets a big part of our day."

She loves country life, gardening, antiquing, cooking and exploring all the nooks and crannies of the Bluegrass for stories, but a large portion of her life is spent tramping around the farm with her dogs. "I guess I'm a certifiable dog nut," she admits. "The empty nest syndrome we found ourselves in a few years ago kind of put us over the top." Besides three Louisiana Catahoulas, she has a pack of French basset hounds that hunt rabbits, and five retired foxhounds who are spending their sunset years very comfortably on the living room chairs. "We're the only people who have two living rooms, one for the people and one for the dogs," she says.

Acknowledgments

Jeff Walter

The success of a book like this fourth edition of *The Insiders' Guide to Lexington and the Kentucky Bluegrass* is, in a way, incremental. That is, we as authors hope that each edition is at least a little bit better than the previous one. We build on the knowledge we've gained in the past while adapting with the changes that the future always brings.

Many people have helped me in my quest to better understand this fine city, and the contributions of those who helped in the early going are not diminished by the passage of time. So I'll continue to thank them, as well as the more recent contributors.

In addition to my eternally understanding wife, Roberta, and my inspiring son, Reece — who, for better or worse, seems to have a lot in common with his old man — I'd like to thank:

My mother and father for instilling in me a love for the written word and for encouraging me to follow my dreams; Jim Niemi and Linda Smith-Niemi for their friendship, emotional support and research assistance; Johnny and Angi Howard for their friendship and well-timed social gatherings, with opportunities to (almost) relive athletic glory days; and Adra Brandt for the "career guidance" that led to my becoming an Insiders' Guide author.

For assorted factual contributions and insights: John Bobel, Rob Bolton, Mary Breeding, John Campbell, Marsha Caton, Audrey Companion, Doug Crutcher, Karen Edelstein, Carolyn Edwards, Don Edwards, LuAnn Farrar, Mike Fields, Doug Gibson, Eric Gregory, Tim Haymaker, Al Isaac, Bruce Isaac, Jim Jordan, Art Lander, Eleanor Leonard, Louie Mack, Andy Mead, Ed Moores, Tina Moorhead, Kent Pearson, Paul Prather, Georgia Ringo, Kay Sargent, Dale Sexton, Howard Snyder, Jan Swauger, Martin Taylor, Fred Trogdon, Walter Tunis, Grady Walter, Ted Walter, Vicki Weesner, Linette Wheeler, Deborah Winograd, Dave Winters, the Lexington Public Library, the Greater Lexington Chamber of Commerce and WRFL; and Sharon Thompson for sharing her recipes.

And, for being such good people to work with, Susan Miller, my co-author for the last two editions; and Ruthie Maslin, my co-author for the first edition; as well as the other people who make things flow so smoothly at The Insiders' Guides Inc.

My sincere apologies to anyone I've forgotten.

Susan Miller

The person who needs to be thanked most abundantly for this book is Ruthie Maslin, the original co-author, whose good writing and amazing accuracy made the job of updating this edition a much easier task. Thanks, Ruthie, for going out of your way to fax me some helpful updates for this edition. And appreciation goes to present co-author Jeff Walter for his great writing style and for being fun to work with. He was still fun this year, even though he took on the daunting task of doing two books at the same time — kicking off the *Insiders Guide to Nashville* along with the Lexington update. Another big thanks to Jessica Meyer at the Lexington Convention and Visitors Bureau for invaluable help and for being the most efficient and nicest PR person in the world. Without the dependable advice and descriptions from *Herald-Leader* restaurant critic Howard Snyder I would have had to eat my way through Lexington. And kudos go to

Peggi Frazier at Bluegrass Auto Club for enthusiastic suggestions and lists of some great stores for the shopping chapter.

Thanks must also go to my family: They never lost their patience when I spent whole days on the phone, and didn't grumble too much when deadlines were near and there wasn't a clean pair of socks in the house. And I'm ashamed of myself but truly proud of my dogs who frequently got tired of waiting to be fed and just learned how to eat out of the bag!

Table of Contents

Directory of Maps

Lexington

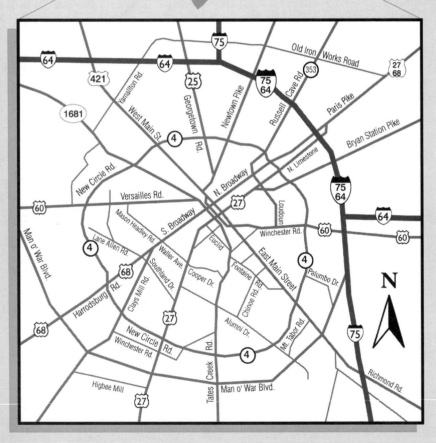

Greater Lexington

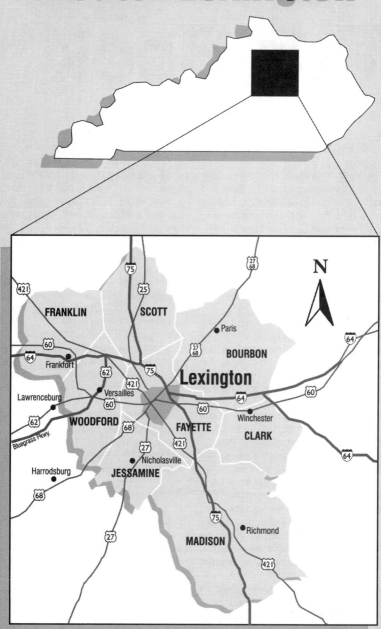

How to Use This Book

This book, like Lexington itself, is a work in progress.

Here's what we mean: The subject of this book is a dynamic entity, ever shifting and adapting. Inevitably, by the time you read *The Insiders' Guide® to Lexington and the Kentucky Bluegrass*, there will be new restaurants, nightclubs and attractions, while others quite likely will have closed their doors or adopted new identities. Frankly, there's not a whole lot we can do about that. Things change. But, with a little effort, you keep your copy of the book updated, as well as personalized.

This is not a sacred text inscribed in stone. Take your pen and mark freely in it to indicate places you have visited, experiences you have had, foods you have sampled, bands you have heard, attractions you have enjoyed. Make notes in the margin to remind you of places you'd like to try again (or perhaps, places where you disagree with your humble authors' assessments). Please do not rely on us as your only source of Lexington knowledge — we are merely your guides on a journey that demands your participation and input.

As a guide, this book begs to be taken with you wherever you go. Don't leave it on a shelf to gather dust or alone in your hotel room where it won't be able to help you in your Bluegrass explorations. Keep it in your glove compartment, under the front seat of your car, in your purse, anywhere it's easily accessible.

You may notice some repetition throughout the book — for example, sites that are listed in more than one chapter. That is intentional. We have designed the book to be user-friendly and flexible, which means you certainly don't have to read it from cover to cover before you embark on your travels through the Bluegrass. Each chapter is self-contained, so you can turn to the Restaurants chapter now if you're looking for a place to get a hearty steak dinner, then turn to the Nightlife chapter when you're ready to paint the town. When you've got a little more time on your hands, sit back and enjoy the more in-depth chapters, like History.

Now, a slight disclaimer: It is conceivable — despite our double- and triple-checking of facts and the thoroughness and diligence of our editor — that you might find (gasp!) a mistake or two in this book. While we hope this is not the case, we also hope that, should you find an error, you will point it out to us so we can correct it for future editions. Address all correspondence to The Insiders' Guides offices:

The Insiders' Guide® to Lexington and the Kentucky Bluegrass
P.O. Box 1718
Helena, MT 59624
or visit our website www.insiders.com

Telephone Service

It may seem strange to have a section on local phone service and how to use it, but as Lexington and its surrounding cities (see our chapter on Lexington's Neighbors) continue to expand toward each other, their phone service needs are changing. It wasn't too long ago that it was long distance to call any of the surrounding towns from Lexington, or vice versa. Now that has changed for some of the towns.

So here's the low-down. Calls between Lexington (basically all the exchanges starting with a "2") and Georgetown (863, 867 and 868 exchanges), Wilmore (858 exchanges), Versailles (873 and 879 exchanges), Midway (846 exchanges) and Nicholasville (885 and 887 exchanges) are all local calls. However, long-distance rates apply when calling between two of these surrounding towns, such as a call between Wilmore and Versailles. The exception to this is calls between Georgetown and Midway which are local calls.

One note about phone numbers listed in this guide: If no area code is given in front of the number, it is a local call from Lexington, but it may not be a local call from everywhere in the Bluegrass area.

Although Lexington is in the 606 area code region, numbers in this book preceded by that area code are long-distance calls from Lexington. Phone numbers in the state's other area code, 502, which includes most of the western half of the state, also are long-distance calls. In other words, any number with an area code in front of it is long distance from

Lexington, and you'll have to dial "1," then the area code and number.

Because newcomers sometimes have difficulty remembering how and when to use the 606 and 502 area codes and which calls are local and long distance, we have strategically placed shaded boxes throughout this text that encapsulate the information in this section.

What's Included in This Book

This book covers not only Lexington and Fayette County, but also the seven counties adjoining Lexington — clockwise from the south, Madison, Jessamine, Woodford, Franklin, Scott, Bourbon and Clark — as well as nearby Franklin County, which contains the state capital, Frankfort. Still, the majority of the places we describe are in Lexington.

In summary, we'd like to encourage you to use this book in whatever manner you find most comfortable — but, above all, *use it*, because we really want to be useful.

As a border state,
Kentucky was ripped
apart, not so much from
actual Civil War battles
as from the
philosophical and
political rifts that
divided families, friends
and business partners.

History

Whiskey, racehorses and burley tobacco. That's what comes to mind for most folks today when they think about Lexington and the Central Kentucky region.

But Lexington's history is a veritable extravaganza of colorful people, exciting events and bitter controversy.

It all started about 500 million years ago, when what is now Lexington and the surrounding Bluegrass region was at the bottom of a large, shallow sea. Today, remnants of that ancient ocean survive in the limestone foundation that underlies most of the region.

Some of the area's earliest inhabitants were the Paleoindians. Arrowheads used by this group of people 10,000 years ago have been found in the Lexington area. The Adena people inhabited the area from about 1000 B.C. to A.D. 1000. However, by the time European settlers first arrived in the area, there were no longer any permanent Indian settlements. The region was used primarily as a hunting ground for numerous tribes including the Iroquois, Cherokee, Wyandot, Kaskaskia, Chippewa and Shawnee.

The first pioneers to view the area as they trekked inexorably westward were awed by the beauty of the countryside, proclaiming it another Eden. The gently rolling hills and lush vegetation seemed to make the area an ideal site for settlement. In fact, the explorations of famous frontiersman Daniel Boone (remember the old TV show?) helped pave the way for the establishment of the first two permanent settlements in Kentucky just a short distance from Lexington at Harrodsburg to the southwest and Boonesborough to the southeast. Both Fort Harrod and Fort Boonesborough have been reconstructed, and thousands of people from across the country visit them each year.

Originally called Masterson's Station, this area was renamed Lexington in 1775 in celebration of the Massachusetts site of the famous Revolutionary War battle. In 1779 Col. Robert Patterson led a group of settlers from Harrodsburg to the Lexington area. They built Fort Lexington to protect themselves from attacks by both the Indians and the British during the Revolutionary War. Fayette County, in which Lexington is located, was formed the following November. In the early 1770s what is now Kentucky was actually part of Fincastle County, Virginia. This area was later divided into Kentucky County, Virginia, out of which Fayette County and two other counties was formed. Fayette County was named for the famous French general Marquis de Lafayette. Lexington became an official city in 1782.

During those early years, Lexington was the site for many "firsts" in American history. In 1780, Transylvania Seminary, now Transylvania University, became the first college chartered west of the Alleghenies. In 1787, the first newspaper west of the Alleghenies, *The Kentucky Gazette*, was published by Lexingtonian John Bradford. And the first performance in America of a Beethoven symphony took place right here in Lexington in 1817.

The late 18th and early 19th centuries saw Lexington transformed from a crude pioneer settlement into a cultivated center of business, agriculture and the arts. One of the agricultural mainstays of that time was the cultivation and manufacture of hemp into rope and bagging for cotton bales. As recently as World War II, hemp used for rope, twine, burlap and cotton bagging played a major role in Bluegrass farming. Today there is a heated debate in Kentucky about whether farmers should be allowed to again grow industrial hemp as an alternative to tobacco crops. While it is now illegal to grow or possess hemp (from which marijuana is derived), it is still widely cultivated in the area.

Among Lexington's preeminent citizens around the turn of the 18th century were the nationally famous portrait painter Matthew Jouett, who did portraits of such famous men as Gen. Lafayette; noted physician Dr. Samuel Brown (who introduced smallpox vaccination into the region); and the renowned statesman and orator Henry Clay, "The Great Compromiser," who moved to Lexington in 1797 from his home state of Virginia. Clay's Lexington estate, Ashland, is open to the public for tours. (For more information on the Ashland estate, see our Attractions chapter.)

Lexington was known in those days as "the Athens of the West." It quickly became the state's largest community as well as a thriving center of commerce and politics. Kentucky's first governor was elected here, and Lexington was also the site of the meeting of the first legislature. The city was the temporary state capital in 1792.

Part of the success and early rapid growth of the city can be attributed to the fact that Lexington was at a sort of crossroads for explorers and travelers. Most Kentucky trails and roads passed near or through the city and, therefore, so did most of the commerce. Lexington's elevated position among Kentucky cities was diminished, however, by the invention of the steam engine and the subsequent increase in importance of riverboat commerce with the South. Through the 1820s and 1830s, river cities Louisville and Cincinnati gradually replaced Lexington as the premier regional town. Nonetheless, the second steam locomotive constructed in the United States was built in Lexington in 1833 by Thomas Barlow and Joseph Burien.

Although it was no longer the queen city of the frontier, Lexington, which was incorporated in 1831, continued to grow and expand its holdings in the Bluegrass region. Eastern Lunatic Asylum, built in 1824 in Lexington, was one of the first psychiatric hospitals in the country. The 1820s also saw the rise in stature of Lexington's Transylvania University. With an emphasis on law and medicine, Transylvania became one of the preeminent universities in the nation. Public education, however, fell by the wayside during the early years, and the first public schools weren't opened until the 1830s.

In 1833 Lexington suffered a major blow as a cholera epidemic wiped out nearly 10 percent of the city's population of 6,000. One of the city's greatest heroes, indentured servant William "King" Solomon, emerged during this epidemic. He repeatedly risked his own life and health by burying the numerous dead left by the epidemic.

In the years leading up to the Civil War, Lexington focused its efforts on the building of roads and, later, a railroad to connect the city with Frankfort and Louisville, all in an attempt to maintain its economic competitiveness with the river cities.

Throughout the middle of the 19th century, the political tension affecting the rest of the country began building in Lexington, where half the population was made up of slaves. By the 1850s, Lexington had grown into one of the major slave markets for the region. Some of the most vehement opposition to this commerce in human flesh came in the voice of ardent abolitionist Cassius Marcellus Clay, a distant cousin of Henry Clay. Cassius Clay published an antislavery newspaper on Mill Street in Lexington, the *True American*, until local slavery proponents shut it down. Clay's paper was surrounded by bitter controversy from the very start. By the time the first issue rolled off the presses in June 1845, Clay was prepared for the worst. The *True American* offices were fortified on the outside with sheet iron, and two small brass cannons as well as an array of other armaments including shot-

www.insiders.com

See this and many other **Insiders' Guide®** destinations online.

Visit us today!

INSIDERS' TIP

The name Kentucky is derived from an Indian word that has been translated as meaning different things, including "land of tomorrow" and "land of meadows."

Photo: Kentucky Department of Parks

Fort Boonesborough was established in 1775 and served as a settling point for many pioneers, including Daniel Boone.

guns and swords were at the ready inside. Clay also rigged an emergency escape route through a trapdoor in the roof and strategically placed powder kegs throughout the establishment so that he could blow up the office if the need arose.

The end of the *True American* did not come violently, however. A vociferous proslavery group of citizens finally succeeded in getting the Lexington Police Court to issue an injunction against Clay and his newspaper, and the offices were shut down just a few months after they opened.

This clash between pro- and antislavery factions was just the beginning of a long and tragic struggle between ideologies that irrevocably changed the face of Kentucky and the nation. As a border state, Kentucky was ripped apart, not so much from actual Civil War battles as from the philosophical and political rifts that divided families, friends and business partners. Hundreds of Lexington citizens joined the armies of both the Confederacy and the Union.

While Lexington's most significant military figures were Confederate soldiers — John C. Breckinridge and the famous cavalry raider John Hunt Morgan — the city was occupied by Union troops for much of the war. Many buildings on the Transylvania University cam-

pus were used as hospitals for Union troops injured during the fighting.

The issue of slavery and the strong adherence to vastly differing political ideologies factionalized the city during the years surrounding the Civil War. The late 19th century found Lexington, along with the rest of the nation, struggling to heal the rifts that cut deep into the lives of nearly every American.

But time passed, and Lexington continued to grow. The federal land grant provisioned by the Morrill Act enabled the state to found the Agricultural and Mechanical College of Kentucky in 1865. This college would grow into the University of Kentucky.

During this time, the local media experienced a spurt of growth as well. The *Thoroughbred Record Weekly* appeared for the first time in Lexington in 1875. In 1888 the first issue of the *Kentucky Leader* (later the *Lexington Leader*) was published as a Republican newspaper. The *Morning Herald* (later the *Lexington Herald*) was first published in 1896. These two newspapers would combine some 80 years later into the present *Lexington Herald-Leader*, which is owned by the Knight-Ridder Company.

The Lexington Opera House, still in operation today in its restored state, was built in

1886. In 1889 the horse- and mule-drawn streetcars that had been used in Lexington since 1882 were replaced by electric streetcars. In the 1890s tobacco edged out hemp as Kentucky's main cash crop: Lexington would later become the world's largest burley tobacco market.

In 1905 Andrew Carnegie donated money to construct an impressive public library in historic Gratz Park. (The old library was renovated in 1991-92 and became home in September 1992 to the Carnegie Center for Literacy & Learning, which houses such programs as Operation Read and The Writer's Voice of the YMCA of Central Kentucky.) Also around the turn of the century, Lexington's own James Lane Allen became one of the nation's premier novelists.

The late 1800s and early 1900s produced some of Lexington's most colorful and progressive women. In 1881 the famous madam Belle Brezing started her first "bawdy house" across the street from the Transylvania University campus. Brezing continued to operate her "red light" establishments in Lexington until she was forced out of business during World War I. Brezing was the inspiration for the character of Belle Watling in Margaret Mitchell's novel *Gone With the Wind*.

This was also the era of reform, and Lexington women quickly moved to the forefront of the suffrage movement, playing important roles in improving conditions for the poor and immigrants. Laura Clay, daughter of Cassius Clay, became a national leader on the issue of women's rights. She organized the Kentucky Equal Rights Association in 1888 and served as its president for the next 24 years, until 1912, and was also a supporter of the temperance movement. Sophonisba Preston Breckinridge became the first woman to be admitted to the Kentucky bar in 1892, and after practicing law in Lexington, she attended the University of Chicago and became the first woman to earn a doctorate in political science.

She also served as president of the American Association of Social Work.

Madeline McDowell Breckinridge, the great-granddaughter of Lucretia Hart and Henry Clay, as well as a descendent of Dr. Ephraim McDowell, used her powerful family's position and her natural leadership abilities to force political change. She achieved needed changes in child labor laws and helped set up a state juvenile court system, a tuberculosis sanatorium, a park system and a playground and model school for poor children.

Despite intense segregation and oppression by such groups as the Ku Klux Klan, Lexington's black community produced many notable artists, doctors and other professionals during the early part of the 20th century. Among these were the sculptor Scott Hathaway, doctors T.T. Wendell and John E. Hunter and jockey Isaac Murphy. However, lynchings were not uncommon during this period, and a Lexington lynch mob created a national stir in 1920 when it tried to storm the Fayette County Courthouse to lynch Will Lockett, a black man accused of murdering a white girl. Governor Edwin Morrow sent in state troops to control the mob, and during the ensuing confrontation, the troops fired on the crowd, killing six people and injuring many others.

It was during this time that Lucy Harth Smith, who would become one of Kentucky's most prominent black leaders, was growing up. After serving as principal of the Booker T. Washington Elementary School, she became the only woman ever to serve as president of the Kentucky Negro Education Association.

The economic havoc that the Great Depression wreaked on much of America during the early years of the 20th century left Lexington fairly unscathed. It was during the first decades of the 1900s that the new racetrack was built at Keeneland, and the Blue Grass Airport began operations in 1942.

Following World War II, Lexington

INSIDERS' TIP

Though Daniel Boone had quite a reputation as an Indian fighter, he reputedly told his son, Nathan, that he was sure he had killed only one Indian in his lifetime of fighting.

experienced a surge of economic growth due to the rapid increase in the number of large companies that moved to the area, including such major firms as Square D, Dixie Cup and the typewriter division of IBM. Between 1954 and 1963, Lexington's employment grew by 260 percent.

Though it was considered a controversial move, a major accomplishment of the 1970s was the merger of the city and county governments in 1974. Throughout the decade, downtown underwent phenomenal physical changes and hundreds of millions of dollars were pumped into development. The Lexington Center, which houses Rupp Arena and the Civic Center shops, was dedicated. The beautifully restored Opera House reopened and put life back into the arts and cultural scene, and the remodeled complexes of Victorian Square and Festival Market added immeasurable appeal to downtown. A huge modern library was built on Main Street, and highrise hotels and office buildings completely changed the skyscape.

On the outskirts of Lexington, during the last two decades, subdivisions, industrial parks, shopping centers and mega office complexes have cropped up at a rate that is alarming for many residents — some of the "urban sprawl " is impinging upon once-isolated horse farms. Lexington has never been more vibrant, but the task of balancing our unique cultural heritage with a sensitive awareness of progress has never been more challenging.

FRANCE

Bring your passport.

Bring your kids.

Exotic destinations, faraway places – there's a lot to be said for them. Meanwhile, what are you doing right now? From hiking and horseback riding to mountain crafts and music, our Eastern Kentucky highlands hold an escape beautiful enough to satisfy your soul.

Affordable enough to share with the whole family. And close enough to enjoy today. Dream vacations in a convenient getaway size. Why put happiness on hold? Call us for your free Great Kentucky Getaway Guide today. (Dept. IGL)

Stop Dreaming. Start Driving.
1 - 8 0 0 - 2 2 5 - 8 7 4 7 or kentuckytourism.com

EDUCATION
PAYS

Area Overview

Lexington, the seat of Fayette County in Central Kentucky, lies in the center of the Bluegrass region, a scenic area widely known as the best place in the world to raise thoroughbred horses. And it also happens to be a fine place to raise families.

The consolidated Lexington-Fayette Urban County, which covers 280 square miles, had a population of 237,611 according to U.S. Census Bureau estimates from July 1, 1996, the latest date for which figures are available. The Lexington metropolitan statistical area, which includes the six bordering counties of Bourbon, Clark, Jessamine, Madison, Scott and Woodford, had a total population of 430,841—an increase of 6.14 percent since 1990 and 16.14 percent since 1980. (These numbers are estimates based on growth since the 1990 Census.) Projected figures from the Greater Lexington Chamber of Commerce show the metro area's population growing by an additional 19,347 people by the year 2000.

"A superior quality of life is often cited by population experts as the main reason for the rapid growth," the Chamber reports. Hey, that's no surprise to us. The Lexington area has earned a national reputation for its quality of life. A recent book, Lee and Saralee Rosenberg's *50 Fabulous Places To Raise Your Family*, included Lexington. The Rosenbergs based their decision on such criteria as accessibility, affordability, climate, crime rates, education quality, ethnic and religious diversity and scenic beauty.

As a result of such factors, people who are born in Greater Lexington (a name we choose to take quite literally), as well as those who move here, are likely to spend the rest of their lives here. For example, many young people from inside and outside the state's borders flock here for their college education and then never go home. Instead, they stay, find jobs and start new Lexington families. Similarly, a number of people within large national and multinational corporations reportedly have turned down better-paying transfers because they didn't want to leave their Kentucky homes. Who can blame them?

Diversity and Contrast

It's easy to characterize the Bluegrass region by the images most closely associated with it: the postcard pictures of green, rolling farmland populated with frolicking thoroughbreds and surrounded by white plank fences; the fields of golden tobacco; the rabid basketball fans screaming "Go Big Blue!" Those are part of the package, to be sure. But there's much, much more. So, while you'll notice that nobody bats an eye when a local radio station's promos call Lexington "the basketball center of the universe," you might also want to consider that this fair city was once known as "the Athens of the West," a late-18th-century hotbed of commercial, political and cultural activity. (For more information on the early days and development of the area, see the History chapter.) In any number of areas, Lexington is a lot more diverse than many newcomers expect, and its diversity continues to increase, as a result of both choice and necessity.

In many ways, Lexington and its surrounding regions comprise a land rife with contradictions. Perhaps that is to be expected in a border state that couldn't decide, as a whole, which side to fight on during the Civil War. The state's ambivalence is understandable when you realize that the presidents of both the Union and the Confederacy are native sons, born less than one year and 100 miles apart. Abraham Lincoln was born February 12, 1809, near Hodgenville, about 80 miles southwest of Lexington. During his presidency, he would periodically return to Lexington with his wife, Mary, to visit his in-laws. Jefferson Davis, Lincoln's adversary during the war, was born June 3, 1808, in Fairview in Todd County, a little farther southwest. Before beginning his military career, Davis spent two years as a student at Lexington's Transylvania University.

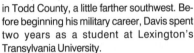

www.insiders.com

See this and many other
Insiders' Guide®
destinations online.

Visit us today!

Although Union soldiers from Kentucky outnumbered Confederates by a three-to-two margin, downtown Lexington features a statue of Gen. John Hunt Morgan atop a stallion. (Over the years, there has been some controversy over the stallion, because Morgan's best-known horse was a mare named Black Bess. Perhaps because of this, a somewhat warped local tradition involves painting bright red a most un-Bess-like portion of the statue stallion's anatomy.)

Here are just a few more examples of Lexington's dual nature:

• While the entire state is generally considered to be in the heart of the Bible Belt, Kentucky achieved its reputation in the international marketplace with what some view as vices: bourbon, tobacco and gambling on horses. According to many accounts, bourbon whiskey was invented by a Baptist minister, the Reverend Elijah Craig of nearby Georgetown.

• While Lexington has many of the conveniences and cultural opportunities of a larger metropolitan area—and is within a little more than an hour's drive from both Louisville, west

on Interstate 64, and Cincinnati, north on Interstate 75—you don't have to travel far to get away from it all on a quiet country road, nature trail or scenic waterway.

• While you can find plenty of eateries serving home-style Kentucky cookin' served up with cheerful Southern hospitality, if you're in a hurry you can also find virtually any kind of fast food you'd want. In fact, Lexington is one of the top fast-food markets in the United States, and several of the nation's leading fast-food chains have headquarters in the state. The city also has its share of finer dining establishments.

A Good Place for Business

Former Governor Wallace Wilkinson caught some flak during his term when he had signs erected on interstate entrance points proclaiming Kentucky "now open for business." How tacky and how mercenary, critics said. Nevertheless, the facts are that the state and Central Kentucky in particular has proven hospitable to a variety of businesses, large and small.

With Louisville to the west and Cincinnati to the north, both roughly 75 miles away, Lexington forms a Golden Triangle containing more than one-third of Kentucky's population and more than half of its manufacturing jobs. In recent years, this area has proved attractive to new, expanding and relocating businesses. The Toyota plant in Georgetown near Lexington is the crown jewel of this Golden Triangle, and it has brought a number of satellite automotive plants to the area.

Advantages of the area as a site for new plants or relocations include railroad access and proximity to two major highways.

What We Mean When We Say "Bluegrass"

Let's talk about bluegrass—all of it.

Close-up

We realize that you might be confused about what the word "bluegrass" means. After all, in this book, we have used it to denote no fewer than four different meanings. Perhaps these explanations will help put things in context.

Bluegrass, the Grass (*poa pratensis*)

When you live in Kentucky, there's a chance that someday, out of the blue, someone from Connecticut or Wyoming or Louisiana will ask you: "Do you really have *blue* grass in Kentucky?" How you choose to answer may depend on your personality, as well as your mood at the time.

If you're not really up to a botanical conversation, you might take the tersely true (though perhaps slightly misleading) route and say, "Yes, we do have bluegrass in Kentucky."

If you're a stickler for accuracy (and have time to go into some detail), you might say something like this: "We do have a plant called bluegrass, scientifically known as *poa pratensis,* but it's really dark green. It does, however, appear to have a bluish tint at certain times, especially in the early morning when the dew is still on the ground. Incidentally, this plant—which thrives on the such limestone in Kentucky's soil and has played a key role in the development of our fine horses and livestock—originated overseas and was brought to North America by English settlers in the first half of the 17th century. It was previously known by such names as 'smooth-stalked meadow grass' and 'white man's foot-grass.'"

— continued on next page

Photo: James Archambeault, courtesy of Lexington Convention and Visitors Bureau

When we say "Bluegrass," we're referring to the stuff that makes Kentucky special.

Or, if you're a sports-minded person (and a smart aleck), you might choose to say: "Yes, which proves that God is a Kentucky Wildcat fan."

"The Bluegrass State"

Because bluegrass adapted so well to Kentucky and so heavily influenced the development of the state's signature animals, the nickname "The Bluegrass State" was almost inevitable. But it's not the only nickname. At various times, Kentucky has also been known as "Land of Tomorrow," "Meadowland" and "Dark and Bloody Ground," all of which have been put forth as possible translations of the Cherokee word that gave the state its name.

Bluegrass, the Region

The term "the Bluegrass," as used to denote one of Kentucky's five primary geographic regions, generally refers to the state's north-central portion, an area of more than 8,000 miles bordered by the Ohio River on the north and west and, on the east and south, by a hilly, rocky, semicircular area known as the Knobs.

The Bluegrass Region, which contains the state's highest concentration of poa pratensis, has been the site of much of the early settlement in Kentucky. It includes Louisville and Lexington, the state's two largest cities, as well as the Northern Kentucky area near Cincinnati, and is home to more than one-half of Kentucky's total population.

Kentucky's other regions are the Eastern Coal Field (also known as the Appalachian Plateau or the Cumberland Plateau); the Pennyroyal Region (or "Pennyrile," as many Kentuckians pronounce it); the Western Coal Field; and the Jackson Purchase Region. In addition, the Knobs are considered by some geographers to be a separate region.

At the heart of the Bluegrass Region is the area referred to throughout this book as Greater Lexington.

Bluegrass, the Music

Bluegrass music is a form of country music generally performed on acoustic stringed instruments including the guitar, banjo, upright bass, mandolin, fiddle and dobro. It typically features high-pitched tenor lead vocals and harmonies. This form of music, also sometimes called mountain music or hillbilly music, evolved from a wealth of diverse influences, including folk, Irish and Scottish ballads and reels, blues, jazz and gospel.

Kentucky has given birth to some of the best-known bluegrass musicians in the world, most notably the late, great Bill Monroe, the "Father of Bluegrass Music," whose band the Blue Grass Boys popularized the style in the 1940s. (For more information on Kentucky musicians, see our close-up "Music: Past, Present and Future," in the Arts chapter.)

Together, east-west Interstate 64 and north-south Interstate 75 put Lexington within 500 miles of two-thirds of the U.S. population. In addition, surrounding counties provide a sizable work force, and the state has shown a farsighted willingness to provide tax breaks and other incentives to attract new businesses. The advantages extend to small businesses as well as big ones, as evidenced by an *Entrepreneur* magazine report that ranked Lexington as number 5 on its list of the 10 best places in the South for small businesses. The rankings considered risk, performance, growth, quality of life and state attitude toward small businesses.

The region's economy was built on agriculture, including corn, hay, soybeans, hemp and livestock in addition to the controversial tobacco. Today, however, the economy is a healthy mixture that also includes manufacturing, retailing and services. Lexington's abil-

Photo: The Lexington Cemetery

Lexington is blessed with a host of natural resources.

ity to weather the Great Depression better than a lot of other American cities has been attributed to the diversity of its economy, and there's more diversity now than ever.

The area is home to a number of thriving manufacturing industries, with more than 50 plants in Fayette County alone. Products include the aforementioned automobiles and automotive accessories, as well as air conditioning, computers, textiles, peanut butter and Dixie Cups. Construction, both commercial and residential, also makes a significant contribution to the economy. Employment opportunities abound in retail, tourism, hospitality, banking, government, education, medicine and communications. The equine industry is also a major employer, providing more than 20,000 jobs throughout the state.

Major employers include the University of Kentucky, the state's largest institution of higher learning; Toyota; the Fayette County Public School System; Lexmark International; the Lexington-Fayette Urban County Government; the Veterans Administration Medical Center; Central Baptist and Saint Joseph hospitals; and Square D.

The role of agriculture in the local and state economy is less significant than it once was, and the controversy over tobacco is likely to bring about even more changes. Kentucky leads the nation in burley production and trails only North Carolina in overall tobacco production. (Bourbon County, part of the Lexington metropolitan statistical area, is Kentucky's tobacco-growing capital; figures from 1992 showed that the county produced 15.1 million pounds — enough to make 2,460 cigarettes for every man, woman, child and infant in the state.) One much-debated alternative to tobacco centers on the possibility of legalizing the cultivation of industrial hemp, which played an important role during Lexington's early years and during World War II, when farmers were encouraged to grow it for rope.

One fortunate aspect of Lexington's industrialization is that it hasn't acquired an "industrial stink." Unlike many American cities with large manufacturing bases, Lexington has been able to attract primarily clean industries that do not cause large amounts of pollution. As a result, if you do happen to smell anything from a Lexington manufacturing plant, it's more than likely than not to be the pleasant aroma of roasted peanuts from Procter & Gamble's Jif peanut butter plant.

Famous Lexingtonians

Lexingtonians have enriched the world in countless ways, providing important contributions to the worlds of politics, business and industry, education, medicine, aerospace, art, literature, music and sports.

Probably Lexington's most famous citizen was Henry Clay, the eloquent and passionate statesman who became known as the Great Compromiser in the early 1800s and who once told the Senate he would "rather be right than be president."

Henry Clay was hardly the only notable personality to emerge from the Lexington area. Another pair of Clays, Cassius Marcellus Clay (Henry's cousin) and his daughter Laura Clay, became widely known for their fiery support of slave emancipation and women's rights, respectively.

Mary Todd, who became Mrs. Abraham Lincoln, was born and reared in Lexington. John Hunt Morgan, whose family moved to Lexington from Alabama when he was 5 or 6, became a Confederate general and the devil-

may-care leader of a band of guerrillas known as Morgan's Raiders. Morgan's nephew, Thomas Hunt Morgan, born in Lexington in 1866, won the 1933 Nobel Prize in physiology, or medicine, for his ground breaking heredity research.

Many other famous people have been born or reared in Lexington, attended school here or achieved some measure of their fame while living in the area. We are proud, in most cases, to call them sons and daughters of Lexington. They include James Lane Allen, a best-selling novelist of the late 19th and early 20th centuries; John C. Breckinridge, who served as Vice President under Buchanan; brothel owner Belle Brezing, who was reportedly the inspiration for Belle Watling in *Gone With the Wind*; businessman and former governor John Y. Brown Jr. and his ex-wife Phyllis George, a former Miss America and television sportscaster; historian Thomas D. Clark; bluegrass banjo legend J.D. Crowe; and painter Henry Faulkner.

Wait! There's more, including Preston and Anita Madden, noted horse-farm owners and party hosts; jazz musician Les McCann; author Ed McClanahan; surrealist photographer Ralph Eugene Meatyard; country star John Michael Montgomery; three-time Kentucky Derby-winning jockey, Isaac Murphy; astronaut Story Musgrave; NBA coach Pat Riley; actor Harry Dean Stanton; novelist Walter Tevis, whose novels *The Hustler* and *The Color of Money* became hit movies; actress Ashley Judd; and Jim Varney, a gifted actor (seriously) who nevertheless is best known as the notoriously stupid Ernest P. "Hey Vern!" Worrell of movies and commercials. And, of course, we can't forget Rick Pitino, the coach who restored the beloved University of Kentucky basketball program to respectability (and a 1996 NCAA title) before leaving at the end of the 1997 season to take over the NBA's Boston Celtics.

INSIDERS' TIP

To appreciate the natural beauty of the Bluegrass, just look for the first dogwood blooms at the start of spring. Or drive south on I-75 on a fall weekend when the leaves are turning gold and orange. Or stop along a quiet country road to savor the Christmas card-like timelessness of a snow-covered horse pasture.

Challenges of Tomorrow

As has been the case in many cities across the country, as Lexington has grown outward and malls and strip shopping centers have proliferated, downtown has suffered. Lexington has taken a number of steps to reverse this trend, with mixed results. Victorian Square and The Market Place were expensive renovations of old downtown buildings into modern shopping and restaurant complexes. The Market Place experienced a prolonged financial struggle before finally closing in the summer of 1994. Two eating establishments, an advertising company and an investment firm are now open in the complex, which is presently called Triangle Center. The adjacent Victorian Square has had its problems, but some tenants, including the Lexington Children's Museum, continue to thrive.

A number of downtown storefronts also have remained vacant for years. In October 1993 the historic but decrepit "Ben Snyder Block" on Main Street was razed after a prolonged debate. To many Lexingtonians, the buildings had come to symbolize a painful choice—preservation or practicality?—with consequences extending far beyond that one block.

On the other hand, downtown Lexington has Rupp Arena and the adjoining Civic Center complex; three top-quality hotels in the Hyatt Regency, the Radisson Plaza Hotel and the Gratz Park Inn; the elegantly restored 1887 Opera House; a beautiful five-story library; a recently built bus station; and three small but scenic parks. It is also the site of the Kentucky World Trade Center, which was created to help in-state businesses grow in the global marketplace.

Tomorrow's business and political leaders can build a solid foundation for successful careers through education in Lexington's public schools, which are among the finest in the state. There are also more than a dozen private schools available, both parochial and independent, in Lexington.

Lexington's public schools, like those elsewhere in the state, are still working hard to meet new requirements set forth in the Kentucky Education Reform Act of 1990, a landmark bill intended to balance inequities among the state's richer and poorer school districts. The act, while controversial, has gained national praise and has been called a model for other states.

The University of Kentucky, the state's largest institution of higher learning, has its main campus here. Lexington is also the home of Transylvania University, a small but nationally respected liberal-arts college that is the oldest institution of higher learning west of the Alleghenies. There are also several business, technical and trade schools within the city.

This brief overview should give you at least an idea of the possibilities that exist for you in Lexington, regardless of how long you plan to stay. The rest of this book will provide more details.

Whether you're just passing through Lexington, planning a vacation visit here or moving to the area—or even if you're a longtime resident who has purchased this book to find out whether you've been missing anything—just relax, take some time to get to know the people and, above all, enjoy yourself. Lexington will be here for a long, long time.

Fayette County and its
six neighbors share
similar histories,
cultures and economies.

Lexington's Neighbors

Lexington has good neighbors, and these communities continue to grow closer together into an area increasingly recognized for its productivity as well as its natural beauty, friendly hospitality and all-around livability. Residents of Lexington's neighboring communities enjoy the benefits of city life along with a small-town atmosphere.

Greater Lexington, or the Lexington metropolitan statistical area, or MSA, as certain bureaucratic types are prone to say, consists of Fayette County and six adjoining counties: Bourbon, Clark and Madison to the east and Scott, Woodford and Jessamine to the west. Most of Scott County is actually north of Fayette County, while most of Madison is south of Fayette.

We have also included Franklin County, which includes the capital city of Frankfort, in this chapter because of its proximity and because, after all, it is Kentucky's capital. Just be aware that Franklin County's population is not included in the figures for the Lexington metropolitan statistical area. Speaking of populations, they continue to grow steadily in Lexington and its neighboring counties, as more and more people discover the benefits of Bluegrass life. The numbers in this chapter are, unless otherwise indicated, 1997 estimates based on growth since the 1990 Census.

The sequence of the county overviews in this chapter is as follows: Madison, Jessamine, Woodford, Franklin, Scott, Bourbon and Clark. We arrived at this order by starting with Madison County, the largest of the six, and then proceeding clockwise around Fayette County, which lies at the center.

Fayette County and its six neighbors share similar histories, cultures and economies. In general, what's good for one community is good for the others through a positive domino effect. A new manufacturing plant in Winchester, for example, will employ a number of Lexingtonians. Thousands of people commute to work from one county to another in the Bluegrass. Many Lexington workers even live outside the metropolitan area and drive an hour or more one way to get to their jobs. Those who do so insist that it's not nearly as tiresome as it might seem. In a big city like New York or Chicago, it can take an hour just to get from one side of town to another. In the Bluegrass, you're at least going to see some pretty scenery during your commute. This chapter provides a general overview of the history, development and current situation of the six surrounding counties plus Franklin County. If you're seeking specific suggestions for places to visit, eat, spend the night, shop and play, see such chapters as Attractions, Restaurants, Accommodations, Shopping and Antiques, Kidstuff and Parks and Recreation.

Madison County — Richmond and Berea

OK, time for a quiz. What do all of the following have in common: one of the nation's first pioneer settlements, the country mansion of an explosive and outspoken 19th-century abolitionist, the site of a famous Civil War battle and the oldest working pottery west of the Alleghenies?

If you don't know the answer, you should take a half-hour drive south from Lexington on

Interstate 75 to Madison County (the location of all the above-mentioned points of interest), where you can find the historic and picturesque towns of Richmond, in the northern part of the county, and Berea, in the southern part.

As Lexington's most immediate southeast neighbors, Richmond and Berea are a pleasant mix of the excitement of the city and the peacefulness and beauty of the foothills of the Appalachian Mountains. While much of the county is agricultural, Richmond and Berea are both college towns with thriving business and industrial bases.

Madison County has about 64,000 residents. It is home to two major institutions of higher learning: Eastern Kentucky University in Richmond and Berea College. Madison County farmers produce some 11 million pounds of tobacco and raise about 64,000 head of cattle each year on the more than 245,000 acres of farmland in the county.

While agriculture service industry forms the backbone of much of the local economy, an increasing industrial base is transforming the Madison County work force. More than a dozen industries with more than 100 employees each now call Madison County home. The growing industrial base includes several automotive products manufacturers, such as Hayes Wheels International (semitruck hubs and brake drums), Sherwin Williams Company (automotive coatings), Process Manufacturing (metal stamping), and Tokiko Manufacturing (shock absorbers for the Ford Motor Company), which aligns nicely with the Toyota plant just outside of Lexington to the north.

Other major Madison County industries include Ajax Magnathermic Corp. (induction heating and melting equipment and industrial and gas dryers), Alcan Aluminum (recycling), Dresser Industries Inc. (pressure gauges), Electronic Assembly Inc. (electronic subassemblies), YUASA-Exide Inc. (industrial batteries), Gibson Greeting Card Inc., NACCO Materials Handling Group Inc. (forklifts), Continental Metal Specialty (metal stamping assemblies, tool and dies), Parker Seal Company (O-ring and shaped seal parts), The

FYI

If no area code is given, it's a local call from Lexington-Fayette County. If an area code is given, whether it's 606 or 502, it's a long-distance call: dial 1, the area code and the number. See the How To Use This Book chapter for detailed information on calling.

Okonite Company (electrical insulated underground wire and cable), American Tape Company, B & H Tool, Kokoku Rubber Inc., and Rand McNally & Co. (distributor of maps, books, etc.). AFG Industries Inc. purchased 60 acres in Richmond Industrial Park South II where construction began in May 1997 for an automotive glass manufacturing plant that will employ 200 people.

Madison County and its two main cities offer the best of both metropolitan and rural lifestyles. With Lexington just a half-hour to the north, two hours to the south and Cincinnati and Louisville within a couple hours' drive, Madison Countians can take advantage of all the best parts of big city living and still be able to return to the quiet beauty of home.

Madison Countians take a great pride in their rich history and traditions. Indigenous arts and crafts produced and marketed in Berea, preserving the fine old traditions of mountain handiwork, are a big drawing card for the nearly 250,000 visitors who come each year to the quiet, rustic town in the foothills of the Appalachian Mountains.

Founded in the mid-1800s by the Rev. John G. Fee and named after the New Testament town where people "received the Word with all readiness of mind," Berea is home to more than 46 arts and crafts galleries, studios and workshops. It is designated the "Folk Arts & Crafts Capital of Kentucky," and many of the finest regional and national artists and craftspeople display their works at three major arts and crafts fairs held at Berea's Indian Fort Theatre in May, July and October. Berea College, which was founded in 1855 as the first interracial college in the South, is also here. (See our Colleges and Universities chapters for more information.)

Madison County is filled with well-preserved examples of period architecture, not to mention a reconstructed fort of frontiersman Daniel Boone. In addition, one of the major battles fought in Kentucky during the Civil War — the Battle of Richmond — is reenacted in Richmond every August.

Established by the Virginia legislature in 1785 (before Kentucky became a state), Madison County is Kentucky's seventh-oldest county and, at 446 square miles, the largest county in Central Kentucky. It was named after James Madison, the fourth U.S. president.

Throughout its 210-year history, Madison County has been home to both the famous and the infamous. Perhaps the area's most famous resident was also one of its earliest: Daniel Boone. Boone and his company of pioneers reached the Kentucky River on April 1, 1775, and began building Kentucky's second settlement, Fort Boonesborough, in what is now the northeastern corner of Madison County. Boone's fort has been reconstructed as a working fort open to the public, featuring blockhouses, cabins and period furnishings. Resident artists offer pioneer craft demonstrations using antique tools from the 18th century.

A little more than a quarter of a century after Boone established his frontier settlements in Kentucky, Madison County received a unique Christmas gift in the form of Christo-

pher "Kit" Carson, who would grow up to become one of the nation's most famous hunters, pathfinders and soldiers. Carson was born December 24, 1809, on Tates Creek Pike just 3 miles from Richmond.

In the northern part of Madison County, you can still tour White Hall, the mansion of famous abolitionist and Kentucky statesman Cassius Marcellus Clay, cousin of Lexington's Henry Clay, "The Great Compromiser." Cassius Clay was one of Kentucky's most colorful historical figures. Known as "The Lion of White Hall," Clay was a noted abolitionist, politician, publisher, U.S. minister to Russia and friend to Abraham Lincoln. He was also instrumental in the founding of Berea College.

In more recent history, baseball Hall of Famer Earle Combs attended Eastern Kentucky University in Richmond before going on to play alongside Babe Ruth for the New York Yankees, where he led the American League in at-bats (648); in hits (231); and in triples in 1927 (23), 1928 (21) and 1930 (22). A debilitating car wreck in 1934 cut short his career as a player, but Combs went on to coach the Yankees, St. Louis Browns, Boston Red Sox and the Philadelphia Phillies. After retiring to Paint Lick, a small community in southern Madison County, Combs died in 1976 and was buried in the Richmond Cemetery.

As the largest county in the Bluegrass, Madison County is, needless to say, chock-full of interesting places to visit. It's impossible to detail them all, but we've given you some of the high points. When visiting the area, be sure to take Richmond's historic downtown walking tour, which showcases some of the most beautiful historic architecture in the area. Information on this tour is available from the Richmond Tourism Commission, (606) 626-8474.

You will also want to spend at least a day in Berea looking through the numerous arts and crafts studios and shops, along with more than a dozen antique shops, all filled with lots of great stuff.

How to Get There

You have three basic routes to get to Madison County, and one involves a ferry. The quickest and easiest route, barring a major accident or construction, is to take I-75 south from Lexington. There are six exits off the interstate in Madison County, two north of Richmond, two Richmond exits and two Berea exits.

You could also take U.S. Highway 25 south from Lexington. You get on this highway from Richmond Road across from Jacobson Park (which is where U.S. 25 cuts off). This is a picturesque ride through the country on a two-lane road. It has entry onto I-75 before and after the Clays Ferry Bridge across the Kentucky River (which is the county line), as well as at several places in Madison County. Staying on U.S. 25 will take you through Richmond south to Berea, where you can again join I-75.

The third option for going to Madison County is much more roundabout, but also more fun if you have the time to do it. Don't

choose this route if you're in a hurry, because the ferry occasionally closes down. Take Tates Creek Road out of Lexington until you come to the Valley View Ferry (about a five-minute ride) across the Kentucky River leading into Madison County.

For more information on Richmond, contact the Richmond Tourism Commission, (606) 626-8474. For more information about Berea, contact the Berea Visitors Center, (800) 598-5263.

Jessamine County — Nicholasville and Wilmore

Jessamine County, like the fragrant jessamine flower, is a creation of great natural beauty. Some of the most awe-inspiring scenery in the Bluegrass can be found within the 177 square miles of this county, formed from Fayette in 1798.

Nicholasville, the county seat, is 12 miles south of Lexington. Because of continuing development on U.S. Highway 27, the main Nicholasville-Lexington corridor, the two cities seem to be growing steadily closer to each other. Idle talk of eventual annexation by Lexington has never been taken seriously, however, because Jessamine Countians are proud of their unique heritage and identity. Although it's nice to be so close to Lexington, where many Jessamine Countians commute to work each day, most of them — believe it or not — probably wouldn't want to live there.

One explanation for the county's name is that it was in recognition of the abundance of jessamine flowers growing along its banks. According to another account, it came from Jessamine Creek, a name bestowed by Virginia settler James Douglas in honor of his beautiful young daughter, Jessamine. While there may be truth in both of these stories, a legend that the girl was scalped by Indians is not supported by historical fact, reports county historian Elexene Cox.

White Hall was the home of abolitionist Cassius Marcellus Clay.

As for the name of the county seat, we know that it was named for Col. George Nicholas, who served in the Revolutionary War and later played a key role in drafting the Kentucky Constitution. It was the Rev. John Metcalfe who named and planned the town, which received its charter in 1812 and was incorporated 25 years later.

More than 90 percent of the county's land is occupied by farms that produce such crops as tobacco, corn, fruit and vegetables and that raise livestock and poultry. The fertile Kentucky River valley in which the county lies helped attract early settlers, who in the late 18th century made hemp a major crop that persisted for three-quarters of a century. At one point, Jessamine County was the largest hemp producer in the state. Proximity to the river — which borders the county on its east, south and west — was also an advantage in the establishment of whiskey distilleries.

The river also made the area an important site to both armies during the Civil War. Union and Confederate troops occupied Nicholasville during the war, and Camp Nelson was established on the river in 1863 as a recruitment center that provided 10,000 black soldiers to the Union Army. As these soldiers brought their families with them, the center became a sanctuary for escaped slave families and thus a symbol of freedom. Despite the Union presence, however, the area was not safe from Confederate Gen. John Hunt Morgan, who stormed into Nicholasville with his cavalry on September 3, 1862 and, within a few hours, recruited 1,000 rebels. Today, Camp Nelson National Cemetery serves as the final resting place for not only Civil War soldiers but also dead from World War I and II and the Korean and Vietnam wars.

According to 1994 population figures, Jessamine County has 33,557 residents, with

INSIDERS' TIP

Thousands of people from Central Kentucky flock to the Living Christmas Tree musical program at Jessamine County's Southland Christian Church each December. The tree is made up of choir members who form the "branches" of the enormous tree that reaches the ceiling of the huge church.

16,121 of those living in Nicholasville. Wilmore, established by the Cincinnati Southern Railroad in the late 19th century and home of Asbury College and Theological Seminary, is the county's only other incorporated town.

Although Nicholasville has in the past been considered a bedroom community of Lexington, Jessamine County has a strong manufacturing base of its own to complement its agriculture. Nearly 2,000 people are employed by about 30 Jessamine County manufacturers, a number of which are located in an industrial park at the southern edge of town.

Some of the larger companies and their products are Sargent & Greenleaf Inc. (high-security locks), Gulf States Paper Corporation (folding cartons), Hospital Specialty Company (sanitary napkins and disposable diapers), Donaldson Company Inc. (dust collectors and fume exhaust equipment), Trim Masters Inc. (automobile seating), Alltech Inc. Biotechnology Center (yeast for distilleries and additives for feed), McKechnie Vehicle Components USA (injection-molded plastics), and McLane Cumberland (food distribution).

Other products manufactured within the county include carbon wire, wood cabinets and other furniture, electrical equipment, tools and dies, packaging film, paint, plastic bottles and clothing.

It is nature, however, that has provided this community with its greatest (second-greatest, if you're counting the people) resources. In addition to the sheer splendor of the palisades area, Jessamine County also has its share of timelessly beautiful horse farms, as is evident during a drive through the countryside. At Keene, a small community 4 miles northwest of Nicholasville, the remains of a late-19th-century Greek Revival-style health spa are on display.

Downtown Nicholasville itself is a historic district, filled with 1800s architecture. The Jessamine County Courthouse lawn holds monuments to Revolutionary War soldiers and to Confederates. The oldest-recorded business in Kentucky, the Valley View Ferry, crosses the Kentucky River between Jessamine County and Madison County, its neighbor to the east. The locals also claim that the first celebration of American independence west of the Allegheny Mountains was held in the county. Incidentally, they still like to celebrate with annual fairs, festivals and parades.

Today Nicholasville revels in its history, even as the clock in the tower of its majestic 19th-century courthouse reminds us all that time marches on. County residents seem to realize that it is possible to pay tribute to the past while living in the present and preparing for the future. They have adapted, preserving the things that are worth preserving.

Consider the tale of Asbury College. It was founded by the Rev. John Wesley Hughes, once-illiterate farm boy-turned-minister who received a heavenly vision of a school. Finding the right location was essential. He turned down one Kentucky site before being invited by a Methodist minister to consider Wilmore. Although the community was then just a railroad whistle stop with a few houses, Hughes found it sufficiently divine. He established his college in 1890, naming it in honor of Francis Asbury, a circuit rider who became the first Methodist bishop in the American colonies. A prosperous little town grew around the college, but in 1909 much of the campus burned. Wilmore residents, fearful of losing their beloved college, pitched in and raised $15,000 to rebuild it on the same site.

Today, Rev. Hughes's impression of Wilmore still holds true, not only for Wilmore but for Jessamine County as a whole. He called it "a model place . . . a good country, fine citizenship, healthful, easily accessible, a quiet place."

INSIDERS' TIP

If traffic is backed up on I-75, U.S. 25 is a good alternate north-south route. It cuts off from Richmond Road across from Jacobson Park and runs south past Berea. There are opportunities to rejoin I-75 at the Madison-Fayette county line, twice before you get to Richmond and then again in Berea.

Photo: Kentucky Department of Parks

Mountain art, crafts and handiwork still thrive in many of the rustic towns that neighbor Lexington to the east.

How To Get There

The most direct route from Lexington to Nicholasville is by U.S. 27 (Nicholasville Road). But if you prefer to travel on winding, two-lane country roads dotted with plank-fenced horse farms — and who doesn't? — you should go by way of U.S. Highway 68 S. (Harrodsburg Road). From Harrodsburg Road, you can head east toward your destination by taking either Ky. Highway 169 or, a few miles farther, Ky. Highway 29.

For more information on opportunities available in Jessamine County, call or visit the Jessamine County Chamber of Commerce, 102 North Main Street in Nicholasville, 887-4351.

Woodford County — Versailles and Midway

One sure way to identify yourself as an outsider in Woodford County is to walk into the county seat speaking French. In other words, when you're in Versailles, Kentucky, the correct pronunciation is "Ver-SALES," not "Vare-SIGH," even though the town was named after the French city where Revolutionary War hero Lafayette attended school. (The county's name also has its basis in the war: it was named in honor of Gen. William Woodford, a Virginia officer who died a prisoner of the British.)

Versailles, which lies about 12 miles west of Lexington on U.S. Highway 60, is closely linked historically and economically to its neighbor. Robert Patterson, who led the expedition that originally settled in Lexington, was also involved in the settling of Versailles. The Virginia legislature created Woodford County from Fayette County in 1788, four years before Kentucky was to become its own state. Versailles was incorporated in 1837.

The Civil War deeply affected Woodford County, as it did much of Kentucky. Confederate forces, aided by the cunning strategies of the omnipresent John Hunt Morgan, briefly occupied Versailles in 1862 after destroying the railroad line and misleading Union troops with bogus telegraph dispatches. Union troops controlled the town both before and after the rebel occupation, at one point guarding every street corner and forbidding the assembly of more than two people. In and near Midway there were also some significant events, most notably the burning of the train station and looting of the town by Confederate guerrillas led by the notorious Marcellus Jerome "Sue Mundy" Clarke and the execution by Union troops of four guerrillas.

Woodford County, which covers 192 square miles, has a population of 21,234, with 7,972 of that total living in Versailles. Midway is the county's other incorporated town; unincorporated communities include Duckers, Faywood, Nonesuch, Pisgah, Troy and Zion Hill.

Today, many Woodford County residents commute to work in Lexington. On the other hand, many people from Lexington and surrounding areas commute to Woodford County, which regularly has the state's lowest rate of unemployment. Major employers within the county include the Osram Sylvania fluorescent lighting plant; Rand McNally & Co., which produces books and maps; and the Texas Instruments thermostat and switch plant.

Woodford County has a rich agricultural history that continues today. The county is one of the state's leading agricultural money-makers. Its limestone-rich soil and rolling land make the area ideal for corn, tobacco, horses, livestock and poultry. It also has a number of horse farms, including such heavyweights as Airdrie Stud, Lane's End, Pin Oak and Three Chimneys. Elizabeth II, queen and thoroughbred breeder, has often visited Lane's End Farm. Its owner, William S. Farish III, is a close friend of former President George Bush, who also has been a frequent visitor.

Like its French namesake, which is famous for its beautiful Palace of Versailles, the Versailles in Central Kentucky is noted for its

FYI

If no area code is given, it's a local call from Lexington-Fayette County. If an area code is given, whether it's 606 or 502, it's a long-distance call: dial 1, the area code and the number. See the How To Use This Book chapter for detailed information on calling.

architecture, particularly the many homes that were built in the early 1800s.

The railroad has played, and continues to play, an important role in the daily life of Woodford County, which, like most of the state, is not embarrassed by nostalgia. From Versailles to charming Midway, where Main Street is divided by train tracks and lined with antique and crafts shops, to the county's rural county roads, a drive through Woodford County is a trip into the past.

Midway, so named because of its location midway between Lexington and the capital city of Frankfort, was the first town in Kentucky to be developed by a railroad company, and its streets were named for members of the Louisville & Nashville Railroad's board of directors. In addition to having 176 buildings on the National Register of Historic Places and plenty of quaint shops where you can buy antiques, crafts and other gifts, Midway is also home to Midway College, the only women's college in Kentucky.

Adding to the county's historical charm are more than a dozen bed and breakfast inns, which are great places to stay for those who want to experience real Southern hospitality in an old-fashioned household setting. (For more information, see our Bed and Breakfast Inns chapter.)

Famous residents of Woodford County have included John J. Crittenden, who served as Kentucky's governor from 1948 to 1950, and Lt. Gen. Field Harris, who commanded the U.S. Marines during World War II and the Korean War.

But the county's most beloved and most controversial son has undoubtedly been Albert B. "Happy" Chandler, who was governor from 1935 to 1939 and 1955 to 1959, and who also served as commissioner of baseball from 1945 to 1951, the period in which Jackie Robinson broke the color barrier and blacks began playing in the major leagues. The Chandler Medical Center at the University of Kentucky is named for him. Unfortunately, the former governor became increasingly controversial in his later years as a member of the University's board of trustees. After he allegedly made racial slurs at a couple of board meetings, many Kentuckians called for his resignation or forced removal from the board. He resisted these efforts and was still a board member when he died at his Versailles home in 1991.

The Chandler family, publisher of *The Woodford Sun,* a weekly newspaper, remains prominent in the county and the state. Ben Chandler, grandson of the former governor, is now Kentucky auditor as well as the newspaper publisher.

Curiously, despite all the significant events in Happy Chandler's life — the good, the bad and the ugly — this author's most vivid memory of the former governor is of his singing, in a voice quavering with emotion, "My Old Kentucky Home" before the start of a UK basketball game.

How To Get There

The most direct route from Lexington to Versailles, by way of U.S. 60 (Versailles Road), is lined with landmarks. Just outside the city limits, you'll go by Calumet Farm on your right and, immediately after that, you'll simultaneously pass Blue Grass Airport on your left and Keeneland on your right. A little farther ahead on your right looms the mysterious castle (see our Kidstuff chapter), which will continue to keep us all guessing until somebody finally buys it and opens it to the public.

For more information on opportunities available in Woodford County, call or visit the Woodford County Chamber of Commerce, 110 N. Main Street in Versailles, 873-5122.

Franklin County — Frankfort

Frankfort, a hilly city nestled on both sides of an S-shaped curve of the Kentucky River, is the site of the creation of Kentucky's laws and a fair amount of its whiskey: (feel free to insert your own punchline here). The city has a storied and colorful history, much of which remains in evidence today. And it's safe to say that history will continue to be made here.

Frankfort, which lies 26 miles northwest of Lexington and has a population of 25,968, is the state capital as well as the seat of Franklin County, population 43,781. The county, formed in 1794 from Mercer, Shelby and Woodford counties, was named for Benjamin Franklin; we'll discuss the origin of the city's name later.

Whatever one might say about today's political maneuverings, they fall short of the drama that marked politics in the late-18th and early 19th centuries. Even the manner of deciding the location of Kentucky's capital would seem to say something — at least to the cynic in each of us — about the state of politics in general. In effect, Frankfort became Kentucky's capital in 1792 because its citizens outbid Lexington and several other towns. Then, as now, money (and real estate) talked.

So did firearms. In January 1809, Lexington's fiery native son Henry Clay became embroiled in a heated debate with Humphrey Marshall, his nemesis in the state House of Representatives, on the subject of British imports. The argument on the House floor degenerated into name-calling and, eventually, a duel on the banks of the Ohio River across from Louisville. Both were wounded, neither seriously. Modern-day political duels are fought with mud, not guns.

It is perhaps unfair to characterize Frankfort only in terms of politics, even though state government has been the leading employer for as long as anyone can remember. Rich farmland constitutes nearly three-quarters of the 212-square-mile county, which also benefits from the manufacture of such products as underwear and automotive parts as well as bourbon (for more information on the latter, see our chapter on Distilleries and Breweries).

In 1751, surveyor Christopher Gist became one of the first pioneers in the area, which was a popular Indian hunting ground, by following an ancient buffalo trace to the Kentucky River. Gist was followed in subsequent years by some of the legends of the pioneer era: John Finley, Daniel Boone, George Rogers Clark. The first settlement, a mile south of present-day Frankfort, was established in 1775 by brothers Hancock and Willis Lee — the namesakes of Leestown Road which runs from Lexington to Frankfort. The city of Leestown thrived for more than 100 years before being absorbed by Frankfort.

The name of Frankfort stemmed from a 1780 Indian attack that killed a pioneer named Stephen Frank. The site of the attack was dubbed Frank's Ford, which was eventually transformed into Frankfort.

In the early part of the 19th century, Frankfort's population was second only to Lexington's among Kentucky towns. Its river location made it a desirable site for manufacturing and shipping a variety of products such as rope, clothing, glass and tools. Its location also made it a prime target of Confederate and Union forces during the Civil War. The rebels occupied the town for about a month in September and October 1862. On June 10 and 11, 1864, Frankfort, then back under Union control, fought off an attack by John Hunt Morgan.

Frankfort's history since then has been marked by adversity as well as by hope. On the negative side are such racially and politically charged events as postwar Ku Klux Klan violence, the 1900 assassination of Democratic gubernatorial candidate William Goebel and continuing revelations of corruption by elected officials. On the plus side are the 1882 opening of the Clinton Street School, an educational landmark for black children, and the founding five years later of the State Normal School for Colored Persons, the teacher-training school that became Kentucky State University. The verdict is still out on the Kentucky Education Reform Act, the complex 1990 legislation that, in the name of equity, has funda-

mentally changed the way the state's school systems operate. (See our Education chapter.)

These and other developments ensure that when Kentuckians think about their future, it will be hard for them to avoid thinking about Frankfort.

How To Get There

To get to Frankfort from Lexington, take U.S. 60 (Versailles Road) east. At the red light on the outskirts of Versailles, where you see a shopping center on your right and a number of fast-food restaurants on both sides of the road, U.S. 60 turns right and heads north. You're about halfway there: It's about 13 more miles to the capital city.

If you'd like a pleasant alternate route, take Leestown Road (U.S. Highway 421) from Lexington. It's two lanes all the way, but you won't mind as you wind past miles of farms bounded by stone and plank fences beneath a shady canopy of old trees. If you're driving, try to remember to keep your eyes on the road. You can take Ky. Highway 1681 (Old Frankfort Pike), which will eventually get you to the capital after lazily winding past Midway and some prime Bluegrass green space.

For more information on opportunities available in Franklin County, call or visit the Frankfort/Franklin County Tourist and Convention Commission, 100 Capitol Avenue, (502) 875-8687.

Scott County — Georgetown, Stamping Ground and Sadieville

Indians. Settlers. A Baptist minister. Bourbon whiskey. George Washington. Buffalo. Railroads. A college. A Japanese auto plant. A National Football League team.

Throw these disparate elements together,

stir with controversy, mix in a couple of obligatory visits by our old friend John Hunt Morgan and, finally, add the likelihood of a happy ending. You've got the makings for one heck of an epic novel — or the true story of Scott County, Kentucky.

Georgetown, the seat of the 286-square-mile county, lies 7 miles north of Lexington, little more than the proverbial stone's throw away on I-75. In fact, Scott County is descended from Fayette County. It was created from Woodford County, an offspring of Fayette County, on June 1, 1792, one of two counties established by Kentucky's first legislature. The county was named for Gen. Charles Scott, governor from 1802 to 1812. The city, named in honor of the first president of the United States, was first called George Town and then Georgetown.

The county population as of 1995 was 27,813, and Georgetown's was 13,353. Tiny Stamping Ground and Sadieville, with just a few hundred people between them, are also incorporated towns in the county.

Since the opening in late 1987 of the Toyota Motor Manufacturing Company's Camry plant, Scott County's contributions to Greater Lexington's economy, and to that of the entire state, have increased exponentially. The original $800 million manufacturing-facility investment has grown to more than $2 billion through an expansion plant and the addition of plants to produce power trains, V-6 engines and Toyota's flagship, Avalon. Toyota, which employs more than 7,000 people in Kentucky, was scheduled to begin production of the new Toyota Sienna minivan in August of 1997.

Although controversy was generated by the generous package of tax breaks, industrial-development bonds funding and other incentives that the state offered to land Toyota, the decision appears to be paying off. Toyota's arrival has helped lure more than 50 automotive-related plants to the state, and the company has made significant contributions to public schools, colleges, universities and charities in the area. Meanwhile, the cars made in Georgetown have several times earned J.D. Power Quality Awards as the best-built cars in the nation.

Scott County's industrial base also includes Johnson Controls' automotive seating plant; The GCA Group, which produces wiring harnesses; Hoover Group, wire products; and The Molding Company, injection molders. The Scott County School System, Georgetown College, Winn-Dixie, city and county government, Scott General Hospital, Kroger and Kmart are also major community employers. The county and the state received another boost in August 1996 when the NFL's Cincinnati Bengals reached a seven-year agreement with Georgetown College to hold their summer training camp at a new facility built by the college. The Bengals, whose home is just 60 miles north of Georgetown, began training here in July 1997. Meanwhile, tourism officials expect the arrangement to bring hundreds of thousands of dollars into the county and more than $2 million into the state. (For more information about the Bengals' training camp, see our Big Blue Basketball and Other Spectator Sports chapter.)

But let's flash back for a moment to earlier times, more than 200 years ago when the area was truly a wild place where buffalo roamed — hence the name Stamping Ground for one of the county's towns — and there was not a sushi bar to be found. The main characteristic of the area then was its untamed beauty: rich and verdant forests, gracefully rolling hillsides, springs. These features were to set the tone for Georgetown's early economy, which remained almost exclusively agricultural until just before the Civil War.

The area's recorded history began in 1774 when a surveyor named John Floyd, a member of a party that was locating land warrants for French and Indian War veterans, discovered a spring near present-day Elkhorn Creek. He named it Royal Spring and claimed 1,000 acres but did not settle there. The probable first settlers in the area were the John McClelland family from Pennsylvania, who built a cabin at Royal Spring in October 1775. In July 1776, as democracy was being born on the East Coast, a group of soldiers and explorers that included Daniel Boone's contemporary Simon Kenton built a fort on the spring bluff. But after an Indian attack on the fort just four days after Christmas in 1776, the settlers took the hint and left.

It wasn't until 1782 that any further settlement was attempted. The Rev. Elijah Craig arrived with some members of his Baptist congregation, intent on founding a settlement called Lebanon. The Virginia legislature incorporated the town in 1784 and six years later renamed it George Town. It officially became Georgetown in 1846.

Rev. Craig was an enterprising sort who held a variety of skills in addition to preaching. He grew hemp for rope, made paper, established a fulling mill for the treatment of cloth and, according to some accounts, invented bourbon whiskey. He also established a school that was a precursor to Georgetown College, the first Baptist college west of the Alleghenies.

The county's farms produced large quantities of livestock, as well as corn, flax, fruits and vegetables and hemp, which soon was supplanted by tobacco as the major crop. Later, manufacturing facilities turned the wealth of raw materials into such goods as whiskey, rope, lumber, paper, flour, meal and cloth.

Scott County's sympathies during the Civil War ran almost 10-to-1 in favor of the Confederacy, and Scott Countian George W. Johnson was even elected Kentucky's provisional Confederate governor in 1861. Nevertheless, John Hunt Morgan and his men made two uninvited visits to Georgetown in 1862 and 1864, wreaking their usual havoc and, on the first occasion, camping for two days on the courthouse lawn.

These raids set back progress a little, but the resilient county quickly recovered with help from the railroads, which provided connections with Louisville, Frankfort, Versailles, Paris, Cincinnati and more distant destinations like Nashville and New Orleans. (Incidentally, if Georgetown residents hold a grudge against Morgan, they don't show it. Each June, more than 500 Civil War buffs gather to reenact one of his raids.) Sadieville was formed in the late 1870s as a shipping connection on the Cincinnati Southern line. Industrialization began to take off in the years after World War II, and

in recent years, Scott County's accessibility via railroads and Interstates 64 and 75 has continued to be instrumental in its industrial development.

Famous Scott Countians, in addition to the ones mentioned earlier in this section, include James Campbell Cantrill, a former state and U.S. representative who in the first part of the century helped bring about more equitable market prices for farmers; and James Fisher Robinson, who served as Kentucky governor from 1862 to '63, the midst of the Civil War.

How To Get There

From Lexington, take I-75 N. That's the quick and easy way. For added enjoyment, however, take U.S. 25 (Georgetown Road).

For more information on opportunities available in Scott County, call or visit the Georgetown-Scott County Tourism Commission, 160 E. Main Street in Georgetown, 863-2547.

Bourbon County — Paris

Just think miles of horse farms (around 100, some of them world famous) where leggy thoroughbreds graze in grassy paddocks bound by black four-board fences and old stone fences, and a pretty downtown Main Street with Victorian buildings where the locals still go to get a haircut. Many downtown businesses have disappeared in the past few years, but there's a heavy concentration of antique shops, homestyle restaurants and boutiques on Main Street, and three excellent bed and breakfasts in town (see our bed and breakfast chapter), indicating Paris is getting serious about attracting more tourists. On the drawing board (and with federal and community funding in place) are plans to lay new brick sidewalks and install period lightposts downtown. The Queen of England had visited this charming county — not once, but three times in the past decade.

INSIDERS' TIP

Central Kentuckians appreciate the crystal-clear taste of Highbridge Spring bottled water from Jessamine County.

Did we say bourbon? Did you fall for the old Kentucky myth that Bourbon County is dry while Christian County is wet? You believed it? Well, so did we. Many historical accounts by reputable Kentucky writers, to this day, say that you can't buy an alcoholic beverage in Bourbon County. We just want to set the record straight: The county is indeed wet and has been since the days of prohibition. You won't have any trouble finding you-know-what in Bourbon County.

As for the famous branchwater that's said to give Kentucky bourbon a little something extra, it's basically regular old stream water. Old-timey Kentuckians thought branchwater (one word) was much more dramatic and had more of a ring to it. It's up in the air which county first produced bourbon but because the beverage was named after the county and because it is known that there were at least 25 distilleries in the county in 1791, residents here think they have a pretty strong case for its point of origin. In addition, the first known advertisement for bourbon appeared in the *Western Citizen*, a Bourbon County newspaper, on June 26, 1821. At any rate, the natives love to sit around on the porch and argue about it.

Paris, the county seat of Bourbon County, is about 15 miles northeast of Lexington in one of the most beautiful regions of the Bluegrass. In fact, Paris and the surrounding countryside seem to typify what people picture in their mind's eye when they think of Bluegrass horse country. Some of the most famous Kentucky horse farms are here, including Claiborne Farm, Stone Farm and Stoner Creek Stud.

While it had some pioneer residents as early as 1776, the town was officially established in 1789 by the Virginia legislature. It was originally called Hopewell after the New Jersey hometown of Lawrence Protzman, who donated 250 acres for the establishment of a county seat in the mid-1780s. The official name was changed to Paris in 1790 to correspond with the naming of the county after the French royal house of Bourbon in appreciation of its help during the Revolutionary War.

Bourbon County was the fifth of nine counties formed by the Virginia Assembly before Kentucky became a state. In fact, Bourbon County was formed from part of Fayette County.

Paris has had its share of famous residents and visitors over the years. Historic Duncan Tavern, built in 1788, hosted pioneer explorers Daniel Boone and Simon Kenton.

In 1798 the Kentucky legislature established the Bourbon Academy in Paris on 6,000 acres of land. Lyle's Female Academy opened for classes in 1806. Just 20 years later, Paris served as a temporary home to a famous American educator, William H. McGuffey, author of the McGuffey Reader, while he was on a break from Washington College.

Paris has another permanent famous inhabitant. John Fox Jr., Bourbon County native and author of such famous local color novels as *The Little Shepherd of Kingdom Come*, is buried in the Paris Cemetery.

Not to be overlooked are Bourbon County's famous animal residents. Among the great thoroughbred racehorses associated with this county are Secretariat (who in 1973 became the first winner of the Triple Crown since Citation in 1948), Riva Ridge and Swale.

Paris has some unique places to eat. Try Amelia's Field Country Inn for country French, or Louie's if you want to rub elbows with the locals.

While horse breeding and tobacco dominate Bourbon County's economy, a handful of manufacturing plants also provide jobs in Paris. However, the county has one of the smallest growth patterns because of a lack of new jobs — and because Paris isn't accessible by interstate or four-lane highway. The two-lane, 20-mile stretch of Paris Pike that connects the town to Lexington boasts some of the most beautiful horse farms in the country, yet it's one of the most heavily traveled and dangerous roads in the Bluegrass because everybody seems to be in a hurry.

To outsiders, Paris is a charming reminder of how small towns used to be: slow-paced and agricultural with residents who have a strong loyalty to their past. We recently attended a Bourbon County Historical Society dinner and one woman at our table proudly announced that her family settled in Bourbon County before Kentucky became a state. This loyalty is what Bourbon County is all about, what makes it unique, and what you'll inevitably feel when you visit.

How To Get There

To get to historic Paris and Bourbon County, take U.S. 68/27 northeast out of Lexington. Also known as Paris Pike, this road meanders through some of the most beautiful horse-farm country in the Bluegrass. Famous horse farms you will pass on the way from Lexington include Gainesway, Greentree Stud, Walmac, C.V. Whitney, Duntreath and Manderly. In total, there are more than a dozen horse farms along Paris Pike.

An added sightseeing bonus is the miles of old hand-laid stone fences that line Paris Pike between Paris and Lexington. Keep in mind that, traffic-wise, it's one of our most dangerous roads because it's only two lanes and it's heavily travelled.

Clark County — Winchester

When you visit Winchester in Clark County, Lexington's closest eastern neighbor (just 16 miles on I-64), don't be surprised to see lots of folks drinking something out of bright green bottles. The soft drink, Ale-8-One, is produced right in Winchester.

Ale-8-One got its name from a name-the-soft-drink contest held in the 1920s by G.L. Wainscott, who developed the formula for the drink. The winning entry was Ale-8-One — "A Late One." The name, and the popularity of the drink, stuck. Ask Clark Countians why they like Ale-8-One more than other soft drink, and they'll be hard-pressed to pinpoint just what it is that makes this drink so unusual. It has a taste reminiscent of ginger ale, but it's less fizzy and less gingery. Actually, it doesn't taste that much like ginger ale at all, yet it doesn't taste like 7UP or Sprite, either. The taste is subtle, understated; it grows on you. The best idea is to buy one — Winchester Insiders say the version in ice-cold 12-ounce returnable bottles tastes best.

If you like the drink enough, you might decide to visit the Ale-8-One bottling plant. It's been bottled in Winchester since 1926. Tours of the plant are offered Monday through Thursday, 8:30 AM to 4:30 PM, and visitors are asked to call in advance, (800) 736-2538, if they want to take the free tour of the plant. The Ale-8-One boutique is open Monday through Friday, 8:30 AM to 4:30 PM. To get there, take the Van Meter Road Exit off I-64 to Carol Road.

However, there is more to Winchester than its soft drinks.

Photo: Berea College Crafts

The Log House Craft Gallery is a showcase for the crafts created at Berea College.

The city and county have a long and rich history as one of the state's oldest settlements. Clark County was established in December 1792, Kentucky's ninth county, the same year Kentucky became a state. John Baker named the city after his hometown of Winchester, Virginia, which was named for the city in England that is home to the beautiful Winchester Cathedral. The county itself was named for one of America's best-known heroes of the American Revolution in the West, Gen. George Rogers Clark.

Some of the earliest inhabitants of the area were the Shawnee, who farmed and hunted on about 3,500 acres in the southeastern part of the county. Archaeologists are still looking for the exact location of the Shawnee village named Eskippakithiki, which means "blue lick," thus named because of the salt-and-sulphur springs that attracted game to the area.

Famed Kentucky statesman Henry Clay gave his first and last Kentucky speeches in Winchester. Clay also practiced law in the Clark County Courthouse.

Clark County is also the birthplace of one of Kentucky's most famous sculptors, Joel Tanner Hart, in 1810. Hart's first experience with sculpting was as a headstone engraver for a local marble company. He later studied in Europe and went on to create some of the state's greatest sculptures, including famous busts of Cassius Marcellus Clay, Andrew Jackson and John Jordan Crittenden, as well as a full statue of Henry Clay that took more than a decade to complete. You can find a historical marker on Mount Sterling Road commemorating Hart's birthplace.

One of Winchester's more recent claims to fame is that much of the movie *The Flim-Flam Man* was filmed in Clark County.

Today, Clark County has about 30,732 residents. While Clark County has a primarily agricultural economy, several major manufacturing plants and companies in Winchester — including Ale-8-One, Sylvania, Leggett & Platt, Winchester Clothing, Quality Manufacturing and Winchester Farm Dairy — provide an industrial base. Many people living in the area work in Lexington, finding the short commute worth the benefits of small-town living.

Clark County is characterized by gently rolling farmland and picturesque cliffs and palisades around the Kentucky River and Boone Creek. (Don't forget, this was Daniel Boone territory!) However, subdivisions are cropping up, seemingly overnight, in rural areas, and in the opposing groups were arguing over development policies in the county.

How to Get There

Getting to Winchester from Lexington is fairly straightforward. Your two basic options are either to take U.S. 60 (Winchester Road) out of Lexington, which is the more scenic route, or to take I-64 W. off I-75 as it passes Lexington — the more direct route. There are two main Winchester exits off I-64.

Except for the usual rush-hour traffic and a few pesky one-way streets downtown, Lexington is very accessible and easy to navigate.

Getting Here, Getting Around

If you're reading this, you're probably either A) trying to figure out how to get here or B) already here and trying to figure out how the heck to get to all the great places we'll be telling you about in the rest of this book. Well, you've come to the right chapter.

On the following pages you will find information on everything from how to drive around Lexington yourself (or how to have someone else drive you around in a bus taxi, limo or horse-drawn carriage) to how to fly in, call anywhere in the surrounding region or ship yourself out (if you are a package).

If you get to the end of the chapter and you're still lost, just remember that you're in the friendly and ultra-hospitable South, and most anyone around would be glad to tell you where to go (no, not like *that*) or at least point you in the right direction. Plus, except for the usual rush-hour traffic and a few pesky one-way streets downtown, Lexington is very accessible and easy to navigate.

Driving

Ah, yes. The Great American Adventure. Give me a full tank of gas and an open highway, and I'll be one happy camper (if you are a happy camper too, check out our Campgrounds chapter). In this section, we'll approach driving in Lexington from the outside in.

Lexington is conveniently situated on the eastern United States' major north-south interstate highway corridor — I-75. This makes it easy to get here from Detroit and Miami and cities in between along the route. There is almost always a heavy flow of traffic on I-75,

and it often increases to problem proportions around holidays, especially the Fourth of July, Labor Day and Thanksgiving. However, work is under way to make the interstate more accommodating to the large volume of traffic it carries each day. I-75 is being widened to six lanes from Georgetown north of Lexington to past Berea south of Lexington.

There are five Lexington exits off I-75. All but one eventually cross New Circle Road, the four-lane road ringing much of Lexington (more about that later). Starting from the south is Exit 104, locally known as the Athens-Boonesborough Exit (Athens is pronounced with an A as in "ape," unlike the traditional pronunciation of the Greek city). Going into Lexington, this road eventually becomes four-lane Richmond Road, which becomes Main Street and takes you right downtown. Depending on the traffic flow, it takes about 15 to 25 minutes to get downtown from I-75. The speed limit decreases from 55 to 45 to 35 the closer you get to downtown.

Next is Exit 108, or Man o' War Boulevard, named after a famous thoroughbred race horse. This is the only exit that doesn't hit New Circle, primarily because Man o' War is itself an arc (outside the ring of New Circle) around much of Lexington — about 16 miles long. It does, however, cross Richmond Road. Man o' War services most of the fast-growing southern section of Lexington, including many of the new subdivisions and apartment complexes, from I-75 to Versailles Road in the west. There are about a dozen stoplights along its route, and the speed limit is 45 or 50 mph (compared to 55 on New Circle), but you can get, for instance, from the interstate to Blue Grass Airport without ever getting into the downtown traffic.

Exit 110 (Winchester Road) is next in line. This is this author's personal favorite route to downtown Lexington, mainly because, while it is busy, the traffic seems to move along fairly well, and you can usually get downtown in about 10 minutes. Speed limits on this four-lane road drop from 55 to 45 around the intersection with New Circle and then to 35 as you approach downtown. A center turning lane prevents folks making left turns from slowing traffic at intersections.

Three miles farther north is Exit 113. This exit leads out of Lexington on Paris Pike or into Lexington on Broadway. Broadway leads into downtown from the northeast past some of the city's most historic buildings, including Transylvania University, the first college west of the Alleghenies, and the Lexington Opera House. If you are heading to an event at Rupp Arena, this is the route to take. Once Broadway crosses Main Street and starts heading out of town to the west, it becomes Harrodsburg Road.

The final exit, 115, is Newtown Pike. This road is not as congested as some of the other feeder routes, but it crosses Main Street northwest of downtown, so you have to backtrack a short distance if you want to go downtown. Newtown Pike takes you past the famous Marriott's Griffin Gate Resort and golf course complex, as well as past Lexmark International, one of Lexington's major manufacturers, producing IBM laser printers, typewriters, office supply equipment and keyboards.

East-west interstate travelers are serviced by I-64, which runs through Louisville. I-64 and I-75 join for about a 7-mile stretch around the

FYI

If no area code is given, it's a local call from Lexington-Fayette County. If an area code is given, whether it's 606 or 502, it's a long-distance call: dial 1, the area code and the number. See the How To Use This Book chapter for detailed information on calling.

northern part of Lexington, splitting off into separate roads just north of Exit 115 and between exits 110 and 113.

Once you're in Lexington, the key navigational feature is New Circle Road. New Circle is like the sun — you can always tell which way you're going in relation to it. Roughly, Lexington is laid out like a giant bicycle wheel with downtown at its hub and "spokes" radiating out as 10 major feeder roads (clockwise from the south): Tates Creek, Nicholasville, Harrodsburg, Versailles, Old Frankfort Pike, Leestown, Newtown Pike, Broadway, Winchester and Richmond. Many of these are named for the surrounding towns they link with Lexington.

Lexington's three major malls are on feeder roads: Fayette Mall on Nicholasville Road, Turfland Mall on Harrodsburg Road and Lexington Mall on Richmond Road. Blue Grass Airport is on Versailles Road.

Nicholasville Road is a little tricky, because Monday through Friday its lanes change directions. From 7 to 9 AM, traffic going into downtown from New Circle gets an extra lane (making three total inbound lanes plus a center turning lane), reducing the traffic going out of town to one lane. This process is reversed from 4 to 6 PM.

Lights across the road at regular intervals indicate which lanes are in use by whom. Green arrows over a lane indicate you can drive in that lane; white, curved arrows identify turn lanes; and a red "X" means the lane is for use by traffic going the opposite direction. It sounds confusing, but it doesn't seem to cause many problems, so don't worry about it too much. If you end up in the wrong lane, plenty of people will honk at you to make you aware of your mistake.

INSIDERS' TIP

Call 233-1111 for updates about road construction in Lexington and surrounding counties, especially Interstate 75 in Madison County which is scheduled to undergo construction through 2000.

Now to downtown and its one-way streets. Most streets are divided into "North" and "South" segments at Main Street and "East" and "West" segments at Limestone Street. Street numbers start at 100 at these intersections and increase in both directions.

Main Street is one way westbound from Vine Street to the Civic Center just past Broadway. Two flanking streets, Short Street to the north and Vine Street to the south, are one-way the other direction. Streets crossing Main Street alternate one-way directions, with the exception of Rose Street, Martin Luther King Boulevard and Broadway, which are two-way north-south roads.

Traveling to the south of Main Street (the general direction of the University of Kentucky campus), streets running parallel to Main Street — Vine, High and Maxwell — alternate one-way directions until Euclid Avenue, which is two-way. To the north of Main Street (toward I-75), generally, the streets are "numbered," such as Second Street, etc., and run in alternating one-way directions.

Again, it sounds confusing, but the layout of downtown is actually fairly logical and straightforward. People are friendly, so if you get lost, just stop somewhere and ask directions.

If you don't want to try to navigate on your own, you can check out one of the following options.

Public Transportation

About 120,000 passenger trips are made on the Lexington Public Transportation System, or LexTran, each month. The Transit Authority of Lexington offers nine main bus routes throughout the city, plus connecting bus routes to the UK campus that run on 25-minute intervals in circular routes.

To get a bus schedule or to have one of the LexTran information clerks help you find which bus to take to get where you want to go, call 253-INFO Monday through Friday, 6 AM to 5:30 PM. Schedules are also available

at the following locations: the Transit Center, 220 Vine Street; Transit Authority office, 109 W. Loudon Avenue; Fayette County Health Department, 650 Newtown Pike; Lexington-Fayette Urban County Government Center, 200 E. Main Street; Turfland Mall information desk, Harrodsburg Road; or on the route's bus.

LexTran bus fares are 80¢ for adults, 40¢ for disabled people and those older than 65 and 60¢ for youth ages 6 to 18. Children younger than 6 ride free. To get the reduced rates, you must present your LexTran ID card, available at the Transit Center or the Transit Authority office Monday through Friday, 8:30 AM to 4:30 PM. Exact change is required, and once you pay the fare, you can get a free transfer to another bus if you need it for a one-way trip.

If you ride the bus a lot, you can save money by purchasing a LexTran pass. Adult monthly passes (unlimited rides) are $30. Passes for the elderly and disabled are $15. Twenty-ride adult passes are $15, and 20-ride youth passes are $10. College students can get a semester pass for $50, and a summer youth pass is available for $30.

Buses run hourly from 5:30 am to 1 am Monday through Saturday. Peak service is between 6 and 9 am and 3 and 6 pm Monday through Friday when buses run every half hour.

LexTran's "Wheels" service, provided in conjunction with the American Red Cross, meets the requirements of the Americans with Disabilities Act by providing door-to-door transportation for the disabled. Call 233-3433 to see if you qualify for this service. The Wheels fare is $1.60 one-way.

LexTran offers free ride service on the University of Kentucky campus route.

Many people working in Lexington live outside the main metropolitan area and commute to work each day. In connection with Bluegrass Area Ridesharing, LexTran offers two commuter options. LexVan is a commuter vanpool leasing service with 15 passenger vans, and it is recommended for people living

INSIDERS' TIP

Whenever possible, avoid Nicholasville and Richmond roads during peak traffic times.

The slower pace and elegant style of a horse-drawn carriage make it an ideal vehicle for exploring the city.

at least 15 miles from the same general employment area. For instance, a group of people living in Richmond (about 25 miles south of Lexington) who all work downtown might get a LexVan group together. This saves money on individual gas and car wear and tear and parking, while at the same time helping the environment by reducing the amount of hydrofluorocarbons being pumped into the ozone layer from automobile exhaust. LexTran will help you get your vanpool together.

Another commuter service is 233-POOL, an office that helps people set up commuter carpools.

Taxis and Limousines

If you want to have someone else drive you around, Lexington has several taxi and limousine options available.

Holiday Cab, Lexington Yellow Cab Wildcat Cab and United Transportation Inc.
708 W. Third St. • 231-8294

With a fleet of 45 propane-powered Chevy Impalas and Ford Crown Victorias, this consolidated taxi company provides service to Lexingtonians 24 hours a day, 365 days a year. The rate is $1.90 for any call, plus $1.60 per mile for up to four people. Discount coupons offering a 20 percent discount for senior citizens and the disabled are available at the main office on W. Third Street.

Gold Shield Limousine Inc.
720 National Ave. • 255-6388

With stretch limousines accommodating up to eight passengers, Gold Shield Limousine Inc. offers hourly and daily limousine, van and luxury sedan rental and a 20-passenger bus. Limousine rates for six-passenger vehicles are $55 per hour (two-hour minimum Sunday through Thursday and three-hour minimum Friday and Saturday) and $550 per day. Rates for eight-passenger limousines are $75 per hour and $750 per day.

For nationwide travel, Gold Shield has an executive coach that seats 23 passengers. This vehicle is equipped with a galley and bar, restroom, TVs, stereo and CD player.

Happy's Limo Service
1167 Commercial Dr. • 252-1541

Happy's Limo Service, with its fleet of one charcoal-grey, one black and two white stretch limousines, services all of Kentucky at a rate of $45 per hour, two-hour minimum. Happy's has a special one-way rate of $125 from Lexington to either the Cincinnati or Louisville airports.

Land Transportation
Bluegrass Field • 255-4981

Land Transportation offers shuttle service to and from Blue Grass Airport, with fares ranging from $17 to $25 in the Lexington area. Stretch limousine service is available throughout Kentucky for $55 per hour with a two-hour minimum.

Rolls-Royce Charters
111 Conn Terrace • 223-3272

Talk about going in style! The walnut-colored Rolls-Royce touring sedan is the only one in a three-state area. Rates are about $40 to $60 per hour depending on number of passengers and destination and the day of the week. Airport transportation to Cincinnati or Louisville is $90.

Carriage Rides

What could be more romantic than a ride with that special someone in an elegant horse-drawn carriage through some of downtown Lexington's most beautiful areas?

Lexington Livery Company
• 259-0000

Lexington Livery gives you and up to three other people at a time a chance to experience Lexington in the mode of days gone by. Carriage rides are offered nearly every night from 7:30 to 10:30 PM during most of the year. Exceptions are nights when there is bad weather January through March.

Carriage rides depart from the Vine Street entrance of the Radisson Hotel and pass through historic Gratz Park and beautiful Triangle Park during the 25-minute tour. The cost is $25 for up to four people. Reservations are not usually necessary, except for peak times at Christmas and New Year's Eve.

Airline and Bus Travel

If you want to come by air or by land, Lexington has plenty of options to offer at Blue Grass Airport through Delta, USAir, United Express, Atlantic Southeast Airlines, Comair, Continental, Trans World Express and Northwest/Mesaba or through Greyhound bus service.

Blue Grass Airport
4000 Versailles Rd. • 254-9336

Five miles west of Lexington in some of the region's lushest horse country, Blue Grass Airport was transferred to the city of Lexington from the U.S. Army Air Corps in 1945. The 1,000-acre site is home to eight regional and national carriers with 100 departures daily to major cities around the country. Connections to international airline service as well as an in-house U.S. Customs department make international travel to and from Lexington convenient as well. In 1998 one million passengers were served.

There are plenty of new things going on at the airport. Valet parking is now offered, a feature that is particularly convenient while a major new parking garage is being built. (Note to passengers departing from Blue Grass Airport: You need to arrive about 15 minutes earlier than usual because of this construction which is scheduled to be completed by the summer of 2000.) There's now a business center and meeting room, restaurants and gift shops, a game room and lounge. You'll also find a small art gallery with rotating exhibits from local artists. Patients who use wheelchairs can rent customized vans through Wheelchair Getaways, 271-6111 or (800) 458-1115, which can deliver the vehicle — and train the customer on vehicle features — right to the front door of the airport.

Greyhound
477 New Circle Rd. N.W. • 299-8804

About nine buses a day go through the Lexington Greyhound bus line station, which is open daily 7:30 AM to 11 PM. Typical one-way rates include $57 from Lexington to Chicago, $94 to New York City and $111 to Tampa. There is a no-smoking policy in effect for the buses.

Greyhound also has a package express service (call 299-0428 for more information) that offers, for instance, same-day delivery to Chicago for $25 for up to 10 pounds and $15 for overnight delivery.

Whether you're a world traveler with a discriminating palate or the head of a family with a limited budget, you'll find a restaurant to suit you in Lexington and its environs.

Restaurants

We hope you're hungry. If not, you're sure to work up a hearty appetite as you explore the Bluegrass. And, whether you're a world traveler with a discriminating palate or the head of a family with a limited budget, you'll find a restaurant to suit you in Lexington and its environs. You may be surprised by our diversity. Anxious to try the "regional" cuisine? We'll try to steer you in the right direction. In the mood for exotic foods from faraway lands? You can find them here, and we'll share our findings with you. Want to know the best places for a thick steak or some fresh seafood? We'll show you where we go.

Obviously, this is a highly subjective chapter. It's not a complete directory and was never intended to be. Personal tastes being what they are, we can't guarantee that you'll agree with everything we say. Similarly, the Bluegrass has many fine restaurants quite deserving of your business that aren't included here.

We had to rely on our existing knowledge, supplemented with occasional input from restaurant critics and friends. The restaurants in this chapter are the ones we personally recommend. If you have a Bluegrass dining experience you'd like to share with us, let us know about it so we can take it into consideration when revising *The Insiders' Guide® to Greater Lexington* for the next edition.

With a few exceptions, we have avoided the big chain restaurants, the reason being that you probably already know about them. The ones we have mentioned are the ones that we 1) think you might not know about or 2) are simply so wild about, we decided to mention them anyway. You might be interested to know, incidentally, that Lexington and Kentucky are the headquarters for a number of popular restaurant chains. Long John Silver's is based in Lexington, as is Fazoli's, a fast-food Italian restaurant that is growing rapidly. In 1993 PoFolks relocated its headquarters from Nashville to Mount Sterling, a town of 5,000 people about 35 miles east of Lexington. Louisville is the corporate home for Kentucky Fried Chicken, Chi-Chi's Mexican restaurants, the Rally's hamburger chain and Papa John's Pizza.

We have some very good chain steakhouses that keep their parking lots filled: Outback, Chop House, Reno's, Texas Roadhouse and Player's Steak and Ale. And we are practically bilingual now that we have well over a dozen authentic Mexican restaurants in various parts of town. They are all good, and you'll leave with pesos in your pocket.

Arirang Garden is a Korean restaurant with a loyal following, and Thai cuisine has definitely caught on, especially around the University of Kentucky campus. We have more than two dozen Chinese restaurants, all reasonable and reliable.

Restaurants in this chapter are organized by type of food served (barbecue, Italian, seafood, steak, etc.) or, in a couple of cases, by environment (bar food, cafeterias). At times the decision was somewhat arbitrary as to which category a restaurant belonged in, but we used our best judgment. We also included a few restaurants outside Greater Lexington but within a reasonable drive.

In case you're wondering what, precisely, we mean by "regional" cuisine, we'll tell you, vaguely, that the term is a little murky. Basically, as we see it, it's food that originated in this region of the country, was perfected here or is associated with these parts. Most people would consider "lamb fries," catfish fried in cornmeal, and fried banana peppers to be regional cuisine; the hot Brown, invented in Louisville, definitely qualifies. You could also make a case for barbecue, although we have listed it as a separate category. Sushi and cannelloni, on the other hand, are definitely not regional cuisine, although you can find excellent versions of them in the Bluegrass (for more information on regional foods and beverages, see our close-up, "A Taste of Kentucky Food and Drink," at the end of this chapter).

If you want to play around a little, peruse our guide for something that strikes your fancy. But if you want to dress up and experience the best we have to offer, pick out a more upscale restaurant under the "American" category or stick strictly to the "Continental" section of this chapter.

Price Code

Our pricing chart is intended as a guide, not as gospel. Menus and prices change. If you order the most expensive entrees on the menu, your check may be higher than suggested here. We have tried to indicate the typical range for dinner for two, not including alcohol beverages, appetizers, dessert, tax or tip.

$	$15 or less
$$	$16 to $25
$$$	$26 to $40
$$$$	$41 and more

If you have any questions about prices or menu offerings, it certainly doesn't hurt to call the restaurant in advance. Most of these restaurants serve beer, wine and mixed drinks, and most accept credit cards (we tell you if a restaurant does not accept credit cards).

Some of the more upscale restaurants suggest making reservations; we have indicated this preference in the appropriate listings. During Keeneland meets and on nights when the University of Kentucky has a basketball or football game, it's a good idea to phone ahead anyway if you want to avoid a long wait.

While dining in the Bluegrass, you'll find that, although Kentucky may technically be a border state, it's brimming with that characteristic commonly known as Southern hospitality. Don't take offense if your waitress calls you "honey" — it just means she's enjoying the opportunity to serve you. And you'll surely enjoy the fine dining experiences that await you here.

In addition, if "fine dining experience" to you connotes quantity as well as quality, you can find a variety of buffet opportunities here. Also, unless we say otherwise our choices are

open for both lunch and dinner daily, and we let you know which spots serve breakfast or offer a late-night menu.

We know you're hungry by now, so dig in. Perhaps we'll see you at one of our favorite establishments. In the meantime, good eatin' (that's Kentuckian for *bon appetit*)!

American and Regional

A.P. Suggins Bar & Grill
$ • 345 Romany Rd. • 268-0709

A.P. Suggins is best-known as a true neighborhood restaurant that probably hasn't fed more than a handful of out-of-towners in its entire lifetime, so that's why we're including it. With its regional cuisine, it's a good place to try a hot Brown (made with country ham, which is not authentic but sure is good), banana peppers or catfish. Or just drop by to rub elbows with the locals and have a burger and brew.

Applebee's Neighborhood Grill & Bar
$ • 4009 Nicholasville Rd. • 271-9393
$ • 2573 Richmond Rd. • 266-3327
$ • Beaumont Center, Harrodsburg and New Circle Rds. • 224-1166
$ • Hamburg Pavilion • Man o' War Blvd. at I-75
$ • Carriage Gate Shopping Center, Richmond • (606) 624-1224
$ • 1525 W. Lexington Ave., Winchester • (606) 737-0111

This increasingly popular chain has earned a reputation as a fun place to eat for kids as well as adults. It's a perfect place to go for appetizers or for a meal, with an emphasis on such satisfying "finger foods" as fajitas and quesadillas; sandwiches, including blackened chicken; and the ever-popular riblet basket. There's also pasta, chicken, steak and seafood and some low-fat items with 6 grams of fat or less (the fat grams are counted for you).

Beaumont Inn
$$ • 638 Beaumont Dr., off U.S. Hwy. 127, Harrodsburg • (606) 734-3381

The stately building, an 1845 Greek Revival brick mansion with Ionic columns, was once the Greenville Female Institute. Since

1918, however, it has been Beaumont Inn, and it is practically synonymous with Kentucky hospitality. The interior is filled with family portraits and heirlooms. The Dedman family has run the inn for four generations, serving such traditional favorites as yellow-legged fried chicken, 2-year-old cured country ham and its famous corn pudding. Lunch and dinner are served during certain seating times; brunch is served on Sunday. The restaurant closes after Christmas and reopens in March.

Boone Tavern
$$ • Main St., Berea • (606) 986-9358

Boone Tavern, at the center of picturesque Berea, is operated by students at nearby Berea College. The dining room is pretty and traditional, and the kids are required to sit up straight (just kidding!). The limited but dependable menu highlights traditional Kentucky cooking in plentiful quantities. The servers will keep you supplied with plenty of vegetables, and you'll probably want a second or even third helping of the signature spoonbread. The tavern is open daily for breakfast, lunch and dinner. Reservations are required, and men must wear jackets at dinner. Unbelievably, if you don't wear one, they'll provide you with one! No alcohol is served.

Buffalo & Dad's
$ • 805 N. Broadway • 252-9325

During the summer you'll often find adult softball teams still in uniform at Buffalo & Dad's chowing down and ordering a beer or two. The menu is surprisingly diverse for a little place with such a laid-back tavern atmosphere. You can get burgers, grilled steaks and pork chops, lamb fries, grilled or blackened swordfish, fried seafood and frog legs and more. And to ensure that you feel at home, the extensive sandwich menu even includes fried bologna sandwiches. Lunch and dinner are served daily; breakfast is served Monday through Saturday.

Cafe Jennifer at The Woodlands
$$ • 111 Woodland Ave. • 255-0709

This pretty restaurant on the ground floor of The Woodlands condominium complex near downtown is one of the most dependable places in town to eat, but many people forget about it because it's so tucked away. With hunter green walls, lots of airy windows with flowered window treatments, white tablecloths and big splashes of art, it's one of the only places to get all our regional specialties: a hot Brown made with country ham; chicken or salmon croquettes; chicken pot pie (on Thursday); and bread pudding for dessert. The menu is extensive and runs the gamut from comfort food (meatloaf, fried chicken and chicken livers) to steaks, seafood and pasta. There's a sort of southern gentility here, yet it's quite casual and relaxed.

Campbell House Inn
$$ • 1375 Harrodsburg Rd. • 255-4281

Traditional Southern fare is the specialty in the dining rooms of this longtime Lexington landmark. From the outside, the original section of the Campbell House complex, with its graceful white columns, gives the impression that it's always been there and always will be. On the inside, the food confirms that idea with such time-honored fare as lamb chops, lamb fries, Southern fried chicken, hot Browns, country ham and frog legs, as well as more mainstream items such as steak, prime rib and seafood. A good Sunday buffet is served from 11:30 AM to 3 PM

deSha's
**$$ • 101 N. Broadway
• 259-3771**

It's hard to miss deSha's, with its prime downtown location at the southeast end of Victorian Square at Main and Broadway. Inside and out, this 1870s structure retains much of its Victorian charm. The dinner menu features steaks, chops, prime rib, chicken and

---

INSIDERS' TIP

Shaker Village of Pleasant Hill is a special place to spend the night and eat Thanksgiving dinner, but make reservations well in advance.

seafood, plus inventive daily specials. Lunch is oriented around tantalizing soups, salads and sandwiches, including a hot Brown. For dinner try Maryland-style crab cakes, vegetarian pizza or chargrilled shrimp. For dessert the lemon icebox pie is worth a trip in itself.

Flag Fork Herb Farm Garden Cafe
$ • 900 N. Broadway
• 252-6837

This wonderful rustic cafe - which is located in an old house brimming over with dried flowers, country accessories, gourmet foods and antiques - is one of Lexington's most unique dining experiences. You can visit for lunch or afternoon dessert and be seated in the Garden Room which overlooks the bird and butterfly garden - or in the more traditional Colonial Fireside Room. There's a bit of tearoom flavor here, and menu choices might include broccoli soup with fresh rosemary; pasta salad with asparagus, toasted walnuts, sundried tomatoes, fresh basil, olive oil and parmesan cheese or Kentucky burgoo (look for the take-home mix in their gourmet food section). For dessert, try the rose geranium cake or strawberry pie. It's open Monday through Saturday for lunch, and for dessert from 2 to 4 PM. Reservations are recommended.

The Dutch Mill and Bake Shop
$ • 927 S. Limestone St.
• 252-6275

For true nostalgia try this little old-fashioned diner, complete with chrome bar stools and big vinyl booths that are eons old. We can't remember when The Dutch Mill wasn't there. Though the present owners have kept all the good old things, they've updated the menu with healthy but creative fare, including vegetarian dishes. They also have a pastry chef who creates outstanding desserts, including the to-die-for pies that the restaurant is famous for.

Merrick Inn
$$ • 3380 Tates Creek Rd. • 269-5417

When we have out-of-town company and want to show them what Kentucky dining is all about, we usually take them to Merrick Inn. You can get plenty of regional cuisine with a few Continental touches. The three formal Williamsburg-style dining rooms have a homey, Colonial-inn atmosphere graced by brass chandeliers, gorgeous wallpaper, working fireplaces and candlelight. Regular entrees include prime rib, Southern fried chicken, seafood and veal, and there are nightly specials. This writer's favorite is melt-in-the-mouth walleye pike. Separate menus are available for the more casual bar and, in warmer weather, for the patio. Reservations are necessary. The Inn is closed on Sundays.

Phil Dunn's Cook Shop
$$$ • 431 Old E. Vine St.
• 231-0099

This downtown cafe has an upbeat, airy feel with big front windows, black-and-white tiles and lots of light wood. It's definitely the place to see and be seen, especially at lunchtime. There's an on-the-premises bakery, and the menu is creative, with entrees like oven-roasted lamb chops over couscous laced with a brunoise of vegetables and tomato concasse, grilled ribeye with a mound of spiced red onion rings, or grilled Long Island duckling over a soy marinated salmon pan-

FYI

If no area code is given, it's a local call from Lexington-Fayette County. If an area code is given, whether it's 606 or 502, it's a long-distance call: dial 1, the area code and the number. See the How To Use This Book chapter for detailed information on calling.

INSIDERS' TIP

Take a drive on a country road and stop at a country store for a sandwich. Cummin's & Son on Athens-Boonesboro Road has "world famous chili dogs," beans and cornbread and a daily hot lunch special.

roasted and served with a pinot grigio and red pepper sauce. There are always daily specials, and the desserts are divine. If you can't get there right away for lunch or dinner, stop by and pick up a loaf of homemade bread or a luscious dessert for dinner. There's also a great Sunday brunch from 11 AM to 2 PM. Reservations are recommended.

Ramsey's Diner

$ • 496 E. High St.
• 259-2708
$ • 4053 Tates Creek Rd.
• 271-2638
$ • Kroger Plaza, Bryan Station and New Circle Rds. • 299-9669
$ • Man o' War Blvd. at Todds Rd.
• 264-9396

Ramsey's serves good, old-fashioned home cooking guaranteed to "stick to your ribs." We're talking really good pot roast, meat loaf, country fried steak and more, served with a huge choice of fresh veggies. Want something different? Try the lemon-yogurt chicken breasts, available as a meal or a sandwich. Ramsey's also has a limited late-night menu.

Rogers Restaurant

$ • 808 S. Broadway • 254-1077

So you're looking for a restaurant with true Kentucky fare? Look no further. This is the place - that is, if you don't mind if the waitresses call you "honey." It's one of Lexington's oldest restaurants, and it might not be the best but, by golly, it won't break the bank, and you'll get a belt-buster of a meal and a good sampling of regional fare. Go for the homemade beer cheese for starters and follow with the wilted leaf-lettuce salad with bacon dressing. Then move on to salmon croquettes, country ham, liver smothered in onions, lamb fries or prime rib for the next course. And don't forget sides of "greasy" green beans, yeast rolls and cornsticks. Dessert? The best in town, hands-down. Try chocolate, coconut or butterscotch cream pie - or the ice cream ball rolled in pecans, then topped with chocolate sauce. And don't forget Saturday morning breakfast with country ham, biscuits, grits, the works. It opens at 9 AM on Saturday, 11 AM Monday through Friday, and it serves all day, right through dinner.

Rosebud Bar & Grill

$ • 121 N. Mill St. • 254-1907

This quaint, cozy-but-tiny downtown bar is the little sister of the more sophisticated La Petit Rose next door, with which it shares the kitchen. Along with good bar food, look for more special fare that might trickle over from big sister next door — like a portabello Caesar salad, fresh mozzarella with tomatoes and basil in balsamic vinaigrette, or baby lamb chops with chutney. There's always a pasta special, too.

Shaker Village Trustees Office Dining Room

$$ • 3500 Lexington Rd.
• (606) 734-5411

Because the Shaker religious sect practiced celibacy, it's no longer around. Fortunately, their dining traditions live on at Shaker Village of Pleasant Hill. The regional fare is served by women in traditional Shaker dress, and it's hearty from start (relish tray) to entree (fried chicken or country ham) to finish (fresh-baked pies such as tongue-tingling Shaker lemon and scrumptious cakes). Three meals a day are served in a Shaker-style dining room, and reservations are required. The dining room closes for three weeks in January, but the Winter Kitchen remains open with a more limited menu.

Springs Inn

$$ • 2020 Harrodsburg Rd. • 277-5751

The dining room at this locally owned motel is renowned for its Southern hospitality, and it's beautifully furnished: brass chandeliers, Queen Anne chairs that scoot up to white-clothed tables and walls covered with framed prints by Kentucky artists. The house specialties are Kentucky standards such as country ham with redeye gravy, lamb fries with cream gravy and the hot Brown, and the salad bar is small but all-out sumptuous. There's also a generous selection of beef, poultry and seafood including whole rainbow trout. If you want a crash course in regional cuisine, try the Wednesday-night Kentucky buffet, which includes burgoo, catfish, country ham, pork roast

with dressing, spoon-bread, bread pudding and more. The Springs is also a well-kept secret for a perfect Kentucky breakfast (country ham, biscuits and gravy, grits, the works). Three meals are served daily, with a lunch buffet every day except Saturday.

Bar Food

Charlie Brown's

$ • 816 Euclid Ave.
• 269-5701

Here's the ultimate in coziness. Sink down in an overstuffed chair or couch near one of two fireplaces in a room lined with bookcases, and you're likely to feel as if you're sitting in the parlor of a friend who lives in an inviting old house. In addition to appetizers and a bunch of burgers and sandwiches — including a turkey burger — there are a few daily specials. During the warmer months, you can relax on the patio out back.

Cheapside Bar & Grill

$$ • 131 Cheapside Dr. • 254-0046

Cheapside describes its menu as "contemporary cuisine with a Southwestern flair." The atmosphere in the bar area, like the building's exterior, is old-fashioned. High ceilings and lots of classic dark woods lend a certain timelessness to the place. The main dining area is more contemporary, with walls graced by minimalist art such as that of local painter and bluesman Rodney Hatfield (a.k.a. Art Snake). When weather permits, the patio is generally filled. Menu highlights are subject to change, but they might include jalapeño black bean soup or smoked salmon wontons as appetizers and smoked-duck and mushroom pasta or a black bean turkey tostada as entrees. Smoked baby back ribs are a specialty.

INSIDERS' TIP

Drop by the snack bar at Hi Acres Pharmacy on Bryan Station Road during lunch for a piece of scrumptious mile-high cream pie: peanut butter, coconut cream, lemon or chocolate.

Hooters

$ • 3101 Richmond Rd. • 269-8521

Forget political correctness and just have a good time. Some folks have criticized this chain restaurant for the short shorts and tight T-shirts worn by the waitresses, but most patrons take it all in fun. This is a great place to watch a ball game on TV with friends while sharing a pitcher of beer and a plate of their famous chicken wings. Other specialties include oysters on the half-shell and steamed clams, and there's also a selection of salads and sandwiches.

Lynagh's Irish Pub & Grill

$, no credit cards • University Plaza Shopping Center, 384 Woodland Ave. • 255-1292

Lynagh's Shamrock Bar & Grill

$ • Patchen Village, off Richmond Rd. • 269-7621

Looking for the best burger in town? Get to one of the Lynagh's locations because it always gets everybody's votes (from newspaper and magazine surveys) for the O'Round, a huge burger — the menu says it's the size of a small hubcap — chargrilled to order and topped with your choice of cheeses. Other standout sandwiches are the ribeye and the T&A, which stands for — guess again — turkey and avocado. Lynagh's also has Guinness on tap, which gives the places extra points and just adds to their basic pub-like atmosphere.

Barbecue

Billy's Bar-B-Q

$ • 101 Cochran Rd. • 269-9593

Billy's is Lexington's original purveyor of Western Kentucky-style hickory-pit barbecue. Although the number of barbecue restaurants has increased severalfold since Billy's opened in 1978, lots of natives still swear this place is the best (including this barbecue nut). You can get barbecue pork, beef, mutton, chicken or pork ribs with traditional side items like baked beans, coleslaw and potato salad (the beans and slaw are top-notch). Billy's also offers several hardwood-grilled items and Kentucky burgoo. And you can bring your own turkey or pig in and have it custom smoked.

Red Hot & Blue

$ • 874 E. High St. • 268-7427

Blues and barbecue complement one another perfectly at this top-notch chain restaurant where the walls are covered with concert posters and photos of blues legends and the music doesn't stop. Memphis-style barbecue specialties include "pulled pig," beef brisket and pork ribs, which you can order "wet" (with sauce) or "dry" (with spices). The side dishes are good, too, especially the sweet-as-candy beans.

Cafeterias, Family and Fast Food

Central Christian Church Cafeteria

$, no credit cards • 205 E. Short St. • 255-3087

For more than 16 years, folks have lined up for home-style breakfasts and lunches in space leased from the Central Christian Church. For about $4 you can get an overloaded plate of home-style food, and there are always plenty of vegetables. The chicken-and-broccoli casserole, chicken livers and salmon croquettes would do your mom proud. The cafeteria serves breakfast and lunch Monday through Friday.

Morrison's Cafeteria

$ • Lexington Mall, Richmond Rd. • 269-3329

Lexington Green off Nicholasville Rd. • 273-4470

At Morrison's you can get salad, entree, two vegetables, bread, drink and dessert at a price that makes it easy to feed the whole family. Quarter broiled chicken, fried and broiled fish, country fried steak and liver and onions are among the regular features.

Kenny Rogers Roasters

$, no credit cards • 4101 Tates Creek Rd. • 245-2585

Turfland Mall • 277-2491

Forget "Lucille" and "The Gambler"; this has nothing to do with Kenny's music. Even headbangers enjoy the enticing roasted chicken served by this relatively new chain.

It's fast food, but it's different. The specialty is chicken marinated in citrus juices and spices, then slow-roasted over a wood fire. This process supposedly produces chicken lower in fat and healthier than the fried kind, but the bottom line is it really is mouth-watering. Some of the side dishes are very good; this author loves the garlic-and-parsley potatoes, coleslaw and steamed veggies, as well as the sweet corn muffins studded with kernels.

Parkette Drive In
$, no credit cards • 1216 New Circle Rd. N.E. • 254-8723

Drive-ins with honest-to-goodness curb service and an old neon sign are a rare breed these days. But the Parkette continues to thrive. Just for nostalgia's sake, pull up to one of the big menu boards and place your order through the speaker. Your food will arrive in minutes. When it opened in 1952, the drive-in was in the boonies; now it's on the phenomenally busy "strip." Today it still serves largely the same menu: "Kentucky Poor Boy" double-decker cheeseburgers, fried chicken and seafood boxes, strawberry pies, cherry Cokes and more. Old-timers from the '60s, like this writer, have to go for a Parkette fix every once in a while. It's closed on Sunday.

Perkins Family Restaurant
$ • 2401 Richmond Rd. • 269-1663

Perkins definitely has the feel of a chain, but it's a good place to take the family for a variety of soups, salads, sandwiches and dinner selections. It's also a favorite late-night spot because it's open 24 hours a day. You'll love the pasta, especially the seafood primavera and the chicken Alfredo, served in edible bread bowls. And it's one of our special favorites for a huge variety of omelets and eggs Benedict — which you can get anytime. An in-house bakery makes breads, gargantuan muffins and desserts piled miles high with gooey stuff that looks great but is not for the faint-of-heart.

Rock-A-Billy Cafe
$ • 2573 Richmond Rd. • 268-9089

Think fun, put on your letter sweater or your poodle skirt and bobbysocks and bop on over to Rock-A-Billy Cafe. This bright, '50s-style soda fountain serves a variety of whimsically named burgers and sandwiches, chili fries and shakes. Your kids will love this place. You big kids will too.

Chinese

August Moon
$$ • 2690 Nicholasville Rd. • 277-8888

Many people like August Moon for its atmosphere, which is more sophisticated than the average Chinese restaurant. The furnishings and service are elegant, and the food is consistently good. The steamed dumplings are sumptuous, and there are an incredible eight soups. Spicy "five-flavored" sauce, a house specialty, is used in several dishes, including seafood, lamb, chicken, pork and steak. Reservations are recommended.

Imperial Hunan
$$ • 1505 New Circle Rd. N.E. • 266-4393
Hunan Chinese Restaurant
$$ • 111 Southland Dr. • 278-3811

These pretty restaurants, in east and south Lexington, respectively, share ownership and menus. The New Circle location, in Woodhill Circle Shopping Center, is a perennial poll-winner as the area's best Oriental restaurant. Specialties include Peking duck and seafood deluxe (shrimp, scallops, crabmeat and lobster with vegetables). The extensive menu of beef, pork, chicken and vegetable dishes makes it hard to choose; fortunately, sharing is customary at Chinese restaurants, so go with several people. Both restaurants offer a Sunday buffet.

Ming Garden
$$ • Richmond Rd. at New Circle Rd. • 268-2688

It could be the year of the pig every year at Ming Garden because this is the place to pig-out on Chinese food. There is a huge buffet every day, and it has the works: appetizers, soups, more entrees than you can imagine and desserts to boot. The quality is usually good, unless you get there just before closing at night when things start fizzling out. And a tip: It's crowded from noon to 1 PM on Fridays and Saturday nights from about 6 to 7 PM.

Panda Garden

$$ • 531 New Circle Rd. N.W. • 299-9798

This restaurant is worth searching out for its nice, crisp decor and its wide range of Chinese fare, including plenty of seafood dishes. Try the crunchy-breaded Phoenix shrimp with a spicy garlic sauce, orange chicken, the Hawaiian duck and chicken bouquet with the chicken pieces cut like flowers and served with vegetables. Peking duck is always available.

Asian Wind

$$ • Palomar Centre, off Man o' War Blvd.
• 223-0060

Billed as a "new generation Chinese restaurant," Wind is a contemporary, refreshing eatery with an emphasis on healthy preparation: low sodium, low fat and no MSG. They have a variety of vegetarian dishes along with "beef" and "chicken" dishes that sure taste like beef and chicken but are actually made from soybeans. Special dishes full of natural flavorings and spices are the gingery shrimp hot pot, succulent shrimp in lobster sauce or the tongue-searing ma-la chicken for the truly adventurous. It's closed on Sunday.

Continental

a la lucie

$$$ • 159 N. Limestone St. • 252-5277

This quaint, quirky little downtown restaurant with a bistro feel was deemed "a Lexington treasure" by one of the *Herald-Leader's* restaurant critics, Howard Snyder, and it's one of our best. From the appetizers, which include three varieties of escargots, through the desserts, a la lucie makes its inventive offerings seem simple. The menu changes periodically, but you can be sure it will always be tantalizing. Recent offerings included an avocado half stuffed with lobster and grapefruit, barbecued duck burrito and Caribbean chicken with peanut sauce and pineapple. Don't go without reservations, especially on weekends. (And don't go on Sundays: A la lucie is closed.)

Amelia's Field Country Inn

$$$$ • 617 Cynthiana Rd., Paris
• (606) 987-5778

One of the bonuses at Amelia's Field is that it's situated in a pretty, old country house in Bourbon County, surrounded by sheep, chickens and flower and herb gardens. Look for wonderful things such as sauteed Dover sole with herbed potato crust, seared saddle of venison with pear and parsnip puree and crisp root vegetables, or salmon with a sweet-hot mustard glaze.

Lunch and dinner are served Thursday through Sunday or by arrangement, and alfresco dining in nice weather is really special here. Reservations are a must. And if you feel like you want to stay forever, there's a bed and breakfast inn upstairs.

The Cafe

$$$ • 355 Romany Rd. • 268-2133

This charming little cafe has one of the most exciting menus around, yet it's so out-of-the-way it often gets overlooked. Our best advice is to seek it out. Located inside a gourmet carryout shop and lunch spot called Scarborough Fare, the upscale Cafe occupies a separate dining room with about 12 tables dressed up with crisp linens and tall, clear-glass vases of fresh flowers. Though it's dimly lit and decidedly romantic, one wall is papered — and spotlighted — with big red roses (very English, as is the owner!). Try the roasted vegetable terrine (another touch of English) as an appetizer or a dinner salad made with caramelized sea scallops, baby lettuce, pancetta, fennel and red onion confit, all drizzled with a lingonberry confit. For entrees you can choose from enticing offerings such as curried, oven-roasted salmon filet served with sun-dried tomato couscous, caramelized apples and leeks; or tenderloin in a Stilton cheese crust with grilled pear wedges and creamed potatoes.

INSIDERS' TIP

The carrot soup at The Atomic Cafe on Limestone Street is a favorite with locals.

There's also a daily "comfort" special for diners looking for something a little more homey. It's open for dinner only from Monday through Saturday.

Cherry Knoll Inn
$$$ • 3975 Lemons Mill Pike • 253-9800

If country dining is your cup of tea, you'll love the Cherry Knoll Inn experience. You dine in the downstairs rooms of a beautiful white-columned Greek Revival house surrounded by horse farms; there are two bed and breakfast rooms upstairs. The small but exciting menu changes regularly but it might include rosemary flank steak with a spicy teriyaki wild mushroom sauce, Atlantic salmon with a honey grape cognac sauce, braised chicken filled with smoked cheese and spinach, or pasta primavera tossed with cherry smoked chicken. Round things out with a chocolate truffle tart in a pistachio nut crust or Cherry Knoll bourbon honey cake and vanilla-bean ice cream for dessert. Dinner is served by reservation only Tuesday through Saturday. The fixed price is $26.

The Coach House
$$$$ • 855 S. Broadway • 252-7777

Under original owner Stanley Demos, The Coach House long ago set the standard for Lexington culinary excellence, and it remains one of Lexington's most elegant restaurants, characterized by paintings in gold leaf frames and big fresh floral bouquets decorating the dining room. The current owner, John B. Du Puy III, continues the fine tradition. The Coach House is famous for its Maryland crab cakes and its curried Crab Demos, which are offered as appetizers. Other specialties include sole "My Way" (created years ago by Demos), rack of lamb and veal Oscar, but there are plenty of innovative entrees available as well. Reservations are recommended; the restaurant is closed on Sundays.

Dudley's
$$$ • 380 S. Mill St. • 252-1010

The centerpiece of historic Dudley Square, a former schoolhouse divided into a number of small businesses, is this comfortably stylish spot. The patio is one of the most popular places in town for a business lunch or an af-ternoon date on a warm spring day. Lunch features a quiche of the day, and there are daily fish and pasta specials at lunch and dinner. The menu is always innovative with entrees such as roasted scallops with vegetables and niçoise sauce. Dudley's serves a Sunday brunch. Reservations are recommended.

Emmett's
$-$$$ • corner of Tates Creek Rd.
and Duval Dr. • 254-4444

This latest star in the Lexington dining scene offers a mix of continental and Kentucky fare (with a bit of "trendy" for good measure) in an attractive old house that has been lovingly restored. Relax by the fire in one of their four dining rooms and try such enticing appetizers as bourbon honey quail or wild mushroom "moon pies." For the main course, there's fresh fish, homemade pasta, chicken (including croquettes) and plenty of wonderful vegetables (corn pudding to die for) and breads like bacon-cheddar cheese-corn muffins. And, of course, the restaurant has its own pastry chef. Emmett's recently added Sunday brunch which might include eggs, hash browns, cheese grits sauteed apples (whoo!), and a choice of pan-fried trout, grilled steak, country ham or sausage. Emmett's is open Monday through Saturday for dinner, on Sunday for brunch. Reservations are recommended.

Ed and Fred's Desert Moon
$$ • 148 Grand Ave. • 231-1161

Ed and Fred's Desert Moon is an eclectic and intriguing blend of Southwestern and nouvelle cuisine, and it has plenty of style. The place is named after its creators' fathers, who financed the place. The restaurant moved to a new location in the spring of 1997, and the decor is now sleek, minimal and modern in gray and black — with splashes of color coming from lots of modern artwork. The menu is slightly limited, but it's fun to go with several people, order a bunch of appetizers and share. From starters such as black-bean enchiladas through entrees such as lime chili pesto linguine and raspberry chicken, there's nothing ordinary here, including specialty pizzas. It's closed on Mondays.

La Petit Rose
$$$ • 125 N. Mill St. • 254-1907

A huge chandelier is the piece de resistance of this classic but creative white-tablecloth cafe which shares a kitchen with its casual counterpart next door, the Rosebud Bar and Grill (see the previous entry in the "American and Regional" section). When you're in the mood for the classics, try filet mignon with hollandaise, tournedos with crabmeat and hollandaise or slow-roasted rosemary Dijon pork loin. Or turn out for their festive theme dinners — which are scheduled once a month or so —where food and wine might revolve around Caribbean cooking or some other exciting culinary region. La Rose is closed on Sundays.

The Mansion at Griffin Gate
$$$$ • 1720 Newtown Rd.
• 231-5152

The Mansion at Griffin Gate is a restored Southern antebellum mansion. You could call it Lexington's version of Tara, and it's definitely in the lineup as one of Lexington's most elegant restaurants. It offers tastefully prepared American and continental cuisine — both traditional and contemporary — with impeccable service, but keep in mind you have to pay for all these special things. Reservations are recommended.

Mason's
$$$$ • 436 S. Ashland Ave.
• 266-8382

Mason's bills its fare as "contemporary world cuisine," and you'd better believe it. This is the quality and style of food you would expect to find in a big city, yet the restaurant is a study in refined coziness:two tiny bistro-ish dining rooms with starched white linen, lots of artwork on creamy-white walls, candlelight and fresh flowers. And the menu will wow you. Look for appetizers such as Vietnamese duck rolls, fresh oysters with a mignonette sauce of minced shallots, cracked pepper and wine vinegar, and entrees such as coffee-glazed quail, grilled filet of beef with ancho pepper rub or pan-seared ahi with a black and white sesame-seed crust. Mason's is open for dinner Monday through Saturday.

Regina's Club and Cafe
$ • 116 N. Upper St. • 255-1277

This modern cafe is distinctively different with its sleek decor (complete with one wall portion covered in "leopard skin" wallpaper) and its eclectic menu, heavy on spicy New Orleans-style fare. There's crayfish ètouffee, gumbo, caponata and shrimp Creole, but there are also pasta dishes topped with delightfully eccentric sauces. For example, there's maque choux sauce which is composed of tasso cream with prosciutto, crayfish, bell peppers and corn; or ropa Vieja, a highly spiced stew made with shredded pork, tomatoes and green and black olives. Lunch is served Monday. Lunch and dinner are served Monday through Friday; dinner is served on Saturday.

Roy and Nadine's
$$ • Palomar Centre, off Man o' War Blvd.
• 223-0797

The busy bar area in the front dining room of this adventurous restaurant gives it a casual feel, but if you can stand all the activity, the food is superb. Owned by a la lucie's Lucie Meyers, this establishment offers such delectables as hummus, olive tapenade and sun-dried tomato spread with toasted pita bread, Indonesian shrimp and basmati rice salad, arugula and seared tuna salad, grilled duck breast, blackened pork tenderloin with apple chutney, marinated flank steak with pickled ginger and green onions and even a grilled portabello sandwich for lunch. You'll miss the festive crowds, but go during off hours to be assured of getting a table. On Sunday, only dinner is served.

Delis

In addition to the terrific delicatessens described below, you can choose from two popular downtown-area delis: **Park Plaza Deli**, 252-0153, 120 E. Main Street, a traditional deli; and **Stella's Deli**, 598 Ballard Street, 252-3263, which is more like an old-fashioned sandwich shop with homemade soups and sandwiches.

For deli meats, cheeses, German bread by the pound and a gazillion gourmet items and party supplies (everything from invitations to plates and napkins to decorations), there's

GIUSEPPE'S

Italian Ristorante & Bar

• Pasta • Fresh Seafood • Steaks • Veal •
• Chicken • Extensive Wine List •

South on Nicholasville Road,
One half-mile past Man-O-War, on the left.
To make dinner plans with us, call: (606) 272-4269

www.giuseppeslexington.com

an astounding variety at the two **Liquor Barns**, 3040 Richmond Road and 921 Beaumont Centre Parkway, 223-1400. They prepare party trays, and also offer gourmet entrees and desserts to go, as well as frozen hors d'oeuvres, pastas, pizzas and desserts and fresh European-style breads, 269-4170.

In addition, all the larger groceries in town have delis with varying selections of meats and cheeses, salads and plate lunches. The Kroger, Winn Dixie and Slone Market delis, for example, have good varieties of hot and cold foods. They can prepare party trays to order and also have ready-to-cook entrees that make it easy for you to throw a dinner party without actually doing that much work.

Claim Jumpers Grinders & Pizza
$ • 200 Bolivar St. • 252-5225
$ • 2222 Coburn Dr. • 269-JUMP

Technically, Claim Jumpers doesn't call itself a deli, but its variety of sandwiches, made with a unique, crusty bread that's baked fresh daily, reminds us of one. Sandwiches including club, Reuben, roast beef, turkey, stromboli, BLT and several others are available in one-third loaf, half-loaf and full-loaf versions. Pizzas, salads, soups, chili and nachos are also available. Hours vary at the two locations. The Bolivar Street shop is in South Hill Station, the other is off Richmond Road.

The Mouse Trap
$ • 3323 Tates Creek Rd. • 269-2958

Check out The Mouse Trap for its pâté including a tasty veal-chicken version. Besides all kinds of domestic and imported cheeses, this deli in the Lansdowne Shoppes has Greek and other salads, delicious smoked salmon spread and more. Its selection of imported crackers, cookies and candies makes it something of a "gourmet supermarket" — and it also has fancy homemade cookies such as almond macaroons. The Mouse Trap, which has an atrium filled with cafe tables in front of the shop for the lunch crowd, also prepares party trays and gift baskets and operates an adjoining cookware and gift shop.

Scarborough Fare
$ • 355 Romany Rd. • 266-8704

The imaginative fare at this "gourmet to go" shop runs from specialty pasta and vegetable salads to entrees and desserts, plus a full lunch menu with imaginative sandwiches and salads prepared to order. Try roast turkey breast with brie or mozzarella and tomato sandwiches, or a grilled eggplant focaccia with pesto, sun-dried tomatoes and provolone. There's also espresso and cappuccino, plus a full catering service and an upscale restaurant in a separate dining room, The Cafe (see its description in the "Continental" section).

Stanley J's New York Style Delicatessen

$, no credit cards • Stonewall Shopping Center, Clays Mill Rd. • 224-3354

In addition to your standard deli offerings such as corned beef and pastrami, Stanley J's makes a variety of ethnic foods in-house, including Indonesian rice with plum sauce and ginger root, tabouli and Greek lemon soup. The ham, baked in Stanley J's own bourbon sauce, is great served on a hot or cold sandwich, and you can also get huge, one-third-pound kosher hot dogs and bagels with lox. And, of course, there's New York cheesecake for dessert.

Italian and Pizza

Bella Notte

$ • 3715 Nicholasville Rd. • 245-1789

This phenomenally popular Italian eatery is the "upscale" creation of the Lexington-based fast food Fazoli's chain. It you ever get past the line that frequently trickles outside, the interior is sort of a festive Italian barn atmosphere — rustic and fun. The red sauces are top notch and the menu is extensive. There are bottles of olive oil to drizzle over crunchy bread while you wait for your meal. It's open all day, so we would suggest going during off hours if you want to avoid the crowds.

Bravo's of Lexington

$$$ • Victorian Square, 401 W. Main St. • 255-2222

Originally called Bravo Pitino, this authentic Italian restaurant was sure to become a hit when it opened, simply because the beloved former UK basketball coach was a partner and the place was modeled after his favorite Big Apple eatery. Rick Pitino has moved on to the Boston Celtics, and the restaurant has long since modified its name, but it still serves elegant cuisine in an atmosphere to match. Tender fried calamari and a filling antipasto are just the beginnings. Entrees include steaks, chicken and veal which can be prepared a variety of ways (piccata, parmigiana, marsala, etc.) and grilled salmon and pasta dishes that might include a savory blend of tomato fettuccine, crabmeat, shrimp and vegetables in a red peppercorn sauce with basil. For the finale, this is one of the only places in town that serves bananas Foster. Reservations are recommended. (It's closed on Sunday.)

Giuseppe's Ristorante Italiano

$$ • 4456 Nicholasville Rd. • 272-4269

Though it looks like a rustic tavern on the outside, the inside of Giuseppe's is a real surprise: attractive and contemporary with a nice bar area and really first-rate Italian food. The veal dishes, spicy shrimp diablo, eggplant Parmesan, manicotti and chicken Marsala are exceptional. But there are more adventurous dishes such as pasta di Vincenzo, a pasta dish tossed with grilled chicken, sun-dried tomatoes, mushrooms, black olives, red onions, olive oil and garlic; or pesce spada alla griglia which is fresh grilled swordfish with pesto butter. Reservations are suggested.

Joe Bologna's

$$ • 120 W. Maxwell • 252-4933

Since moving into a beautifully restored old church building several years ago, Joe B's, as it is affectionately known, is no longer the dive (in the best sense of the word) it used to be when it was just up the street at the corner of Maxwell and Limestone. The scratchy old jukebox has been replaced with a CD jukebox, and stained-glass windows let the sun shine in. One thing that hasn't changed, however, is the fantastic pizza, considered by many people to be the best in town, which is available in traditional round, Sicilian pan and specialty versions. You can also get meat or vegetable lasagna, manicotti and other pasta dishes, salads and sandwiches. Whatever you order, start off with one of Joe B's famous bread sticks (if you're on a diet, you can get the garlic butter on the side).

Paisano's

$$ • 2417 Nicholasville Rd. • 277-5321
$$ • 1765 Alexandria Dr. • 260-7722

This hideaway in the inconspicuous Stone Square shopping center features all the traditional Italian favorites, from pasta and pizza to veal, chicken, seafood and steak. Baked ziti, eggplant Parmesan and Florentine rolls (available with or without meat) are among the specialties. A real highlight is Paisano's chicken, cooked with artichokes, black olives and sun-dried tomatoes in a piccata sauce — all served over angel-hair pasta. Paisano's opened a second restaurant on Alexandria Drive in October of 1997.

Pizzeria Uno
$$ • 2547 Richmond Rd. • 266-8667

This chain, which originated in Chicago, specializes in Chicago-style deep-dish pizza that is rich, rich, rich. Freshly made dough and choice ingredients make such creations as the spinoccoli (spinach and broccoli) and the four-cheese exceptional. Uno's also serves pasta, steaks, ribs, chicken and burgers.

Portabella's
$ • Man o' War Place, off Richmond Rd.
• 266-6836

Just think Italian cafe atmosphere with bottles of olive oil and vinegars and baskets of vegetables as part of the decor. The specialty of this casual restaurant with an open kitchen is delectable chargrilled Portobello mushrooms, tasty and meaty, along with a complete lineup of pasta dishes, steaks, wood-oven pizzas, strombolis and big specialty salads — and finish off with tiramisu and a cup of espresso or cappuccino. Mamma mia! An Insider's tip: One of the owners is a former restaurant critic, so doesn't that tell you something?

Asian-American

Pacific Pearl
$$$ • Chinoe Village Shopping Center
• 266-1611

It's hard to categorize Pacific Pearl because it's a little wild and wonderful in its decor and menu — all modern and colorful (a bit of an understatement) with a terrifically adventurous menu that is billed as "Far (Out) East Meets West." First, let's talk about the decor. The color scheme is — are you ready? — purple, fuschia, turquoise and gold, but it all comes together in an attractive, if futuristic, way. Let's just say Judy Jetson would definitely dine here. Keep in mind this is the enterprise of Lucie and Roy Meyers, creators of two of the most popular and original restaurants in town, a la lucie and Roy and Nadine's, so they know what they are doing here. The menu is a mixture of Chinese and Thai creations with an American twist. There are plenty of traditional Asian dishes but look for some of the exciting compromises such as coconut fried lobster with sweet and sour sauce, barbecued salmon with orange sesame glaze or grilled double-thick pork chop with honey sambal chile glaze. What more can we say? You'll just have to go.

Japanese

Nagasaki Inn
$$$ • 435 Redding Rd. • 272-1858

If you've never been to a Japanese steakhouse, you should know that it's more than a dining experience — it's a show. At least that's the case with Nagasaki Inn, which prepares steak, seafood, chicken and vegetables right in front of you. The action takes place at large tables, where your party is likely to be seated with another party or two; for extra enjoyment, go with a large group. Nagasaki moved to a spacious new location early in 1997. The sushi is better than ever in this new modern dining room which utilizes lots of natural wood and stone in its decor.

Tachibana
$$$ • 785 Newtown Ct. • 254-1911

This is Toyota's place — what more recommendation do you need? The location just off I-75 makes it a quick commute for executives from the Georgetown plant. And, especially if you're in the mood for sushi, it's worth a drive from anywhere else in Central Kentucky. Especially recommended are the tuna rolls and the yellowtail, a form of mackerel. And if, like Travis Tritt, you like your sushi

---

INSIDERS' TIP

Try the fried dill pickles at Billy's Bar-B-Q in Chevy Chase.

Southern fried, you can go the tempura route with deep-fried seafood and veggies. Tachibana also has a room where you can get Japanese steakhouse-style cuisine, show and all. (The restaurant is closed on Sundays.)

Mexican

Jalapeño's

$$ • 285 New Circle Rd. N.W. • 299-8299
$$ • 1050 S. Broadway • 281-5171

Jalapeño's two locations are standouts in the south-of-the-border lineup, offering traditional favorites as well as some truly inventive creations, all served amid festive surroundings. The camarones Acapulcos — shrimp stuffed with polano pepper and cheese, rolled in bacon and grilled — are mind-blowingly delicious. The marinated baked chicken wrapped in banana leaves gets high marks as does the gulf shrimp blanketed in creamy chipotle pepper sauce. All the basics are available, as well. Ole!

Rincon Mexicano

$ • 818 Euclid Ave. • 268-8160
3501 Lansdown Dr. •245-4679

In a city blessed with an abundance of good, authentic Mexican cooking, this cozy little second-floor restaurant above Charlie Brown's holds its ground. If you like your Mexican food really hot, you must try the chile Colorado, tender chunks of beef in a fiery red sauce served with flour tortillas. Rincon Mexicano, which translates as "Mexican corner," also offers several steak dinners and vegetarian combination dinners, as well as a good mole and seven kinds of fajitas with meats or seafood cooked over an open flame mesquite grill. Plus, all the traditional favorites are available.

Mi Mexico

$ • 818 New Circle Rd. • 253-0690

The menu goes on forever at this truly Mexican restaurant which has operated at locations all over town — and in nearby towns — and has finally settled in at an attractive building that really looks like a Mexican restaurant with a stucco-like exterior and lots or arched windows and doorways. There's even an out-door patio where you can enjoy Mexican steaks, fajitas, mole dishes, chile Colorado, or peppers stuffed with potatoes and cheese. Of course, there are enchiladas, burritos, tacos and all those "C" things: chimichangas, chalupas and chilaquiles.

Seafood

Charlie's Fresh Seafood & Carry-Out Market

$ • 928 Winchester Rd. • 255-6005

You can't eat at Charlie's, and even the carryout menu is very limited, but you can't beat the price or the generous portions. Whitefish sandwiches and shrimp, oyster and clam lunches are the extent of the menu, and they are a bit of a well-kept secret. This small market, however, has a bounty of fresh and frozen seafood — including oysters, shrimp, tuna, halibut, salmon, swordfish, Alaskan king crab legs, crawfish tails and more — for wholesale and retail.

Hall's on the River

$$ • 1225 Athens-Boonesboro Rd. near Boonesborough • 255-8105

Hall's may be most famous for its beer cheese, its fried banana peppers and its location on the Kentucky River, but fried catfish is king here. The rustic drive to Hall's is one of the reasons for going. Besides seafood, there are pasta dishes, chicken and steaks. For something really original — and also very good — try the beer cheese soup.

Linc's, Springfield

$$ • 1007 Lincoln Park Rd., near Springfield • (606) 336-7493

Linc's lovers don't mind driving nearly an hour to reach this homey seafood haven off Ky. Highway 555. Shrimp, oysters, scallops, catfish and frog legs are highlights, and there is a selection of broiled seafood items. A big draw are the Friday and Saturday night buffets of crab legs, steamed and fried shrimp, oysters on the half-shell, fried and broiled whitefish, barbecue ribs and more. Non-seafood menu items include ribeye and filet mignon.

New Orleans House
$$$$ • 1510 Newtown Pike • 254-3474

Be sure to wear loose-fitting clothing when you visit the New Orleans House in Griffin Gate Plaza. And be sure to take your appetite with you. This isn't your typical seafood buffet, with the emphasis on fried fish. At New Orleans House, most of the seafood is broiled, Louisiana style. The buffet's "cold" station features Norwegian smoked salmon, peel-and-eat shrimp and oysters on the half-shell. Then there's Alaskan crab legs, tasty broiled scallops, steamed shrimp and clams, mussels cooked in wine, frog legs and much more. It's open for dinner only. Reservations are required.

Steakhouses

Columbia Steak House
$$ • 201 N. Limestone St. • 253-3135
$$ • 1425 Alexandria Dr. • 233-4185
$$ • 2750 Richmond Rd. • 268-1666

The Columbia Steak House special — a thick, round tenderloin of beef broiled to order in garlic butter — has been one of Lexington's finest steaks for decades. In fact, it's the only entree this author has ever ordered here, even though T-bones, prime rib, lamb fries, chicken and seafood also are available. The Diego salad, a simple mixture of lettuce and tomatoes mixed in big bags with a secret seasoning, is a must. The original Limestone location has the funkiest and best old-time roadhouse atmosphere with seating by longtime maître d', Smitty.

Logan's Roadhouse
$$ • 1224 Harrodsburg Rd. • 252-4307

This Western-style saloon/steakhouse is the forerunner of roadhouse-type restaurants that have popped up all over town. The restaurant charcoal-grills steaks, ribs, chicken and seafood in plain view in the center of the restaurant. Everybody seems to love the trendy baked sweet potatoes served here. The hot, freshly baked bread is also a must. On weekend nights, the place is packed, but waiting isn't so bad if you can find a seat in the bar, where they'll give you a bucket of peanuts in the shell to tide you over. Just for the record,

Logan's is the very first place in Lexington to encourage diners to throw their peanut shells on the floor. Now there are a half-dozen chain restaurants that have followed suit.

Malone's
$-$$$ • The Lansdowne Shoppes, Tates Creek Rd. • 335-6500

It's located in an upscale shopping center and has a bit of a "clubby" feel (dark woods, gold leaf mirrors, nice lighting), but it's always so crowded and festive, Malone's is more like a busy neighborhood restaurant.

Steaks are the showpiece here, but there's so much more: delicious seafood (walleye pike is a standout), scrumptious salads (try the Greek), chicken, pasta and more. If you're looking for prime rib, this is the place. And if you stop by for lunch, to avoid the crowds, ask to eat in the bar area. .

Other Ethnic

The Atomic Cafe
$$ • 265 N. Limestone St. • 254-1969

This author has never been to the Caribbean, but when he does, he hopes he can find conch fritters, coconut shrimp and jerk chicken as good as those served here. Owner Linda Hoff wanted to remind people of their island vacations, so she created a casual restaurant and bar featuring a huge tropical mural, reggae music and menu items adapted from Jamaica, the Bahamas, the West Indies and other exotic locales. The Atomic Cafe also has plenty of options for vegetarians, such as Latin carrot soup from Cuba, an eggplant "caviar" appetizer from Trinidad and a vegetarian sampler dinner. Key-lime cheesecake is one of several tempting desserts. Check out the pretty patio in warm weather. The Atomic Cafe is open for dinner only, and it's closed on Sundays.

Bangkok House
$ • 275 Euclid Ave. • 226-9711

Don't be fooled by Bangkok House's inconspicuous location — beneath a Baskin-Robbins in a shopping center near UK's Memorial Coliseum. It's an inexpensive and highly popular restaurant serving authentic Thai specialties like Thailand's national dish pad Thai and much more. Entrees include chicken, pork, beef, shrimp, squid and vegetables, each of which is available stir-fried several different ways. (The menu lists them by the type of seasoning — curry, ginger, chili, garlic, basil, etc. — used to prepare them.) Many of the dishes are spicy, but there are plenty of choices for those with milder palates. Bangkok House is open for lunch and dinner Monday through Saturday and for dinner Sunday.

Furlongs
$$ • 735 E. Main St. • 266-9000

If you like Cajun, this is the place. The lively menu includes a huge array of Louisiana fare: fried crayfish tails, etouffee and gumbo, Po' Boys, grilled andouille, red beans and rice, gumbo, jambalaya. Whew-eee! Then there's grilled quail and baked duck and about two dozen other dishes.

If you prefer bluegrass to bayou fare, there are steaks, chicken and seafood, too. There's also bread pudding and peanut butter pie for dessert. The atmosphere is cozy and casual in this cute little brick building that has been home to about a dozen restaurants in the past decade or so, but we think this one is here to stay. There's even a cozy fireplace — as if the food didn't provide enough heat. C'est si bon!

Jewel of India
$ • 504 Euclid Ave. • 252-5010

You might leave this little Indian "diner" in tears because its delicious vegetarian buffet includes some tongue-searing items. So make sure you have some sweet chutney, yogurt and rice on your plate to balance the taste, and have some cold water on hand. If you want meat, you can order curried chicken, tandoori chicken or goat from a separate menu.

And you want to talk about personal service? On the author's first visit, planned as a business lunch, he and his companion were joined by the proprietors for an illuminating discussion of Hinduism.

Jozo's Bayou Gumbo
$, no credit cards • 4053 Tates Creek Rd.
• 273-9229
$ • 384 Woodland Ave. • 254-7047
$ • 115 Locust Hill Dr. • 268-4700
$ • 3061 Fieldstone Way • 296-4262

One of the great things about Cajun and Creole food is that even the names of the dishes are a treat for the tongue. Jambalaya. Gumbo. Chicken fricassee. Shrimp ètouffee. They all just seem to roll musically off the tongue. And wait until you taste them. They call this fast food, and there are only a few tables, but with generous servings and bayou bargain prices that even a college student can afford, Jozo's (pronounced YO-zoes) will give you more than you can eat for about $5. Thank goodness for those take-home boxes! All dishes are served over rice and include crusty French garlic bread. Crawfish and alligator are available in season, and Jozo's has some of the best chili in town. For dessert, treat yourself to a slice of peanut-butter pie or a rich praline.

Kashmir Indian Restaurant
$$ • 341 South Limestone St. • 233-3060

It may seem surprising to find three Indian restaurants in a city the size of Lexington, but Kashmir, the latest entry in the field, appears likely to be here for the long haul. Readers of *ACE* magazine voted it Lexington's best new restaurant in 1997. The aroma of fresh-baked Indian breads and exotic spices, wafting out from the former location of Bluegrass Billiards near the UK campus, will reach you well before you reach the door. Inside you'll face a tempting selection of vegetarian and non-vegetarian choices, plus several appetizers and more than a dozen kinds of bread.

Curry, saag, korma and vindaloo (different styles of Indian cooking) dishes are available

---

INSIDERS' TIP

The best 1950s-style restaurant in town is the Dutch Mill on Limestone Street, across from the University of Kentucky campus. The homemade pies and desserts are a special treat.

A Taste of Kentucky Food and Drink

When you're dining in the Bluegrass, it's quite possible that you will encounter certain menu items that, while not unpronounceable like some snooty French dish, are simply unfamiliar to you — things like "lamb fries," for example, or "hot Browns." Should you order them, or should you steer clear? And just what do we mean when we talk about "country ham" — are we trying to distinguish it from pork raised in the city? This close-up is designed to help you answer such questions.

Close-up

From the perspective of worldwide culinary recognition, Colonel Harland Sanders' "finger-lickin'-good" creation might be the food that most people associate with Kentucky. If you go to Corbin, about 80 miles south of Lexington, you can visit the very first KFC establishment, which opened in 1930. But if your knowledge of Kentucky cuisine is limited to fried chicken, you're in for a surprise. (Sanders, incidentally, was born in Indiana. As any market researcher worth his salt will tell you, however, "Indiana Fried Chicken" would never have flown.)

A number of influences, including American Indian, Irish, Scottish, French and German, have come together to create the smorgasbord of tastes known as Kentucky cuisine, regional cuisine or "country cookin'." All in all, it's hearty fare, heavy on the meat and potatoes. And second helpings are encouraged!

Restaurants offering regional cooking are likely to serve such delicacies as fried catfish, country ham with beaten biscuits and redeye gravy, grits, fried chicken, barbecue and burgoo. It's true that many of these dishes can be found throughout the South, but Kentucky cooks take special pride in the way they prepare these delicacies. More recent additions to the state's diverse menu include beer cheese, fried banana peppers and the aforementioned hot Brown.

With good bourbon in such plentiful supply, the native liquor is used not only as a beverage but also as a flavoring agent for a number of recipes. Commercially bottled preparations such as bourbon steak sauce can be found in groceries throughout the state, and Kentucky-made chocolate candies sweetened with bourbon are popular around the country, especially during the holidays.

Lexington Herald-Leader food writer Sharon Thompson has graciously shared a handful of the Kentucky-style recipes she has accumulated over the years, and we have included them in this chapter just in case you're inclined to whip up a few of these dishes yourself. As with just about any regional dish, numerous variations are possible, so you may see different versions of these recipes elsewhere. Experiment with your own versions; we don't care.

Of course, if Bluegrass cuisine is a new experience for you, you may feel more comfortable letting the so-called experts

Photo: Kentucky Travel and Tourism

Kentucky country ham is cured for six months to three years.

do the cooking. Either way, do sample some Kentucky-style home cookin'. While everything on our varied menu may not be to your liking, you'd have to be a mighty picky eater not to find something that suits your fancy, especially when it's served with such fine hospitality. If you leave a Bluegrass dinner table hungry, it's nobody's fault but your own.

Country Ham

A Kentucky country ham is distinguished from your run-of-the-meal variety by its preparation, which involves curing with salt or sugar for a period of anywhere from six months to three years. Before you cook your country ham, you'll first want to remove some of the salt it acquired in curing (not necessary when the ham is sugar-cured) and restore moisture lost in the aging process. To accomplish this, the ham is usually boiled instead of baked. Some cooks set a glaze on the outside by baking it briefly after boiling. Here's one way to fix a country ham.

> 10- to 16-pound aged country ham
> ½ cup cider vinegar
> 1 bottle beer or 1½ cups ginger ale (optional)
> Whole cloves (optional)
> 1 cup brown sugar
> ¼ cup cornmeal
> 1 tablespoon dry mustard
> 1 tablespoon freshly ground black pepper
> 2 or 3 tablespoons bourbon, pineapple juice or apple juice

Put the ham under cold running water and scrub with a stiff brush to remove any loose mold. Place the ham in a large container and add cold water to cover. Allow to soak for 24 hours.

Drain the water and scrub the ham again, then wipe with a cloth soaked in vinegar to remove any remaining mold.

Place the ham in a large kettle or deep roasting pan with enough water to cover it completely. Add the vinegar and beer, if desired, to help neutralize the salt flavor.

Bring to a boil, cover and simmer gently for 3 to 3½ hours. Keep the ham covered with liquid by adding boiling water as needed. The ham is done when the small crossbone in the shank is pulled out easily.

Let the ham cool to room temperature in its cooking liquid. This will take several hours.

Preheat the oven to 400 degrees.

Remove the cooled ham from the liquid. Cut off all of the rind except for a small band around the shank end that will serve as a handle when carving.

Trim off the fat, leaving only a ¼- to ½-inch-thick layer. You may score the fat in a diamond pattern.

To glaze the ham: In a bowl, mix together the brown sugar, cornmeal, mustard and pepper. Moisten the mixture with the bourbon.

Spread the mixture over the ham and bake for 20 minutes or until the glaze is bubbly and nicely browned. Watch the ham carefully during glazing to make sure the glaze doesn't burn; pour a cup or two of water into the pan if necessary.

Country ham is best served at room temperature, sliced very thin with the grain. Eat it with biscuits.

If you want redeye gravy with your country ham, fry it instead of baking it. After boiling, slice the ham into thicker slices and fry it in a skillet. Take the juice left from frying,

— continued on next page

stir in a little water (use your own judgment) and, if desired, a spoonful of brewed coffee (no grounds, please). Spoon the mixture over your ham and biscuits.

Burgoo

The meat in burgoo, according to a popular joke, consists of "whatever didn't make it across the road the night before." That's a bit of an exaggeration, but the truth is you can add virtually any type of domestic or wild beast that you might imagine. The policy on vegetables is also quite liberal. This concoction — something like a thick and spicy vegetable soup or beef stew — is tasty and filling. It's popular at Kentucky race tracks and is especially good on cool evenings.

There are a number of theories about the origin of burgoo. Although the name is the same, this slow-cooked, labor-intensive and ultimately satisfying delicacy is not to be confused with the thick but bland oatmeal gruel once served to sailors, who quite likely went wild with gastronomic abandon whenever they reached shore. No, tasty Kentucky-style burgoo apparently was the creation of rugged, hearty 19th-century folks who filled their continuously simmering stockpots with the bounty from the men's hunting trips: squirrel, rabbit, venison, fowl and sometimes even bear.

Gus Jaubert, a member of Gen. John Hunt Morgan's cavalry, is sometimes credited with first using the word "burgoo" for meat-and-vegetable stew, which he prepared for the troops in massive quantities from field rations. Variations of Jaubert's dish later became a hit at political rallies, and that tradition has continued. J.T. Looney, a Lexington grocer and Jaubert protégé, later became known as "the burgoo king." In 1932, a horse named Burgoo King won the Kentucky Derby and the Preakness.

It is common knowledge that you should always make enough burgoo to serve an army. The following recipe, which contains nothing you have to go out and shoot, was created to serve "at least 25" — or six to eight members of this author's family.

- **2 pounds lamb shank, bone in**
- **2 fresh pork knuckles, about 1½ pounds**
- **1 veal shank, about 2¼ pounds**
- **5 pounds of beef shank, bone in**
- **4 to 4¼ quarts of water**
- **2 teaspoons salt**
- **2 bay leaves**
- **Handful of celery tops**
- **1 tablespoon black peppercorns**
- **3 dried red pepper pods (optional)**
- **1 large onion, quartered**
- **3 to 4 cloves garlic, peeled**

Put all the meat and bones in a 12- to 15-quart kettle with a lid. The bone-in beef shank is a huge piece; unless your pot is huge, you'll probably need to cut the meat off the bone in two or three pieces so both the bone and the meat will fit comfortably into the pot.

Cover all the meat and bones with water. Add all the other ingredients. Bring to a slow boil, skim, lower the heat, cover and simmer for 2½ to 3 hours, until the meat is falling off the bones.

Take the pot off the heat and let it cool. Take out the meat and strain the broth. Discard any gristle on the meat.

With a small spoon or knife, dig any lingering marrow out of the bones and put it, along with any loose marrow, back into the stock. Discard the bones. Refrigerate the stock and the meat separately in covered bowls. The next day the stock will have jelled, and the top layer of fat can be removed. Return the stock to the pot and bring slowly to a high simmer. Then add:

3½- to 4-pound chicken, cut in quarters
2 cups diced carrots
2 cups diced onion
2 cups diced celery
2 cups diced green peppers

Let simmer, partially covered, for an hour. Take out the chicken and set it aside to cool slightly. To the still-simmering stock, add:

4 cups diced potatoes

In about 15 minutes, when the chicken is cool enough to handle, pull off and discard the skin and bones, cut the chicken into small pieces and put it back into the pot along with:

All of the reserved meat, shredded or finely chopped
4 cloves garlic, minced
6 cups fresh corn kernels, or three 10-ounce frozen packages
4 cups baby lima beans, or two 10-ounce frozen packages
4 cups okra, or two 10-ounce frozen packages, cut into 1-inch pieces
1-pound can tomato puree
4 cups tomatoes, skinned and chopped, or 2 pounds canned plum tomatoes, drained

Stir all these ingredients together while they simmer about 15 minutes, until the lima beans are cooked and the okra has thickened the stew. Now it's seasoning time, that crucial point at which you mold the character of your burgoo — and it should go without saying that you want your burgoo to have character. You will need the following:

3 tablespoons Worcestershire sauce
2 teaspoons salt to taste (optional)
Cayenne pepper to taste
Black pepper to taste
Tabasco sauce to taste
1 bunch curly parsley, stems removed and leaves minced

Add everything except the parsley. Burgoo is supposed to be on the fiery side, so be liberal with the Tabasco sauce, while taking into consideration the tolerance levels of your guests and yourself. Cook gently for about 10 more minutes, stirring to blend the flavors. Stir in the parsley and serve with biscuits.

The Hot Brown

The hot Brown, an open-faced sandwich made with turkey and cheese, is so named because, 1) it was created at the Brown Hotel in Louisville in the 1920s and 2) it is served hot.

In later years, various chefs at the Brown Hotel introduced their own hot Brown variations. The recipe that follows is for the original hot Brown.

4 ounces butter
Flour to make a roux (about 6 tablespoons)
3 to 3½ cups milk
1 beaten egg
6 tablespoons grated Parmesan cheese
1 ounce whipped cream (optional)
Salt and pepper to taste

— continued on next page

Slices of roast turkey
8 to 12 slices of toast (may be trimmed)
Extra Parmesan for topping
2 strips cooked bacon

Melt butter and enough flour to make a reasonable roux (enough to absorb all of the butter). Add milk and Parmesan cheese. Add egg to thicken sauce, but do not allow to boil.

Remove from heat. Fold in whipped cream. Add salt and pepper to taste.

For each hot Brown, place two slices of toast on a metal or flameproof dish. Cover the toast with a liberal amount of turkey. Pour a generous amount of sauce over the turkey and toast. Sprinkle with additional Parmesan cheese.

Place entire dish under broiler until the sauce is speckled brown and bubbly.

Remove from broiler, cross two pieces of bacon on top and serve immediately. Makes 4 servings.

Subsequent versions of the hot Brown have included such variations as sliced chicken or country ham instead of turkey, Romano and American cheeses, sherry and tomato, to name a few. Today you can order some version of the hot Brown just about anywhere you go in Kentucky.

Beer Cheese

Beer cheese, which varies in spiciness according to the maker, is popular when served with crackers or veggies as a snack or an appetizer. Here's one of many versions.

1 pound aged cheddar cheese
1 pound natural Swiss cheese
1 cup beer
1 teaspoon dry mustard
2 teaspoons Worcestershire sauce
Red pepper to taste, or a little chopped jalapeno pepper
Garlic to taste

Grate cheese; mix in a little garlic, pepper, dry mustard and Worcestershire sauce. Gradually beat in enough beer until smooth (a food processor works best for the proper consistency). Serve at room temperature. Makes about 1 quart.

Corn Pudding

Kentucky pioneers, influenced by the Indians, displayed endless creativity in finding new uses for corn, a staple in their gardens and on their tables. Today corn is consumed on the cob, off the cob, in cornbread and "Johnny cakes," as hominy and grits and in many other forms, including as grain for livestock and as a key ingredient in the mash that is fermented to make bourbon.

Corn pudding is a rich casserole that Harrodsburg's long-lived Beaumont Inn has down to an art form. Here's how Beaumont Inn makes its legendary corn pudding.

2 cups white whole-kernel corn, or fresh corn cut off the cob
4 eggs
8 level tablespoons flour
1 quart milk
4 rounded teaspoons sugar
4 tablespoons butter, melted
1 teaspoon salt

Stir into the corn the flour, salt, sugar and butter. Beat the eggs well; put them into the milk, then stir into the corn and put into a pan or Pyrex dish. Bake at 450 degrees for 40 to 45 minutes.

Stir vigorously with long-pronged fork three times, about 10 minutes apart, while baking, disturbing the top as little as possible.

Lamb Fries

Warning: If you're easily offended or grossed out, please skip this section.

Lamb fries are a Kentucky delicacy, but they're not for the squeamish. They're tasty enough — until you learn that they are actually, ahem, lamb testicles, sliced thin, breaded, fried and served with cream gravy. Despite the origin of the dish, sometimes called "Kentucky mountain oysters," it remains popular enough that a number of restaurants throughout the Bluegrass offer lamb fries on their menus. Everyone can't be ordering them for the first time. Some people are simply nuts about them.

We don't have a recipe for lamb fries to share with you, but you can get them at the Campbell House, Columbia's, the Springs Inn, The Coach House and many other fine dining establishments in the Bluegrass.

The Mint Julep

As a whole, Kentuckians and visitors alike are ambivalent about the mint julep, a Kentucky beverage tradition and the "official" drink of the Kentucky Derby. "It's a terrible thing to do to good bourbon" is a typical complaint. A joke recipe for the drink instructs the unsuspecting novice to — after preparing the needed mint syrup from mint leaves, sugar and water — throw the sticky-sweet mixture away and drink the bourbon straight or on the rocks.

Nevertheless, thousands of mint juleps are served each year on the first Saturday in May at Churchill Downs and at weekend Derby parties around the Bluegrass (our editor corrected us here and said that this concoction is served all over the country during Derby parties, as she had had "only a couple" at such a party in Richmond, Virginia). Again, there are many variations, the merits of which can be hotly debated. Anita Madden, the queen of Derby parties, uses this recipe:

1/3 cup sugar
2 tablespoons mint syrup (instructions follow)
1½ to 2 ounces bourbon
Crushed ice
Fresh mint
Powdered sugar

To make mint syrup, bruise a "whole handful" of mint leaves and combine with the sugar dissolved in 1 cup water. Boil for 5 minutes and strain.

Pour mint syrup in sterling silver cup. Add bourbon. Mix.

Fill cup with crushed ice. Rub fresh mint around rim of cup.

For garnish, dip fresh mint sprig in powdered sugar and insert in ice.

Chocolate Chip-and-Nut Pie

Another popular Bluegrass dessert is the Derby Pie®, a rich, chocolate chip-and-nut-filled trademark of Louisville-based Kern's Kitchen. Rivaling this treat in popularity are its many generic versions, known by a variety of names including Kentucky pie, Pegasus pie, Keeneland pie and Run for the Roses pie. Kern's Kitchen does not take trademark infringement lightly.

— continued on next page

This variation is known as Oldham pie.

> ¼ cup margarine (not butter)
> 1 cup sugar
> 3 eggs
> ¼ teaspoon salt
> ¾ cup light corn syrup
> 1 teaspoon vanilla
> ½ cup chocolate chips
> ½ cup chopped black walnuts
> 2 tablespoons bourbon
> 1 unbaked pie shell

Cream margarine. Add sugar and beat with a mixer. Add eggs and syrup. Then add salt and vanilla. Mix well. Add chocolate chips, nuts and bourbon. Pour into pie crust. Bake at 350 degrees for 45 minutes. Serve warm with whipped cream.

Bourbon Balls

Even teetotalers enjoy a bourbon ball or six during the holidays. Rebecca Gooch and Ruth Hanly, the founders of Rebecca-Ruth Candies in Frankfort, are credited with inventing bourbon balls. Variations are many, and the choice of bourbon is up to the cook. Here's one recipe.

> 1 cup chopped pecans
> 4 tablespoons bourbon
> 1 stick butter or margarine
> 1 pound powdered sugar
> ½ box semisweet chocolate
> ½ rectangle paraffin

Combine pecans and bourbon and allow to sit for 3 hours. Cream butter and powdered sugar with mixer, adding pecan mixture. Roll in small balls and chill. Melt chocolate in double boiler, adding shaved paraffin. Dip balls into chocolate mixture, using fork. Put on waxed paper to dry.

Bread Pudding

One of the things Kentuckians have a knack for is making a meal out of bread — as in biscuits and gravy, which should go down in the good eating hall of fame. So it's no wonder we also make a dessert with bread, and call it bread pudding. We can't claim to have created bread pudding, but we sure can claim to make the best version imaginable when we top it with bourbon sauce. It should be designated our state dessert.

Though every self-respecting Kentuckian claims it as a favorite, just a handful of restaurants serve bread pudding.

The Woodlands Grille makes a version with an extra ingredient — buttermilk — that makes it sublime. Here's the Woodlands' recipe, scaled down from restaurant proportions.

> 8 slices of white bread
> 4 eggs
> 1½ cups of whole milk
> ½ cup buttermilk
> ½ cup granulated sugar
> Nutmeg and cinnamon to taste
> 1 stick of butter, plus 1 tablespoon for topping
> 1 cup of powdered sugar
> 2 tablespoons of bourbon

Preheat oven to 350 degrees. Cut crusts off bread, then cut into cubes and place in 1½-quart casserole that has been generously buttered. Sprinkle with nutmeg and cinnamon and toss. Lightly beat eggs, then add sugar, milk and buttermilk and beat lightly after each addition.

Pour over bread, making sure all cubes are moistened. Dot with the tablespoon of butter and bake for 1 hour, or until top is lightly brown.

To make sauce, heat the stick of butter over low heat until melted. Add the powdered sugar and whip until smooth. Add bourbon, blend and serve about 1 tablespoon over each portion of pudding. The amount of bourbon can be adjusted to your taste.

in chicken and lamb versions. If you like a little fire, go for the spicy vindaloo; those less adventurous will like the milder, but just as tasty, saag dishes, cooked with spinach. Kashmir offers a buffet from noon to 3 PM Saturday and Sunday.

Marikka's
$$ • 411 Southland Dr. • 277-9801

German restaurants have always been risky ventures in Lexington, but Marikka's has been going strong for more than two years now. One reason for the success is the authentic German cuisine — including Wiener schnitzel, jaegerschnitzel, sauerbraten, knackwurst and bratwurst — cooked up by Marikka Tackett from family recipes. If they would just keep real mashed potatoes on the menu, the place would be just about perfect. The adjoining bar is a beer lover's dream, with more than 300 brews from around the world and a billiard table.

Natasha's Cafe
$ • 304 Southland Dr. • 277-8412

Natasha Williams, a Russian native, and her American husband, Gene, opened Natasha's Cafe and Boutique in December 1991. The tiny cafe features Russian and Greek dishes and exotic coffees — and since coffee houses have become trendy in Lexington in the past couple of years, Natasha's also functions as a true coffee house. Vegetarian specials include an Armenian cheese roll filled with feta and cream cheeses, black olives, green peppers and cilantro. Try the Turkish coffee or the Turkish coffee milkshake. The adjoining boutique has great clothing, gifts and jewelry from around the world. It's closed on Sundays.

The Oasis
$, no credit cards • 868-B E. High St. in Chevy Chase Place • 268-0414

This Mediterranean restaurant has plenty of options for the meat-lover and vegetarian alike. Greek specialties include gyros, spinach pie, tabouli, falafel and stuffed grape leaves. Do not even think of visiting without ordering the creamy cumin-laced lentil soup. It's open for lunch-only on Sundays.

Old San Juan
$ • 247 Surfside Dr. • 278-2682

Had a good Cuban sandwich lately? You know, with roast pork, ham, cheese, butter and pickles all between two slices of crusty Cuban bread? No, it's not exactly low-cholesterol, but you should have one anyway. Or at least a bowl of black beans and rice with a side order of fried plantains. Come as you are. Old San Juan is nothing fancy, just a few tables at the front of a Cuban/Puerto Rican grocery. The owners are friendly, the food is cheap, daily specials are offered and you can't get a good Cuban sandwich just anywhere, you know.

Siam Thai Restaurant
$ • 126 New Circle Rd. N.E. • 231-7975

Siam Thai is a basic, no-frills spot with a big following that specializes in spicy dishes such as Thai chili and pad Thai, both of which are available with chicken, pork, beef or shrimp. The spring roll appetizer is a good way to start things off. Vegetarian dishes are also available.

Taj Mahal Indian Cuisine
$$ • 925 Newtown Pk. • 225-9634

It may be tucked away in an Econo Lodge,

but this is definitely not your typical motel food. Exotic Indian dishes like curry, masala and vindaloo are available with chicken, lamb or shrimp; you'll also find a number of vegetarian selections. All meals are served with long-grain basmati rice; be sure to try some nan (leavened white flour bread) or other Indian breads. Our favorite entree is the wonderful tandoori chicken, which is marinated in yogurt and freshly ground spices, then broiled in a charcoal clay oven. It ends up colored bright red, with a delicious smoky flavor. You can also order mulligatawny (remember the hilarious "soup Nazi" episode of "Seinfeld"?), a traditional Indian soup made with chicken and lentils.

We're crazy about Taj Mahal's daily lunch buffet, which offers a representative sampling of the menu. We also like Ali, the friendly and jovial server who, during an earlier job at a posh Washington, D.C., restaurant, was once voted waiter of the year. He's fond of telling diners at the buffet, "Remember, it's all you can eat; if you eat less than that, we charge you double." Taj Mahal is open Tuesday through Saturday.

Yats'
$ • 200 Bolivar St. • 254-8128

New Orleans-style dining in Lexington owes much to Yats' owner Joe Vuskovich, a former Big Easy resident whose recipes have also enlivened the menus of Jozo's Bayou Gumbo, which he has since sold, and Regina's. Yats', in the South Hill Station complex, is an informal and inexpensive place where you can sample a continually changing menu of Cajun, Creole and other imaginative creations, most of which are served over pasta.

At this writing, the menu included pasta jambalaya, Caribbean pasta ropa Vieja, white chili, pasta maque choux and (sometimes) crayfish. Sandwich lovers should try the Yatwich, which is sauteed turkey, vegetables, spices and olive oil on focaccia bread. During happy hour — 11 AM to 1 PM and 5 PM to 7 PM — you can get any dish and a domestic beer for $5. The menu defines a "yat," incidentally, as "a person, usually an off-the-wall fun-lovin' person, who grew up in or near the French Quarter in New Orleans." Yats' is open Monday through Saturday.

Vegetarian

Alfalfa
$ • 557 S. Limestone St. • 253-0014

This restaurant across from the main entrance to the University of Kentucky gained its reputation in the '60s as a primarily vegetarian hangout for the coffeehouse crowd. Times have changed since then, and so have the patrons, but they keep coming back. And Alfalfa continues to serve old favorites (both vegetarian and carnivorian) as well as inventive new creations. You'll find everything on the menu from babagannoush to hoppin' John. The Saturday and Sunday brunch is a specialty, and Alfalfa also has international nights. Call to get on the mailing list.

Everybody's Natural Foods & Deli
$ • 503 Euclid Ave. • 255-4162

During lunchtime at Everybody's, a storefront cafe with shelves of health-food products lining the walls, you'll find everybody from suit-and-tie professionals to hippie types in tie-dyes and sandals. The food is healthy, cheap, and interesting and there are daily specials, including hot vegetarian and vegan specials. Regular offerings include a meatless whole-grain "veggie burger"; tofu, falafel and tuna salad (dolphin-safe, of course) sandwiches (especially the veggie delight with fresh crunchy veggies and tahini); pasta salad; and tabouli. And don't forget to try their smoothies (healthy milkshakes!). Everybody's is open every day for lunch and dinner.

Delivery

Want a restaurant meal but don't feel like going out? Your options aren't limited to that old standby, pizza. Here are a couple of alternatives.

Cafe Express
$ • 277-9777

Menu items from nearly three dozen restaurants are available from Cafe Express. Order steak, prime rib, Chinese, Mexican, Italian, barbecue, sandwiches and more, and it will generally be delivered in less than an hour.

Hay and soybeans are important crops in Kentucky.

Drivers use insulated Mylar bags to keep the food warm. You pay a delivery charge of $3.50 if you live within the designated delivery area and an additional 75¢ for each mile outside it. Gratuity is included on lunch orders Monday through Friday only; a 15 percent tip is customary at other times. Pick up a menu book at any participating restaurant, or call Cafe Express and one will be mailed to you.

Columbia Steak Express
$ • Park Hills Shopping Center, 3120 Pimlico Pkwy. • 272-9600

Steaks (including Columbia Steak House's famous tenderloin in garlic sauce), tenderloin tips, ribs, grilled chicken, burgers, salads and side dishes are available with a $6 minimum order in an area between Nicholasville and Winchester roads and to all Lexington hospitals.

Steak-Out
$$ • 125 Southland Dr. • 277-2669
$$ • 112 Mount Tabor Rd. • 269-1000

Steak-Out offers a variety of charbroiled items including steaks, chicken and burgers, along with side dishes, generally delivered in a half-hour to 45 minutes. The current delivery area is between Versailles and Richmond roads out to Man o' War Boulevard.

T.M. Riders
$ • 1670 Bryan Station Rd., Kroger's Plaza • 299-1880
$ • 1080 S. Broadway, Simpson Center • 255-2448
$ • 4750 Hartland Pkwy., Hartland Village • 273-0100

This Tex-Mex "outfit" just about has all of Lexington covered with two more stores on

---

INSIDERS' TIP

If you're in the mood for a burger, try Lynagh's.

Transylvania University is the oldest college west of the Alleghenies.

the drawing board for Nicholasville and Richmond roads by the end of 1997. All of your Mexican favorites are available, along with steak dinners, sandwiches and kids meals. There's a $6 minimum on lunch orders, $10 minimum on dinner orders.

Caterers

It isn't difficult to find a caterer around here. What's hard is choosing one. Whether your event is a wedding reception, a corporate luncheon or a Super Bowl party, you'll find a wide range of businesses that specialize in catering. In addition, nearly three dozen restaurants of all types — from fried chicken to pizza to haute cuisine — also provide catering services. Check the Yellow Pages under "caterers," and you'll probably find someone who can provide the appropriate food for your party or just

---

INSIDERS' TIP

For an old-fashioned milkshake and old-fashioned atmosphere, visit Kelly's Grill and Ice Cream on Southland Drive.

call your favorite restaurant. We've listed a few with different specialties or services to get you started.

Central Catering
1050 Newtown Pike • 321-8561

Mike and Debbie Silvey made the delicious homestyle fare at downtown's Central Cafeteria an institution before they sold it and went into the catering business full time. They still do homestyle, as well as upscale, at your place or theirs. Their place is the spacious Fasig-Tipton sales pavilion (where thoroughbred horse sales are held several times a year) where their kitchen is located.

Phil Dunn's CookShop
431 Old E. Vine St. • 231-0099

Phil Dunn is one of Lexington's most popular and most seasoned (we couldn't resist, but he has been in demand for more that 15 years!) caterers, specializing in upscale, creative dining and wonderful pastries and desserts, all prepared in his popular restaurant and bakery, the CookShop. He'll do a carryout dinner for four people or a sit-down dinner for 400 anywhere in town.

Something Special Catering and Flowers by Jerry Hester
16 Mentelle Park • 266-5551

Just leave it to Jerry Hester and he'll prepare fare for an intimate dinner party for six or a picnic for 200 people. The best part is he'll make everything look wonderful with the most creative decorating and fresh flowers.

Bleu Ribbon Hospitality
255 Romany Rd. • 266-8704

Kate Savage catered the prestigious Lexington Ball in 1996 and 1997 for more than 600 people, so you can guess her capabilities. This busy Englishwoman also offers gourmet carryout and an upscale restaurant, The Cafe, at the same location as her catering business.

There's enough variety on Lexington's nightlife scene to at least keep you groovin' (or whatever you're doing) past midnight.

Nightlife

They basically roll up the sidewalks at 1 AM, which means you'll probably beat the cows home. But, until you find out where those blasted bovines are partying, you'll have to either deal with the early closing times or find an "after hours" club. (We have three such places in this chapter — Spurs, The Bar and Vertigo — serving wildly different clientele.) In the meantime, there's enough variety on Lexington's nightlife scene to at least keep you groovin' (or whatever you're doing) past midnight.

You can dance or simply listen to music provided by live bands or by disc jockeys. Take in a rock show at one of the area's major concert venues. Shoot some pool. Play bingo while benefiting a local charity. See a first-run blockbuster movie or an avant-garde foreign film. Laugh at a nationally touring comedian. (For information about pool, bingo and bowling, see our Recreation chapter. For information about live theater, see our Arts chapter.)

Keep in mind that you must be 21 years of age to gain admittance to Lexington's nightclubs. There are some exceptions, such as restaurants that serve food late and feature entertainment. If you're thinking about using a fake ID, take our advice: Don't do it. Local bartenders and bouncers have become increasingly sophisticated in their ability to detect frauds, and you could cause yourself a major hassle. Similarly, you should know that driving under the influence is taken very seriously by the Lexington police department its special Traffic Alcohol Patrol, which monitors the streets in a fleet of unmarked Ford Crown Victorias.

Concerts and Shows

For lovers of music and culture, living in Lexington means there's almost always some high-quality entertainment going on within easy driving distance. If Lexington doesn't have

much going on, Louisville or Cincinnati usually will. Most of the major rock and country tours hit one of these three cities, as do Broadway touring productions and other shows.

Tickets to many area concerts can be ordered by calling TicketMaster at 281-6644, a local number.

To keep up-to-date on the rock 'n' roll concert scene in the area, call WKQQ's concert line, a recording, at 259-3398.

Rupp Arena
430 W. Vine St. • 233-4567
Ticket information • 233-3566
Charge-A-Tick • 233-3535

If there's a more popular year-round public place in the Bluegrass, somebody's gonna have to tell us about it. First, of course, you have Kentucky Wildcat basketball, which packs the 23,000-seat arena roughly 15 times a year. Then you have an impressive schedule of concerts and shows featuring some of the biggest names in the biz. Highlights of recent years, for example, have included the Eagles, Garth Brooks, Rod Stewart, Aerosmith, Clint Black with Wynonna, Metallica, Reba McEntire with Central Kentucky's own John Michael Montgomery, Bruce Springsteen, Vince Gill and Mary Chapin Carpenter.

The Kentucky Theatre
214 E. Main St. • 231-6997

If you haven't heard about the theater's highly successful Troubadour Concert Series, then you don't know what you've been missing. The series, organized by local folkie Michael Johnathon and his Troubador Project, has featured the likes of Bill Monroe, Merle Haggard, Waylon Jennings, John Prine, Steve Earle, Guy Clark, Townes Van Zandt, Joan Baez, Richie Havens, Don McLean, Leon Redbone, Leo Kottke, Nanci Griffith, John Hiatt, Allison Krauss & Union Station, and many others, playing mostly acoustic music in an intimate atmosphere. You gotta be there! (For more about The Kentucky, see the "Cinema" section in this chapter.)

Bogart's
2621 Vine St., Cincinnati
• (513) 872-8801, after 11 AM,
Concert line recording, (513) 281-8400

This comfortable 1,300-seat venue near the University of Cincinnati features a wide range of artists who, for assorted reasons, don't play arenas. Some of them are up-and-coming stars, some are veterans whose arena days are behind them, still others are bands with cult followings or "alternative" heavyweights. In recent years, for example, you could have caught such artists as B.B. King, Warren Zevon, Los Lobos, Smashing Pumpkins, The Lemonheads and De La Soul. If someone you like is playing Bogart's, it's well worth the drive from Lexington.

Riverbend Music Center
6295 Kellogg Ave., Cincinnati
• (513) 232-6220

Riverbend is nestled, appropriately enough, in a bend in the Ohio River. Concertgoers can choose covered pavilion seats or save a few bucks and sit farther away from the stage on the sloping lawn. This highly popular place for summer concerts covers all the bases, from pop, rock and country to blues, jazz, Big Band and even comedy. Jimmy Buffett plays several sold-out shows every summer. Other hot tickets recently have included the Eagles, Eric Clapton, Steely Dan, Sting, Van Halen, Bette Midler, Tony Bennett, Bonnie Raitt, Elton John, and the Lollapalooza and Lillith Fair festivals.

Kentucky Center for the Arts
5 Riverfront Plaza, Louisville
• (502) 562-0100 tickets, (502) 584-7777

The beautiful Kentucky Center for the Arts building, on Main Street between Fifth and Sixth streets, offers a variety of cultural opportunities. With 2,479-seat Whitney Hall; Bomhard Theater, which seats 622; and the

flexible MeX black-box theater, which can seat up to 139, the center has something for everyone. Five resident groups — Stage One, the Broadway Series, the Louisville Ballet, the Louisville Orchestra and the Kentucky Opera — present several programs apiece each year. The center's award-winning Lonesome Pine Specials series, which airs on Kentucky Educational Television and on other public TV stations around the country, has featured critically acclaimed folk, blues, jazz and world music artists from around the globe.

The Crown
100 Broadway,
Cincinnati, Ohio
• (513) 241-1818

The former Riverfront Coliseum underwent an extensive remodeling in 1997, reopening in grand fashion with a new name for an October concert by the reunited Fleetwood Mac. The Crown, with a capacity of 16,000, is also home to the Cincinnati Cyclones professional hockey team and the Cincinnati Silverbacks pro soccer team.

Freedom Hall
Kentucky Fair and Exposition Center, Louisville
• (502) 367-5001

Freedom Hall is a longtime favorite venue for pop, rock and country concerts and athletic events. The University of Louisville basketball team plays its home games here. It seats 19,800 at full capacity.

Louisville Gardens
525 W. Muhammad Ali Blvd., Louisville
• (502) 587-3800, (502) 584-7777 tickets
by phone

Louisville Gardens, which seats a maximum of 6,850, plays host to pop, rock and country concerts and other events.

Norton Center for the Arts
Centre College, Danville • (606) 236-4692

This often-overlooked treasure, in a town with a population of 12,500 about a half-hour from Lexington, offers a wealth of big-city

---

FYI

If no area code is given, it's a local call from Lexington-Fayette County. If an area code is given, whether it's 606 or 502, it's a long-distance call: dial 1, the area code and the number. See the How To Use This Book chapter for detailed information on calling.

culture. Ballet. Opera. Tony Award-winning Broadway musicals and plays. Orchestra concerts. Classical soloists. Jazz. A classic-film series. The Norton Center's consistently top-notch offerings are not surprising when you consider Centre College's nationally acknowledged academic reputation and the fact that the school has produced vice presidents, U.S. Supreme Court justices and many other leaders in all walks of life.

Bars, Nightclubs, Restaurants, Coffeehouses

There's no question that live club music in Lexington has suffered some major blows in the last couple of years, with the closing of the alternative haven The Wrocklage, longtime rock 'n' roll stalwart JDI (Jefferson Davis Inn) and the newer House of Heresy; The Wrocklage and Heresy in particular produced some downright legendary shows in their time. Local musicians grumble that it's dang near impossible to make a living playing in this town, and that may be so. Still, for those who are willing to venture out at night — and not just on the weekend — there are ample opportunities to catch not only local and regional talent but also some fine national touring acts.

Unless otherwise indicated, all the nightspots in this section have a full bar. Most, but not all have a cover charge (exceptions are noted), which generally runs between $2 and $5, more for special engagements or major acts.

A note about the organization of this section: Because many of Lexington's more popular nightclubs — especially the ones offering live music — often fit into several categories, we've chosen to merely list them alphabetically rather than rack our brains (and fight with ourselves) over which category to force them into.

A1A Sandbar & Grille
367 E. Main St. • 231-7263

One of A1A's biggest challenges since moving downtown in 1994 from its original location (Wilhite Drive off Nicholasville Road) has been avoiding complaints from nearby residents about noise levels. But, at this writing, manager Greg Hardin was working on ways to contain the music while expanding the capacity of his live-music bar and the variety of his clientele, which now falls largely into the 25-35 age range.

He should be successful, because A1A — which is actually three bars in one — does offer something for almost everybody. Riptides, the live-music room, seats 800 and will seat 1,000 once the expansion is complete; it features regional and occasionally national bands. You'll also find a disco bar and a sports bar, where you can catch your favorite sports on big-screen TV or play interactive trivia, pool or darts. A1A is also known for its volleyball leagues, in season.

Alfalfa Restaurant
557 S. Limestone St. • 253-0014

Low-key acoustic music ranging from folk, pop and jazz to Appalachian bluegrass and New Age is performed in an intimate coffeehouse atmosphere at this perennially popular restaurant, long a favorite among vegetarians and vegans (see our Restaurants chapter). Live performances are held from 8 PM to 10 PM Friday and Saturday night. The mostly adult clientele is varied: singles, couples, groups, UK professors and lawyers (the UK law school is across the street). There's never a cover charge.

The Atomic Cafe
265 N. Limestone St. • 254-1969

Weather permitting, this popular Caribbean eatery (see our Restaurants chapter) offers live entertainment on its spacious and breezy patio Friday and Saturday night. The music is appropriate: reggae, salsa, merengue and

---

INSIDERS' TIP

The incredible Joseph-Beth Booksellers is open until 11 PM on Friday and Saturday.

other island sounds from regional bands. Relax, mon!

Austin City Saloon
2350 Woodhill Shopping Center • 266-6891

Country music fans who appreciate history-in-the-making will appreciate the fact that this is where rising star John Michael Montgomery got his start. To show his appreciation, he filmed his video for "Beer and Bones" here. Montgomery has moved on to the big time, but Austin City Saloon continues its long tradition as one of the top places in Lexington to catch local country bands. The shopping center is near the Richmond Road Exit off New Circle Road.

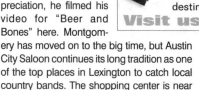

www.insiders.com
See this and many other
Insiders' Guide®
destinations online.
Visit us today!

The Bar
224 E. Main St. • 255-1551

The Bar, once known as Johnny Angel's, is a long-lived downtown nightclub that serves a primarily gay clientele. Patrons dance to industrial and dance music played by a disc jockey in a discotheque atmosphere, and shows by female impersonators are featured on Friday and Saturday night. The Bar is actually three bars: a lounge, a disco and a show bar. There's no cover charge for the lounge, but you'll pay $3 to dance in the disco, $3 for the drag show or $4 (Friday) and $5 (Saturday) for both. Friday and Saturday also feature "after hours" (no alcohol) where you can dance from 1 to 3:30 AM for $3 (no charge if you're already there).

Blue Moon Oldies Saloon
815 Euclid Ave. • 268-0001

Dance cheek to cheek with your baby while a DJ spins hits from the '50s, '60s and '70s at this Chevy Chase nightclub that's popular with folks who remember when the songs were cool the first time around. If you dig dancing

to the original versions of the oldies, this is the place to be in Lexington.

Boardwalk Restaurant and Lounge
1479 Boardwalk • 254-6170

Boardwalk, which has a honky-tonk atmosphere, offers live entertainment Friday, Saturday and Sunday nights featuring the Lanny Murphy Band. Sunday evening is jam session, which means you can get up and play or sing with the band, if you're so inclined. There's never a cover charge.

The Cafe Joseph-Beth at Joseph-Beth Booksellers
The Mall at Lexington Green • 273-2911 bookstore, 271-0062 cafe

The Cafe Joseph-Beth, just part of one of the coolest bookstores you'll find anywhere (see our Shopping chapter), is a popular spot for literate singles who spurn the bar scene and want to chat over a cup of espresso and a pastry. The bookstore is also a great place to take the whole family at night. The kids can visit the expanded children's section while you browse the books, the extensive selection of newspapers and magazines or the large CD and cassette section. In addition, Joseph-Beth, which is open until 11 PM Friday and Saturday nights, features live acoustic music from 7 to 9 PM Friday on the patio, weather permitting, and Saturday inside.

The Campbell House
1375 Harrodsburg Rd. • 255-4281

The Campbell House nightlife is primarily aimed at an older crowd, but anyone is welcome. There's piano music from 7 to 9 PM Monday through Saturday in the dining room. In the Gallery Lounge, karaoke lets you be the singer from 7 to 9 PM Tuesday through Friday, followed by a variety band until closing.

INSIDERS' TIP

Country music fans will enjoy Austin City Saloon, where John Michael Montgomery got his start.

Cheapside Bar & Grill
131 Cheapside • 254-0046

Blues, R&B, jazz and occasionally zydeco, as well as rock, are the musical cornerstones of this immensely popular bar and restaurant in the heart of downtown. It can sometimes be a yuppie haven, but when the music is hot — as it generally is — the clientele is diverse and sometimes sweaty, especially those who crowd into the tiny dance area in front of the band. The bar section is a dark, loud, smoky joint and packed on weekends, literally standing room only — you'll have to be lucky or quick to snag a table. When the weather is nice, the action spills out onto a brick patio and upstairs "Oasis" deck (check out the awesome mural) where you can have a conversation without screaming. Cheapside also is known for its inventive Southwestern-tinged menu. Simultaneously hip and down-to-earth.

Circle H
9079 Old Richmond Rd., Clays Ferry
• 263-9944

Country stars such as Keith Whitley and Alan Jackson, in town for concerts, have been spotted sitting in with the band at the Circle H. But even without celebrity cameos, this bar on the Kentucky River at Clays Ferry would be a hot place for country music. Owner Earl Watkins and his County Line band play Thursday through Saturday. The joint is closed the rest of the week because, as Watkins says, "I like my four-day weekends."

The Coach House
855 S. Broadway • 252-7777

As a restaurant, The Coach House is renowned for its elegant atmosphere and cuisine (see our Restaurants chapter). Its lounge, on the other hand, is not as well known — but that is rapidly changing. Every Friday and Saturday night from 7:30 to 11:30 PM, you can enjoy jazz, and occasionally pop, from some of the top musicians in the region. Drummer

Dave McWhorter and his jazz trio are regulars. The lounge, expanded in August 1997, is dark and romantic, with white tablecloths, candles, a fireplace and a bandstand. Dinner is served, but you don't have to eat. And while there's no cover, it's a good idea to make reservations, as word is getting out and the place is often packed.

Comedy off Broadway
Lexington Green • 271-5653

Lexington's only nightly spot for live comedy moved from its downtown North Broadway location in 1994, necessitating a name change from Comedy on Broadway. The location has changed to the Nicholasville road mall with the green roof, but the laughs are still here, with some of the nation's top touring comedians.

The atmosphere is as intimate and laugh-friendly as anything you'll see on cable television. A warning: If you're easily embarrassed, don't sit near the stage, as some comedians tend to single out individuals for ridicule. And would-be hecklers take heed: No matter how witty you might think you are, it's hard to win a verbal battle when the other guy has a microphone and you don't. Tuesday through Thursday, Comedy off Broadway has one show, at 8 PM. Friday shows are at 8 and 10 PM. Saturday shows are at 7 and 9:15 PM, with an optional 11:30 PM show if the first two sell out. Cover charge generally ranges from $5 to $8, more for special engagements. Reservations are suggested.

Common Grounds Coffee House
343 E. High St. • 233-9761

Common Grounds' new owners, who took over in July 1997, have brought back live acoustic entertainment on most weekends. It may be folk, Celtic, bluegrass or something else. Cover charge ranges from nothing to $3. Each Monday from 8 to 10 PM is open-mike night.

INSIDERS' TIP

Carmike Cinemas, 3151 Maple Leaf Drive, offers 10 discount movies — $1 Monday through Thursday and $1.50 Friday through Sunday.

From bingo and billiards to concerts and karaoke, Lexington offers
plenty of opportunities to shake, rattle or roll.

Continental Inn
801 New Circle Rd. N.E. • 299-5281

Honkers Tavern features Top 40, blues and variety dance bands for a mixed crowd. Downstairs at the Someplace Else lounge, a DJ spins the hits for a slightly younger crowd.

Gazebo Lounge
At Doubletree Guest Suites
2601 Richmond Rd. • 268-0060

Doubletree Guest Suites was formerly the French Quarter Suites Hotel, and the new owners have retained the Bourbon Street ambience in the Gazebo Lounge. The courtyard-like atmosphere is casual, with a fountain, trees, a gazebo bar and wrought-iron tables and chairs sprinkled around the band area, where area jazz musicians perform. There's no cover

The Grapevine
4101 Tates Creek Rd. • 273-7788

This popular gathering place and restaurant in Tates Creek Centre is especially packed on Sunday evenings, when Troy Lee Gentry plays host to open microphone night. The music is mostly country covers, with a fair amount of rock 'n' roll and with the occasional original thrown in. You can catch live entertainment Wednesday, Friday, Saturday and Sunday night.

Looney Tune Saloon/Neon Moon
509 W. Main St. • 255-2822

Two clubs in one make up this two-level downtown nightclub that has had several previous incarnations. Downstairs the Looney Tune Saloon, which opened in November 1996, offers "dueling pianos." The atmosphere is fun and occasionally rowdy, as the pianists take requests from the '70s to today, while encouraging sing-along crowd participation. Upstairs is the Neon Moon, a country line-dance bar with live DJ. A $4 cover charge

admits you to both clubs, and there's no cover Wednesdays. In addition, ladies and their dates get in free Thursdays. Reservations are accepted but not required.

Lynagh's Music Club
388 Woodland Ave. • 255-6614

Just two doors down from the great hamburgers at Lynagh's Irish Pub & Grill, in University Plaza Shopping Center near the UK campus, is one of the top music venues in town, with live entertainment every night except Sunday. Like the Pub & Grill, the Music Club is owned by John Lynaugh. Originally opened as a blues venue, Lynagh's gradually began expanding its repertoire to include a wider range of music, including funk-metal, rock 'n' roll and country. Lynagh's has also regularly featured exceptional national roots-music acts such as Wilco, Jimmie Dale Gilmore, John Hammond, Dale Watson, Junior Brown, Iris DeMent and Jason and the Scorchers.

Millennium
156 W. Main St. • 225-9194

Millennium is a large (14,000-square-foot) club with two levels. The lower level has a traditional look with a bandstand for live rock' n' roll. Upstairs is a dance-mix bar with corrugated-panel walls, a DJ and laser lights to accompany the pounding music.

Millennium, which draws a mixed, largely single crowd, is open Wednesday through Saturday nights.

The Springs Inn
2020 Harrodsburg Rd. • 277-5751

The Springtide Lounge here is a happening place for anyone who appreciates a variety of danceable music. Live music Wednesday through Saturday features the house band, The Rotations. The clientele is generally 35 and older.

INSIDERS' TIP

For a nice, romantic, cheap (OK, free) date, it's hard to beat a nighttime stroll around Triangle Park. Sit for a spell and gaze at the well-lighted fountains of water cascading down a series of steps.

Spurs
2320 Palumbo Dr. • 266-0890

Spurs might best be described as a bar for country insomniacs. It's open Thursday through Saturday nights, and it basically stays open all night — until 4 or 5 AM. No alcohol is served, but you can bring your own beer. Brad Alford and his house band generally take the stage about 2 AM; before that you can line dance on one of the city's largest dance floors, with lessons available early in the evening. The decor is a mix of Western and Southern, with longhorns, cowboy hats and Confederate flags. Cover is a bit steep — $6 Thursday and $10 Friday and Saturday — but the owners say they had to raise the price because the crowds were getting too big.

Two Keys Tavern
333 S. Limestone St. • 254-5000

The Keys, a popular hangout for college students and others since it opened in the 1920s, is at the corner of the University of Kentucky campus. Today it's a sports bar with 35 televisions and four satellites, which means that on Sundays during football season you can watch every blessed NFL game. Original and cover bands play rock 'n' roll Wednesday through Saturday night. On Tuesday night, you can catch national comedians at radio station WKQQ's "Laugh Track Live." The bar menu includes burgers, sandwiches, soups, salads and specials.

Vertigo
123 W. Main St. • 226-9904

Vertigo, an upscale dance club with DJ, prides itself on its casual atmosphere, friendliness and "totally mixed" (but mostly 25 and older) clientele, which varies widely from night to night depending on the entertainment. One night it's '70s music; another '80s; another, techno and industrial. Though it was voted "best lesbian/gay/alternative bar" by the readers of *ACE Magazine*, that tag can be misleading, say the owners, who welcome everybody. The former retail store is dark, mysterious and highlighted by a huge, 160-pound disco ball and a stunning variety of artwork supplied by Medusa, a local antique store. There's also a lounge area where people can get away for quieter conversation.

Cinema

There are dozens of places in Lexington to catch a movie. Most of them fall into the category of multi-screen corporate "cine-plexes." We won't list them here; check your newspaper for schedule information. But there's one "real" theater, and we'd really like to tell you about it.

The Kentucky Theatre
214 E. Main St. • 231-6997

This beloved downtown landmark is the place to go for foreign, offbeat, cult and classic films that don't generally hit your conventional cinemas. The Kentucky, as it's affectionately known, is a grand, 810-seat theater in the old-fashioned tradition, as evidenced by the large marquee out front. And despite its elegance, it's still cheaper than most cinemas: $4.50 for first-run films and $3.75 for all others, including the special midnight showings on Friday and Saturday nights.

When it opened in 1922 amid great fanfare, The Kentucky was a luxurious 1,100-seater complete with oil paintings, plush carpeting, tapestries, mirrored doors, a marble foyer, hand-carved woodwork and more. It underwent major renovations in the 1950s and 1980s, and was closed for more than four years after a fire in a next-door restaurant caused heavy smoke damage to the theater. Vocal support from the community led to The Kentucky's restoration (including the enlargement of the stage, which reduced the number of seats by about 300) and subsequent reopening in April 1992. It has since returned to

---

INSIDERS' TIP

Let off a little steam by engaging in high-tech warfare at Laser Quest. And on weekends Laser Quest is open until midnight (see our Kidstuff chapter).

Photo: Lexington Herald-Leader

After nearly four years of repairs from a fire, the Kentucky Theatre
downtown reopened to a sell-out crowd in 1992.

its status as a local treasure that you should not overlook.

In addition to movies you won't see anywhere else in town, The Kentucky is also home to the Troubador Concert Series (see the "Concerts and Shows" section in this chapter).

Cinema Grill
Lexington Mall, Richmond Road
• 266-4104

You won't get to see brand new releases, but you can catch up on the ones you haven't seen (for $3) - PLUS have dinner while you watch. It's mostly burgers, sandwiches, salads and pizza, but it's a novelty and great fun.

Call for films and times, then arrive at least a half hour early to get your order in.

Shocking Revelations

Psst! It's only fair to mention that Lexington does have several establishments at which young — and, in some cases, not so young — women shed a good portion of their clothing. If you're inclined to visit this sort of place, you'll find your way there one way or another. This author, unfortunately, can provide no additional information lest he arouse the suspicions and/or wrath of his generally understanding wife. Watch your newspaper for details.

According to some estimates, Kentucky produces 70 percent of the world's distilled spirits.

Distilleries and Breweries

Kentucky's claim to drinking fame is bourbon, not beer. But that could be changing, as Lexington is following the nationwide trend of proliferating microbreweries that brew small quantities of premium beer on the premises and, in many cases, serve it along with food.

Meanwhile, the state remains the top producer of bourbon whiskey, which was recognized by Congress in 1964 as a distinctly American product. That means no "bourbon whiskey" can be imported into this country. The potent brew is distinguished from other whiskeys in that the mash used to make it contains at least 51 percent corn.

Bourbon is distilled in a number of Kentucky towns, including Frankfort, Lawrenceburg, Louisville, Loretto and Bardstown, which is often referred to as "Bourbon Capital of the World." But we still have many counties that are "dry" - where bourbon cannot be legally sold.

A number of Kentucky counties, including Scott, Bourbon and Jefferson, claim to be the first production site bourbon whiskey. Many claim it was Georgetown minister Elijah Craig who first stumbled upon the secret, but there are several other people who might also have done it first — including one Jacob Spears of, appropriately enough, Bourbon County. At this point in time, it seems unlikely that we will ever know the truth. So, to paraphrase a once-popular beer commercial, "Why ask who?"

Because early settlers used whiskey as currency, converting the state's plentiful supply of corn into spirits made sound economic sense. The limestone-purified water in the area was an added benefit. As a result, distilleries have long played a major role in the Kentucky economy. As early as 1775 or 1776, whiskey was being distilled in the territory that is now Kentucky, and the Old Pepper Whiskey distillery was established in Lexington in 1780.

The number of distilleries has declined significantly since the early 19th century, when as many as 2,200 were producing whiskey in the state. Even today, with distilleries numbering in two digits instead of four, however, Kentucky continues to be the nation's largest producer of distilled spirits, including not only whiskey but also vodka, gin, brandy and assorted liqueurs. According to some estimates, the state produces 70 percent of the world's distilled spirits.

Distilleries

Here are just a few area distilleries where you can get a glimpse into the making of one of the state's most famous products. None are in Lexington, but all are within easy driving distance. Even for people who don't imbibe, these tours provide a fascinating look into an integral facet of Kentucky's history and economy.

Jim Beam Distillery
K.Y. Hwy. 245, Clermont • (502) 543-9877

Free tours are offered seven days a week at Jim Beam's American Outpost, adjacent to the distillery, which celebrated its 200th year in 1995. Although the distillery itself is not open for tours, you can see a 10-minute film on how bourbon is made and take a short walking tour that includes the Beam family home and what is said to be the oldest moonshine in the country. Hours are 9 AM to 4:30 PM Monday through Saturday and 1 to 4 PM Sunday. To get to Clermont, take the Bluegrass Parkway to the first Bardstown exit, get on Ky. Highway 245 and follow it about 18 miles to the distillery.

Heaven Hill Distilleries
1064 Loretto Rd., Bardstown
• **(502) 348-3921**

Heaven Hill, which bills itself as "America's largest family-owned distillery," produces Evan Williams bourbon whiskey as well as other distilled spirits. Despite a devastating fire in 1996, Heaven Hill is operational and offering tours. The free tours cover the entire bottling process, and visitors can take home a souvenir barrel bung (the barrel's cork or stopper) soaked in bourbon. Take the Bluegrass Parkway to the first Bardstown exit and then take Ky. Highway 49 to Heaven Hill.

Labrot & Graham Distillery
7855 McCracken Pike, Versailles
• **879-1812**

Labrot & Graham Distillery, owned by Brown-Forman, boasts a history going back to Elijah Pepper, one of the first distillers of bourbon whiskey. After moving from Virginia to Woodford County in 1797, Pepper started a distillery, then moved to the current location on Glenn's Creek in 1812. James Graham and Leopold Labrot bought the property in 1878 and gave the distillery its current name.

The distillery now produces small batches (five barrels a day) of Woodford Reserve, a pricey premium brand of bourbon. Compare that with 500 barrels a day produced by the Early Times distillery also operated by Brown-Forman. The property includes a wide-porched visitors center featuring exhibits and a video.

Free tours are offered at 10 and 11 AM and at 1, 2 and 3 PM Tuesday through Saturday. To get to Labrot & Graham, take U.S. Highway 60 (Versailles Road) past the city of Versailles toward Frankfort. Just past the intersection of U.S. 60 and K.Y. Highway 1685, turn left onto Grassy Spring Road. Follow this winding road until it dead ends at McCracken Pike. Turn right, and look for the L&G sign on the left side of the road after about 200 yards.

The Leestown Company
1001 Wilkinson Blvd.,
Frankfort • **(502) 223-7641**

Bourbon production began as early as 1869 on the site of this facility, which touts itself as "America's largest distillery" as well as one of its oldest. The company produces several Ancient Age bourbons plus a number of popular single-barrel bourbons, including the award-winning Blanton brand. Free tours are offered on the hour from 9 AM to 2 PM Monday through Friday year round. You'll see a video and walk through parts of five buildings, including bottling, warehouse and the Blanton building.

Maker's Mark Distillery
3350 Burks Spring Rd., Loretto
• **(502) 865-2099**

Although family-owned Maker's Mark produces just 38 barrels of whiskey—or "whisky," as the Samuels family prefers to spell it—at peak capacity, it has gained an international reputation for smoothness. A variety of publications, including *Esquire* magazine, have sung its praises. Please note that the Maker's Mark product is not bourbon; one difference is that mild winter wheat is used in place of the more common rye.

Free tours are offered on the half hour from 10:30 AM to 3:30 PM Monday through Saturday, except in January and February, when

FYI

If no area code is given, it's a local call from Lexington-Fayette County. If an area code is given, whether it's 606 or 502, it's a long-distance call: dial 1, the area code and the number. See the How To Use This Book chapter for detailed information on calling.

INSIDERS' TIP

The legal age to consume alcoholic beverages in Kentucky is 21.

the distillery is closed Saturdays. Tours include the still house, where the smooth, award-winning whiskey is made; the bottling house, which includes the wax-dipping operation; and the warehouse.

To get to the distillery from Lexington, take the Bluegrass Parkway to the first Springfield exit (Exit 42) and go left toward Springfield. At Springfield, take a right onto U.S. Highway 150, go for about a mile, then turn left onto Ky. Highway 152. Go about 11 miles until the road becomes Ky. 49, and continue for about a mile into Loretto. There, Ky. 49 runs into Ky. Highway 52, which you take east for about 2.5 miles. Turn left on Burks Spring Road, which will take you to Maker's Mark.

There's a dispute as to which Kentucky county was the first to produce bourbon.

Wild Turkey Distillery
1525 Tyrone Rd., Lawrenceburg
• (502) 839-4544

This distillery has been drawing attention since before 1893, when bourbon made by the Ripy brothers was selected from more than 400 whiskeys to represent Kentucky at the World's Fair. After Prohibition was repealed, the Ripy Distillery was reopened. It now makes the famous 8-year-old, 101 proof Wild Turkey and related brands.

Free tours are conducted Monday through Friday at 9 AM, 10:30 AM, 12:30 PM and 2:30 PM; the distillery is closed the first week of January and the last two weeks of July. Groups of 20 or more should make reservations. To get there from Lexington, take U.S. 60 W. to Versailles, then get on U.S. Highway 62 W. and follow the signs.

Breweries

Lexington Brewing Company
401 Cross St. • 252-6004

Calcium-rich limestone water is harder than other types of waters; brewing with it allows the various flavors to "coat the inside of the

Photo: Lee P. Thomas, courtesy of the Lexington Convention and Visitors Bureau

Many local distilleries offer free tours.

mouth," giving the drinker a more "vivid perception of the beer," says Brian J. Miller, brewmaster at Lexington Brewing Company. Thus the company's Limestone products benefit from the same limestone deposits that give our thoroughbred sturdy yet aerodynamically designed skeleton; make bluegrass grow; and add to the distinctive taste of Kentucky bourbon.

Lexington Brewing's process, which is in the English style, results in a beer that is crisper, with a little more bite. Lexington Brewing Company was the third microbrewery to open in Lexington, but the first to bottle beer for sale in stores. It began brewing on-site in October 1996; earlier, beginning in July 1995, it had been selling kegs brewed under contract by an Indianapolis microbrewery. Bottling began in January 1997. Three flagship ales—the original 1897 Amber Lager, Limestone Pale Ale and Limestone Dark Ale—make up the heart of Lexington Brewing's output.

Quarterly seasonal ales, such as an Oktoberfest, a winter bock and a Limestone Hefeweisen (unfiltered wheat beer), also make appearances through the year.

While the company has a capacity for brewing 12,000 to 13,000 barrels a year, its planned output for 1997 was just 1,500 barrels. Free tours (including free samples) of the facility off West Maxwell are offered during business hours. Tours last 15 minutes and up, according to how long somebody wants to stay and look at the tanks, says President Bill Ambrose, who founded the locally owned company with four partners in 1994. Reservations are not required, but "if you're coming with a large group, you might call and give us a few minutes' warning."

Lexington City Brewery
1050 South Broadway • 259-2739

Lexington's first brewery after Prohibition,

Lexington City Brewery takes pride in local history, and that pride is reflected in the names of its products. Belle Brezing is a light beer named for the famed brothel madam; Burley Red is an amber ale honoring the state's tobacco tradition; Winner's Gold, a European-style golden ale, is a salute to horse racing; and Smiley Pete, a dark, British-style stout, is named for Lexington's last "town dog." In addition, a different seasonal brew is on tap once a month, and other, "specialty" brews show up sporadically.

Lexington City Brewery, which opened in November 1995, is a brewpub that seats 300 people and serves a range of menu items. For information on the food served at Lexington City Brewery, see our Restaurants chapter. Lexington City Brewery is not related to Lexington Brewing Company, which at one time sought to prevent the use of the similar-sounding name. It is owned by City Breweries Investment Corporation, a California-based firm that also operates microbreweries in Mobile and Birmingham, Alabama, and Baton Rouge, Louisiana.

Brewmaster Kevin Banta said the brewery was making about 1,200 barrels in 1997, significantly less than its full capacity of 3,000 barrels. None of the beer is bottled or canned, but half-barrel and quarter-barrel kegs are available for sale. Tours are available on request.

Oldenberg Brewery
I-75 at Buttermilk Pike, Fort Mitchell
• **(606) 341-2804**

Oldenberg's distinctive beers are bottled and sold in a growing number of locations around the country. With the demise of Oldenbergy's Holy Grail brewpub and restaurant in Lexington, you'll have to take I-75 north to Exit 186, 5 miles south of Cincinnati in Northern Kentucky, to experience this microbrew at its source.

Daily tours include the microbrewery and the American Museum of Brewing History & Arts, which has more than 500,000 bits of brewing beer memorabilia; and a tasting of Oldenberg products. Oldenbergy periodically offers "beer schools" and "beer camps" for the true connoisseur.

Also of Interest

The Oscar Getz
Museum of Whiskey History
114 N. Fifth St., Bardstown
• **(502) 348-2999**

This museum contains a collection of whiskey artifacts and documents, including Abraham Lincoln's liquor license for a tavern he operated in Illinois in 1833. You can also see an authentic moonshine still, numerous antique bottles and jugs and memorabilia relating to Carrie Nation, the Kentucky-born woman who traveled throughout the country with a hatchet in her bid to eliminate the evils of alcohol.

The whiskey museum is housed, along with the Bardstown Historical Museum, in historic Spalding Hall. Hours are 9 AM to 5 PM Monday through Saturday and 1 to 5 PM Sunday, from May 1 through October 31. From November 1 to April 30, the museum is open from 10 AM to 4 PM Tuesday through Saturday and 1 to 4 PM Sunday. Admission is free.

Lexington's more than 50 hotels and motels have more than 6,000 rooms and suites available for visitors to the area.

Hotels and Motels

From a New Orleans-style inn to resort hotels with golf courses and fine dining to your more traditional kids, pets and pool motels on the interstate, Lexington is likely to have an accommodation option that will suit your needs.

Lexington's more than 50 hotels and motels have more than 6,000 rooms and suites available for visitors to the area. While Lexington is not typically known as a resort area, we do have a nationally known resort hotel and golf club, Marriott's Griffin Gate, which features a championship 18-hole golf course designed by Rees Jones and listed by *Golf Digest* as one of the 75 top resort golf courses in the country. For more information about this course, see our Golf chapter. For more information about accommodations not detailed here, contact the Lexington Convention & Visitors Bureau at 233-7299 or (800) 84-LEX-KY.

One note of warning: There are times during the year, especially in spring and fall, when Lexington's hotels and motels are pretty well all booked, and many even raise their rates temporarily. This usually happens on weekends when there is a University of Kentucky home football or basketball game and horse racing or horse sales going on at the same time. Lexington is also host to a number of large conventions throughout the year, so it is advisable to call ahead early for reservations.

We have listed hotels and motels in alphabetical order, and while we haven't listed every accommodation, there is a good representation of lodging from high end to economical. If you have a favorite chain hotel, check the Yellow Pages of the phone book; if it's Motel 6 you're looking for, we have those too. And don't forget to check out our Bed & Breakfast chapter for even more accommodations.

Price Code

Keep in mind that some rates are based on availability. The average nightly rates for two adults at the hotels and motels listed in this section are indicated by a dollar sign ($) ranking in the following chart. Also, the hotels and motels in this chapter accept all or most major credit cards.

$	$25 to $50
$$	$51 to $75
$$$	$76 to $100
$$$$	$101 to $125
$$$$$	$126 to $150

Best Western Regency of Lexington
$$ • 2241 Elkhorn Rd.
• 293-2202, (800) 528-1234

Convenience, attractive rooms, a complimentary, deluxe continental breakfast and a lot of fast food and regional cuisine restaurants within close walking distance are some of the perks of staying at the Best Western Regency/Lexington Inn.

In addition, you get cable TV and movies in your room, access to a coin laundry and a recreation area that has an outdoor pool, sauna and whirlpool. There is a computer-accessible phone line in each room, as well as fax services.

Best Western Regency/Lexington Inn has 112 guest rooms. A special rate is offered mid-December through the first of March, and a senior citizens discount is also available.

Bluegrass Suites
$$ • 2400 Buena Vista Dr.
• 293-6113

The Bluegrass Suites is tailored to the business traveler; it offers meeting rooms, a business center and airport shuttle transportation. All rooms have refrigerators and work desks. Suites have separate living rooms with mini-refrigerators, coffee pots and hair dryers. Deluxe suites also have two TVs, as well as an extra sleeper sofa. There's a small exercise room, a lounge and several restaurants within walking distance. Guests receive a complimentary deluxe continental breakfast.

Campbell House Inn, Suites and Golf Club
$$ • 1375 Harrodsburg Rd.
• 255-4281, (800) 354-9235

A longtime Lexington tradition, this complex has a lot to offer its guests. There's an 18-hole golf course adjacent to the hotel (greens fees apply). But you may also want to play tennis on one of the hotel's two courts or swim in either the indoor pool or the heated outdoor pool. An exercise room is also available, and some of the suites even have cooking facilities for guests who desire extended stays.

There are two restaurants with entrees priced in the $9 to $20 range, as well as a coffee shop, lounge and live entertainment. The hotel has 300 rooms with 70 suites.

FYI

If no area code is given, it's a local call from Lexington-Fayette County. If an area code is given, whether it's 606 or 502, it's a long-distance call: dial 1, the area code and the number. See the How To Use This Book chapter for detailed information on calling.

Continental Inn
$-$$ • 801 New Circle Rd. N.E.
• 299-5281, (800) 432-9288

With all the things going on at Continental Inn, you could book a room, be entertained and never have to leave the hotel. This big complex has 325 rooms and six suites, some of them overlooking a year-round tropical pool pavilion. Rooms have satellite TV, but you don't have to go more than a few steps for a meal or live entertainment. Honker's Tavern has a live band every Friday, Saturday and Sunday, and the Some Place Else lounge features disco music. The inn has facilities to handle everything from wedding receptions to conventions. It's about five minutes from downtown and less than five minutes from Interstate 75. You can even bring your pet along.

Courtyard by Marriott
$$$ • 775 Newtown Ct. • 253-4646

Located conveniently near both I-75 and downtown Lexington, the Courtyard by Marriott gives you easy access to the greater Lexington area. The Courtyard is in an ideal setting on a quiet side street off one of the main feeder roads from I-75 into Lexington. You can feel free from the hustle and bustle of traffic while still being accessible to most area attractions.

Fairfield Inn
$$ • 3050 Lakecrest Circle
• 224-3338

This 2-year-old inn is Marriott's economy lodging, but it has plenty to offer. All 63 rooms have king- or queen-size beds, or you may choose king suites with microwaves and refrigerators. The inn has no restaurant, but Applebee's is within walking distance.

Marriott's Fairfield Inn is just a stone's throw from New Circle Road, and it's less than 10 minutes to Keeneland, Bluegrass Airport, downtown and Fayette Mall, as well as two new shopping centers within walking distance, Palomar and Beaumont Centre. Frequent visitors can take advantage of the 13th-night-free

Travel Club, which is honored at any Tharaldson accommodation.

The inn also has rooms for the physically handicapped as well as nonsmokers' rooms. Pets are not permitted.

Gratz Park Inn
$$$$ • 120 W. Second St. • 231-1777, (800) 227-4362

This downtown hotel is the top of the line if you want an upscale place to stay with plenty of traditional atmosphere. In the heart of one of Lexington's most historic districts (just a few blocks from Transylvania University, the first college west of the Alleghenies), the inn is surrounded by some of the finest and most historic architecture in town.

Another plus about staying at this inn: It's just a couple of blocks from Main Street, so you have the convenience of being downtown plus the quiet and peacefulness of staying in a more residential area. Chauffeur service to and from the airport is offered.

The Gratz Park Inn has 38 rooms and six suites furnished in 19th-century antique reproductions, complete with sherry in crystal decanters. Guests receive a Continental breakfast, and soups, salads and sandwiches are served in the bar area. An excellent continental restaurant, Johnathan's, is also at the Gratz Park Inn.

Hampton Inn
$$ • 2251 Elkhorn Rd. • 299-2613

Hampton Inn is a stone's throw from I-75 and a nice place to stay if you're in the market for a clean, comfortable, moderately priced motel.

You can enjoy movies and cable TV in your room, take a dip in the indoor heated pool or work out in the exercise room. Then, when you get hungry, choose from several restaurants within close walking distance, ranging from fast food to country cuisine. A continental breakfast is provided.

Hampton Inn has 125 units. Pets are not permitted.

Harley Hotel
$$ • 2143 N. Broadway • 299-1261, (800) 321-2323

If you're looking for lots of ways to recreate without leaving your hotel, the Harley Hotel is the place to be. A heated outdoor pool, an indoor pool, a wading pool for the kids, saunas, a whirlpool, a putting green, volleyball and shuffleboard courts, an exercise room and two lighted tennis courts will keep even the most active traveler busy.

A dining room, with entrees priced from $7 to $14, is in the hotel lobby, and you can also get a cocktail and enjoy live entertainment there.

Harley Hotel has 146 rooms and one suite and offers a discount for senior citizens. No pets are allowed.

Hilton Suites of Lexington Green
$$$$ • 3195 Nicholasville Rd. • 271-4000, (800) 367-HSLG

This hotel is especially unique because you are right in the heart of some of the best shopping in town. Lexington Green shopping complex features a number of excellent stores (including Joseph-Beth Booksellers, one of the largest bookstores in the region), and many restaurants. Fayette Mall, the second largest mall in the state, is within walking distance. Add to that the popular comedy club Comedy Off Broadway, three major movie theaters and

---

INSIDERS' TIP

When you're in the right part of Lexington and the wind is blowing your way, you can step outside and breathe in the rich, warm, tantalizing aroma of roasted peanuts. This is the smell of Jif peanut butter being made at the Procter & Gamble plant on Winchester Road.

at least a dozen restaurants ranging from fast food to Mexican, Italian and Chinese, and you're talking major convenience.

If you don't want to set foot outside your hotel, you can enjoy food and drinks at Polo's Cafe and Chukker's Lounge right inside the hotel or order pizza from room service (the hotel has its own Pizza Hut franchise). The Hilton has 174 suites where you can get free or pay movies, or swim at the indoor pool or use the sauna, whirlpool and exercise room. Pets are not allowed, but kids can stay free with their parents. Parents can even check out games, books and toys for the kids at the Vacation Station. For guests with disabilities the Hilton has 10 specially designed suites, two equipped with roll-in showers.

Holiday Inn Express
$$ • 2221 Elkhorn Rd. • 293-0047

Four of this hotel's 60 rooms are Jacuzzi suites; the rest of the rooms have all the ba-

sics, plus more: on-demand movies, cable TV, computer-accessible phone lines in rooms and a complimentary deluxe continental breakfast. There's an indoor pool and whirlpool, plus plenty of restaurants nearby. It's about five minutes to downtown and a stone's throw from I-75. For each 20 rooms reserved, guests receive one free room.

Holiday Inn North
$$$ • 1950 Newtown Pike
• 233-0512, (800) HOLIDAY

With its convenient location just off I-75, Holiday Inn-North is easily accessible to most of the big area attractions, including the Kentucky Horse Park just to the north. For golfers, it is an ideal location adjacent to the nationally ranked Griffin Gate Golf Club. There is also a putting green at the hotel.

The Holidome recreation center includes an indoor heated pool, sauna, whirlpool and exercise room. And a restaurant, with entrees

Photo: Kentucky Department of State Parks

A visit with his cousins at Federal Hill inspired Stephen Foster to write the ballad "My Old Kentucky Home."

priced from $8 to $13, and The Post lounge in the hotel mean you really don't have to go far to get anything you'll need during your stay.

Holiday Inn South
$$ • 5532 Athens-Boonesboro Rd.
• 263-5241

Just off Lexington's southernmost I-75 exit (hence the name), Holiday Inn South offers all the perks at a pretty reasonable rate.

The new Holidome has an indoor pool and exercise equipment, plus cable TV, free and pay movies, an outdoor pool, sauna and whirl-pool. You can even bring your pet.

A dining room — entrees priced from $8 to $13 — is off the lobby, and in the lounge you can also have a cocktail and enjoy nation-ally-booked entertainment.

Hyatt Regency Lexington
$$$$$ • 400 W. Vine St. • 253-1234

If you want to stay right downtown where

Business & Pleasure

FEEL THE HYATT TOUCH.™

401 West High Street
Lexington, KY 40507
606-253-1234 or
800-233-1234

With 365 luxurious rooms and professionally-organized conference rooms and meeting facilities, the Hyatt Regency Lexington is perfectly suited for your visit to the Bluegrass.

Plan on breakfast in bed, dinner at the Glass Garden, and a tete-a-tete over cocktails by the Hyatt's fireplace.

The quality of service and style you expect from the name Hyatt Regency. We add the Bluegrass hospitality.

all the action is, from college basketball to harness racing to banking, Hyatt Regency Lexington is your place. It sits in the heart of downtown and is attached to the Civic Center, a shopping and restaurant complex and Rupp Arena, home to major rock 'n' roll and country music acts as well as the nationally ranked University of Kentucky Wildcats basketball games. Appropriately, there's a sports bar called Hytops.

The Glass Garden restaurant, in the hotel lobby, is well known for its sumptuous Sunday brunch and Kentucky The Restaurant serves upscale American fare for dinner only. Plus you get free and pay movies and cable TV in your room and access to a heated indoor pool and health club. Pets are not allowed.

Hyatt Regency Lexington has 365 guest rooms (one for each day of the year, if you wanted to stay that long), plus nine suites. Senior citizens discounts are available.

The Kentucky Inn
$$ • 525 Waller Ave.
• 254-1177, (800) 221-6652

If you're looking for a comfortable, no-frills place just off Harrodsburg Road and less than a mile from the University of Kentucky football stadium, this is it. It's also across the street from St. Joseph Hospital (the inn is owned by the hospital), and is close to downtown and the Red Mile harness racing track. Convention and banquet facilities are available, and the inn offers a medical discount. The inn has an outdoor pool, cable TV and a restaurant and lounge. Small pets are allowed for a $5 fee.

INSIDERS' TIP

The old fieldstone sheep fences that line much of Paris Pike are a familiar sight for Lexingtonians.

Knights Inn/Lexington North
$ • 1935 Stanton Way • 231-0232

This pleasant inn has 113 rooms with cable TV and Jacuzzis, and it's near I-64 and I-75 as well as New Circle Road, so it's easy to get to shopping areas. Knights Inn is also one of the closest hotels to the Kentucky Horse Park. The complex has an outdoor pool, a restaurant and even a meeting room for business guests. Pets are allowed, and seniors receive a discount.

La Quinta Motor Inn
$ • 1919 Stanton Way
• 231-7551, (800) 531-5900

Just off I-75 near the Griffin Gate Golf Club, La Quinta Motor Inn offers travelers convenience, comfort and cable TV, plus a continental breakfast.

The 130-unit motel has a heated pool, and you can bring your pet (though not to the pool). A restaurant is located opposite the motel, and several others are nearby, offering a nice choice in places to eat. This is a pleasant, comfortable place to stay.

The rates are pretty reasonable, too, and are even slightly lower from mid-November to February.

Marriott's Griffin Gate Resort and Golf Club
$$$$ • 1800 Newtown Pike
• 231-5100, (800) 228-9290

Marriott's Griffin Gate is the ultimate place to stay in Lexington, especially if you're an avid golfer. In addition to sporting one of the finest 18-hole championship golf courses in the nation, this resort hotel and elegant restaurant, The Mansion, offer Lexington guests all the creature comforts, with a lot of luxuries thrown in for good measure.

Located near the intersection of highways I-64 and I-75 and just 15 minutes from the Blue Grass Airport, Marriott's Griffin Gate has 388 guest rooms and 21 luxurious suites. In addition to the golf course, there are three lighted tennis courts, indoor and outdoor swimming pools, a hydrotherapy pool and a health club. You can even get a massage when you're through recreating.

When you get hungry, the resort has several dining options. The Mansion features el-

egant dining in a restored 19th-century home that looks a lot like a Southern movie set. JW's Steakhouse specializes in steaks and seafood, Griffin Gate Gardens features family-style dining, and Pegasus Lounge offers dancing and entertainment in the evenings.

If you're in town on business, Marriott's Griffin Gate has 14 meeting rooms that can accommodate 12 to 1,400 people. The resort also offers complimentary van service to and from the airport.

As you might expect, you do have to pay for all these conveniences. Rates depend on the number of people and how far in advance you make your reservation. The resort offers special weekend and event packages throughout the year. Some of the services, such as massages, cost extra. Pets also cost $20 extra per stay.

Radisson Plaza Hotel
$$$$$ • 369 W. Vine St.
• 231-9000, (800) 333-3333

Because it's downtown, the Radisson is an ideal combination of comfort, convenience and accessibility to the Lexington business and financial district. Equidistant from I-75 and Blue Grass Airport, the Radisson has all the perks that make it even better, in some cases, than a home away from home. A multi-million dollar renovaton was completed in 1998.

Just across the street from Rupp Arena and the Civic Center, the Radisson is surrounded by unique shopping and dining opportunities. Picturesque Triangle Park, with its dazzling lighted fountains, fronts one side of the hotel, and horse-drawn carriage rides through Lexington's historic district leave from the hotel's Vine Street entrance.

In addition, during your stay at the Radisson, you have free and pay movies in your room and use of an indoor pool, sauna, whirlpool and exercise room.

Health club privileges are available for an additional fee. Transportation to and from Blue Grass Airport is provided to guests as well.

The Radisson's fine dining restaurant — Cafe on the Park, overlooking Triangle Park — is off the lobby, and in the evenings, you can enjoy live entertainment in Spirits Lounge or or relax at the Bigg Blue Martini Bar.

The Radisson has 367 guest units. Pets are not allowed.

Residence Inn by Marriott
$$$$$ • 1080 Newtown Pike • 231-6191

The Residence Inn by Marriott truly offers all the comforts of your home away from home. Its 80 suites are spacious and beautifully decorated, and some guests use this inn for stays of more than 30 days. Many units have fireplaces, and some have two bathrooms. All apartments have refrigerators, cable TV and movies. VCRs are available for rental.

For recreation, you can use the heated pool, whirlpool and sports court. Several nearby restaurants, including one next door, make eating out convenient.

Pets are allowed, but a substantial deposit is required for a short-term stay. Rates are slightly higher during the Keeneland race meets in April and October.

Sheraton Suites
$$$$ • 2601 Richmond Rd.
• 268-0060, (800) 262-3774

Lexington's Sheraton hotel takes you back to the quaint Southern charm of New Orleans. From the indoor courtyard filled with exotic trees, fountains and wrought-iron furnishings to the live jazz performances each weekend, this hotel offers its guests a unique and charming accommodation option.

Ideally located just 10 minutes from I-75 and from downtown, Sheraton Suites are near many unusual and interesting restaurants and shopping areas, including Lexington Mall.

The hotel's 155 suites feature hot tubs and refrigerators as well as free and pay movies. Many rooms open onto the picturesque courtyard. A swimming pool and exercise room give you a great opportunity to work out or just ease away tension. When you get hungry, Tippedore's Restaurant in the lobby features

American and Cajun cuisine, and guests are treated to a complimentary breakfast buffet. There's even more of a French Quarter feel on Friday and Saturday nights, when live jazz is performed in the Gazebo Lounge.

Shoney's Inn-Lexington
$ • 2753 Richmond Rd.
• 269-4999, (800) 222-2222

Right in the heart of one of Lexington's prime shopping, business and restaurant districts, Shoney's Inn is convenient, comfortable and affordable. Shoney's Restaurant is next to the motel, but if you're in the mood for something more exotic, you can dine at nearby Italian, Oriental and steakhouse restaurants.

The 100-room Shoney's Inn also has an outdoor pool, cable TV and movies in your room. Kids younger than 18 stay free with their parents. There is free coffee, but no room service is available. Pets aren't allowed. A senior citizens discount is available.

The Springs Inn
$$ • 2020 Harrodsburg Rd.
• 277-5751, (800) 354-9503

The Springs is one of Lexington's old, traditional establishments that has been renovated in the past few years. Rooms are comfortable, grounds are pretty and the dining room is "true Kentucky" — hand-painted walls, white-clothed tables, Queen Anne dining chairs and regional specialties such as country ham, Southern fried chicken and hot Browns.

The inn has a heated outdoor pool, and Turfland Mall is just across the road. It's easy to get to most of the area attractions, especially Keeneland and Shakertown, from the inn. Meeting facilities are available; pets are not allowed.

Wyndham Garden Hotel
$$ • 1938 Stanton Way • 259-1311

This pleasant 177-unit hotel has large, comfortable rooms, and it's near I-75 and the Kentucky Horse Park. Among the amenities are a coffee pot in your room and a free happy-hour buffet in the lounge from 5 to 8 PM weekdays for any guest older than 21. There's also a full-service restaurant with entrees in the $9 to $14 range. Kids stay free with parents (no age limit), and there are indoor and outdoor pools. Airport transportation is available; no pets are allowed.

A heated indoor pool, a whirlpool and an exercise room are available, as are free and pay movies in your room, and you can use the coin laundry.

Berea

Boone Tavern Hotel
$$ • corner of Main and Prospect Sts.
• 986-9358, (800)366-9358

Located in College Square of picturesque Berea, the legendary Boone Tavern Hotel and Tavern have welcomed guests since 1909. From its white-columned porch with summer flowers and rocking chairs to its comfortable rooms furnished with Early American-style furniture and hand woven items made by students in Berea College's craft programs, it's an experience in Kentucky hospitality. The hotel features 59 air-conditioned rooms and a beautifully furnished lobby area with wingback chairs and portraits of past college presidents where guests can sit and read or play old-fashioned board games. Most of the pleasant hotel and tavern employees are students in the college labor program that requires them to work 10-15 hours weekly to help pay for their tuition. Within a short walk from the hotel there are craft shops brimming over with fine crafts made by students and local artisans. The college, just across the street, offers interesting tours of its campus, including shops where the crafts are produced. The tavern serves three meals daily, and it's known far and wide for spoonbread which is served at lunch and dinner. It's about 30 miles from Lexington and about a five minute drive from I-75. (For more information see our Restaurants and Attractions chapters.)

There's been a bed and breakfast boom in the Bluegrass area in the last couple of years.

Bed and Breakfast Inns

Most of them don't sport the kidney-shaped swimming pool with a slide for the kids. And you'd be hard-pressed to find soda or ice machines out in the hall.

But there's a certain charm about staying in a bed and breakfast inn that just can't be matched by your superhighway, kids-eat-free motel chains. The absence of humming, neon-lit food and drink machines is a big part of that charm. The "and" in the name also plays a big role: You get a meal with your room.

Bed and breakfast inns are places where you can feel free from the drudgery of daily, hand-to-mouth existence, yet still feel at home when you're on the road. There's been a bed and breakfast boom in the Bluegrass area in the last couple of years.

The ones mentioned here are in Lexington or in towns in the surrounding counties (see our chapter on Lexington's Neighbors). We haven't tried to list every inn because there are dozens out there, but we have listed some of the most popular ones, plus a few of our favorites. The nice thing about bed and breakfast owners is most of them will refer you to someone else's establishment if they are booked. You can also use one of the reservation services we have listed because they can just possibly match you up to exactly what you're looking for. Because there are so many bed and breakfast inns, we have listed Lexington first, then the surrounding towns. All of them accept major credit cards unless noted.

Bed & Breakfast Association of Kentucky
1026 Russell St., Covington
• **(606) 281-4255, (800) 292-2632**

Nearly 200 bed and breakfast inns in all parts of the state are listed by this organization, so call for a free brochure and map.

Bluegrass Bed & Breakfast Reservation Service
Rt. 1, Box 263, Versailles, Ky. 40383
• **873-3208**

If you're looking for a place in our famous countryside, call Bluegrass Bed & Breakfast Reservation Service, which represents about 20 lodgings. Most of the inns are on farms and list exclusively with this service, so you might not find them on your own. Plus, talking to owner Betsy Pratt is a good way to get a personal match-up to exactly what you're looking for. There is no fee to use this reservation service.

INSIDERS' TIP

Some people who just want a nice getaway spend a night in a country bed and breakfast right in their own county.

Lexington

A True Inn
$$-$$$$ • 467 W. Second St., Lexington
• 252-6166, (800) 374-6151

You'll discover wonderful architectural details — a turret, stained- and leaded-glass windows, ornately carved mantels (even in the guest rooms), original chandeliers and front and back gardens — in this big Richardsonian Romanesque house, which was built in 1843 as a Greek Revival residence in downtown Lexington then remodeled in 1890. The bedrooms have tall ceilings, four-poster beds with quilts and big private baths. Breakfast is served in a formal dining room, sunroom or in the garden. A favorite spot for summertime guests to relax is the homey front porch with ferns and white wicker looking out over a pretty, old downtown neighborhood.

The Brand House
$$-$$$ • 461 N. Limestone St., Lexington • 226-9464

If you're looking for a historic home in downtown Lexington, The Brand House is a luxurious choice. The Federal-style house is a Lexington landmark and has been written about in many architectural books about Kentucky. Each of the five guest rooms has been meticulously remodeled and professionally decorated with a mix of antiques and reproductions. There are elegant bed dressings (with dozens of pillows!), stylish color schemes and lavish modernized bathrooms with private whirlpool baths. A full gourmet breakfast is served in the formal dining room with incredibly tall ceilings and a romantic chandelier,

and public rooms include a drawing room and a billiard room. Many downtown attractions are within a short walking distance. Kids older than 12 are welcome. Pets aren't allowed but the owners of the Brand House will make kennel arrangements.

Cherry Knoll Inn
$$ • 3975 Lemons Mill Rd., Lexington • 253-9800, (800) 804-0617

Built in 1855 and situated on 28 acres of beautiful Bluegrass farmland, this white-columned Greek Revival house is listed on the National Register of Historic Places. Two spacious guest rooms with private baths have their own entrance, and a real highlight is an upstairs veranda that overlooks acres and acres of horses grazing in the Kentucky sunshine. In warm weather guests can enjoy either a full or continental breakfast outdoors, and dinner is also served in the downstairs dining rooms Tuesday through Saturday. A conference room is available, as well as catering for special events. Pets are not allowed, but kids are.

Halifax Lane Farm
$$ • 1201 North Yarnallton Rd., Lexington • 225-5485

If you want to stay in "horse country," you might as well do it right and stay in a barn. We do mean barn, but not what you're probably thinking. Owner Bill Shaw, a real estate broker who specialized is construction of barn and home combinations, added a spacious loft to a 50-year-old foaling barn. The upstairs den and kitchen combination is open and airy with hunter green walls, pumpkin-hued wooden floors and traditional furnishings. Two bed-

---

FYI

If no area code is given, it's a local call from Lexington-Fayette County. If an area code is given, whether it's 606 or 502, it's a long-distance call: dial 1, the area code and the number. See the How To Use This Book chapter for detailed information on calling.

INSIDERS' TIP

Many bed and breakfast owners with pretty historic houses in small towns around Lexington rent them for weddings, parties and other special events. Unfortunately, this kind of use is restricted in Lexington.

rooms are modern and comfortable, with plush carpeting and a big shared bath. There's a small parlor for socializing. The big bonuses are the big windows that look out over miles of horse farms. Children (and horses!) are welcome but dogs and cats must stay at home because of Halifax Lane's "cast if characters," A full breakfast is served every day. It's about ten minutes from downtown and Keeneland.

Homewood Farm
$-$$$ • 5301 Bethel Rd., Lexington • 255-2814

Homewood, on a peaceful 300-acre cattle and horse farm, has been owned by the same family since 1846. Bob and Anne Young moved out of their old house and built a new country house, charmingly traditional in style and especially designed for bed and breakfast guests. You may choose from a private suite with a living room, dining room and kitchen or one of the two guest rooms, each with a private bath and its own entrance. Highlights are furnishings of traditional antiques and Oriental rugs, a 12-acre yard with perennial gardens and old trees and a big front porch filled with antique wicker where you can enjoy the country life. The innkeepers will serve you a country breakfast in a breakfast room overlooking a pond and horse paddock. Young children and pets aren't accepted. Homewood also has a 1,200-square-foot unit with a bedroom, a living room and a kitchen that is geared toward corporate use. Weekly and monthly rates are available.

Silver Springs
$$$ • 3710 Leestown Pike, Lexington • 255-1784

You'll feel like part of the family in this big, homey, Federal-style house. It's spacious and cheerful with big, sunny windows, gleaming hardwood floors and a mixture of antiques. The two upstairs bedrooms are very roomy and both have sitting areas. The Oak Room has a brass bed, oak furniture, quilts and afghans. The West Room is a little more formal with a king-size bed, dressing table and white brocade sofa and chairs. The two rooms share a large bath.

Outside you can stretch your legs on the 21-acre horse farm, meander through the pe-

rennial garden or just relax in a swing or hammock underneath the shade of old trees. Silver Springs is just a five-minute drive from downtown. Call if you want to bring children or pets.

Swann's Nest at Cygnet Farm
$$-$$$$ • 3463 Rosalie Ln., Lexington • 226-0095

Though the Southern-style house with big white columns is only a couple decades old, it has the feel of an aging mansion. Completely hidden from the road by a long tree-lined drive, Swann's Nest is a study in comfortable elegance. Floors have plush carpeting, and furnishings in the pretty bedrooms are tasteful and traditional; all have private baths. A wing built on the back of the house offers big, airy suites with a balcony that overlooks a garden pond and perennial beds. In the main part of the house, guests are invited to relax in a family room with comfy furnishings and a fireplace. A generous continental breakfast is set out for guests in the big kitchen, and the breakfast area that overlooks the back yard seems to be the hub of the house. Situated on a small farm on a moderately developed residential lane just on the outskirts of Lexington, Swann's Nest is close to Keeneland Race Track and has the feeling of being much farther out of town. Young children and pets must stay home.

Richmond

Barnes Mill Guest House
$ • 1268 Barnes Mill Rd., Richmond • (606) 623-5509

This Victorian home built in the early 1900s has been lovingly restored, and, if you like Victorian collectibles, you'll feel right at home in this cheerful house. It's cozy and pretty, and breakfast always includes plump loaves of homemade bread, bacon, sausage, eggs, muffins and maybe even biscuits and gravy — all served in a dining room with a lacy tablecloth and pretty dishes. The rooms are small with old-fashioned furnishings, neat as a pin. Barnes Mill Road is less than a mile from I-75, yet the backyard overlooks peaceful cattle farms. Children 12 and older are welcome, but pets can't visit.

Bennett House
**$$-$$$ • 419 W. Main St., Richmond
• 625-0097**

This Victorian Romanesque house in downtown Richmond has towering ceilings, an impressive cherry staircase, gleaming wood floors and big, airy rooms furnished with eclectic antiques. There's even a room in the turret furnished with twin beds. A full continental breakfast is served to guests, and the common rooms are filled with work by local artists. The house can also be rented for private functions and is especially popular for artists' receptions. Children aren't encouraged, and pets must stay home. The house has a smoke-free environment.

Harrodsburg

Canaan Land
**$-$$, no credit cards
• 4355 Lexington Rd., Harrodsburg
• (606) 734-3984**

You can snuggle up in one of Canaan Land's feather beds and read if you want to, but the outdoors will beckon. The inn has a swimming pool and hot tub, woods to hike and two flocks of sheep to tend on a 185-acre secluded farm. There are also cows, goats, donkeys, a miniature horse and other assorted creatures, and guests can even help with the chores. Shaker Village is less than 3 miles away. You can have a room in the 1795 brick farmhouse, furnished with primitives, or in a big reconstructed log house. And one of the best parts is a llama named Max that gives guests kisses. Rooms have either private or shared baths. Older children are welcome; pets must stay home.

Nicholasville

Cedar Haven Farm
**$, no credit cards • 2380 Bethel Rd.,
Nicholasville • 858-3849**

Cedar Haven Farm bed and breakfast inn is on a working Bluegrass farm. The two-story house is new and offers one room with a private bath and one with a shared bath. You'll find all the charms of a country setting here,

including fresh-baked breads and homegrown fruits and vegetables. This is a family-oriented inn with a cozy front porch and lots of wide-open spaces where kids and pets are welcome with prior permission.

O'Neal Log Cabin
**$$ • 1626 Delaney Ferry Rd.,
Nicholasville • 223-4730**

Daniel Boone probably didn't sleep here, but scout and sharpshooter George O'Neal did! This 1820 reconstructed log house has all its original charm but it also has a bath with a whirlpool, air conditioning, a full kitchen, a living room and two bedrooms, so it's ideal for a family that loves a getaway in the country. Furniture includes period antiques and pieces made by owner Jim Humphrey. Guests are provided with a stocked refrigerator, homemade granola and freshly baked breads for breakfast.

By the way, if it rains, the owners guarantee you a good night's sleep because the cabin has a tin roof! Children are welcome, and pets are accepted on an individual basis.

Sandusky House
**$$ • 1626 Delaney Ferry Rd.,
Nicholasville • 223-4730**

Sandusky House features three private guest rooms in a wonderful country setting. The elegant Greek Revival house was built in 1850, and guests particularly love its winding staircase, big windows that overlook the countryside and porches with rocking chairs, both upstairs and downstairs. The home is furnished with a mixture of traditional and country antiques. A full breakfast is served in the formal dining room. The farm on which it stands was part of a 1780 land grant from Patrick Henry to Revolutionary War hero Jacob Sandusky. Kids 12 and older are welcome. Pets aren't allowed, but owners can make kennel arrangements.

Paris

Amelia's Field Country Inn
**$$-$$$ • Cynthiana Rd. (U.S. 27), Paris
• (606) 987-5778**

Just think "movie set" and you'll get the idea of Amelia's Field: an early 1900s Colonial

Photo: Kentucky Department of Parks

Many area bed and breakfasts are furnished with period antiques.

Revival country house with purple clematis curling up the porch posts, organic vegetables growing with the flowers and vegetables in the front circle, chickens clucking, ewes bleating — you get the picture. The colorful guest rooms (sky blue, lemon yellow, parrot green, peach) are filled with family antiques and even a bit of whimsy, and private bathrooms border on romantic. In addition, country French-style lunches and dinners are served Thursday through Sunday. Children are welcome; pets are restricted because of the farm animals.

Pleasant Place
$$ • 515 Pleasant St., Paris
• (606) 987-5546

Nestled in a historical neighborhood just one block from Main Street, Bourbon House is filled with 1890s Victorian charm. Two rooms furnished with English antiques are available with private baths. For visitors who just can't

leave the present behind, there are color TVs in the guest rooms as well as an office area with computer and fax machine. A full breakfast is served in the dining room, and guests especially like to linger on the screened-in front porch or meander through Pleasant Place's "secret garden." Young children are not encouraged; pets can't visit.

Rosedale
$$-$$$ • 1917 Cypress St., Paris
• (606) 987-1845

"Genteel" is a good word to describe this lovely Italianate house built in 1862. It's in town but cozily tucked away on 3 secluded acres where you can play bocce ball, croquet or just relax on a hammock. Furnished with antiques and Oriental rugs, Rosedale has four guest rooms with pencil-post beds and private baths, and guests have access to a parlor and library with working fireplaces. Children older than

12 are welcome; arrangements can be made to board your pet nearby.

Perryville

Elmwood Inn
$$$ • 205 E. Fourth St., Perryville • (606) 332-2400

Time has stood still in the sleepy little town of Perryville, where this white-columned, pre-Civil War mansion sits amid 100-year-old sweet gum and maple trees. The floors squeak old secrets for sure because this wonderful old house has had many lives. It functioned as a residence, a private school, a hospital during the Civil War, a popular regional restaurant and now it's a beautifully remodeled bed and breakfast inn and English tearoom. Elmwood's two suites are furnished with English and American antiques, and each has a sitting room and private bath. A complete English afternoon tea is served Thursday, Friday and Saturday at 2 and 4 PM by reservation. Children age 6 and older are welcome; pets must stay home. Elmwood has a totally smoke-free environment.

www.insiders.com

See this and many other **Insiders' Guide®** destinations online.

Visit us today!

Versailles

B & B at Sills Inn
$-$$$ • 270 Montgomery Ave., Versailles • 873-4478, (800) 526-9801

This bustling inn features more than a dozen rooms. Double whirlpool-bath suites and a full gourmet breakfast are some of the perks of staying at B & B at Sills Inn, which is in a big yellow Victorian house with a homey front porch and wicker furniture on a street filled with other old-fashioned houses and lots of trees. The guest rooms, with big windows and honey-hued wood floors, all have themes.

You can stay in the nautical room, the Victorian room or the English room. Furnishings include Victorian antiques, stylish wallpaper and window treatments and interesting bathrooms, many with claw-foot tubs and whirlpool baths. A new addition behind the main house features more modern rooms. A full gourmet breakfast is served in a bright, airy dining room. Kids are not encouraged, and pets and smoking are not allowed.

Rose Hill Inn
$$-$$$ • 233 Rose Hill, Versailles • 873-5957

This Kentucky Gothic-style house was built in the early 1800s, and it definitely rates a 10 on the curb-appeal scale with its fairy-tale style, huge yard and romantic old trees. The three attractive guest rooms are furnished with a mix of antiques, and guests enjoy pretty stained-glass windows throughout the house, original hardwood floors, a formal parlor, a library and an upstairs sitting room in this spacious house. Families will like staying in the quaint old cottage (the old summer kitchen) behind the main house; it has two full-size beds, a sitting room, a kitchen and a front porch complete with a swing. Kids are welcome; pets are allowed to visit in the cottage. The house is in a beautiful historic neighborhood close to downtown.

Shepherd Place
$$ • 31 Heritage Rd., Versailles • 873-7843

Centrally located just 4 miles west of Keeneland race track and the Lexington airport, 10 miles from downtown Lexington and just outside the pretty little town of Versailles, Shepherd Place combines the charm of country living with the convenience of the city in a black-shuttered, white-brick house that was built before the Civil War. The inn has two

---

INSIDERS' TIP

Most bed and breakfast owners are glad to show you around, even if you don't plan to stay.

Photo: Norman Drake

A mallard duck awaits his mate.

guest rooms, each with a private bath, and as a bonus, there are sheep right outside your bedroom window. In fact, you can even order a sweater while you're there, and it might even be knitted with wool from those sheep. This historic house and surrounding acreage are situated in front of an attractive subdivision with traditional-style houses. Pets and kids are not allowed.

Tyrone Pike Bed & Breakfast
$-$$$ • 3820 Tyrone Pike, Versailles • 873-2408

Two guest suites with private baths are available in this contemporary house surrounded by horse farms. Rooms are quaint and cozy with down comforters and canopy and sleigh beds. One suite includes a private entrance, a kitchenette and a claw-footed soaking tub in the bathroom. A full gourmet breakfast is served. Children are welcome, and a crib and toy chest are available for guest use. Pets are accepted on an individual basis. The house is about 15 minutes from Keeneland and Bluegrass Airport.

Western Fields Guest Cottage
$$$$ • 5108 Ford's Mill Rd., Versailles • (800) 600-4935

You can really get away to the peaceful countryside in this private little brick house with a big cozy kitchen (with a stocked refrigerator for breakfast), two bedrooms, a study, a living room and enough sleeping room for seven people. The house is decorated with fine American crafts, much of it made by your hostess Deborah Banta-Westerfield who is a raku artist.

Kids are welcome and there are friendly llamas on the adjoining farm (you can even take a llama trek). Deborah also has a studio and gallery where she sells her work along with the work of other artists from around the country. There's a resident cottage cat, a gas grill on the patio and lots of trees and wide open spaces. Pets are welcome.

Midway

Holly Hill Inn
$$ • 426 N. Winter St., Midway • 846-4732

This pretty Victorian house in the sleepy little town of Midway has a big front porch complete with swings and old shade trees. Two guest rooms are furnished with a mixture of antiques, and a full-service dining room serves "Kentucky gourmet" lunches and dinners Tuesday through Saturday. A continental breakfast is served in the dining room. Kids are welcome, but pets must say home.

Keene

Stone Paddock Farm
**$$$-$$$$ • Keene-Troy Pike, Keene
• 885-6637**

This Williamsburg-style house was built in the present century, but the home and surrounding farm are picture-perfect. The curving driveway meanders through mature trees to an impressive two-story house. Furnishings are antique, but there's a comfortable, posh feeling with deep carpets, pretty wallpaper, rich color schemes and even a hot tub in the corner of the bedroom suite. Guests can rock on the back porch, fish in the pond or go on a nature walk on the surrounding 48 acres. A full breakfast is served in the traditional dining room, and the hostess will even prepare a candlelight dinner on request. Pets are not accepted; inquire about children.

Georgetown

Blackridge Hall
**$$$-$$$$ • 4055 Paris Pike, Georgetown
• 863-2069, (800) 768-9308**

With its three private rooms and two private suites with whirlpool baths, Blackridge Hall offers the charm of an old Southern mansion mixed with the luxury of modern amenities because the 10,000-square-foot Georgian-style house is newly built with all the authentic details. Even better, it's in the middle of thoroughbred country. There are six guest rooms, two with whirlpool baths. (All rooms have private bathrooms.) Rooms are elegant and formal, and a gourmet breakfast is served in the dining room with silver, china and candlelight. Kids and pets are not allowed.

Chimneys
**$$-$$$ • 528 E. Main St., Georgetown
• (502) 863-2766**

For pure history, this Greek Revival house slips you back to the 1840s with its wonderful architectural details and fine antiques. A three-room suite features two bedrooms, a large den and a private bath, all furnished with antiques of the 1870s. The large den has a fox-hunting theme, and the private bath has a whirlpool tub. A second suite is decorated in a romantic rose theme with a private bath. A gourmet breakfast is featured, and guests have access to a garage for their cars. Children are not encouraged, and pets are not allowed.

Jordan Farm
**$$$, no credit cards
• 4091 Newtown Pike, Georgetown
• 863-1944**

This unique bed and breakfast inn is in a newly built, two-story "carriage house" on a Central Kentucky horse farm. A nearby fishing lake and acres of beautiful Bluegrass countryside enhance your stay in this idyllic spot, and if you visit in spring, you might even want to watch one of the farm's mares foal.

Jordan Farm has three guest rooms, each with a hot tub, wet bar and private bath. The owners say some guests have even gone into the horse business after visiting here, and some come just to see how a horse farm is operated. Kids are not encouraged, and pets are not allowed.

Log Cabin
**$$ • 350 N. Broadway, Georgetown
• 863-3514**

Though it's right in town, Log Cabin bed and breakfast inn offers a unique frontier perspective. Built around 1809, this Kentucky log cabin has chinked walls and primitive furniture, along with a fireplace and fully equipped kitchen. Its central location — just 5 miles from the Kentucky Horse Park and 12 miles from Lexington — makes it an ideal vacation spot. Log Cabin has two bedrooms, and if you want to spend Christmas in pioneer style, the cabin is all decked out in holiday decorations. Kids and pets are welcome.

INSIDERS' TIP

One of the best ways to get up close and personal with Lexington's famous horses is to stay in a bed and breakfast on a horse farm.

Pineapple Inn
$-$$ • 645 S. Broadway, Georgetown • 868-5453

Built in 1876, Pineapple Inn is listed on the National Registry of Historic Places. This big, elegant house is right in town and is filled with antiques, so it just sets the stage for antique shopping in Kentucky's "antique capital," Georgetown's designated title. It features a wonderful Country French dining room where a big breakfast is served, a large living room and four guest rooms — three with private baths and one with a spa. Pets are not allowed, but kids older than 12 are welcome.

Wilmore

Scott Station Inn
$ • 305 E. Main St., Wilmore • 858-0121

This century-old farmhouse features six guest rooms, each done in a different style, from a sewing loft to an Oriental theme. Scott Station is a family-oriented bed and breakfast inn, featuring a playroom with videos and games for the kids. Four of the rooms have private baths; two rooms share a bath. This bed and breakfast is especially popular with guests visiting students at Asbury College in Wilmore. Pets are not allowed.

Stearns

Marcum-Porter House
$-$$ • 35 Hume Dr., Stearns • (606) 376-2242

This homey frame company house was built by the Stearns Coal and Lumber Company in 1902 as one of the rental houses pro-vided for its employees. The five-bedroom house has been in the same family since that time, and one of the owners, Patricia Porter Newton, says the house is much the same as it's always been, "with mother's and grandmother's furniture." The rooms have antique beds (with new custom bedding), and a full breakfast is served in the dining room. Now painted blue with cream trim, the charming house is surrounded by old shrubs and perennial gardens "planted by grandfather."

Stearns is in the heart of the Daniel Boone National Forest and the Big South Fork National River and Recreation Area; Cumberland Falls State Resort Park is only 20 miles away, so expect plenty of great scenery. The inn is open April through October or by special arrangement. Children are welcome, but pets must stay home.

Cynthiana

Seldon Renaker Inn
$ • 24 S. Walnut St., Cynthiana • (606) 234-3752

If you like the feel of a small town, this inn is nestled right in downtown Cynthiana. Built in 1885 by Seldon Renaker, this two-story brick residence has been used as a boarding house, tea room, dress shop and doctor's offices. The three bedrooms of this elegant house, which was remodeled in 1987, have tall ceilings and carpeting and are furnished with a mixture of antiques. Each guest room has a private bath.

Guests are invited to mingle in the gathering room, formerly the original parlor of the old house. A "continental plus" breakfast is served in the dining room. Children are welcome; pets are not allowed.

Kentucky has one of
the finest state park
systems in the nation,
along with a widely
varied geography
featuring mountains,
rivers, lake systems
and forests.

Campgrounds

One of Kentucky's biggest claims to fame is the magnificence and purity of its natural resources. Having one of the finest state parks systems in the nation, along with a widely varied geography featuring mountains, rivers, lake systems and forests, makes the outdoors in Kentucky a delight for the whole family. A fairly temperate climate makes camping enjoyable throughout much of the year.

There are dozens of campgrounds in the Bluegrass area, and we've provided only a partial listing here. For more information, call the Kentucky Department of Travel at (800) 225-TRIP.

In addition to many privately owned campgrounds in the region, the state parks system runs 28 parks with campsites equipped with utility hookups and dump stations. Primitive sites are also available at many of the parks.

Following is a list of some of the state parks in the I-75 and I-64 regions. Most of these campgrounds are within 2 to 3 hours of Lexington and are readily accessible from the interstate.

Rates for camping in state parks are $8.50 to $16 a night for two people at sites with utility hookups and $8.50 to $10.50 for primitive sites, depending on the season and the day of the week. Each additional person older than age 16 is charged $1 more. There is a 15 percent discount for senior citizens. Some campgrounds do not accept reservations, but it'd still be wise to call and see if any big events are going on in the area that might cause the campground to fill up.

Privately owned and operated campgrounds in Central Kentucky follow the state parks listings. For more information on sports and recreational activities at area state parks, see The Great Outdoors chapter.

State Parks

Kincaid Lake State Park
Ky. Hwy. 159, Falmouth
• (606) 654-3531

Located northeast of Lexington, Kincaid Lake State Park features 84 camping sites with utilities on its 850 acres. The campground is overlooks the 183-acre Kincaid Lake and has a pool, multipurpose building and boat dock. Drinking water, flush toilets and showers are also available. It is open from April 1 through October 31.

Kincaid Lake State Park also has 125 primitive camping sites. To get there from Lexington, take Interstate 75 N. and Ky. Highway 330, Exit 14 off I-75, to Morgan and on to Falmouth.

Big Bone Lick State Park
3380 Beaver Rd., Union • (606) 384-3522

The prehistoric world meets the present at Big Bone Lick State Park, where thousands of years ago great herds of giant mastodons, mammoths and bison came to enjoy the warm salt springs in the area.

This 525-acre park has year-round camping at 62 sites with utilities. Fishing, hiking and swimming in the park pool are some of the recreational activities the whole family will enjoy. To get there, take the Ky. Highway 338 Exit (180) off I-75.

INSIDERS' TIP

A good way to spend a Sunday afternoon is to take a hike through Raven Run Nature Sanctuary. Stop to enjoy the breathtaking view of the Kentucky River palisades.

General Butler State Resort Park
1608 Ky. Hwy 227, Carrollton
• (502) 732-4384, (800) 325-0078

Featuring the state parks system's only snow ski area, General Butler State Resort Park is an ideal site for year-round outdoor recreation. The park offers 20 acres of ski trails, a large lake for summer activities, a nine-hole golf course, tennis courts and a pool. General Butler also has 111 campsites with utilities that are available throughout the year.

To get to General Butler State Resort Park, 44 miles northeast of Louisville, take the Carrollton Exit off Interstate 71. To get to I-71, take Interstate 64 W. from Lexington to Louisville.

Levi Jackson Wilderness Road State Park
998 Levi Jackson Mill Rd., London • (606) 878-8000

Step back in time 200 years as you visit historic Levi Jackson Wilderness Road State Park, which is located on two pioneer trails: Boone's Trace, blazed by Daniel Boone from the Cumberland Gap to the Kentucky River, and the Wilderness Road, which led the way for more than 200,000 settlers into Kentucky.

Levi Jackson Wilderness Road State Park has 146 campsites with utilities and 15 group camping cabins, all of which are available year round on the park's 896 acres. To get there, take I-75 S. from Lexington to Exit 38, just south of London.

General Burnside State Park
U.S. Hwy. 27 S., Burnside
• (606) 561-4192, (606) 561-4104

Kentucky's only island park, General Burnside's 430 acres are located amid the beautiful waters of Lake Cumberland, southwest of Lexington. The area was patrolled by Union General Ambrose Burnside and his troops during the Civil War. Today, the park is ideal for many outdoor activities, including boating, golfing, fishing and swimming.

General Burnside State Park has 94 camp sites with utilities and 16 primitive sites, all of which are available April 1 through October 31. Each campsite has a fire pit and metal grill, picnic table and paved tent pad. To get there, take U.S. 27 S. from Lexington, through Somerset to the park.

Cumberland Falls State Resort Park
7351 Ky. 90, Corbin
• (606) 528-4121, (800) 325-0063

A magnificent 60-foot waterfall that boasts the only moonbow in this hemisphere is the crowning glory of Cumberland Falls State Resort Park. Whitewater rafting, fishing, horseback riding and hiking are just a few of the outdoor activities you can enjoy during your stay at this unusual state park.

Cumberland Falls State Resort Park has 50 campsites with utilities that are available April through October.

Fort Boonesborough State Park
4375 Boonesboro Rd., Richmond • (606) 527-3131

Camping at the site of Daniel Boone's second pioneer settlement is a unique way to experience and enjoy this part of American history. A reconstruction of Boone's fort here along the Kentucky River, as well as fishing, boating, miniature golf and a new swimming pool, make Fort Boonesborough State Park a great family park.

There are 167 campsites with utilities on this 153-acre park. To get there, take Exit 95 off I-75 and go east on Ky. Highway 627.

Pine Mountain State Resort Park
1050 State Park Rd., Pineville
• (606) 337-3066, (800) 325-1712

Atop a mountain overlooking Kentucky Ridge State Forest, Pine Mountain State Resort Park became Kentucky's first state park in 1924. The Mountain Laurel Festival is held here the last weekend of every May when the beautiful laurel blossoms are in full bloom.

There are 24 tent camping sites at this

FYI
If no area code is given, it's a local call from Lexington-Fayette County. If an area code is given, whether it's 606 or 502, it's a long-distance call: dial 1, the area code and the number. See the How To Use This Book chapter for detailed information on calling.

Campgrounds in the area offer sites with or without utilities.

1,519-acre park located 15 miles north of Middlesboro off U.S. Highway 25 E. in Pineville. The park's open from April through October.

Blue Licks Battlefield State Park
U.S. Hwy. 68, Mount Olivet
• (606) 289-5507

The site of the last battle of the Revolutionary War in Kentucky, Blue Licks Battlefield State Park offers miniature golf, hiking and swimming to its visitors. There are 51 sites with utilities at this 150-acre park located northeast of Lexington on U.S. Highway 68. It's open April through October.

Natural Bridge State Resort Park
Ky. 11, Slade • (606) 663-2214,
(800) 325-1710

A spectacular sandstone arch 78 feet long and 65 feet high gives Natural Bridge State

Resort Park its name. The park's 18 miles of hiking trails have some of the most spectacular views in the state. You can hike up to the bridge or take the sky lift.

This 1,900-acre park in the heart of the Daniel Boone National Forest, has 95 campsites with utilities and 10 primitive sites that are open from March through November. To get there, take I-64 E. from Lexington to the Mountain Parkway and then to Ky. 11.

Greenbo Lake State Park
Ky. Hwy. 1, Greenup
• (606) 473-7324, (800) 325-0083

Another hiker's paradise, Greenbo Lake State Park covers 3,300 acres of secluded forests in Greenup County, home of the late poet Jesse Stuart. Fishing, especially for rainbow trout and largemouth bass, is a favorite activity at this beautiful state park.

Greenbo State Park has 64 campsites with utilities, and they are available April 1 through October 31. There are also 35 primitive sites open during the same time as the other campsites. To get here, take I-64 E. from Lexington to the Grayson Exit and then to Ky. 1.

Privately Owned Campgrounds

Privately owned and operated campgrounds also abound in the Central Kentucky area. Those in the immediate Lexington area are listed below by the town nearest to where they are located. Most of these campgrounds are not as scenic as those at the state parks, but they are usually more accessible to main roads and cities.

www.insiders.com

See this and many other **Insiders' Guide®** destinations online.

Visit us today!

Lexington

Kentucky Horse Park
4089 Iron Works Pike• 259-4257

Located at the exciting Kentucky Horse Park (folks camping here get a discount off admission to the horse park), this campground features a number of amenities, including a pool, dump stations, tennis and basketball courts, volleyball, horseshoes and a recreation area.

There are 260 campsites with utilities at the Kentucky Horse Park. Rates April 1 through October 31 are $15 a night (including water and electricity) for up to four people. November 1 through March 31, rates drop to $11.50 a night for up to four people. There is a $1 charge for each additional person. Primitive sites are available for $9. Senior citizens get a discount— rates are $12 in peak season, $9 off-season. To get there, take Exit 120 off of I-75.

A word of advice: You can't make reservations, and when there are special events at the park, the campground frequently fills up. Just call first.

Berea

Oh! Kentucky Campground
1142 Ky. Hwy. 21 W., Berea
• (606) 986-1150

Oh! Kentucky is located in the beautiful foothills of the Appalachian Mountains in the Folk Arts and Crafts Capital of Kentucky. Amenities at the park include two pools, basketball courts, an activities room and plenty of nearby churches.

Oh! Kentucky Campground has 90 sites with utilities and a number of primitive sites. For two people, rates are $7 a night for tent sites, $11 a night for sites with electric and water and $13 a night for electric, water and sewer hookups. Electric heat or air conditioning is $2 nightly. Each additional person costs $1.

Walnut Meadow
1201 Paint Lick Rd., Berea
• (606) 986-6180

If you're planning on camping with a large group of people (for a family reunion, for instance), Walnut Meadow is the place to stay. The campground can provide entertainment and a potluck dinner for groups of 25 or more.

But even if you're just camping with the family or friends, this Berea campground offers amenities such as a pool, volleyball court, playground, laundry and bathhouse. Additionally, a building called "the Barn" is available for use by campers for grilling out or holding gatherings. The Barn is also equipped with a small kitchen so you can prepare food for your group as well.

Walnut Meadow has about 100 sites with

INSIDERS' TIP

Kentucky is the only state bounded in three directions by rivers, and more than one-fourth of the state's population lives on a river.

utilities. Rates for sites with full hookups (water, electric and sewer) are $14 a night. For electric and water only, the rate is $13 a night. These rates are based on two adults; anyone older than 8 years old is charged an additional $2; children younger than 8 stay for free. To get here, take I-75 S. from Lexington to Exit 76.

Renfro Valley

Renfro Valley RV Park
U.S. Hwy. 25, Renfro Valley
• **(606) 256-2638, (800) 765-7464**

Renfro Valley has a convenient campground that's a short walk from Renfro Village and the nationally famous Barn Dance. The newly renovated campground has electric, sewer and water hookups, a dump station and cable TV for a straight rate of $21 a night. It's open all year.

Frankfort

Elkhorn Campground
165 Scruggs Ln., Frankfort
• **(502) 695-9154**

Adjacent to picturesque Elkhorn Creek, Elkhorn Campground offers campers all the comforts of home away from home. There's a swimming pool, miniature golf, shuffleboard, a playground, a basketball court, volleyball, horseshoes and video games. An on-site camp store with food and supplies and a laundry facility are among the other creature comforts.

The 125 campsites with utilities at Elkhorn Campground are priced as follows: $15 a night with water and electric; $17.50 a night with water, electric and sewer; and $19.50 a night with water, electric, sewer and cable TV hookups.

Kentucky River Campground
1489 Steele Branch Rd., Frankfort
• **(502) 227-2465**

With its prime location on the banks of the beautiful Kentucky River, Kentucky River Campground is ideal for those who enjoy water sports. An on-site boat ramp allows campers to play on the river during the day, then return immediately to their traveling "homes." Campground features include basketball courts, picnic shelters, volleyball and horseshoes as well as a Laundromat and supply store. The campground is open from April through October and during the winter, weather permitting.

Kentucky River Campground has 104 sites with utilities. Rates are $15 a night with water, sewer and electric, $80 per week and $200 per month.

Still Waters Campground
249 Strohmeier Rd., Frankfort
• **(502) 223-8896**

Still Waters Campground is located on Elkhorn Creek and the Kentucky River. Water sports play a big part in activities at this campground. Boats and canoes are available for rent, and on weekends when there is a new moon or full moon, the campground leads a guided starlight or moonlight "float" with a cookout after. The cost is $13. Other campground amenities include volleyball, horseshoes, croquet, Frisbee golf, a bathhouse and a dump station.

Open April through October, Still Waters Campground has 29 sites with utilities and 32 primitive sites. Rates are $7 a night for primitive sites, $9 a night with water and electric, $10 to 13 a night with water, electric, air conditioning and sewer hook-up.

If you're determined, and you have a full day to spend, it's possible to sample the scope of what the area has to offer in the way of stores, shops, boutiques, malls and studios.

Shopping and Antiques

If you're into shopping, you're probably pretty serious about it, and, rather than skimming through a long introduction, you'd prefer we get right to the good stuff.

So here's the lowdown on the Greater Lexington shopping scene. In one day of good shopping in the area, you could purchase hand-painted dolls from Russia, pottery made from local clay, a pair of jockey's racing silks and even a 19th-century armoire. In terms of variety and sheer number of shopping possibilities, Lexington and the surrounding area are a retail paradise.

In terms of superlatives, the area boasts several unusual ones, including the oldest continuously working pottery west of the Alleghenies (Bybee Pottery), the second largest mall in the state (Fayette Mall) and, for what it's worth, a Wal-Mart with the state's largest retaining wall in front of it (on Richmond Road).

This chapter loosely groups shopping options by location, with the exception of antiques stores and shops and sporting goods stores, which are listed together under specific category headings.

If you're determined, and you have a full day to spend, it's possible to sample the scope of what the area has to offer in the way of stores, shops, boutiques, malls and studios. But you will probably enjoy local shopping more if you are able to spend a few days and divide your shopping excursions into categories.

For instance, you might want to take the better part of a day to go to Berea, about 40 miles south of Lexington, and browse through the dozens of antiques stores and malls and the many working arts and crafts studios. Then you could take another day to do Lexington's malls, a day to spend in the new Hambur Pavilion and another for downtown shopping, etc.

The following listings should give you a taste of what is out there, waiting for you to find it — that special dress or pair of brass candlesticks or hand-woven shawl you just can't live without. There are many more shopping centers out there; we haven't included every one of then, but we have included the largest ones — certainly enough to get you started. So grab your credit cards and your walking shoes and forge on!

Lexington

Downtown

Lexington's downtown shopping district is filled with interesting and unique shopping experiences. There are also many charming restaurants and cafes, as well as several beautiful city parks for you to enjoy on your downtown shopping excursion.

This shopping district is perhaps most obviously noted for the duo of shopping "centers" that anchor W. Main Street surrounding Triangle Park and Rupp Arena. These are Victorian Square and the Civic Center Shops. The area has a couple of parking areas where you can park free with a validation from one of the businesses in these centers.

However, not all downtown shops are in this concentrated area. Dudley Square, south of Main Street; the Clay Avenue Shops, off E. Main Street; and specialty shops carrying everything from Peruvian beads to used Levi's are scattered throughout the area.

Downtown Shopping Centers

Civic Center Shops
410 W. Vine St. • 233-4567

At the Civic Center Shops, you can browse for hours, stop for something delicious to eat at the food court and then browse again. Among the dozens of shops and specialty boutiques, you'll find jewelry, books, antiques, art, clothing and University of Kentucky Wildcat items and the new UK Basketball Museum.

Artique, on the Main Street level, is a colorful store filled with the creations of more than 700 American artists and craftspeople. You'll find everything from blown glass and wood accessories to whimsical and equine art, jewelry, pottery, Appalachian crafts and other unique gift items.

Illusions carries a line of equine and equestrian-themed clothing and accessories, from hand-painted denim to silk jackets, sunglasses and jewelry.

Crystal, china, jewelry, sterling silver flatware, mint julep cups and Limoges and cloisonné boxes are among the treasures you'll find at Lafayette Galleries.

If you're looking to satisfy your sweet tooth, Old Kentucky Chocolates, on the second level of the Civic Center Shops, is the place to go. Specialties of this confection connection include bourbon chocolates and bourbon cherries as well as its famous pulled cream candies.

Fragrance Garden has all kinds of good-smelling bath oils, soaps and specialty gift baskets. Orvis has plenty of "sporty" clothing and accessories, and Logan's carries tradi-tional cloths for men and women. To finish off an outfit, visit Sheila's Fine Jewelry.

Clay Avenue Shops
Just off E. Main St. on Clay Ave.

This unique shopping area has taken over the houses in a residential area, giving the shops, boutiques and businesses a homey charm. You can find just about everything here in the way of gifts and specialty items, from the practical to the unusual.

Animal Crackers carries a nice line of children's clothing from layette to preteen and prep. There is also a selection of baby and birthday party gifts. Among the services Animal Crackers offers its customers are baby registry, layaway and monogramming.

Peggy's Gifts & Antiques has a wide range of fine gift items, varying both in type and in price. You can find that special gift for someone at a price you can afford, whether it's luxury bath oil or hand-painted ceramic bowls from Louisiana. Unique jewelry, home accessories and furniture are also featured, as well as plenty of items with a "bunny" theme.

If you love designer shoes and accessories, visit Alfred James and the adjoining shop, AJ's, for casual women's clothing.

From personalized stationery to paper by the pound, The Paperweight Inc. features practically every imaginable writing-related item. Unusual colors and styles of stationery, pens, photo albums and greeting cards are also available. The Paperweight is the place to shop for invitations — the store has a whole section of blank, decorative invitations that it can print custom print for you. Woodland Park Bookstore offers scholarly and uncommon books. Linens Limited has furnishings for bed, bath and table - from practical to luxurious. (They have all those yummy, romantic things we see

---

INSIDERS' TIP

Keep an eye out for ducks crossing the road in front of Lexington Mall on Richmond Road.

in magazines, but never know where to buy.) Look for Williamsburg crystal and accessories, Royal Creamware from England, gorgeous table linens from Europe (and beyond), wonderful towels, as well as interesting and unique gifts and antiques you won't see anywhere else in town. There's also a monogram service, as well as a bridal registry.

If you're looking for unusual items to complement your porch or garden, Through the Garden Gate features a great variety of unique objects, from handcrafted decorative pieces and garden supplies to statuary and garden tools — and a huge selection of flags to hang from the front porch.

Old East Vine Shops
400 Old E. Vine St.

Two blocks south of Main Street, in the renovated Taylor Tire building, is Worlds Apart, a unique clothing store for women that features its own original lines of sportswear. If you love designer shoes and accessories, visit AlfredJames. Surgener Jewelers has fine and gold-filled jewelry, plus all those watches on our wish lists: Omega, Baume & Mercier and Rolex. And Crystal on Vine will dazzle you with hundreds of crystal items, including Waterford, small silver gift items, picture frames, and dinnerware (including Spode).

Victorian Square
401 W. Main St. • 252-7575

This block of restored Victorian buildings with more than a dozen specialty shops is a quaint and charming addition to the downtown shopping scene. Gifts with an equine or Kentucky theme, fine clothing, jewelry and beautiful gift items and collectibles are among the items you'll find in this pretty complex. Two good restaurants, Bravo's and deSha's, are also here. And don't forget that Artist's Attic studios and galleries, where you can watch artists at work, is on the fourth floor.

Talbots Surplus Store on the first level offers a great discount—50 to 70 percent—on misses' dresses and sportswear sizes 4 to 20 and petite sizes 2 to 14. Talbots also has belts, scarves and accessories, as well as children's clothing and some home furnishings and gift items.

Howard & Miller Clothiers to Gentlemen

carries classic menswear from such designers as Corbin, Southwick, Robert Talbott and Kenneth Gordon.

The Acorn has very nice traditional women's clothing, especially skirts, blouses and sweaters.

Victorian Square also has a Laura Ashley store with home furnishings. And if you have the kids along, don't forget it's the home of the Lexington Children's Museum (see our Kidstuff chapter).

Woodland Avenue Shops
Woodland Ave. at intersections of
E. High and E. Maxwell Sts.

This small shopping area is more specialized, and, because it's within walking distance of the University of Kentucky campus, it's popular with students and faculty. You can find everything from rare books to futons to Birkenstocks here. Find garden accessories and neat home decorating items at Delaware River Trading Company. Bibliophiles should check out the Black Swan Book Store then, maybe drop in for a piece of mile-high pie at Missy's Pie Shop or an old-fashioned "meat-and-three" dinner (meat and three vegetables, that is) at Ramsey's Diner. The complex also has a clothing consignment shop, a bicycle shop, a custom leather shop, a futon store, a needlepoint shop, plus beautiful home decorating accessories at Decoratifs.

Other Downtown Shopping

African Marketplace
Robert H. Williams Cultural Center,
644 Georgetown St. • 255-5066

The African Marketplace, featuring Afrocentric and authentic African art, jewelry, fabric, books, accessories, food and decorative items for the home, is usually held the first Saturday of the month from noon to 6 PM but times may vary. The selections change monthly, often featuring the works of a particular artist or native jewelry and art from visitors from various African nations.

Black Market
319 S. Ashland Ave. • 269-3968

The rare and hard-to-find jewelry, home

decorations, clothing and accessories you can purchase at the Black Market are not illegal, although they are unusual. This fun shop is packed full of great stuff at reasonable prices. The jewelry and accessories from around the world are diverse and interesting enough to suit even the most discriminating shopper.

J&H Lan-Mark
515 W. Main St. • 254-7613

J&H Lan-Mark is the place to get your Carhartt coveralls, rag wool socks and long johns. This great — and practical — clothing center carries many lines of well-known outdoor clothing such as Woolrich and Ruff Hewn, hiking boots and other recreational footwear. J&H Lan-Mark also features camping and other outdoor recreational equipment. You'll find a second store on Moore Drive off Nicholasville Road.

Saturday-Sunday Market
601 W. Main St. • 255-7495

This is the best-kept secret downtown because it doesn't have a listing in the phone book and it's only open on Saturday and Sunday. Our best advice: GO. It's absolutely brimming over with reproduction English furniture and accessories, as well as quite a few eclectic items, all at discounted prices. You'll find quite a collection of wonderful "barnyard" and animal oil paintings in ornate gold leaf frames, unique lamps, sculptures, candlesticks, objets d'art (fake, of course!) and on and on. You always bump into (literally, because it's so jam-packed) decorators with their clients here.

The Unfinished Universe
525 W. Short St. • 252-3289

The restoration, repair and refinishing of fine antiques is the specialty of The Unfinished Universe. The store also carries a line of custom-made tools and refinishing supplies.

Man o' War Boulevard and I-75 Area

Hamburg Pavilion
Man o' War Blvd at I-75

This long-awaited shopping complex, built on property which was part of the well-known Hamburg Place horse farm, takes a good day to visit. Anchored by the mega-grocery and department store Meijer's, it boasts Target, Garden Ridge, Goody's, Old Navy, Pier 1, Barnes & Noble Booksellers (with Starbuck's coffee in its cafe, surely meaning we have finally arrived!), PETsMART and a half dozen more stores with shoes, sporting goods, bed and bath furnishings, bath and body products, home furnishings, party supplies, and much more on the way. Whew! And don't worry about getting hungry because there are seven sit-down or fast food restaurants at this writing, including Friday's, Applebee's and Max & Erma's. If you shop until you drop, there are also four new hotels on the drawing board near the complex: Courtyard By Marriott, scheduled to open in March, 1999; Hilton Garden Inn, scheduled for June, 1999; Sleep Inn, scheduled for early spring of 1999; and Townplace Suites, scheduled for late 1999.

Tates Creek Road Area

Chevy Chase
Along Euclid Ave. and High St.

Chevy Chase has true neighborhood appeal. It's one of Lexington's oldest and most unique shopping districts where you can buy everything from French pastries and barbecue to silk flower arrangements, Oriental rugs

---

INSIDERS' TIP

Lexingtonians love shopping for fresh produce at the Farmer's Market.

and designer clothing and shoes and children's clothes. It's also a virtual eating enclave — with American, Mexican, French and Middle Eastern restaurants, plus two great barbecue establishments and two of the city's best restaurants for lunch: The Pampered Chef with cozy European appeal and Mason's with a bistro feel. Chevy Chase covers several blocks of shops and businesses in the Ashland Avenue, High Street, Euclid Avenue and Tates Creek Road areas.

In Chevy Chase Place, Dana Kelly Oriental Rugs has been in operation longer than any Oriental rug gallery in the area. A few doors down, Best of Flowers has pretty gifts and designs some of the city's best floral arrangements.

Chatters, 312 S. Ashland Avenue, is a kids' specialty store with a wide and colorful array of clothing, accessories and gift items for the young folks in your life.

While you're shopping for young folks, don't miss the wonderful children's bookstore the Owl and the Pussycat, 316 S. Ashland Avenue. Around the corner in the 800 block of East High Street is The Front Porch featuring party supplies, stationery and home decorating accessories, and Oram's Florist is one of Lexington's oldest florists.

On Euclid Avenue is Sew Fine, a great place to get your clothes altered. They specialize in wedding dresses. You can even own a sequined gown — for one night anyway — by renting at Glitter for Rent.

Chevy Chase also has an art gallery, liquor store, supermarket, drugstore, paperback book exchange, laundromat, French bakery, hardware store, banks, gas stations and pubs — and four barber shops. In addition, there are several interior design and home accessory shops. It's a convenient way to do a lot of your shopping and business in one handy spot.

The Lansdowne Shoppes
3369 Tates Creek Rd. • 276-5415

At The Lansdowne Shoppes, you can get everything from your groceries to a new outfit. This shopping center also features a card shop, pet store, liquor store, gift shop, veterinary

Area malls carry everything from fine clothing to equine art.

clinic and hair salon. Embry's Petites is a boutique featuring designer clothing for women. Old Kentucky Chocolates is not the place to frequent if you want to shop at Embry's Petites, however.

Don't miss the good-looking women's clothes at The Cotton Patch and Temptations. You can shop for classy jewelry at Lansdowne Diamond Gallery, and if you want to show off that jewelry on a exciting trip, make your reservations at Lexington Travel Center. Don't miss all the gourmet goodies, fat deli sandwiches and cheeses at The Mouse Trap with its new front atrium for casual dining. And you'll get hooked on A Gift Affair and The Mole Hole with all their neat accessories and "must haves."

Tates Creek Centre
4104 Tates Creek Rd. • 253-0000

Located at the intersection of Tates Creek Road with Man o' War Boulevard, Tates Creek Centre is one of Lexington's newer shopping centers. A supermarket, video rental store, coffee shop and restaurants help generate a consistently high volume of shoppers, many of whom are drawn from the surrounding residential areas.

Tates Creek Centre has a variety of unique small shops. Another location of The Front Porch is here and has a colorful collection of party and gift supplies, from candies to beautiful wrappings and balloons. Logan's is a clothing store for men, featuring top-of-the-line suits, sport coats, dress shirts, sportswear and accessories for the well-dressed man. Candles & More carries bed and bath products, oil lamps, candles and decorative accessories, corporate gifts, even a bridal registry.

Tates Creek Centre is also home to a number of popular Lexington eateries, including Jozo's, Ramsey's and Pad-Thai Restaurant.

All the utilitarian stores are there too: hardware, photo, dry cleaners, mail center, pet supplies and veterinarian, paint and sporting goods, plus banking and plenty of fast-food spots.

Nicholasville Road Area

The Boot Store
3090 Lexington Rd. • 885-6629

If you're looking for Western boots, saddle up and get on out to Nicholasville Road, just across the Jessamine-Fayette county line. The Boot Store is the place to go for fancy boots, country-western furniture and men's and women's Western clothing. The Boot Store carries 123 different styles of hats, as well as a full line of belt buckles, accessories and custom-made boots. You'll definitely be in the Boot Scootin' Boogie mood when you leave.

Fayette Mall
3473 Nicholasville Rd. • 272-3493

Recent additions to and expansion of Fayette Mall have turned it into the second largest shopping mall in the state. More than 120 department stores, specialty shops, businesses and restaurants make their home in Fayette Mall. It is almost like a self-contained community — you could come to the mall when it opens at 10 AM Monday through Saturday, stay 'til it closes at 9 PM and still not experience all that Fayette Mall has to offer. It's also open on Sunday from noon to 6 PM.

Fayette Mall is anchored by four large department stores — McAlpin's, JCPenney, Lazarus and Sears. Thirty-four more stores carry men's and women's apparel; these include Dawahares, Talbots, Casual Corner, New Way Boot Shop, Embry's, Lane Bryant, Victoria's Secret, The Limited and The Gap. In addition, there are home accessory and kitchen stores, a movie store, even "body" stores with lotions and potions. By the time this book goes to print, Eddie Bauer will be open, along with Williams - Sonoma.

Fayette Mall also has a cinema complex and game room, not to mention the Pavilion Food Court, which has 11 fast-food restaurants serving everything from Mexican and German to Italian and American. You can

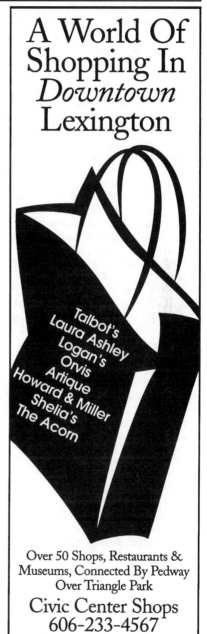

browse through dozens of specialty shops, check out the latest in computers and electronics, get your car fixed, book a cruise around the world, go to a movie or wind down at Waldenbooks.

The Mall at Lexington Green
3199 Nicholasville Rd. • 245-1513

You can't miss The Mall at Lexington Green. It's big, and it has a big, bright green roof under which you'll find all kinds of fun shopping opportunities, as well as great things to eat.

Leather Inc. features fine luggage and leather goods, ranging from garment bags and carry-ons to attaches, briefcases, Pullmans and wheel-aways and coach handbags. Tumi and Hartmann are among the fine lines Leather Inc. carries.

For the bibliophile, Joseph-Beth Booksellers is a book heaven with more than 100,000 titles in stock, not to mention hundreds of magazines. In fact, it's so huge, it has actually become a tourist attraction (as well as a hangout for the singles crowd). You can have a sandwich or a cup of coffee and dessert, or a full scale gourmet dinner in the adjoining restaurant, Cafe Joseph-Beth, or get your children fired up about reading at Joseph-Beth Kids, a special section just for junior bibliophiles.

For wonderful gift items or just plain fun, browse through Artique's eclectic array of art, jewelry and decorative accessories or Touch of Kentucky with lots of horse-themed items and photographs. Diamond Faux has "priceless" jewels (Only you will know just how priceless they are!).

Two restaurants in Lexington Green, Regatta Seafood and Ruby Tuesday's, overlook a pretty lake; you can also dine at Morrison's Cafeteria or the popular Tony Roma's - A Place for Ribs.

Natasha's Cafe and Boutique
304 Southland Dr. • 277-8412

With a selection of unique and unusual items from more than 50 countries, Natasha's is a treasure trove of jewelry, delightful ethnic clothing and native crafts. After you've purchased that perfect gypsy skirt, an African blow gun or a set of Russian nesting dolls, you can enjoy a cup of Turkish coffee or a bowl of borscht from Natasha's little cafe area.

Regency Centre
2300 block of Nicholasville Rd.

One of the newer additions to the Nicholasville Road shopping area, Regency Centre shops carry a variety of goods including GTE phones, golf clothes, clubs and supplies, discount clothing and books. The shopping center also includes a supermarket and restaurants.

If you're shopping for clothes, and you're looking for a bargain, you may just find it in one of the Regency Centre shops. TJ Maxx offers discounts on a huge selection of clothing and household decorating items for the entire family, while Hit or Miss features women's clothing, and S&K Famous Brands offers men's designer clothing at reduced prices.

Michaels is a potpourri of supplies for weddings, parties, silk floral arranging and crafts and art. Hobby Town USA has everything to fit your favorite pastimes, from kites and model cars to collectibles, such as baseball and basketball cards. The Gift Box has wonderful country accessories and gifts.

Zandale Shopping Center
2200 block of Nicholasville Rd.
• 278-5495

Zandale has a wide range of retail stores and services: You can purchase toiletries at Walgreen's drugstore, knitting and needlepoint supplies at The Eye of the Needle or country ham and beaten biscuits at the homey little gourmet grocery store called Critchfield's. You can also shop for jewelry, shoes, tobacco and health foods, as well as have your shoes repaired, get your clothes cleaned, pick up a birthday cake, mail a package and deposit your paycheck. When you get hungry, there are also several places to eat, including Mandarin Chinese restaurant and Fazoli's.

Howard-Knight Tall & Big carries fine sports and dresswear for large men. And if you're interested in sewing, Fabric Fair Textile Outlet is a bonanza of fabric at discount prices. Educator's Delight is a favorite place for teachers and parents to find materials to help their kids learn.

Richmond Road Area

Lexington Mall
2349 Richmond Rd. • 269-5393

Anchored by a large department store, Dillard's, and the Home Depot, which opened in 1998, Lexington Mall is a nice, moderate-size mall small enough to offer easy access yet large enough to have a wide range of retail stores, restaurants and businesses. At this writing, the mall has a lot of empty storefronts, but it still offers a nice variety of stores. You'll find tapes and CDs, shoes, eyeglasses, books and jewelry, and discounted women's fashions. There is also a movie theater, Cinema Grill, and video arcade, as well as several places to grab a bite to eat.

Romany Road Shops
Romany Rd. in Chevy Chase

Talk about one-stop shopping in a small area: You can cash a check at Central Bank, get your dog's vaccinations at Romany Road Animal Clinic, drop your dry cleaning off at Hart's Laundry, have a prescription filled at Wheeler's Pharmacy (while you wait, you might want to grab a pimento-cheese sandwich at the lunch counter), pick up some new window shades at Blue Grass Shade Company, browse through dresses and pretty sweaters at Sweaters & Such and pick up some gourmet goodies for dinner at Scarborough Fare specialty food shop. Whew! In addition, you can grocery shop, get a gourmet ice-cream cone, order flowers, have a picture framed, get a haircut, gets some tips on decorating your house and even fill your car up with gas. Run home, drop off the dog and all your purchases and return for dinner at gourmet eatery called The Cafe or the casual A.P. Suggins

(see our Restaurants chapter for particulars). There's not much traffic in this residential neighborhood shopping enclave, except in Kroger's parking lot, and the pace is relatively slow. Life is good, isn't it?

Harrodsburg Road Area

Turfland Mall
2033 Harrodsburg Rd. • 276-4411

For nearly three decades, Turfland Mall has been one of Lexington's shopping main-stays and it underwent a major renovaton in 1998. With about 35 shops and stores, including two large anchor department stores — Dillard's and Montgomery Ward — Turfland Mall has something for everyone, including the kids. A movie theater, an arcade and kiddie rides will keep even the youngest shopper happy.

Turfland Mall hosts a number of promotional shows and exhibits throughout the year, ranging from antiques and arts and crafts to baseball cards. There are several shoe stores, Waldenbooks, Fashion Bug Plus and Fashion Shop with discounted women's fashions, and a unique store with all kinds of fun things called Spencer Gifts. And keep in mind the old-fashioned Walgreen Drugstore is open 24 hours a day, seven days a week.

Elsewhere

Richmond Mall
Eastern Bypass, Richmond
• (606) 623-2111

From sporting goods stores like Allied and Sports Sensations to shoes, men's and women's specialty stores such as Maurice's

---

INSIDERS' TIP

Weisenberger Mills, in a scenic location at 2545 Weisenberger Road near Midway, makes and sells 70 products, including many types of flour and mixes for hushpuppies, biscuits and pancakes. The historic water-powered flour mill, the oldest commercial mill in Kentucky, is in its fifth generation of operation by the Weisenberger family. Please take note that, although you are welcome to visit the tiny sales space, you cannot tour the mill.

and Stoneworth Shirt Company, you can find it here. This mall is anchored by JCPenney and Goody's Family Clothing, but you can also find books (at The Little Professor Book Center), records, hats, jewelry, country home furnishings, toys, records, greeting cards, crafts, candles, fabrics and shoes, shoes, shoes. When you get tired of shopping, you can catch a movie or eat at the food court.

Food and Specialty Shops

Cosmo's
808 E. High St. • 335-5533

Based on upscale food markets on the West Coast and in New York, Cosmo's carries all kinds of gourmet foods. From fresh European breads baked in their own bakery to dozens of prepared foods sold by the pound, it's a gourmand's paradise. Imported cheeses and meats are a highlight, along with fresh flowers and herbs and locally grown produce.

There's an espresso bar and several cafe tables that are always full, and don't forget it for all your catering needs.

Factory Stores of America Outlet Center
Exits 125 and 126 off I-75, Georgetown • (800) SHOP-USA

This outlet mall has more than 30 factory-direct outlets that offer 30 to 70 percent off regular retail prices. Among the name-brand clothing outlets are Duck Head Outlet, Levi's Outlet by Designs, Bon Worth Factory Outlet, Bass and Revere outlets, Bugle Boy, Van Heusen and Aileen Factory Outlet.

Carolina Pottery has a mind-boggling array of great stuff for your apartment or house — silk flowers, wicker baskets, brassware, dishes, linens and tons more. The Black & Decker outlet specializes in the sale of factory-reconditioned, discontinued, excess and blemished-carton power tools and appliances. Socks Galore & More stocks more than 60,000 pairs of socks priced 25 to 80 percent below retail. Other outlet bargains: ribbon, handbags, boots, paper, linens, cookware and sunglasses.

Flag Fork Herb Farm
900 N. Broadway • 233-7381

Fill a rustic old cottage with fruit preserves, old-fashioned relishes, soup mixes, seasonings, herbal wreaths and arrangements, antiques, Christmas items throughout the year and herbal gardening supplies and you have this great shopping experience. The shop features Kentucky gourmet gift baskets filled with fine food and gift items from across the Commonwealth. There's a small room filled with hundreds of rubber stamps (it's easy to get hooked here), along with paper and envelopes for making your own personalized stationary or note cards. And don't forget to have lunch or dessert in the Garden Cafe which overlooks the bird and butterfly garden, or in the more rustic Colonial Fireside Room.

The Galleria and Equestrian Collectables
868 E. High St. • 269-2000

The Galleria is an exquisite store filled with everything from French Limoges porcelains and Italian pottery to English bone china and crystal from France. It's wonderful for gifts and it's no wonder many brides-to-be are registered here. Inside The Galleria is another upscale collection of beautiful things called Equestrian Collectables. It specializes in equine art — oils, watercolors and charcoals, as well as bronzes. There's also beautiful gold and silver jewelry.

Great Harvest Bread Company
Beaumont Centre, 3735 Harrodsburg Rd. • 223-7603
Idle Hour Center, 2200 Richmond Rd. • 266-2915

Made from flour stone-milled each morning, Great Harvest Bread Company's fresh-baked loaves are absolutely addictive. From sunflower whole-wheat and nut-raisin cinnamon rolls dripping with butter and brown sugar to loaves of herb bread, sourdough bread and special seasonal breads such as country cheddar and basil Parmesan, Great Harvest's baked goods are too delicious to pass up. And — are you ready for this? — several of the varieties are fat-free. The store doesn't brag about this, so you just need to check the labels. Bread prices range from about $2 to $4 per loaf, and other items, such as muffins, cookies, honey and gift baskets, are available.

Julie's Closet
111 Woodland Ave., The Woodlands
• 281-5661

Look for romantic reproduction silver bathroom accessories, huge silver trays that look like they came right out of the British Colonial period, picture frames, unique jewelry and belts, gorgeous tapestry bags, funny greeting cards, and all kinds of whimsical items like "sleeping cats" that are almost breathing! (They're actually made out of rabbit fur.)

Keeneland Paddock Shop
Keeneland Race Course,
4201 Versailles Rd. • 254-3412

Don't think of visiting Keeneland without a peek into their gift shop because it's one of the best around for "horsey" items: great artwork, jewelry, clothes and ball hats with the classy Keeneland logo and dozens of home accessories. You can also pick up any number of small souvenir gifts.

The Lexington Gift Mart
383 E. Main St. • 254-7140

The aromatic candles are intoxicating when you step through the door of this "delicious" downtown shop. Besides furniture, there are exquisite brocade and tapestry pillows, all kinds of aromatherapy products, handpainted items, porcelains, picture frames and pottery. The candles are artistic as well as functional. (Can you tell we love them?)

The Nash Collection
843 Lane Allen Rd. • 276-0161

John and Vivian Nash have always been interested in fine art. When they opened the Nash Collection in the summer of 1994, they fulfilled one of their longtime dreams — to own a gallery for spectacular works of handmade art by artists from around the world. The Nashes designed this gallery and showroom to have an uncluttered, museum ambiance. Display areas focus on specific types of art, from higher-end glass, metal and wood sculpture to functional glass and signed paintings.

The gallery provides people in Central Kentucky with access to international artists. Special orders and commissions from specific artists can be arranged through the gallery.

Berea

Up to this point, our shopping chapter has focused on Lexington businesses, but we felt the section would be incomplete without mentioning the one-of-a-kind shopping experience you'll have in "The Folk Arts & Crafts Capital of Kentucky."

About 40 miles south of Lexington on I-75, Berea is nationally known for the more than 60 arts and crafts studios, galleries, shops and antiques shops that line the streets of this charming town set in the foothills of the Appalachian Mountains. Visiting Berea always makes this writer want to come home and wear gauzy skirts, weave baskets and live off the land.

While many of Berea's working craft studios and shops are clustered in two main areas — historic Old Town and College Square — a lot of others are scattered throughout town. Part of the fun of shopping in Berea is discovering a unique shop on a quiet side street or just outside of town on a country lane. And most of the shop owners love to explain their skills to visitors.

Information about Berea artists and craftspeople, as well as antiques shops and malls, and maps of where to find them is available at the Berea Welcome Center, (800) 598-5263, which is in the old L & N railroad depot at 201 N. Broadway.

While it's not practical to detail every shop in Berea, we'll give you a taste of the scope of the treasures you'll discover in this delightful town. Berea artists and craftspeople create dozens of traditional and contemporary pieces of art, pottery, jewelry and weaving each year. During your shopping tour of Berea, you can also find stained-glass art, Shaker furniture and boxes, hand-carved wooden spoons and utensils, hand-forged knives, Windsor chairs, blown glass, quilts, dulcimers made from native woods and turned wooden bowls.

As for the finest, most beautiful things from the past, you'll find many of them in Berea's more than 15 antiques shops and malls. From

Photo: *Lexington Herald Leader*

Home-grown products from tomatoes to flowers are
available at Lexington's Farmer's Market.

Michler's Florist and Greenhouse

Michler's Greenhouse is the kind of place we have to visit about once a month for our plant fix. It's untamed in the most charming way: There are plants tucked everywhere: under benches, in the corners, hanging overhead and lurking underfoot. It's a little exotic, too, because you never know what species you might meet around the next corner when you meander through the old-fashioned greenhouses that are nearing a century old.

Close-up

John Michler's the president of this fourth-genera-tion family business. He's the one in the T-shirt and old jeans, with long hair and a little plant dirt under the fingernails. He's more often then not carrying a box full of plants to a customer's car. He's the one who'll grin and expound on the happy profusion of plant life. "We take the plant zoo approach," he jokes. Don't for a minute think this laid-back attitude in any way diminishes Michler's knowledge and passion for plants. "He is a true plantsman," says Beverly Fortune, garden columnist for the *Lexington Herald-Leader*. "When you go in, you just connect on another level because he's so non-intimidating and you can learn so much. It's like I love plants, and you love plants, and off we go!"

The variety of plants that Michler grows is astounding. He estimates there are 150 different herbs and 300 to 500 kinds of perennials, including a broad assortment of native plants and wildflowers. In addition, there are dozens of different annuals, water plants, house plants, bulbs — all in the old Aylesford neighborhood near downtown. "We have a taste for the unusual but a respect for tradition," Michler explains. "We like to keep a strong relationship with the past."

This respect for the past includes keeping the old greenhouses that were built by Michler's great grandfather who started in the nursery business at this site in 1901. The oldest structure, built in 1905, still has the original glass panels, cast-iron gutters and hand-crank ventilators. It's supported by a frame of bald cypress. A second green-

— continued on next page

Photo: Norman Drake

Michler's still uses greenhouses built when the business first started in the early 1900s.

house was built in 1907, yet another in 1935. "People see these old greenhouses as not being efficient," explains Michler. "But we just solved that problem with plant selection. We choose plants that will adapt." All this respect for tradition has not gone unnoticed. Michler's received a 1997 Special Preservation Award from Lexington's Historic Preservation Commission for the greenhouses. The buildings are also on the National Historic Register.

Michler wants his greenhouse to be an informal teaching facility. "I wish I had had a place like this to go when I was first learning," he said. "This is a good place for people to come who just want to learn about unusual and useful plants and see what they look like." Fortune says there's this magical attraction at the greenhouses. "People who love plants just know as soon as they walk in," she says. "You always see somebody you know and like. And you can go in with absolutely no intention of buying anything, but you prowl around and invariably find five things that you need for your garden, and pretty soon you're out the door with a box full."

Michler fully expects to keep things low key — quaint old greenhouses with healthy plants tumbling everywhere, he and his family comfortably settled in the old Michler home next door, no great need to modernize. "Maybe it's because we're in the middle of a neighborhood, but it just seems that the world comes to me," he says. Is it any wonder?

porcelain, china and glassware to toys, advertising pieces, lamps, trunks and furniture, Berea is an antiques lover's dream come true. Information on local antiques shops and malls is also available at the Berea Welcome Center.

Antiques

In case you didn't know it, you're in Antiquing Country! The Central Kentucky region is one rich in heritage and an appreciation for the fine craftsmanship of the past. So it's not surprising to find that there are 200 antiques shops in the area, more than a dozen of them in Lexington. Several of Lexington's antiques dealers are open by appointment only, and some shops feature antiques as part of their inventory along with gift items and home furnishings.

Additionally, there are big antique shows throughout the year at several area locations, including the Lexington Loose Leaf Tobacco Warehouse on Angliana Avenue (call 255-7309 for show dates which run from spring through fall) where you'll find a lot of country and primitive furniture and plenty of collectibles; and Heritage Hall in Rupp Arena on Main Street beside the Civic Center Shops where you just might find a good antique mixed in with all the fudge and tool booths.

If you like antique malls brimming with furniture and collectibles, grab the car keys and head straight to Main Street in either Georgetown or Nicholasville, the antique mall capitals of the region. And a couple of counties away in Lancaster is Lancaster Antique Market, 792-4536, with good country antiques. For more antiques, be sure and check out other surrounding towns, including Versailles, Paris and Midway's Railroad Street.

In this section, we describe some of the bigger antiques shops and malls, as well as some of the shops that specialize in certain items. However, anyone who is an antiques shopper knows you often have to check out a lot of places before you find exactly what you're looking for. Of course, that's half the fun.

Antique & Modern Firearms
2263 Nicholasville Rd. • 276-1419

If you are interested in antique guns, rifles and related items, Antique & Modern Firearms is the place for you. In addition to their selection of the most-collected firearms in the world — Colt firearms and Winchester rifles — the shop also has Civil War guns and related accoutrements, including swords, holsters, bayonets and bullets. The Kentucky Rifle, a frontier firearm, is also popular among collectors, and Antique & Modern Firearms carries a selection of these, along with powder horns, bullet molds and related items.

Antique Mall at Todd's Square
535 W. Short St. • 252-0296

Showcasing the collections of about 20 area dealers, the Antique Mall at Todd's Square has vintage clothing, quilts, jewelry, clocks, glassware, silver, furniture, dolls and old advertising pieces.

Bluegrass Antique Market
760 Winchester Rd. • 258-2105

This attractive antique mall has booths arranged loosely like room settings - with everything from Victorian and country furniture to signed Stickley pieces and 50s-style dinettes and jukeboxes. You can also find jewelry,

glassware and china, pottery, silver, and some really interesting items, such as handbags and pillows made from Oriental rugs. If it's a secretary or mahogany dining room table and chairs you're looking for, you can find those there, too.

Boone's Antiques
4996 Old Versailles Rd. • 254-5335

With 27,000 square feet of showroom space, Boone's is another place that could be a good daytrip destination. Whatever you make it, you won't want to leave once you get there. Look for American, European, English and Oriental antiques, along with Country French, wonderful oil paintings, brass, copper, reproduction pewter, Oriental rugs and lots of scrubbed pine pieces. We've amassed an

Photo: Lee Thomas, courtesy of the Lexington Convention and Visitors Bureau

Local folk art and crafts make great keepsakes of your visit.

entire blue-and-white porcelain plate collection from Boone's in the past 10 years.

Heritage Antiques
380 E. Main St. • 253-1035

Local antiques buffs check this shop out frequently because the inventory constantly changes. You'll find everything from Early American to French and Empire pieces, plus all kinds of things in between. The shop buys complete estate holdings, so you're liable to find everything from used furniture to that odd piece you've been looking for. We've found good buys on Oriental runners and old pewter — and currently have an eye on a wonderful old linen press. To locate the shop, just look for the "knights" in armor in front of the store.

Irish Acres Gallery of Antiques
4205 Fords Mill Rd., Nonesuch
• 873-7235

This antiques gallery is as unique as the name of the little town in which it is located. Just south of Versailles off U.S. Highway 33, Irish Acres is a sprawling, 32,000-square-foot complex with more than 50 showrooms of antiques and collectibles. Dolls, toys, lamps, glassware, furniture, marbles, vintage clothing — the list is endless. Actually, going to Irish Acres would make a nice daytrip. You can browse through some of the antiques showrooms, then take a break for lunch in the on-site restaurant, The Glitz, before shopping some more. Lunch is served, and reservations are necessary. (If you don't have lunch in The Glitz or Crystal Alley, at least peek in. It more than lives up to its name!) Irish Acres is closed Sunday and Monday.

Jo & Travis Rawlings
311 and 402 S. Winter St., Midway
• 846-4550

This is one of those "by appointment" shops you should check out if you're in the market for a chest of drawers, which is the house specialty. The last time we visited, the shop also had two handsome sugar chests. This is another dealer who can help you find a specific piece you've been looking for. The shop also has a nice selection of old brass candlesticks, and Travis Rawlings' special talent is furniture restoration.

Kindred's Antiques in the Country
7376 Old Danville Pike, Nicholasville
• 887-2256

There is always a good selection of early country and formal furniture in this rustic old church with sunny yellow walls and brass chandeliers. The specialties here are chests, sideboards, corner cupboards, grandfather clocks and blanket chests, as well as custom-made reproductions. A bonus: The shop shares the grounds with a wildlife sanctuary, so it's great fun to visit. And if you're looking for some special piece, let the owners know, and they'll help you find it.

D. Lehman & Sons
100 N. Winter Street, Midway • 846-4513

Lehman's carries one of the best collections of fine antiques, including American furniture, old silver and brass. What makes the shop even more interesting is a big selection of new gifts and home accessories mixed in with the antiques. It's a great place to shop for a special gift.

Lexington Antique Gallery
637 E. Main St. • 231-8197

The specialties at this upscale mall are 18th- and 19th-century American and English furniture, fine porcelain, coin silver, paintings, linens, antique sewing accessories, garden accessories and Oriental rugs. With about two dozen dealers here, the variety and quality are outstanding.

Mike Maloney Antiques
303 Southland Dr. • 275-1934

The owners say their strong suit is that they have a mixture of everything here — Oriental rugs, period furniture, accessories, and every once in a while some items from the '50s, like a chrome dinette set.

Meadowthorpe Antique Mall
1463 Leestown Rd. • 225-3966

You'll find mostly furniture at this mall, including primitive and country and a nice selection of oak. And you don't even have to leave for lunch because there's a tea room with sandwiches, salad, and desserts inside the mall.

Sporting Goods

Allsports
3559 Nicholasville Rd. • 272-8656

Allsports carries a large selection of athletic equipment and clothing. The store is in Fayette Mall.

Bob Daniels Sporting Goods
1400 Alexandria Dr. • 255-0104

Bob Daniels serves individual athletes and teams with a variety of equipment and apparel. Monogramming, silk screening and trophies are also available.

Brendamour's Sporting Goods
3563 Nicholasville Rd. • 272-9005

Brendamour's, in the newer section of Fayette Mall, offers a selection of sporting and exercise equipment.

Court Sports
385 S. Limestone St. • 255-5125

Court Sports specializes in athletic shoes and apparel.

Evans Firearms & Archery
117 Southland Dr. • 277-7770

Evans Firearms & Archery carries loads of hunting and shooting supplies, including tree stands and gun safes. Practice on the indoor archery range; successful hunters can use the taxidermy service.

John's Run/Walk Shop
317 S. Ashland Ave. • 269-8313

Serious runners, joggers and walkers know they can get expert help from the specialists at John's Run/Walk Shop. Owner John Sensenig even gets referrals from doctors whose patients are having foot or leg problems. It's also the best place to pick up information about racing and walking events.

Jumbo Sports
3650 Boston Rd. • 223-4211

Jumbo Sports, formerly Sports Unlimited,

is the biggest sporting goods store in Central Kentucky. It offers equipment and apparel for practically any athletic or outdoor activity you can imagine.

Kentucky Sporting Goods
501 W. Main St. • 252-5825

Kentucky Sporting Goods, across from Rupp Arena, specializes in team uniforms and carries all major brands and types of athletic shoes.

The Locker Room Sporting Goods
739 Lane Allen Rd. • 276-1101, 278-2702

The Locker Room caters to teams, offering uniforms, team equipment and team discounts. It also has a large selection of Russell sweats, screen printing and monogramming, plus umpire equipment.

Nevada Bob's Discount Golf
101 Mt. Tabor Rd. • 269-4443

Nevada Bob's offers a huge selection of golf equipment, plus club fitting and repair and an indoor hitting net.

Pannell Swim Shop
Fayette Place, Nicholasville Road • 272-7946

Pannell Swim Shop carries, swimsuits, caps, goggles, bags, sweats — "practically anything in the aquatics apparel industry."

Phillip Gall's
1555 New Circle Rd. N.E. • 266-0469

Phillip Gall's specializes in camping, outdoor and ski equipment.

Play It Again Sports
3140 Richmond Rd. • 269-4556

Play It Again Sports, which sells both new and used sports equipment, pays cash for used gear. It specializes in golf, hockey, baseball and exercise equipment and also has a selection of in-line skates.

The Pro Image
2339 Richmond Rd. • 268-4734

The Pro Image has a wide selection of athletic footwear and licensed team logo apparel.

We've got animals and arts and astronauts . . . balls and books and bugs . . . a castle and climbing and clowns . . . dinosaurs and drama and driving . . . magic and music and Mickey Mouse . . . playgrounds and parades and pumpkins . . . and much more.

Kidstuff

Oh, to be a kid again!

Lexington is a great place to be a kid (or to be like one). Most of the attractions mentioned in this section are open to all ages. To fit in, all you need is a willingness to have fun and the ability to approach life as an adventure.

If you're a parent, you'll be happy to know that your children can learn while they're having fun at many of these places, such as the Lexington Children's Museum, the Lexington Public Library, Safety City and the YMCA and YWCA. Heck, you might even learn a few things yourself.

We have gone the extra mile to lend some perspective to this section of the book. We consulted a recognized expert on children's activities: a genuine boy with fun on his mind. The resulting selection of things to do is versatile enough to satisfy almost any interest — even interests that are accompanied by short attention spans. Most of the attractions mentioned in this section are within the confines of Lexington proper; there's nothing more than two hours away.

We've got animals and arts and astronauts . . . balls and books and bugs . . . a castle and climbing and clowns . . . dinosaurs and drama and driving . . . magic and music and Mickey Mouse . . . playgrounds and parades and pumpkins. We could go on, but by now you're probably about ready to pile into the station wagon with your family and start exploring the area on your own, so we'll cut to the chase.

First, a note of explanation: Some of the children's attractions listed could easily have been included in other parts of the book, such as the Shopping chapter. Some are mentioned elsewhere. Because of their appeal to the younger set, however, we thought it appropriate to include them here. For additional activities that the entire family can enjoy, refer to the sections on attractions, campgrounds, parks and recreation, sports, fishing, horses, museums, the arts and, frankly, just about anything else.

As we said, Lexington is a great place to be a kid. So here are the details on a bunch of neat stuff for Bluegrass kids to do.

Action and Adventure

Creative Playgrounds

Lexington has four outdoor creative playgrounds — huge, wooden structures packed with nooks, crannies and physical challenges that can keep easily bored kids occupied for hours while causing their parents to say, "Why didn't they have neat stuff like this when I was a kid?" Creative playgrounds are far more elaborate than the traditional playground equipment older folks grew up with. You'll find such features as tunnels, multiple levels, ramps, bridges and ladders that children can literally "lose" themselves in — great for playing hide-and-seek! The newest of these playgrounds, built by community volunteers, lies between Dunbar Community Center and Russell Elementary School on W. Fifth Street. The others are at Shillito Park (off Reynolds Road), Jacobson Park (Athens-Boonesboro Road) and Picadome Elementary School (Harrodsburg and Clays Mill roads).

Kids Place Indoor Adventure Playground
3992 W. Tiverton Ct. • 272-5433

Kids Place, in the Lexington Athletic Center, bills itself as "the world's largest indoor playground." We can't vouch for that, since there are a couple of indoor playgrounds in Singapore that we have yet to visit. We can tell you, however, that kids love it. The two-story-high playground, which fills an entire gymnasium, includes three slides, three "ball baths," a rope bridge, a "Tarzan climb" and plenty of other climbing and jumping activities. After-school, day-care and summer programs are available, and it's also a great place for a birthday party. Admission, which ranges from $4.95

to $5.95 depending on the time, includes unlimited play. (Admission includes an adult and one child.)

Laser Quest
224 Bolivar St. • 225-1742

Looking for a way to vent some of your pent-up anger? Put down that handgun and head for Laser Quest, which provides a thrilling but safe outlet for all your shoot-'em-up tendencies. Laser Quest, located in a renovated warehouse at the edge of the University of Kentucky campus, is space-age warfare á la Star Wars, and it's good fun for kids and adults of all ages. Participants, equipped with laser guns and sensors, set out on a mission amid a dark labyrinth filled with enemies intent on deactivating them. Points are gained and lost depending on number of foes hit and number of times hit by foes. Generally, you're on your own, but sometimes team play is offered. The cost is $6 for a 20-minute game or "mission"; with $25 annual membership, you play for $5 a game.

Hours are Monday through Thursdays from 6 PM to 10 PM, Friday from 3 PM to midnight, Saturday from noon to midnight, and Sunday from 1 PM to 9 PM. Laser Quest opens early on school holidays and extends its hours during the summer, so call ahead of time for special hours.

One caution: During peak times (like weekends and when school is out), you may face as much as a two-hour wait. May the force be with you.

Entertainment Xpress
230 North Plaza Drive, Nicholasville
• 887-0359

This family fun park, located on 5.7 acres just off U.S. 27, offers a wealth of outdoor and indoor activities. Outside, you can enjoy go-kart racing on a figure-8 track, two 18-hole miniature golf courses, basketball games (on a regular court or with funky "bank shot" goals), batting cages and sand volleyball. Inside, you'll find a two-story arcade jammed with pinball and video games. There's also a laser tag game played in an inflatable, seven-chamber "moonwalk" building. Admission is free; charges vary per activity. (You can get a 3-hour, unlimited-play wristband for $15.)

Hours are Monday through Thursday from 1 PM to 11 PM, Friday and Saturday from 11 AM to midnight, and Sunday from 1 PM to 9 PM.

YMCA of Central Kentucky
239 E. High St. • 254-9622
YWCA of Lexington
1060 Cross Keys Rd.
• 276-4457

The "Y" is a great place for the whole family to get in shape or just have fun. For more information, see our Parks and Recreation chapter.

"How Can We Be Learning When We're Having So Much Fun?"

Aviation Museum of Kentucky
Hangar Dr. • 231-1219

Take to the skies at this unique museum where more than a dozen vintage airplanes are on display, along with a flight simulator to help pilot wannabes get the feel of the controls. There's also a Cessna 150 that kids can climb in and explore, as well as a big collection of airplane memorabilia and a gift shop.

Each June and July the museum hosts an

FYI

If no area code is given, it's a local call from Lexington-Fayette County. If an area code is given, whether it's 606 or 502, it's a long-distance call: dial 1, the area code and the number. See the How To Use This Book chapter for detailed information on calling.

A flight simulator at the Lexington Children's Museum strikes the fancy of a young visitor.

aviation camp for kids age 9 to 14. Call for more information or to sign up.

The museum is open Tuesday and Thursday through Saturday from 10 AM to 5 PM and Sunday from 1 to 5 PM. Cost of admission is $3 for adults, $1.50 for students any age, free for kids under 6.

To get to the museum, turn off Versailles Road (U.S 60) onto Man o' War Boulevard, then turn right on Airport Drive. The museum is located off Airport Drive on Hangar Drive.

Lexington Children's Museum
401 West Main St., Victorian Square
• 258-3256

"Hands-on" is the rule at this two-story, 14,000-square-foot museum. Kids can explore a cave, walk on the moon, participate in an archaeological dig, sit in an actual military flight simulator, wander through a huge model of the human heart and lungs, fight a fire on Main Street, visit foreign countries and travel back in time — and still be home for supper.

Other enjoyable activities include blowing giant soap bubbles, walking across the keys of a large floor piano like Tom Hanks did in the movie *Big*, rolling around the floor inside a giant turtle shell on wheels and trying to solve a series of brain-twisting puzzles. Enthralled children might not even realize they're learning about subjects like anatomy, archaeology, biology, geography, history, physics and social studies. And most adults we know could stand to brush up on a few of those subjects as well. Whatever your age, visit the Children's Museum, even if you have to rent a kid for a few hours.

The museum is open on weekdays 10 AM to 6 PM, Saturday from 10 AM to 5 PM and Sunday from 1 PM to 5 PM. It's closed on Mondays from Labor Day to Memorial Day. Admission is $3, free for those 2 and younger.

Living Arts & Science Center
362 N. Martin Luther King Blvd. • 252-5222

The Living Arts & Science Center, which celebrated its 25th birthday in 1993, was created to promote education in the arts and sciences for young people. Ask your kids if they care. Didn't think so. Now, ask them if they'd like to go to a big, old house where it's cool to touch things and they can draw or paint or make their own masks or cartoons or wander around outside in a natural urban habitat with birds and bats and other wild things. OK, now, that's better!

Since 1970 the center has been in the Kinkead House, an antebellum mansion that's on the National Register of Historic Landmarks. In its 7,000 square feet of indoor space, you'll find two art galleries featuring local artists, a science gallery with hands-on exhibits, a library, classrooms, a darkroom and a media center. Through an ever-changing variety of art and science classes — sculpture, bugs, cooking, pottery, ecology, outer space, dinosaurs and calligraphy, to name just a few — children are encouraged to express themselves, ask questions and solve problems creatively.

Class fees range from $40 and up. Exhibits are free to all. Hours are 9 AM to 4 PM, Monday through Friday. Between Labor Day and Memorial Day, it's also open from 10 AM to 2 PM on Saturday.

Lexington Children's Theatre
418 West Short Street • 254-4546

Lexington Children's Theatre, a professional company that has been around since 1938, presents eight fully staged plays each season for children and their parents. A special touring company performs for school groups around the state. Productions in recent years have included *Romeo and Juliet*, *Peter Pan*, *Androcles and the Lion*, *The Jungle Book* and *Most Valuable Player*, the Jackie Robinson story. Dickens' holiday classic, *A Christmas Carol*, is performed annually. The nonprofit theater group also has the Acting Company for Teens and a number of educational programs in its new home, Victorian Square. Call for a schedule and ticket information.

Safety City
1160 Red Mile Pl. • 258-3636

A miniature version of Lexington is the scene for a 4½-hour course that teaches children some of the most important lessons they'll ever learn. Safety City, which cost $400,000 to build, is the first such facility in Kentucky and probably the finest one in the country.

The highlight comes when the little ones get to drive miniature, battery-powered cars through a residential section and a downtown area, complete with sidewalks and working traffic signals. There's even a small-scale, two-story "Big Blue" office tower. Children watch a short film on safety, which teaches them about fire prevention, looking "left-right-left" before crossing the street, calling 911 and not talking to strangers, among other things.

A warning: Safety City is open to groups only, by appointment only. Most pupils in Fayette County Public Schools participate in the program when they are in first or second grade.

Down on the Farm

Garrett's Orchard & Country Market
3360 Shannon Run Rd. (Ky. Hwy. 1967)
• 873-3819

The ideal time to visit Garrett's is on a fall Saturday afternoon a week or two before Halloween. The air is crisp but not too cool, the sun is shining, leaves are turning, kids are planning jack-o'-lanterns, and you're mulling the idea of taking a thermos of hot spiced cider to tonight's UK football game.

So you go to Garrett's, where the kids pick out their own pumpkins. After sampling some fresh, free cider, you buy a couple of gallons along with some spices and seven-bean-soup mix and Indian corn and a caramel apple and a few other things. If you're lucky, you might even get to see the cider being made.

Added bonus: the scenic drive. Just go out Versailles Road, turn left across from the castle (see below) and follow the signs for 3.5 miles.

Garrett's opens in mid-May for the start of strawberry season and remains open until Christmas. Seasonal hours are 8 AM to 6 PM Monday through Saturday and noon to 6 PM Sunday.

"The Castle"
U.S. 60 between Lexington and Versailles

Technically, this isn't a kids' attraction, or even an attraction at all. You can't go in it or even get any closer than 300 yards from it without trespassing, so we can't tell you what it's like on the inside.

But the anachronistic Gothic structure,

which sometimes has cattle grazing on the sloping hill in front of it, has been the subject of more speculation than any other building in the Bluegrass, and it's great fuel for a child's imagination. (Just ask your kids to make up their own stories about what might be going on inside those walls.) Visitors stop along the highway daily to have their pictures taken in front of the castle, which businessman Rex Martin began building in 1969 for his wife. They have long since divorced, and the castle, which has been mentioned as a possible museum site, has been for sale for many years. You probably can't afford it, but check it out on the way to Garrett's Orchard & Country Market (see above).

Double Stink Hog Farm
3181 Newtown Road, Georgetown
• 868-9703

Don't let the smelly name fool you. While this farm, run by brothers Tom and Howard Fister, once was a commercial pig farm, its focus is now on plants rather than livestock. But there's plenty here to keep the kids interested, especially during the fall (more on that in a moment). The nursery opens in April, offering a variety of bedding plants; in summer you can get homegrown sweet corn, tomatoes and other produce. Then comes Pumpkinfest — which translates into fun for the entire family. Pumpkinfest, which runs over three weekends in late September and October, features horse-drawn hayrides, the opportunity to pick your own pumpkin from the patch, a petting zoo with farm animals as well as more exotic creatures like llamas and wallabies, pig races, pony and camel rides, crafts and more. If you get hungry, you can feast on grilled steak and chicken sandwiches, hot dogs and fresh-baked apples pies. There is no charge for admission, although activities such as hay rides and the petting zoo will cost you a buck or two a person. Many area schools take groups of pupils to Double Stink for Pumpkinfest.

Barefoot Cove at Kentucky Kingdom features slides, a sunken sub and a pirate ship.

Clowns, Pets and Puppets

Cambo the Clown
• 272-2515

Cambo the Clown, a graduate of the Ringling Brothers and Barnum & Bailey Clown College, keeps the children entertained with juggling, magic, balloon animals and nonsense. He's available for birthday parties, picnics, festivals and other events.

Lighter Than Air
136 Southland Dr. • 272-7777

Clown shows. Magic. Fire eating. Balloon animals and decorations. Owner Johnathan Pinczewski can bring it all to your place, with shows tailored to any age group, including adults. Prices range from $65 to $150. Lighter Than Air's offerings also include singing telegrams and other deliveries. Pinczewski, who teaches clowning, balloon decorating and fire eating, also sells animal balloons and other party accessories at his store.

Party Pets
7376 Old U.S. 27, Nicholasville • 887-2256

For a party everyone will remember, Party Pets will bring the zoo to you. From monkeys, llamas, pygmy goats, pot-bellied pigs and fuzzy creatures like rabbits and baby ducks, Party Pets will provide them. Call for information and prices.

Tuppenny Puppets
236 Forest Park Rd. • 277-9493

For a real old-fashioned puppet show — complete with hand-glove puppets and marionettes — let John and Liz Skelton come to your event and bring their cast of characters. John is a musician and Liz is a teacher, so they are naturals at writing scripts and planning music that will thrill a group of kids. There's also juggling and magic, and their shows are especially popular during the Christmas season. Call for more information.

Parades

Lexington has a number of annual parades, including Christmas and St. Patrick's Day, and Lexington's neighbors also like a good parade now and then. See our Festivals and Annual Events chapter for more details.

Fun in (the) Store

The Disney Store
Fayette Mall (McAlpin's wing) • 271-6077

This shop is the place to find the latest in official Disney merchandise ranging from Mickey Mouse watches and clothing to dolls and figurines. Youngsters and their parents are captivated from the moment they enter this colorful world where big video screens feature clips and music from Disney films. You can also stock up on videocassettes of those movies, from classics like *Old Yeller* to more recent gems like *Beauty and the Beast*. When the store opened in 1993 at the Nicholasville

Road mall, people were waiting in line to get in; it's a small world, after all.

Joseph-Beth Kids
The Mall at Lexington Green • 271-4031

The expansion at Joseph-Beth Booksellers has resulted in more things for everybody, and kids are no exception. The children's section now has its own entrance, its own phone number and a wide selection of books and other fun/educational items for all ages. There's even a comfortable "amphitheater" area where the little ones can sit and read, and special readings and other programs are also offered. The mall is at Nicholasville and New Circle roads. (For more information on Joseph-Beth, see the Shopping chapter.)

Natural Wonders
Fayette Mall, Nicholasville Rd. • 245-2313

This eclectic shop is filled with unusual books, puzzles, games and toys, many of them relating to nature and science. Sure-to-please gifts recommended by our discerning Kidstuff consultant include rear-vision sunglasses, real wooden boomerangs, "squiggly writer" pens, holograms, kaleidoscopes and plenty of dinosaur merchandise.

Toys R Us
South Park Shopping Center • 271-6374

Sure, it's a big chain. But our child consultant calls it "the most amazing toy store in Lexington," and he usually knows what he's talking about.

Toys R Us also includes an extensive selection of board games as well as Nintendo and Sega Genesis cartridges. The shopping center is off Nicholasville Road.

Zany Brainy
119 Reynolds Rd. • 245-8697

Adults will wish they were kids again, and kids will never want to leave this fun yet educational place. It's also a chain, but it's so unique, we have to mention it. Besides all kinds of interactive, non-violent toys, puzzles, games and "junior software," there are planned activities at the store every single day for children of various ages. And to make things just about perfect, there's a small movie theater with regularly scheduled shows, a reading station where parents are encouraged to sit and read with their kids, and even computer stations.

Fun with Food

Chuck E. Cheese's
1555 New Circle Rd. N.E. • 268-1800

This franchise pizza restaurant is a popular site for birthday parties. The motto is "where a kid can be a kid"; fittingly, food is secondary to entertainment. The play area offers a range of games and activities, including a pit filled with plastic balls where young ones can burrow to their hearts' content. In front of a dining area filled with long tables, a stage features a mechanical animal rock band led by Chuck E. himself. Chuck, a giant mouse, also wanders about, greeting children and singing "Happy Birthday."

Not Too Far Away

Amusement Parks

Although there are no amusement parks in the immediate Lexington area, two very good ones are located less than two hours away.

Kentucky Kingdom
Kentucky Fair and Exposition Center, Louisville • (800) SCREAMS

Kentucky Kingdom, at the Kentucky Fair and Exposition Center, offers more than 40 acres of fun. Some of it is too scary for the smallest kids, but there's more than enough to satisfy all ages, whether you like your thrills wild or mild. The park is a little more than an hour's drive from Lexington. For more information, see our Attractions chapter.

Paramount's Kings Island
Kings Mills, Ohio, off I-71 • (513) 398-5600

About 24 miles north of Cincinnati lies a longtime regional favorite. Paramount's Kings

Island has several world-class roller-coasters, a water park, roaming Hanna-Barbera cartoon characters and much more. For more information, see our Attractions chapter.

Zoos

As with amusement parks, Lexington doesn't have its own zoo, unless you count the end zone at a UK football game. But you have only to go as far as Louisville or Cincinnati to find a good one.

Louisville Zoo
1100 Trevilian Way • (502) 459-2181

The Louisville Zoo has nearly 400 breeds of animals, a rain forest re-creation, live shows and much more. For more information, see our Attractions chapter.

Cincinnati Zoo and Botanical Park
3400 Vine St. • (513) 281-4700

A white tiger collection and outdoor gorillas are just part of the appeal of Cincinnati Zoo. For more information, see our Attractions chapter.

Wolf Run Zoo and Education Center
7376 Old U.S. 27, Nicholasville • 887-2256

This mini-zoo (and animal refuge) in the country has lions, monkeys, hybrid wolves, foxes, deer, a llama and an emu, along with pot-bellied pigs and an assortment of farm animals, cats and dogs. Many of these animals have been adopted after being abandoned or nursed back to health after being injured.

The animals are housed in a fun, farm setting — so pack a lunch, take a camera and plan on spending an afternoon. Hours vary according to seasons, so be sure and call first, especially if you want to take a group. A $2 donation goes toward buying food for the animals.

Kentucky's state parks system is widely recognized as one of the finest, if not THE finest, in the nation. We have 44 state parks.

Parks and Recreation

Go fly a kite.

If that doesn't interest you, sign up for a basketball or soccer league. Fish. Swim. Hang upside down on a jungle gym. Walk, jog or run. Play tennis. Sail or pedal across a peaceful lake. Play a friendly, or not so friendly, game of softball. Enjoy a quiet picnic or an enthusiastic family reunion. Learn how to tap dance.

In Lexington and surrounding areas, your recreation possibilities are virtually unlimited. Whether you prefer active or passive recreation, you can most likely find what you're looking for in the Bluegrass. In many cases, you'll find city-run programs offering what you want; in other cases, you'll have to look elsewhere. But you'll probably find it somewhere.

If you're the outdoorsy type, you're really in luck. Whatever type of outdoors activity you prefer, you can find it here in Central Kentucky or within about 2 hours' drive. Hunting. Fishing. Hiking. Camping (see our Campgrounds chapter for details). Swimming. Boating. Spelunking (a fancy word for crawling around in caves).

"There are no finer forests in the world than the natural parks of the 'Blue-grass region' of Kentucky," wrote Cassius Marcellus Clay in his 1886 autobiography. We know what he means. The good Lord has blessed Kentucky with a generous supply of natural beauty in the form of lush woodlands, rolling hills and valleys, scenic waterways, spectacular rock formations and vast caves — all of which cry out to anyone who enjoys communing with the outdoors.

Kentucky's state parks system is widely recognized as one of the finest, if not THE finest, in the nation. We have 44 state parks, the majority of which have facilities for outdoors activities. Some of them are listed in this chapter, and you'll find others under Daytrips and Weekend Getaways. The state also has one excellent national park, Mammoth Cave.

Remember that this is not an exhaustive list of recreational opportunities, though there's probably enough here to exhaust you. But no matter how you like to "recreate," you'll find something you like in this chapter. It may be indoors or outdoors, in town or in the country, ultra-physical or a little more passive, on land or in water or even in the air. We've got it. This chapter looks at a variety of activities in a variety of locations, including public parks, playgrounds and programs; popular waterways; state parks; indoor facilities; and even a few bars.

Public Parks, Playgrounds and Programs

Division of Parks and Recreation
545 N. Upper Street • 288-2900, 253-2384 24-hour recorded hotline

Lexington has a generous supply of green parks and playgrounds filled with activities for all ages. Parks and Recreation, a division of the Lexington-Fayette Urban County Government, is responsible for operating and maintaining nearly 100 parks on more than 3,000 acres in Fayette County.

The division also offers, sponsors or co-sponsors a wide range of athletic leagues; instructional and recreational programs, including after-school classes, at Lexington elementary schools and community centers; and annual events for children and adults.

Special recreation programs are available for individuals with disabilities and special needs.

After-school youth classes, which vary seasonally and from site to site, include arts and crafts, ballet, baton, creative dance, drama, modern dance, sports activities, tap dance and tumbling. Costs for the youth classes are nominal, about $6 for a 10-week class. Adult classes, which cost a little more than the youth programs but are still reasonable, include art, ballroom dance, ceramics, clogging, crafts, fencing, pottery and step aerobics.

Athletically speaking, Parks and Recreation offers adult and youth softball, youth T-ball and baseball, youth football and cheerleading, youth and adult basketball, tennis, volleyball, and other activities. For sign-up times, watch for announcements in the newspaper or at your child's school, or call the department. The office is open Monday through Friday from 8 AM until 5 PM.

Parks and Recreation also maintains and operates four public golf courses (see our Golf chapter).

Below, we have described some of Lexington's larger and more popular parks. There are many more, but we couldn't list them all. If you live in Lexington, there's bound to be at least one in your vicinity, and others may be on their way. Don't feel bad if your neighborhood park isn't mentioned here. In fact, you may want to let it remain your little secret; we love parks, and some of them get a little crowded at peak times.

Castlewood Park
201 Castlewood Dr.

In addition to a community center offering a range of activities, Castlewood Park has a swimming pool, basketball courts and baseball and softball fields.

Douglass Park
726-798 Georgetown St.

Mention Douglass Park to many Lexingtonians, and two words come to mind: Dirt Bowl. Now, to be fair, this 27-acre park about a mile north of downtown has plenty more to offer, including a swimming pool and facilities for baseball, football, tennis and volleyball. But its claim to fame, especially among much of the African American community, is the Dirt Bowl Summer Basketball League. Since its founding in 1967, the Dirt Bowl has featured a number of UK basketball stars and other high-grade players, some of whom have played in the NBA. Former Wildcats Jack Givens, James Lee, Dirk Minniefield and Melvin Turpin and Duke's Vince Taylor are among the stars who have left their marks on the court here. The Dirt Bowl's climax comes in July, when Super Sunday draws thousands of people to watch the games amid a festive atmosphere.

FYI

If no area code is given, it's a local call from Lexington-Fayette County. If an area code is given, whether it's 606 or 502, it's a long-distance call: dial 1, the area code and the number. See the How To Use This Book chapter for detailed information on calling.

Garden Springs Park
2005 Dogwood Dr.

This 4½-acre park in southwest Lexington is easily accessible from Garden Springs Drive; just turn into the Garden Springs Elementary School parking lot and drive to the back of the school. You'll find two baseball diamonds, a pool, a batting cage and more.

Idle Hour Park
212 St. Ann Dr., behind Lexington Mall

With several basketball courts, this park is a popular spot for competitive hoops action. It also has baseball, softball and football fields, tennis courts, a picnic area and a playground.

Jacobson Park
4001 Athens-Boonesboro Rd.

Drive into this 216-acre park on practically any Sunday afternoon and you'll quickly realize how popular it is. An attractive, 47-acre lake provides opportunities for fishing (license required), sailing or captaining a two-passenger pedal boat, which can be rented at the marina. The park also contains Lexington's newest and largest creative playground (see our Kidstuff chapter). And Jacobson is a great place to fly a kite. Seven picnic shelters, some of which have electricity, can be reserved by calling the Division of Parks and Recreation at 288-2900. The cost is $15 a day.

Jacobson Park also contains Camp Kearney, a two-week summer day camp for children. Four sessions are offered, with the first beginning in mid-June and the last beginning at the end of July. Times vary, but are generally from about 8:30 AM to 4:30 PM. The cost is $50, which includes transportation, lunch, snacks, insurance and supplies. Scholarships are available.

Masterson Station Park
3051 Leestown Rd.

Equestrian programs, including horseback riding lessons, clinics and lectures, are among the offerings of this 660-acre park (see the Horse Country chapter for more information). You'll also find an entertainment area where concerts are sometimes performed, fields for soccer and football and a jogging and walking trail. Masterson Station, which has picnic areas and dog runs, is also the site of the Bluegrass Lions Club Fair each June. Masterson, like Jacobson, is ideal for kite flying.

Shillito Park
3399 Brunswick Dr., off Reynolds Rd.

You can almost work up a sweat just thinking about this 120-acre park behind Fayette Mall. It has numerous softball, baseball, soccer and football fields, 13 tennis courts (the most of any public park in Lexington), a 50-meter swimming pool and a fitness trail. Picnic shelters with tables and grills can be reserved. Shillito Park is also home to one of the city's creative playgrounds (see our Kidstuff chapter).

Veterans Park at Hickman Creek
off Tates Creek Rd. just south of Man o' War Blvd.

This still-developing park, one of Lexington's newest, consists of 200 acres with spectacular vistas of hillsides, woods, meandering streams and spacious meadows. The park features a "passive" recreation area with bicycle and jogging trails, picnic shelters, play equipment and benches. The "active" recreational facilities include ball diamonds and tennis and basketball courts.

Woodland Park
601 E. High St.

This park near downtown is an athletic and cultural magnet. In addition to a swimming pool, basketball and tennis courts, football and soccer fields, volleyball, playground equipment and picnic areas, Woodland Park also features an amphitheater that is used for Ballet under the Stars and other events (see our Arts chapter).

YMCAs/YWCAs

YMCA of Central Kentucky
239 E. High St. • 254-9622
560 Eureka Springs Dr. • 266-9622
220 E. Maple St., Nicholasville • 885-5013

The "Y," as always, is a great place for the whole family get in shape or just have fun. The YMCA's mission is "to put Christian principles into practice through programs that help kids succeed in life, help adults improve themselves, and bring families closer together," and it offers an array of programs for children and adults.

The High Street facility has a 25-meter indoor pool, gymnasium, aerobics room, Stairmasters, rowing machines, Nautilus and Paramount machines, free weights, indoor track, three racquetball/handball courts, Lifecycles, treadmills, nursery and a men's health center with steam room, sauna, whirlpool and laundry service.

The South Lexington facility (Eureka Springs) has three gymnasiums, aerobics room, co-ed sauna, universal weights, free weights, Stairmasters, rowing machines, treadmills, Lifecycles and nursery.

The Nicholasville facility is more of a community center that offers programs throughout Jessamine County.

Programs at the Lexington Ys include recreational leagues in basketball, soccer and other sports; swimming lessons and lifeguard certification; scuba instruction; CPR and first aid; classes in golf, tennis and martial arts; summer camps for youth; cheerleading; aerobics and yoga; and much more. You can even learn how to baby-sit, cook or dance country-western style. Call or drop by for a detailed program guide.

YWCA of Lexington
1060 Cross Keys Rd. • 276-4457

The YWCA, whose mission is "the empowerment of women and girls and the elimination of racism," provides programs to women, men and children of all ages. Facilities include a 25-meter heated indoor/outdoor pool, activity and meeting rooms, sauna and steam room, weight room with universal weights, stairclimber machine, treadmill and bicycles; men's and women's locker rooms; two outdoor basketball courts; and a volleyball court.

YWCA programs include aerobics, private and group swimming and aquatics classes and water aerobics, cardiovascular workouts, step training, yoga and more. The Flippers are a competitive swim team for ages 8 and older. After-school programs and summer day camps for children and teens are also available.

Participatory Activities

Leagues

Leagues in such sports as baseball, softball, volleyball, tennis and other sports are offered through the Division of Parks and Recreation of the Lexington-Fayette Urban County Government and the YMCA, both of which have detailed program guides available. Adults and youths can choose from other options as well. In many cases, adults can join as individuals or as teams; you may want to get together with a bunch of friends or a group from your workplace. Many churches also have their own leagues. Finally, watch the newspaper for news of sign-ups for T-ball, Little League and other sports leagues. If your child is in school, he or she will probably bring home notices about leagues in or near your neighborhood.

Call Parks and Recreation at 288-2900, the YMCA at 254-9622 (High Street) or 266-9622 (Eureka Springs Drive).

Batting Practice

The Ball Diamond
150 Dennis Dr. • 277-6305

The Ball Diamond, which bills itself as "Kentucky's largest indoor batting range," appeals to virtually all ages with its variety of instructional and recreational activities and leagues. For sports-minded boys and girls, it is a popular site for birthday parties. Children can play whiffleball on an indoor diamond that quickly converts to a basketball court, take batting practice in a cage with a pitching machine, practice their putts on a small artificial green or play one of a handful of pinball and video games. Prices vary.

The Ball Diamond is open 2 to 10 PM weekdays, 10 AM to 2 PM Saturday and 1 to 5 PM Sunday.

Bingo

To quote Clint Eastwood: Do you feel lucky? If so, you might want to head over to one of the following two places. Even if you don't feel lucky, you'll be helping a good cause.

Bluegrass Bingo Center
3340 Holwyn Rd. • 223-9467

The Bluegrass Bingo Center, off Clays Mill Road in south Lexington, has games sponsored by a variety of nonprofit organizations, which reap the benefits. There's play every night, with doors opening at 6 PM, "early bird"

www.insiders.com

See this and many other **Insiders' Guide®** destinations online.

Visit us today!

INSIDERS' TIP

With their wide open areas, Masterson Station and Jacobson Parks are both great places to fly a kite.

games at 7 and main events starting at 7:30. Price and winning amounts vary from night to night.

Jackpot Bingo Center
129 Eastland Shopping Center • 258-2363

Charities benefiting from games at Jackpot Bingo Center include local high schools and the Kidney Foundation. It costs $10 for the basic main-event pack, consisting of eight games. There are other options as well, including $26 for all 20 games on a given night.

Prize amounts are $50 for the early bird games. Other games pay varying amounts from $50 to $200 with a jackpot coverall of $1,000, and winner-takes-all pays according to how many people are playing. Pull tabs are also available for $1, with varying prize amounts. Games start at 7 each night, with doors opening at 5:30. Friday and Saturday nights feature a midnight session; Saturday and Sunday afternoon sessions start at 2.

Bicycling

Lexington cyclists have been pushing for more trails for years. So far, only a handful of roads are marked with bicycle lanes or designated for bicycle use. They are Rose Street, Alumni Drive and Bellefonte Drive, all of which run partly on the University of Kentucky cam-

pus, and Old Squires Road, which is closed to automobiles.

A number of city parks have bike trails, where traffic isn't a problem at all. These include Kirklevington, Lansdowne, Merrick, Veterans and Waverly. Most Lexington neighborhoods also feature wide streets suitable for safe cycling, if proper caution is exercised. And people who like to get away from the suburban traffic and into a more scenic environment enjoy such roads as Walnut Hill, Delong and Old Richmond, as well as Parker's Mill and any other rural road with "Mill" in its name.

Those who really like roughing it prefer mountain biking on their rugged, thick-tired vehicles. Mountain biking trails can be found at Cave Run Lake near Morehead, (606) 784-6428; in the Daniel Boone National Forest near London, (606) 864-4163; and at Red River Gorge in Stanton, (606) 663-2852.

Boating and Fishing

Kentucky Department of Fish & Wildlife Resources
1 Game Farm Rd., Frankfort
• (502) 564-4336

Kentucky has more miles of running streams than any other state except Alaska.

Photo: Natural Bridge State Resort Park

Thousands of years of erosion created this sandstone arch at Natural Bridge State Resort Park.

We have more than 50 man-made reservoirs, which provide us with recreational opportunities, fish, flood control, our water supplies and electricity.

Kentucky's waters are suited for a wide range of boats and activities. More than 100 marinas statewide provide docking space for motorboats, houseboats and pontoons, and rentals of all kinds are available. In addition, you'll find ample opportunities for canoeing, kayaking, rafting, sailing and water skiing.

Kentucky anglers love to pursue bass, which are abundant here. The spotted bass, the state's official game fish, is known nationwide as the Kentucky bass. Largemouth and smallmouth bass are also popular targets. But there's much more — more than 200 native species, at least 40 of which are considered game fish — in Kentucky waters.

It's a good state for catfish (and you haven't eaten fish until you've had Kentucky-style catfish pan-fried in cornmeal; see "A Taste of Kentucky Food and Drink" in our Restaurants chapter). Other favorites are crappie, bluegill, muskie and walleye. The Kentucky Department of Fish and Wildlife Resources, through its fisheries division, has also introduced brown trout and rainbow trout into state streams. Kentucky's fishing season is year round. Size and creel limits, which vary from site to site, are generally posted. For more information about fishing and wildlife in the state, call the Kentucky Department of Fish & Wildlife between 8 AM and 4:30 PM Monday through Friday.

Kentucky River

Many sections of the Kentucky River in the Bluegrass area, particularly between Boonesborough and Frankfort, are used extensively for fishing and boating. This area is notable for its palisades, scenic limestone cliffs that rise high above the river.

From Lexington, the nearest operational Kentucky River boat ramp is at Clays Ferry.

Take Interstate 75 south about 15 miles and get off at Exit 99. The ramp is below the bridge.

Area Creeks

Elkhorn Creek's three forks — Forks of the Elkhorn, North Elkhorn Creek and South Elkhorn Creek — branch through Fayette, Franklin, Scott and Woodford counties, emptying into the Kentucky River in Franklin County. The fishing and other characteristics of the Elkhorn vary from fork to fork. Benson Creek in Franklin County, like the Elkhorn, flows into the Kentucky River.

Stoner Creek, in Bourbon County, winds through picturesque horse-farm country, including Claiborne and Stone farms, on its way to the Licking River. In this peaceful setting, ideal for fishing, you're also likely to see ducks, muskrats, raccoons and other animals.

At Stoner Creek Dock, 387 Chambers Street, Paris, you can rent canoes, fishing boats with trolling motors and pedal boats. Or you can bring your own boat and use one of two ramps for $3. To get to the dock, take Paris Pike out of Lexington into downtown Paris. When you get to where the road becomes one-way, near a Hardee's, turn right at the first stoplight. Go one block, turn left onto Pleasant and then right onto Duncan. At the next four-way stop, veer onto Scott Avenue. Chambers Street is the third street on the left, and you'll see Stoner Creek Dock's sign.

Herrington Lake

Herrington Lake, a 1,860-acre reservoir created in 1925 when Kentucky Utilities dammed the Dix River, was Kentucky's first major lake. This popular site for fishing and boating touches Boyle, Garrard and Mercer counties in Central Kentucky and is about 30 miles south of Lexington.

To get to Herrington Lake, take U.S. Highway 27 (Nicholasville Road) south. Once you cross the Kentucky River at Camp Nelson, your route will depend on which of the nearly dozen

---

INSIDERS' TIP

The little bluegill is, pound for pound, one of the toughest fighting fish in Kentucky waters. He's worth the fight, though, because he makes a fine meal.

marinas you're going to. The two closest marinas, reached via Ky. Highway 152, are Kamp Kennedy, (606) 548-2101, open year round; and Chimney Rock, (606) 748-9065, March through October. The newest, Herrington Marina (606) 548-2282, year round, opened in April 1993; to get there, turn right from U.S. 27 onto Ky. Highway 1355 4.5 miles past the bridge, drive through Homestead Herrington subdivision and follow the signs.

Other major marinas are Sims Mid-Lake (606) 748-5520, April through October; and Gwinn Island Fishing Resort (606) 236-4286, April through October.

Taylorsville Lake State Park
• (502) 477-8766

This relatively young lake, on Ky. Highway 44 near Taylorsville in Spencer County, was created in 1982. To get to the marina, take Interstate 64 W. to the second Shelbyville exit and go south on Ky. Highway 55; when you hit Ky. 44, you're practically there. You can also take the Bluegrass Parkway to the Bloomfield Exit and get on Ky. 55 there. Try both ways and choose your favorite; frankly, there's not that much difference. If you're in a big hurry, you probably shouldn't go to the lake anyway. Call for more information.

Cave Run Lake

This man-made lake is renowned for its muskie fishing. Cave Run, which lies on the Bath-Rowan county line, has two marinas that operate year round: Longbow, (606) 768-2929, on Ky. Highway 1274 near Frenchburg; and Scott Creek, (606) 784-9666, on Ky. Highway 801 near Morehead. Take I-64 E. to either the Frenchburg or Morehead exit, which will be approximately an hour's drive, and then follow the signs.

Grayson Lake State Park

An impoundment of the Little Sandy River in 1968 created a 1,500-acre lake in Carter and Elliott counties. Grayson Lake has long been popular for fishing and other water activities. Take I-64 E. from Lexington to the Grayson Exit, about 100 miles, and follow the signs. Grayson Lake Marina, (606) 474-4513, is on Ky. Highway 7.

Lake Cumberland
State Resort Park

This park, near Jamestown in Russell County about 100 miles south of Lexington, offers some of the best fishing in the state. To get there, take U.S. 27 south to Somerset, then go west on the Cumberland Parkway. Take the Jamestown-Russell Springs exit and get on U.S. Highway 127 S., which will take you straight into the park. The State Dock is open year round.

Bill's Live Fish Farm
1588 Carrick Pike, Georgetown • 863-4269

This pay-to-fish lake is a good place to expose the family to the joys of fishing with minimal hassle and drive time. No license is required. Five ponds are stocked with farm-raised channel catfish ranging from 1½ pounds up to three or four pounds. You pay only for what you catch, and you can have your fish cleaned and filleted for an additional charge.

Bill's Live Fish Farm is open March through October from 8 AM until dark. To get there from Lexington, take Russell Cave Road out of town for about 11 miles — a scenic drive, by the way — until you come to Carrick Pike. Turn left onto Carrick and go about 2 more miles, and you'll find Bill's on your right.

Fish & Wildlife Game Farm
U.S. 60, Frankfort • (502) 564-5448

Two fishing lakes are available at this site operated by the state Department Fish and Wildlife Resources. There is no charge, but you do need a license. When you get tired of fishing, you can check out bears, buffalo, cougars, coyotes, deer and other wildlife native to the state. The game farm is open daily from dawn to dusk.

Bowling

Collins Bowling Center —
Eastland
786 New Circle Rd. • 252-3429

Eastland Lanes, as it's commonly called, has 44 lanes with automated scoring, a game room, lounge, snack bar and pizza bar. During non-summer months, league play is heavy at night, so it's a good idea to call first. If you're in a league, your kids can chill, at no charge, in a supervised playroom while you're bowling.

Collins Bowling Center — Southland
205 Southland Dr. • 277-5746

Southland Lanes, Eastland's sister, has 40 lanes with automated scoring, a game room, lounge and snack bar. There's also a free supervised playroom for children of league bowlers.

Joyland Bowl & Park
2361 Paris Pike • 293-0529

Joyland, once the site of an amusement park, still offers its share of fun with 36 lanes with automated scoring. Various pinball and video games are located around the building. There's also a lounge, snack bar, pro shop and nursery.

Climbing

There are mountains and hills all over the place. Before you begin any serious climbing, however, it's a really good idea to have some instruction.

Climb Time
2416 Over Dr. • 253-3673

Climb Time, Lexington's only rock climbing specialty shop, has 20 walls — including a 50-foot "lead" wall — offering indoor challenges for beginners to experts. In-store experts provide free instruction and advice on all aspects of rock climbing and gear, and you can buy your shoes, ropes, hardware and other equipment (including books and magazines) here as well. Climb Time also has group packages and organizes guided climbing expeditions to the Red River Gorge. Climb Time is open every day but Monday. Hours are 5 to 11 PM Tuesday, 11 AM to 11 PM Wednesday through Friday, and 11 AM to 9 PM Saturday and Sunday.

Fitness and Health Clubs

Prices and membership in Lexington's fitness and health clubs can vary widely, even within a particular club, as many offer different levels of membership. Your best bet is to determine what kinds of facilities, equipment, activities and programs best suit your needs, then shop around. For a regular, single membership, you'll pay anywhere from $20 to $75 a month; the higher prices tend to be the ones that offer not only exercise and weight facilities but also such features as basketball and racquetball courts and swimming pools. Most offer group, family and corporate packages and occasional specials. In addition, most clubs will allow you to pay by the visit, an option that will cost you between $5 and $10 each time.

Hours also vary from day to day and club to club. At some clubs, the hours you can use the facilities depends on the type of membership you have. On weekdays, clubs generally open between 5 AM and 6 AM and close between 9 PM and 11 PM, with shorter weekend hours. All clubs are co-ed unless otherwise indicated. (See the write-ups for the YMCA and YWCA previously in the chapter.)

Fitness Now
151 W. Zandale Dr. • 276-1151

Step aerobics, Stairmasters machines, Supercircuit training equipment, Lifecycles exercise bikes and treadmills are among the options at Fitness Now, behind Ethan Allen off Nicholasville Road. You can also play basketball and racquet ball, or relax in a dry sauna. Fitness Now is open 24 hours Monday through Friday and 9 AM to 6 PM Saturday and Sunday.

Glenn Ford's Fitness Center
2100 Oxford Cir. • 252-5121

Ford's, a popular Lexington workout spot since 1981, has certified staff experts in personal and team training, along with a fully equipped aerobic and weight facility. The center is just off Versailles Road in Cardinal Valley.

Jazzercise Center of Lexington
3323 Partner Place • 223-1441

If you love aerobic exercise with music, then Jazzercise just might be what you're looking for. Four instructors offer co-ed classes performed to the rhythm of a variety of musical styles, including jazz, country, pop and even rap. Choose from several options, from four-week unlimited to 12 or 16 classes in a

Photo: Norman Drake

Keep our parks green, and yellow, and orange.
Please pick up your trash and debris.

month at your convenience. The operators are flexible, so if you miss a week due to vacation or illness you can reschedule. Babysitting is available during most classes.

Lexington Athletic Club
3992 W. Tiverton Ct. • 273-3163

Since 1984, entire families have been benefiting from the diverse facilities at Lexington Athletic Club, popularly known as LAC. You'll find aerobics, basketball, a huge indoor track, free weights, an indoor pool, racquetball and a cardio center. Relax in a whirlpool, sauna or steam facility, or get that summer look in one of the tanning beds. Various fitness programs, including ones specially designed for seniors, are available. LAC is also home to the Kid's Place indoor playground (see Kidstuff).

Jefferson Fitness Club
535 W. Second St. • 255-2582

Established in a former downtown YMCA facility in 1986, Jefferson Fitness Club is a medically based health and wellness facility open to the general public as well as to businesses and corporations. Besides complete exercise facilities, JFC's staff can perform individual fitness and clinical assessments, or the staff can set up consultations at compa-

nies that wish to offer health assessments to their employees.

Besides a broad range of exercise equipment, JFC's facilities include a Junior Olympic swimming pool, sauna, steam room, whirlpool, laundry service, aerobics, water aerobics, yoga, a gymnasium and indoor track.

Memberships are divided into gold, silver and bronze levels, according to how many features of the club a member wishes to use. Prices range from $30 monthly for unlimited water and floor aerobic classes to $69 monthly (plus $25 initiation fee) for a single adult. You can joint by the month or by the year.

Lexington Sports Club
230 W. Main St. • 281-5110

Readers of the *Lane Report*, a monthly Lexington business magazine in 1996 voted Lexington Sports Club the city's top health club. For what it's worth, it's also at the highest altitude, on the seventh floor of Lexington Financial Center parking garage downtown.

Lexington Sports Club's diverse features include Cybex and Nautilus equipment for resistance training, treadmills, Stairmasters, bicycles, cross-country ski machines, rowing machines, cardio equipment, aerobics studio with suspended wood floor, indoor track, half-court basketball, two squash courts, two racquetball courts and 20-meter lap pool. Men's and women's locker rooms include sauna, steam and whirlpool area. The Players Lounge restaurant serves a variety of foods and beverages.

Powerhouse Gym, Aerobics and Fitness
3460 Richmond Rd. • 263-5444

Powerhouse features aerobics, a cardiovascular area, Cybex and BodyMaster weight equipment, free weights, treadmills, bikes, steppers, Wolff tanning beds and more. Forty aerobics classes are offered each week. Free babysitting is available, too.

Shapes New Dimensions Health & Fitness Center
3220 Nicholasville Rd., South Park Shopping Center • 273-6881
1575 Winchester Rd., Village East Shopping Center • 299-8441
3120 Pimlico Pkwy., Suite 18A, Park Hills Center • 273-1558

Shapes, with three locations, has been serving Lexington since 1980. While South Park and Park Hills are exclusively for women, the newer Village East location is designed for the entire family. Offerings include more than 90 aerobic classes weekly, Cybex and Universal machines, free weights, cardio areas, crossrobics programs, tanning, sauna and whirlpool. Free individualized programs and child care are also available.

World Gym
2929 Richmond Rd. • 269-2492
World Gym Aerobics & Fitness
1859 Alexandria Dr. • 276-2492

World Gym's two Lexington locations offer full aerobic classes, personal trainers, full-size cardio deck, free weights and eight types of weight machines, exercise bikes, step machines, treadmills and free child care for members. In addition, the Richmond Road location

has a basketball court, hair and nail salon, saunas and cafe.

Hiking

With all the woodlands throughout Kentucky, hiking and backpacking come naturally. For maximum viewing satisfaction, may we suggest an autumn expedition. In the fall, especially during October, our trees explode into a kaleidoscope of vibrant reds, oranges and yellows. Of course, you can find scenes of great beauty any time and anywhere in the state, including three extremely popular areas not far from Lexington. In fact, the first of these areas is in Fayette County.

Raven Run Nature Sanctuary
5888 Jacks Creek Pike • 272-6105

Raven Run, which recently acquired additional land giving it a total of nearly 500 acres, has 7 miles of hiking trails. History and nature peacefully coexist in this sanctuary highlighting the beauty of the Kentucky River palisades region. You can find nearly 400 species of wildflowers — sorry, no picking of plants, so future hikers can enjoy them — growing amid Raven Run's meadows and woodlands and along its creek beds.

The aesthetic highlight is probably the Kentucky River overlook, which provides a stunning view of the palisades from more than 100 feet above the river. Rock fences, a lime kiln, part of a mill and other artifacts from the state's pioneer days are also found within the boundaries of Raven Run. The sanctuary's nature center features displays and exhibits of the area's flora and fauna and maps of the trails. A number of special programs, including night hikes and group activities, are available.

Raven Run is open Wednesday through Sunday year round. Hours vary by season and sometimes are subject to weather and trail conditions. Before visiting, particularly on weekends, call to be sure Raven Run is open.

To get to Raven Run Nature Sanctuary from

INSIDERS' TIP

For great outdoor basketball competition, check out the Dirt Bowl Summer League at Douglass Park.

Photo: Natural Bridge State Resort Park

State and national parks in the Bluegrass contain miles
of hiking trails and innumerable scenic overlooks.

Lexington, take Tates Creek Road south until you reach the tiny community of Spears, distinguished by a gas station and a grocery. You'll see a sign pointing the way: Make a sharp left turn onto Spears Road, go about 1.5 miles until the road runs into Jacks Creek Pike, turn right, and Raven Run is ahead on your left.

Stonewall Historic Nature Park
Cornwall Dr.

Lexington's first historic nature park, dedicated in September 1994, lies between Stonewall Elementary School and a subdivision in southwest Lexington. There's not a lot to do here other than walk, jog or merely commune with nature, but that's plenty. Five wooded trails, a winding creek and a variety of trees and plants dating back to Lexington's frontier days contribute to the quiet natural beauty of this park, the brainchild of the Stonewall Community Association.

Natural Bridge State Resort Park
Slade • (606) 663-2214, (800) 325-1710 reservations

You can easily combine these next two sites into one trip. Natural Bridge is a 65-foot-high, 78-foot-long arch constructed of sandstone, with no artificial ingredients added, through thousands of years of erosion. If you think the bridge is awesome from the ground, wait until you look down from atop it. You have a choice of how to get there: Hike a mile and a half or take a sky lift. We suggest the hike.

Natural Bridge, part of the Daniel Boone National Forest, is in Powell County. To get there from Lexington, 57 miles away, take I-64 E. to the Mountain Parkway, get off at Exit 33 and follow the signs.

The lodge and dining room, incidentally, are among the most popular in Kentucky's park system.

Red River Gorge, Slade

On the other side of the Mountain Parkway, just a few minutes from Natural Bridge, is the Red River Gorge Geological Area. This entire area is filled with scenery that you can't miss and wouldn't want to, whether you're walking or driving. A 30-mile scenic drive circles through the area, providing breathtak-ing views of the Red River as it winds through the gorge. If you really want to exercise your hiking skills, take on nearby the Clifty Wilderness hiking trail, which is as rugged as its name implies.

Horseback Riding

For a list of facilities offering horseback riding, see our Horse Country chapter.

Ice Skating

Lexington Ice Center
560 Eureka Springs Dr. • 269-5681

A wide range of sporting activities is available at Lexington's only spot for ice skating (except for those rare occasions when your backyard pond freezes solid). Lessons are available for would-be ice skaters. If ice skating isn't your idea of fun, you can play in one of three gymnasiums, pray for a hole-in-one on one of three 18-hole miniature courses with biblical themes, step up to the plate in a batting cage or head for the game room. Prices vary.

This fun place is also the site of the University of Kentucky hockey team's home games Friday at midnight in season.

Martial Arts

Sin Thé Gym and Karate School
284 Gold Rush Rd. • 275-2148

Sin Kwang Thé, a grandmaster (10th-degree black belt) from China, founded this school, Lexington's oldest, in 1965. Instructor Bill Leonard, a 7th degree black belt who has studied with Thé for 30 years, teaches Shaolin-Do, the oldest, most complete martial art in the world, as well as Tai-Chi. The gym includes a weight room.

Tae Kwon Do Plus Karate Center
3120 Pimlico Pkwy. • 245-1733
3735 Harrodsburg Rd. • 223-2842

Instructor Rick Lewis, at the Pimlico location, works closely with Brian Chewning at the Harrodsburg Road location, in the Palomar Centre, to ensure a consistent regimen.

Courses, offered for fitness and self-defense, emphasize self-esteem, character, artistic skill and positive work and academic values.

Tinn's Karate
510 Codell Dr. • 266-3734

Tinn's specializes in adult private instruction in street - practical self defense with an emphasis on Ken - Jitsu.

Pool and Billiards

Yesterdays
410 W. Vine St. • 231-8889

Owner Karen McCool bills Yesterdays, on the ground floor of Civic Center, as an "upscale pool hall" for baby boomers of both sexes. Twelve furniture-style pool tables allow for lots of simultaneous action. The club also serves food and drink and features constant blues music on the sound system. Pool is $3 per hour per person.

The Rack Club
235 Woodhill Dr. • 266-9942

The Rack Club, also a restaurant and bar, has twelve tables — two 9-footers and 10 8-footers. You can play for $2.50 an hour a person. After 3 PM you must be 21 or over unless with a parent. Other options include dart boards, a pair of pinball machines and a Fooseball table. Live bands play Friday and Saturday nights.

Gullett's Family Billiard
952 Winchester Rd. • 252-4229

Pay $2 and hour per person at this family pool hall, which has 10 tables, pinball and video games. The menu is casual: hot dogs, burgers, pizza; beer is available. Gullett's is open until 1 AM six nights a week and closed on Sunday.

Steepleton Billiard Center
1431 Leestown Rd. • 252-9135

Since the death of Toby Kavanaugh in 1994 and the subsequent demise of his popular Bluegrass Billiards near campus, Steepleton's is the oldest poolroom in Lexington. It's also the largest, with a total of 19 tables, including bar-style tables, 8-footers and 9-foot snooker tables. Steepleton's Louisville factory has been making fine tables under the Steepleton name since 1910, and they're for sale here. A bar adjoins the poolroom. Pool is $2 an hour per person.

Buster's
164 W. Main St. • 231-5076

Buster's downtown has seven pool tables, darts and a pop-a-game in an atmosphere described as "kind of alternative." There's no food, but many varieties of beer and a great jukebox. Pool is $5 an hour per table

Roller Skating

Champ's Rollerdrome
2555 Palumbo Dr. • 268-3888

Champ's, Lexington's only roller-skating rink, is another frequent site of birthday parties. A disc jockey keeps things interesting, periodically interrupting the regular action for special activities such as adult skating, backwards skating, the limbo and the hokey-pokey. Rental skates and individual lessons are available, and novice skaters with sore posteriors can take a break with a large selection of video games.

Running and Walking Groups

Todds Road Stumblers
• 268-2701

Todds Road Stumblers, a nonprofit group founded in 1975 by Alex Campbell, is the largest running organization in Central Kentucky. It's a very informal group, with no dues or anything: Simply meet, run and then socialize for a while if you like. During nice weather, as many as 100 people meet between 7 and 8 AM Saturday at the clubhouse on Todds Road to run. Six-, 9-, 12- and 15-mile courses are marked off on rolling hills in the country. First-time completers of the 6-mile course receive a free Todds Road T-shirt. Afterward, coffee and donuts are served in the clubhouse. Those who are interested in joining should call Becky Reinhold at 268-2701.

Lexington Striders
1530 Nicholasville Rd. • 278-6072

You may have seen them at Turfland Mall, walking purposefully through the corridors without stopping to shop. They are the Lexington Striders, and although the group mainly consists of senior citizens, it's open to all ages. The Striders were formed in the mid-'80s as a club designed to help people enjoy walking. At their peak, they numbered about 400 strong, and there are still more than 100 members. They walk at their own convenience (but often in groups), documenting their miles on pocket calendar forms.

Every other Thursday, they report their mileage totals, updating their individual progress charts. The club awards certificates, pins, prices and gift certificates. The Striders' "season" runs from September through May. The club usually holds a kickoff event in the fall and a picnic in mid-July. For more information, call Martha McFarland at the Lexington Senior Citizens Center, 278-6072. (See our Activities and Services for Older Adults chapter for more things senior citizens can do in Lexington.)

Scuba Diving and Snorkeling

Prices for open-water scuba classes generally start around $150, plus $125 or so for the actual open-water diving sessions leading to certification.

New Horizons Diving Center
2577 Regency Rd. • 277-1234

New Horizons, which has been offering diving instruction since 1983, is certified as a five-star facility by the Professional Association of Dive Instructors. Manager Bryan Bates says the center is a full-service dive center, which means it also functions as a travel agency: "We can teach you how to use the equipment, sell you the equipment, send you on trips to use the equipment and even work on the equipment if the need arises."

The basic open-water course is five days over a two-week period — each session consisting of two hours of classroom work followed by two hours in the water. New Horizons, owned by Neil McEachin, conducts its sessions at the Lancaster Aquatics Facility at the University of Kentucky, where it also teaches a scuba curriculum for course credit. Divers can choose to do their actual open-water diving in Kentucky's Laurel Lake or in the Caribbean.

Kentucky Diving Headquarters
3928 Shelbyville Rd., Louisville
• (502) 897-6481, (800) 383-6480

Kentucky Diving Headquarters has been certifying new scuba divers since 1973 and since 1984 has owned and operated Valentine's Dive Center in Harbour Island, Bahamas. The company's scuba program, taught year round by certified instructors, consists of three weeks of classes (two a week), followed by a weekend of open-water training held in either a local quarry or northern Florida, depending on water temperatures. The multimedia curriculum combines textbooks, workbooks, videos, classroom presentations and practical experience in the pool. Private instruction is available. Kentucky Diving Headquarters also has a variety of scuba equipment, photographic equipment and commercial dive gear for sale.

Skydiving and Parachute Jumping

Greene County Sport Parachute Center
215 Airport Rd., Bardstown
• (502) 348-9531

If you like falling out of planes, or have ever thought about trying it, Greene County

---

Horseback riding is a popular pastime in the Bluegrass.

Sport Parachute Center may be just what you're looking for. All training is done on state-of-the-art square parachute systems, and instructors have 25 years of experience. Tandem parachute training and jumping, in which you are attached to an instructor, is available, as are beginner classes. A tandem-jump student session — a 45-minute training session followed by a jump — will coast you $165. The first-jump static-line course, a 6-hour class followed by a solo jump, is $135; after that, the cost is $40 per jump, gear included. Green County Sport Parachute Center is open Saturday and Sunday and, during Daylight Savings Time, on Wednesday.

Snow Skiing

Kentucky isn't exactly known as skiers' paradise, but a number of slopes at surrounding states are within reasonable driving range, two to seven hours. (Ski Butler, Kentucky's only ski area closed this year.) Eighty-five to 100 percent of the snow at these resorts is artificial, which means you don't have to rely on the weather to visit the slopes in the winter.

All have lessons available, and most offer night skiing, at least on weekends.

Below we've listed some of the most popular spots among Kentucky skiers.

Perfect North Slopes
Lawrenceburg, Ind. • (812) 537-3754

Perfect North, which offers 16 trails and three chairlifts, is just 25 minutes northwest of Cincinnati. To get there, take I-75 N. to Interstate 275 W., then take Indiana Highway 50 to Indiana Highway 1 north and follow the signs for 5 miles.

Ski Paoli Peaks
Paoli, Ind. • (812) 723-4696

Ski Paoli Peaks has 13 trails for all skill levels, with four lifts. Take I-64 W. through Louisville, then exit at Greenville-Paoli and go 39 miles along Indiana Highway 150.

Clear Fork Ski Area
Butler, Ohio • (419) 883-2000

This area, about four hours from Lexington, is an hour north of Columbus off I-75. It has six trails and three chairlifts.

Ober Gatlinburg
Gatlinburg, Tenn. • (423) 436-5423

This five-trail, two-lift facility lies within Great Smoky Mountains National Park and is a popular year-round resort. Take I-75 S. through Knoxville and follow the signs into the Smokies.

Snowshoe/Silver Creek
Slaty Fork, W.Va. • (304) 572-1000

This pair of sister resorts, with about 50 trails and 11 lifts, is a seven-hour haul from Lexington. Nevertheless, both Snowshoe and Silver Creek are extremely popular with Bluegrass skiers who have long weekends available.

Soccer

Soccer has really taken off in the Bluegrass in recent years, especially among youth. Leagues are offered through the YMCA (see details in the YMCA/YWCA section) and LYSA.

Lexington Youth Soccer Association
• 223-5632

Lexington Youth Soccer Association, or LYSA, offers recreational and "select" competitive leagues for children ages 5 and up, as well as adult leagues. It has about 2,000 participants in Lexington.

Spelunking

Mammoth Cave National Park
Cave City • (502) 758-2328

The surface area of this highly popular tourist site about 130 miles south of Lexington covers 80 square miles, but that is literally just scratching the surface. Mammoth Cave, the centerpiece of Kentucky's only national park, is part of the world's longest cave system — more than 330 miles of underground passages. During the summer, as many as nine guided tours are offered, including one that's accessible to disabled visitors. Structure your visit to fit your own interests, physical abilities and sense of adventure. For the more adventurous, a guided "wild cave" tour through unlighted portions of Mammoth Cave provides more of a true caving experience.

Often called one of the wonders of the Western Hemisphere, Mammoth Cave was named a World Heritage Site by the United Nations in 1981. In recent years, it has drawn nearly 2 million annual visitors, who come to see such awe-inspiring sights as Floyd Collins Crystal Lake, Crystal Lake, Frozen Niagara and, of course, the multilevel main cave. You'll find stalactites, stalagmites and numerous other types of rock formations. Echo River, which runs through Mammoth Cave and is still making changes to it, is home to rare, eyeless fish.

Mammoth Cave's history is nearly as intriguing as its features. Evidence shows that prehistoric Indians visited the cave. According to some accounts, a hunter in pursuit of a wounded bear in the late 1700s was the first white person to discover the cave. During the war of 1812, a commercial saltpeter-mining operation provided gunpowder for the American troops. A few years later, the public was flocking to take in the cave's natural splendor. It became a national park, the nation's 26th, in July 1941.

Crystal Cave was discovered in 1917 by Floyd Collins, a good spelunker with a fatally bad run of luck. Collins received worldwide attention in February 1925 when he became trapped in Sand Cave while trying to find a passage linking it with Crystal Cave. Pinned in a narrow passageway by a rock that would-be rescuers could not reach, he eventually died.

If that kind of story keeps you out of caves, we're sorry for telling you; stay on the guided tours and you'll be fine, and you'll be glad you took the tour. But even if you steadfastly refuse to set foot in a cave, you'll still enjoy the park. You can hike more than 70 miles of forest trails, camp and take a canoe or cruise boat down the Green River. And there are plenty of picnic shelters.

To get to Mammoth Cave from Lexington, take U.S. Highway 60 W. (Versailles Road) to the Bluegrass Parkway, get on I-65 S. at Elizabethtown, then take the Cave City Exit.

Carter Caves State Resort Park
Ky. Hwy. 182, Olive Hill • (606) 286-4411, (800) 325-0059 reservations

More than 20 caves, some of them still

uncharted, are scattered about this park's 1,350 acres. The squeamish might want to avoid Bat Cave, which is home to thousands of protected Indiana bats. Other caves include Laurel Cave; Cascade Caverns, which features a 30-foot underground waterfall; and Saltpeter Cave. Both Bat Cave and Cascade Caverns are designated state nature preserves.

Like Mammoth Cave National Park, Carter Caves includes attractions for a variety of skill and tolerance levels. If you don't mind crawling on your hands and knees with only a flashlight to lead the way, you can truly find great adventure and rekindle that forgotten pioneer spirit. Just pretend you're a modern-day Tom Sawyer or Becky Thatcher (although they didn't have flashlights).

Still other caves can be found on private land in the vicinity. If you're up to a real challenge, track down a local who can tell you about Jarvie Roark's Cave, a multilevel labyrinth that will seriously test your stamina and your orientation skills. Just be sure to get permission from the landowner to explore the cave.

Other activities include camping, fishing, canoeing and hiking. Carter Caves also has a lodge, cottages, swimming pool, golf course and tennis courts.

To get to Carter Caves from Lexington, take I-64 E. for about 80 miles to the first Olive Hill exit and follow the signs.

Swimming

There's a lot of water in this chapter: lakes, rivers, streams and creeks, much of it suitable for swimming. Or you may prefer pools. Different backstrokes for different folks, you know. (Often you can find both kinds of swimming opportunities in the same place; for example, many state parks with lakes also contain swimming pools.) In addition, you'll find indoor pools at the YMCA, YWCA, Lexington Athletic Club and Lexington Sports Club, all of which have been described in this chapter. During the summer, the Division of Parks and Recreation operates 14 swimming pools. These facilities are categorized in one of three ways (see below).

Hours for the Parks and Recreation pools are 10 AM to 8 PM Monday through Saturday and 1 to 8 PM Sunday for Avon, Cardinal Val-

ley, Garden Springs, Berry Hill, Constitution, Douglass, Shillito, Tates Creek and Woodland; noon to 6 PM Monday through Saturday and 1 to 6 PM for Dixie, Duncan and Marlboro; and 10 AM to 9 PM Monday through Saturday and 1 to 9 PM Sunday for Castlewood and Southland.

Season passes are available at all locations for $25 a person or $75 a family.

Neighborhood Pools
- Avon, 5751 Briar Hill Pk.
- Cardinal Valley, 2077 Cambridge Dr.
- Dixie, 1850 Eastland Pkwy.
- Duncan, 530 N. Limestone St.
- Garden Springs, 2005 Dogwood Dr.
- Marlboro, 561 Benton Rd.

These facilities have a baby pool, bathhouse and picnic shelter, as well as a main pool ranging in depth from 3 feet to 5 feet. Admission is $2, $1 for people 15 and younger.

Olympic and mini-Olympic Pools
- Berry Hill, 3489 Buckhorn Dr.
- Constitution, 1670 Old Paris Pk.
- Douglass, 726 Georgetown St.
- Shillito, 3399 Brunswick Dr.
- Tates Creek, 1400 Gainesway Dr.

Berry Hill, Constitution and Douglass are 25 meters long and have diving wells. Shillito and Tates Creek are 50 meters long and have diving boards. Admission is $2, $1 for people 15 and younger.

Family Aquatic Centers
- Castlewood, 201 Castlewood Dr.
- Southland, 600 Laramie Dr.
- Woodland, 601 E. High St.

These three pools were upgraded for the 1996 summer season. Southland has a three-loop slide and a "teardrop" or "umbrella" fountain in the center. It also has a huge baby pool loaded with play features. Woodland has three separate pools: a diving well with a 3-meter board, a lap pool and a play pool that is 2½ feet at its deepest. The play pool features a pirate ship surrounded by alligators. Castlewood has an octopus and a one-loop slide as well as a diving board. Admission to the Family Aquatic Centers is $2.50, $1.50 for people 15 and younger.

Tennis

Tennis courts are all over Lexington, most notably in city parks and at apartment complexes. There's bound to be one near you. The Division of Parks and Recreation has 27 facilities equipped with tennis courts; 13 of these are at Shillito Park (see the "Public Parks, Playgrounds and Programs" section of this chapter).

Volleyball

In addition to Parks and Recreation and YMCA leagues (see the "Public Parks, Playgrounds and Programs" section of this chapter), some bars have been getting into the volleyball scene.

A1A Sandbar & Grille
367 E. Main St. • 231-7263

A1A, whose outdoor volleyball courts see plenty of action, is known for its competitive leagues, which are held five nights a week in spring, summer and fall. There are different levels to match your skills. Call the bar for more information.

Marikka's Restaurant und Bier Stube
411 Southland Dr. • 275-1925

You might not associate German food with volleyball, but the two are a match at Marikka's (which, incidentally, has more than 300 beers). There are no leagues, just informal play when weather permits and enough people are interested.

Whitewater Rafting

Kentucky Division of Water
14 Reilly Road, Frankfort • (502) 564-3410

Paddlers can test their skills in the over 114 miles of designated Kentucky Wild Rivers — scenic, undeveloped and free-flowing sections of nine rivers, ranging from smooth to Class V whitewater. Parts of the 75-mile-long Rockcastle River, the Red River Gorge area of the Red River, the Cumberland Falls area of the Cumberland River and the Green River are among the best. Information on Kentucky's Wild Rivers, including outfitters who offer whitewater excursions, is available through the Kentucky Division of Water.

Annual Athletic Events

In the Bluegrass it seems there's always some major athletic event going on. The annual ones listed below, while hardly the only events, are representative because they offer something for people of all ages and ability levels. If you live in Lexington, you have no excuse for not having a good time.

Bluegrass 10,000

The Bluegrass 10,000 foot race, sponsored by Parks and Recreation in conjunction with the *Lexington Herald-Leader*, is held every July 4 and is open to all ages. Many families participate, some of them with strollers. Although many participants will be going all out to finish in the fastest time possible, others take a more casual approach and do it for the enjoyment. In addition to the 10,000-meter (about 6.25 miles) race around the streets of downtown Lexington, there also is a "fun run," as well as other related events. This popular race annually attracts thousands of runners from Kentucky and other states. We guarantee that between now and next July 4 you will have ample opportunities to register and get your very own commemorative Bluegrass 10,000 T-shirt.

A Midsummer Night's Run

A Midsummer Night's Run, which turned 10 years old in 1994, is sponsored by Central Baptist Hospital. The main event is a 5-kilometer race, but there are several other activities, including a 1-mile fun walk/run, a Baby Derby, fastest-kid-in-town contest and entertainment. A Midsummer Night's Run is held downtown each year in late August. Watch the newspaper for details.

Bluegrass State Games

These annual summer and winter events are our own version of the Olympics. The Bluegrass State Games, started in August 1985, constitute the state's largest amateur sporting event. They are open to all ages and skill levels. Games are held over one or two weekends across various locations around the state, depending on the sport. Participants, who must be Kentucky residents, are limited to one sport, but they can participate in as many events as they desire in that one sport. For more information, call the Bluegrass State Games office at 255-0336.

Lexington Senior Games

These games for Lexington residents 55 and older are a more low-key version of the Olympics. The Lexington Senior Games feature not only competition in such events as basketball shooting, billiards, bowling, cards, croquet, fishing, horseshoes, shuffleboard and table tennis but also social events such as a nature walk, a party and a dance. For more information call 288-2900.

Kentucky Special Olympics

Kentucky began holding this statewide competition for mentally retarded people in 1970. Leading up to the state championships in June, as many as 12,000 participants ages 8 through adult compete in 22 sports, including swimming, diving, track and field, weight lifting, gymnastics and bowling. Every four years, qualifiers are eligible to participate in the International Special Olympics. This competition helps develop self-esteem among the competitors; and, as anyone who's ever been involved as a volunteer or spectator will tell you, it's a very rewarding cause — rewarding enough, in fact, to warm the heart of the most jaded sports fan. For more information, call 273-1480.

Our gently rolling hills,
so ideal for horses, also
make the Bluegrass a
naturally appealing
place for golf.

Golf

PGA veteran Gary Player, two-time winner of Lexington's sadly departed Bank One Senior Golf Classic, told a local TV reporter after his 1993 victory: "This is my favorite spot on the tour. I don't care where we go; this is my favorite spot because I am a great lover of horses. Actually, I am a horse nut. Sometimes when you're not from an area, you notice things that others don't. I've traveled more than any athlete that's ever lived, and I've never seen a more beautiful part of the world (than) right here in Lexington."

Our gently rolling hills, so ideal for horses, also make the Bluegrass a naturally appealing place for golf, and the number of courses continues to grow. This area has given rise to a number of outstanding professional golfers.

Gay Brewer grew up in Lexington, working as a caddie, winning a record three straight state high school championships at Lafayette High School from 1949 to 1951, attending the University of Kentucky and distinguishing himself as an amateur before going on to become a persistent PGA champion.

Myra Van Hoose Blackwelder is a Lexington native who learned golf at Big Elm Country Club (now the Campbell House course) and won four consecutive state high school championships while at Lafayette. Fort Knox native Larry Gilbert, former club pro at The Champions, is a longtime Lexington resident. Russ Cochran grew up in Paducah but attended the University of Kentucky before beginning his PGA career. From elsewhere in the state have come such notables as Frank Beard and Jodie Mudd.

In its 15 years of existence, the annual Senior Classic attracted such heavyweights as Player, Jack Nicklaus, Arnold Palmer, Lee Trevino and Chi Chi Rodriguez. Unfortunately, the tournament was eliminated so the PGA's SENIOR TOUR could negotiate with larger markets that could pay larger purses. Kearney Hill Links, site of the Senior Classic from 1990 to 1997, added another feather to its cap in 1997 when it welcomed the U.S. Amateur Public Links Championship. In 1993, the University of Kentucky was host of the NCAA Men's Golf Championships, played at The Champions course in Jessamine County. The Children's Charity Classic, an annual event since 1982, regularly attracts a lineup of television, movie and sports stars who have teed off to raise nearly $1 million for charity.

Area courses fall into three general categories: public, semiprivate and private. We have devoted most of this chapter to the public and semiprivate courses. Four public courses — the regulation Kearney Hill Links, Lakeside and Tates Creek, plus par 3 Meadowbrook — are owned and operated by the Lexington-Fayette Urban County Government's Division of Parks and Recreation. The Lexington City Championships are played each year at the three regulation municipal courses.

Some of the remaining public courses offer memberships, which basically amount to prepaid greens fees. The semiprivate courses are open to the public, but members are given first priority for tee times. The private courses, which include country clubs, are open only to members and their guests.

The only private course we have covered in this chapter is The Champions Golf Club, which we have mentioned solely because of its prominence as a tournament course. Lexington also has a number of country club courses, which are open only to members and their guests.

All yardage figures are measured from the back tees. Unless otherwise indicated, all courses are 18 holes and all rental carts are electric. Please note that fees listed in this chapter were as of July 1997 and are subject to change.

Public and Semiprivate Courses

Lexington

Avon Golf Course
5751 Briar Hill Rd. • 299-8356

This nine-hole course, formerly owned by the U.S. Army, has been public since 1995. It's par 36 over 3,300 yards. The course is fairly flat and easy to walk; a couple of holes have lakes to negotiate. Greens fees are $10; seniors can play for $3 until 3 PM Monday through Friday. Carts are $7 a person.

Campbell House Inn, Suites & Golf Club
Parkway Dr., off Harrodsburg Rd. • 254-3631

The Campbell House golf course formerly was part of Big Elm Country Club. The inn bought the property in 1990 and changed the course from private to semiprivate. There are now about 200 members, who get dibs on tee times, but anyone can play here. The 6,300-yard, par 70 course is marked by speedy little greens and plenty of water hazards. Fees, including cart, are $30 weekdays and $35 weekends.

Note: In summer 1997 the owners put the property on the market, and it may be under new ownership by the time you read this.

Kearney Hill Links
3403 Kearney Rd. (off Georgetown Rd.) • 253-1981

Since its opening in October 1989, this 6,987-yard, par 72 municipal course has quickly acquired a reputation for excellence. Designed by noted course architects Pete and P.B. Dye, Kearney Hill Links has been rated by *Golf Digest* as the fourth-best golf course in Kentucky and as one of the top 100 places to play in the country. From 1990 to 1997, it played host to the high-profile Bank One Se-

FYI

If no area code is given, it's a local call from Lexington-Fayette County. If an area code is given, whether it's 606 or 502, it's a long-distance call: dial 1, the area code and the number. See the How To Use This Book chapter for detailed information on calling.

nior Golf Classic, and it was the site of the 1997 U.S. Amateur Public Links Championship. The Scottish-style course has a large, undulating green subject to wind variations that affect the way it plays. Water comes into play on five holes, including holes 15 and 16, which also feature Pete Dye's signature railroad ties. Greens fees are $20 for 18 holes; cart rentals are $8.

Lakeside Golf Course
Richmond Rd. • 263-5315

This 6,844-yard, par 72 municipal course alongside Jacobson Park's lake is one of the area's most popular. The 18th hole is one of the three longest in the state at 653 yards. For 18 holes, the greens fee is $10; seniors and juniors (18 and younger) can play for $3 until 3 PM weekdays. A cart will cost you an extra $7.

Marriott's Griffin Gate Golf Club
1800 Newtown Pike • 288-6193

This 6,300-yard, par 72, semiprivate course was the site of the Senior Classic for seven years before the tournament was moved to Kearney Hill Links. It is characterized by gently rolling hills, with water on nine holes. Four sets of tees make the course adaptable to a variety of skill levels. Greens fees are $52 Monday through Thursday and $62 Friday through Sunday. Daily after 2 PM and on weekends after 4 PM, $32 lets you play to your heart's content.

Meadowbrook Golf Course
400 Wilson Downing Rd. • 272-3115

This 2,235-yard municipal course is par 55 (17 par 3 holes and one par 4). The slightly rolling terrain makes Meadowbrook a nice, relaxing course to learn the game or to hone your iron and putter skills. The greens fee is $7. Seniors and juniors (18 and younger) can play for $3 until 3 PM weekdays; women can play for $4 on Tuesday. Pull cart rental is $2. You can also rent a bag with 3-, 5-, 7- and 9-irons, a putter and a 3-wood for $5; ID is required.

Players Club
4850 Leestown Rd. • 255-1011

The semiprivate Players Club has steadily grown since it opened as an 18-hole course in 1992, then grew to 27, and now has 36 holes. It now has 27 holes, and plans are to have 36 sometime in 1998. There are three distinct par 36 nines: The Island, at 3,218 yards, with an 8th hole that may be the only island hole in the state; The Lake, at 3,286 yards; and The Creek, at 3,309 yards. Numerous ponds and lakes and more than 100 sand traps add a tough dimension to the course, especially from the most distant tees (there are five sets per hole). Players Club was designed by owner Danny McQueen, who also has been involved in the design of the Andover Golf & Country Club and Cabin Brook courses. Weekday greens fees for 18 holes are $30 with cart and $21 without; for nine holes the cost is $18 with cart and $13 without. On weekends, carts are mandatory, and the total cost is $33 for 18 holes or $20 for nine holes.

Tates Creek Golf Course
Gainesway Dr. • 272-3428

This hilly municipal course is 6,240 yards, par 72. Water comes into play on two holes with water. Greens fees are $10 for 18 holes; the 60-and-older and 18-and-younger crowds can play for $3 Monday through Friday before 3 PM. Cart rental is $7 per person. Reservations can be made one week in advance for three-somes and foursomes; singles and twosomes are scheduled from a daily standby list.

Richmond

Gibson Bay Golf Course
2000 Gibson Bay Dr., Richmond
• (606) 623-0225

This beautiful Michael Hurzdan-designed public course in Richmond opened in 1992. It's a long and hilly, 7,113-yard, par 72 course with lots of sand traps, water hazards, trees and elevation changes. Fees, which include

Photo: *Lexington Herald-Leader*

Golf pro Gay Brewer, who grew up in Lexington, used to return to the area for the annual Bank One Senior Golf Classic at Kearney Hill.

cart, are $20.50 weekdays and $26.50 weekends.

Nicholasville

Connemara Golf Course
2327 Lexington Rd., Nicholasville
• 885-4331

Connemara, a converted horse farm on a rolling hillside between Lexington and Nicholasville on U.S. 27, is designed for enjoyment rather than difficulty, with open fairways and few traps. But this 6,533-yard, par 71 public course does present a challenge with a pair of 450-plus-yard par 4s and a 572-yard par 5. Though the course is public, it does have members, who can reserve tee times up to a week in advance; nonmembers can make reservations no more than five days in advance. Fees, which include carts, are $24 for 18 holes weekdays and $28 on weekends. Or take advantage of the "twilight special": After 5 PM, it's $16 during the week and $21 on weekends.

www.insiders.com
See this and many other **Insiders' Guide®** destinations online.
Visit us today!

High Point Golf Course
1215 High Point Dr., off Union Mill Rd.
(Ky. Hwy. 169), Nicholasville • 887-4614

High Point, another former horse farm, is a 6,100-yard, par 71 course. It maintains a horse-farm atmosphere with three lakes, several creeks and three natural springs. The longest hole is the 15th, at 507 yards. High Point is a public course that offers memberships. Green fees, which include cart, are $20 for 18 holes and $13 for nine holes on weekdays and, on weekends and holidays, $23 for 18 holes and $18 for nine holes.

Plantation Links Golf Center
2080 Lexington Rd., Nicholasville
• 885-1254

Plantation Links, a 3,100-yard, par 56 public course across the road from Toyota on Nicholasville, is a short 18-hole course designed to provide plenty of challenges in a shorter playing time. The owners call it "executive par 3," with two par 4 holes thrown in.

It also includes a heated driving range. Memberships are available for the course and the practice facility. Plantation Links also has the area's first nine-hole, bent-grass putting course. Green fees for 18 holes are $16 to ride, $10 to walk; if you're an early bird, you can play for $11 with cart before 9 AM weekdays.

Versailles

Cabin Brook Golf Course
2260 Lexington Rd. (U.S. 60), Versailles
• 873-8404

This public course, opened around 1970, is mostly flat, but its fairways are lined with pine trees. The 7,000-yard course is par 72. Memberships are available. Weekday greens fees are $12 for 18 holes; on weekends it costs $14. Cart rental is $8.

Frankfort

Juniper Hills Golf Course
800 Louisville Rd., Frankfort
• (502) 875-8559

Built-up greens present a challenge on this 6,147-yard, par 70 public course. The terrain is slightly hilly, with one water hole. Memberships are available. Fees are $10 for 18 holes, $6 for nine. A cart is $10 more.

Georgetown

Longview Golf Course
3243 Frankfort Pk., Georgetown
• 863-2165, (800) 572-0210

Longview was private when it opened in the early '70s but went semiprivate around 1994. It's a rolling, 6,559-yard, par 72 course with water coming into play on four holes. The shifting fee structure is a little confusing, with prices varying from a low of $11 to walk nine holes on weekdays to a high of $25 to ride 18 holes on weekends. Call for specifics. Walking is not allowed until after 1 PM on weekends.

Dogwood blooms stretch in the afternoon sunlight.

Paris

Houston Oaks Golf Course
4285 Lexington Rd., Paris • (606) 987-5600

This semiprivate course, which opened in July 1996, is rolling and scenic, with plenty of trees, creeks, lakes and even some links-style holes. Water comes into play on 13 holes. The par 72 course covers 6,932 yards. Fees for 18 holes are $16 during week and $19 on weekends, with cart available for $9 more. To play nine holes, you'll pay $10 weekdays and $11 weekends, plus $5 if you want a cart.

Shady Brook Golf
444 Hutchinson Rd., Paris
• (606) 987-1544

This 2,632-yard public course is par 35 for its nine holes. It's a fairly flat course, but trees and three water holes keep things interesting. Weekday greens fees are $7 to walk nine, $11 to ride 9, $11 to walk 18 (playing the course twice) and $10 to ride 18. On weekends, it's $6 to walk nine, $10 to ride nine, $15 to ride 18 before 2 PM and $17 to ride 18 after 2 PM.

Winchester

Sportland Golf Course
U.S. 60, Winchester • (800) 273-5001

This rolling, par 72 course about 10 miles east of Lexington measures 6,828 yards. There's a lake on the 18th hole, and a small creek running through the center of the course comes into play on five holes. Greens fees vary: Weekends, with a cart, the cost is $25.50 for one duffer and $38 for two. Weekdays, with an even number in the group, it's $12.50 per person; otherwise it's $15 each. Without a cart, the fees are $10 on weekdays, $13 on weekends and holidays.

Southwind Golf Course & Sports Bar
2480 New Boonesboro Rd., Winchester
• (606) 744-0375

Southwind, a semiprivate course, opened in 1992. It's a 6,265-yard, par 71 course marked by hills, three sand traps and water on four holes. Weekday fees are $14.25 for 18 holes or $9 for nine with a cart; walkers can pay $10

INSIDERS' TIP

Kearney Hill Links has been rated one of the top 100 courses in the country.

for unlimited play. On weekends it's $21 for 18 holes or $14 for nine; walkers can pay $14 for unlimited play. You must have a tee time to play on weekends and holidays.

teur. The 1994 U.S. Senior Amateur Championship will be played at the course September 12 through 17. This course has tight fairways, plenty of hazards and a high slope rating.

Private Courses

Instruction

The Champions Golf Club
20 Avenue of Champions, Nicholasville
• 223-7275

Since opening in June 1988, The Champions, a 7,081-yard, par 72 course, has twice been the site of the Kentucky Open and has also been host to the U.S. Senior Individual Challenge and the Women's Western Ama-

Man O' War Golf Learning Center
Man o' War Blvd. at Parkers Mill Rd.
• 259-4653

Man O' War Golf Learning Center provides a number of tools to help you improve your game year round. Two putting greens, including one that covers 9,000 square feet; more than 300 yards of grass teeing area; a "short

Photo: Lexington Herald-Leader

Lexington native and former LPGA pro Myra Van Hoose Blackwelder learned to golf at what is now the Campbell House course.

game" area and a video instruction room are among the facilities. Four instructors are available during the summer, two during the winter. Range fees are $7 for a large bucket of balls, $5 for small. A short game is $11. There is no charge for using the putting area. Memberships are available.

Better Golf for Everyone
332 Colony Blvd. • 269-7628
Outside Lexington • (800) 264-7628
John Rood offers year-round indoor/outdoor instruction. Group discounts are available.

Practice Ranges and Miniature Golf

Lexington

Joby's Driving Range
2751 Palumbo Dr. • 263-4151
Joby's has grass tees and three sizes of buckets: small $3.50, medium $4.25 and large $5. Lessons are available at $25 for a 45-minute session.

Lexington Ice & Recreation Center
560 Eureka Springs Dr. • 269-5681
A biblical theme highlights 54 holes of miniature golf. The cost for 18 holes is $3.95, or you can have unlimited play for $5.95.

Tee It Up Golf Range
4400 Athens-Boonesboro Rd. • 263-2152
Tee It Up has a grass-tee driving range, with $4, $6 and $10 buckets of balls. There's also a putting green and pro shop. Lessons are available at $30 for ½-hour, $50 for an hour from retired PGA pros Gordon Leishman and Mike Dudley.

White Haven Golf Inc.
100 Dabney Dr. • 263-5310
White Haven, just off Richmond Road, offers 18 holes of miniature golf for $2.50 per game. There's also a driving range with grass tees; a bucket of balls ranges from $3.25 to $5.25 depending on the size.

Nicholasville

Entertainment Xpress
230 N. Plaza Dr., Nicholasville • 887-0359
Two 18-hole miniature golf courses are among the activities for all ages at this new entertainment complex. Golf is $4.50 per game, or for $15 you can get an "all-day card" that lets you not only putt but also enjoy go-kart racing, batting cages and more. See our Kidstuff chapter for more information.

Yes, Great Lexington continues to grow and develop and adapt in its role as a sports lover's paradise

Big Blue Basketball and Other Spectator Sports

It's an exciting time to be a sports fan in Kentucky!

Of course, that is almost always the case, but now the air is especially rich with change, excitement and the unknown. Call it a time of transition for Kentucky sports.

First of all, you have the most loved team in the state, the University of Kentucky basketball Wildcats (a.k.a. Big Blue), embarking on a great adventure with a new coach after a national championship in 1996 and a second-place finish in 1997.

Then you have UK's football team (the "other" Wildcats) also breaking in a new coach, one who has revitalized the Cats' long-stagnant game by (gasp!) putting the ball in the air.

And then there's that professional team playing its home games in Rupp Arena — the Kentucky Thoroughblades, a farm team of the National Hockey League's San Jose Sharks. It seems that Lexington, basketball center of the universe, has quickly grown pretty fond of ice hockey as well.

Nearby Georgetown College, which has always fielded competitive football teams, has created its own excitement by becoming the site of the Cincinnati Bengals' summer training camp.

Yes, Greater Lexington continues to grow and develop and adapt in its role as a sports lover's paradise. Although a bid by a high-profile group of business people and citizens to bring professional baseball to town recently fizzled — at least for now — you'll still find plenty of athletic action around here.

And that's good, because throughout Kentucky, people take their sports seriously. Whether the sport in question is one of the big three — basketball, football and baseball — or among the many other athletic possibilities, people in this part of the country root hard for their favorite teams and play hard when they're actually competing.

This chapter covers spectator sports. Horse racing, however, is in the Horse Country chapter. Participant sports are covered in our Parks and Recreation chapters and our Golf chapter.

Basketball

Organized baseball came to Kentucky in 1865 at the end of the Civil War, and football followed about 15 years later. Basketball, on the other hand, wasn't even "invented" until 1891. But that doesn't matter. Only a few years after James Naismith first hung a peach basket from a Massachusetts gymnasium balcony, basketball became king in Lexington and in the rest of the state.

For as long as anyone can remember, high school teams from the mountains of Eastern Kentucky, the bluegrass of Central Kentucky, the coal fields of Western Kentucky and all points in between have competed fiercely for the right be one of the "Sweet Sixteen" competing in the state championship tournament.

March Madness, the name often used to describe the postseason NCAA basketball tournament, also applies to the boys' state high school tournament, which used to rotate between Lexington's Rupp Arena and Louisville's Freedom Hall but is now held only at Rupp Arena. The tournament field, commonly known as the Sweet Sixteen, is made up of the winner of each of the 16 regions in the state. (The girls' state high school tournament is also held each March, with the site changing from year to year.) For many of these kids, a lifelong dream has been to go on to play for the Kentucky Wildcats.

Kentucky Wildcats

When it comes to basketball, Lexington is truly a championship town. Hanging from the rafters of Rupp Arena are six blue-and-white national championship banners earned by the University of Kentucky's Wildcats (plus banner after banner signifying conference cham-

pionships, Final Four appearances and other, smaller victories). The latest of the six championships came at the end of the 1995-96 season, when Kentucky beat Syracuse for the title. One season later, the Cats came close to repeating before falling to Arizona in the championship game.

After the 1996-97 season, Coach Rick Pitino — who had come from the National Basketball Association's New York Knicks in 1989 to rebuild a UK program that was in shambles — accepted an offer to return to the NBA and coach the Boston Celtics. Many Kentucky fans were heartbroken, having grown quite fond of Pitino, a flashy, Armani-suit-wearing New Yawk Italian-American. At the same time, most seemed to understand the ultra-competitive coach's desire for new challenges, as well as the allure of a 10-year contract worth $70 million and a role in the front office (he's also president of the Celtics organization). And with two former Wildcats, Antoine Walker and 1997 draftee Ron Mercer, now on the Boston roster, look for plenty of new Celtics fans in the Bluegrass.

In his second season at UK is Orlando "Tubby" Smith, a former Pitino assistant at UK and the school's first black coach. Smith has big shoes to fill. In his eight seasons at UK, Pitino's teams compiled a record of 219-50 (a winning percentage of more than 81 percent), captured five Southeastern Conference Tournament titles, went to the Final Four three times and barely missed another time, won a national championship and was national runner-up. But Smith was highly recommended for the job by his predecessor and many others, having spent six years establishing winning ways as a head coach at Tulsa (four years) and Georgia (two years) after leaving his post

FYI

If no area code is given, it's a local call from Lexington-Fayette County. If an area code is given, whether it's 606 or 502, it's a long-distance call: dial 1, the area code and the number. See the How To Use This Book chapter for detailed information on calling.

INSIDERS' TIP

When planning social events, be careful to avoid scheduling conflicts with UK basketball games. If you don't, your friends may skip your wedding, or show up with headphones and a mini-TV.

as Wildcat assistant coach. In those six years, Smith's teams compiled an overall record of 124-62 and made four consecutive NCAA post-season appearances. Right on the mark, Smith led the UK Wildcats to an NCAA title in the 1997-98 season. At this writing, in the 1998-99 season, the Wildcats have won another Southeastern Conference title and are in the third round of the NCAA tournament.

Smith's challenge is to continue a Wildcat legacy that, while tainted by some unfortunate scandals over the years, remains one of the proudest and winningest in college athletics. The names associated with Kentucky basketball could fill a Who's Who; we'll name some of the most notable. There's Adolph Rupp, the legendary "baron" of the Kentucky Wildcats whose record as the winningest coach in college basketball stood for years until 1997, when North Carolina's Dean Smith finally passed him . . . Carey Spicer, an All-America member of Rupp's first UK team in 1930-31 . . . Ellis Johnson, an exceptional athlete who led Ashland High School to the 1928 national championship (yes, they really had such a thing in high school back then) and then, at UK, was a basketball All-American in addition to starring in football, baseball and track.

There was Rupp's "Fabulous Five" — Cliff Barker, Ralph Beard, Alex Groza, Wah Wah Jones and Kenny Rollins — the team that won the 1947-48 NCAA championship and then the Olympic gold medal. In 1965-66 came "Rupp's Runts," who came within one game of an NCAA title; that team featured such notables as Pat Riley and Louie Dampier. Other stars have included Cliff Hagan, Cotton Nash, Dan Issel, Jack Givens, Sam Bowie, Kenny Walker, Rex Chapman, Jamal Mashburn and Ron Mercer. And that's a mere sampling.

Perhaps no UK team played with more heart against greater odds than did the 1991-92 Wildcat team, led by a core of Kentucky natives who chose to stay with the team while it served a two-year NCAA probation for illegal payments to players. Homegrown boys Richie Farmer, John Pelphrey, Deron Feldhaus and fellow senior Sean Woods of Indianapolis anchored a team that came within a miraculous last-second shot of beating Duke in the regional finals of the NCAA Tournament and advancing to the Final Four. In an exceptional break with school policy, UK retired the jerseys of the four seniors at the end of the season.

University of Kentucky Basketball Museum
Lexington Center, 410 W. Vine St.
• 225-5670, (800)269-1953

It's been over 20 years in the planning stages, but the $5.5 million high-tech UK museum next to Rupp Arena finally opened early in 1999 and, boy, was it worth the wait!

The 10,000 square foot museum has a replica of Rupp Arena's center court, and a virtual basketball court where visitors can play one-on-one with former UK players.

Fans can sit in a broadcaster's booth, go behind the scenes to visit a locker room, and even hang out in a replica of a 1950s-style diner where fans used to gather to listen to UK games on the radio.

Of course, there's a surround-screen show, computer kiosks and dozens of other hands-on, interactive attractions.

The museum is open from 10 AM to 7 PM Monday through Saturday, from noon to 5 PM Sunday. Admission is $7.50 for adults, $6 for senior citizens and students, $5 for children 7-12, and free for kids 6 and younger.

Rupp Arena
430 W. Vine St. • 257-1818 for tickets

Unless you are a student, have season tickets or are willing to pay scalpers' prices, gaining access to a Wildcat basketball game at the hallowed, 23,000-seat shrine called Rupp Arena will most likely be difficult. Although scalping, or selling tickets at prices higher than face value, is illegal in Kentucky, violations are

---

INSIDERS' TIP

Kentucky's 104-103 overtime loss to Duke in the NCAA regional finals is considered by many to be the greatest college basketball game ever played.

frequent and fairly blatant. Fortunately, the majority of UK basketball games are televised.

Although the Kentucky Wildcats play their home games at Rupp Arena, the facility is owned by Lexington Center Corporation and is not on the campus. Calling the Rupp Arena phone number won't help you get UK basketball tickets. Call the ticket office at Memorial Coliseum, which is located at Avenue of Champions.

During the last year of the Pitino era at Kentucky, university officials and interested citizens began talking about building a bigger, on-campus arena, replete with corporate sky boxes and other trappings of today's ritziest sports showplaces. But, with the departure of Pitino, the issue appears dead — at least for now.

Midnight Madness

If you don't have the money, connections or luck to procure UK basketball tickets, you still have a chance to see the Cats live. Your free opportunity comes in the form of "Midnight Madness," an annual October event that lives up to its name. Midnight Madness is the first practice session of the year, and it's scheduled to begin at the earliest possible moment allowed under NCAA regulations (the Saturday closest to October 15 each year).

Should you be hardy enough to accept the Midnight Madness challenge, you should head for the on-campus Memorial Coliseum, the Cats' practice facility and former home court, as soon as possible. Once there, you'll find a crowd of eager fans already waiting, some of them covered with cobwebs, in hopes of snaring a prime location among the coliseum's 11,000 seats.

Kentucky Lady Kats

Memorial Coliseum, Avenue of Champions • 257-1818 for tickets

The University of Kentucky women's basketball team is coached by Bernadette Mattox, who under Rick Pitino became the first female assistant basketball coach for a men's NCAA Division I team. Mattox held that position for four seasons beginning in 1990 before leaving to become the women's head coach. She replaced Sharon Fanning, whose contract was not renewed after eight seasons and a total record of 134-97, including a 14-14 performance her first season.

One of Mattox's first actions as women's coach was to change the team nickname from Lady Kats to Wildcats, matching the men's team name. New name or not, the going was tough in her first two seasons: The team went 8-19 in both the 1995-96 and 1996-97 seasons, but hit its stride with the winningest season ever and a run in the NCAA tournament in the 1998-99 season.

The Wildcats, whose past stars include Lee Ann Wise and Valerie Still, play their home games at Memorial Coliseum on campus. Tickets are readily available at the door.

Baseball

Kentucky Bat Cats

The UK baseball team, coached by Keith Madison, plays its home games in the Shively Field complex off Cooper Drive on campus. Tickets are available at the gate for $2 and $5. Check newspapers for schedule information.

Cincinnati Reds
Riverfront Stadium,
Pete Rose Way, Cincinnati
• (513) 421-4510, ext. 300 for tickets

The major-league Cincinnati Reds, who won the World Series in 1990 and were on their way to a division pennant before the strike ended the 1994 season, have struggled since. Depending on Interstate 75 traffic, you can generally make it from Lexington to a Reds game in around an hour and a half.

The 80-game regular season runs from early October to mid-April. Tickets are $15, $12 and $9 ($7.50 for children 12 and younger).

Kentucky Cool Cats
Lexington Ice Center, 560 Eureka
Springs Dr.

The University of Kentucky Cool Cats, the college team formed in 1983, draw a loyal and often rowdy crowd that has at times numbered more than 1,000 to their home games at the Lexington Ice Center. Not bad, especially considering that the games are played at midnight. Of course, that was before Lexington had a pro team; attendance has fallen some since the arrival of the Thoroughblades.

Tickets are available at the door for $4. Check the newspaper for schedule information.

Football

Kentucky Wildcats

With Hal Mumme in his second year of coaching, many Wildcat fans feel better about football than they have in years.

True, some fans wondered if the athletics department knew what it was doing when it hired Hal Mumme, coach at Valdosta State University, a Division II school, over several better-known prospects. After all, Division I-A, where Kentucky plays, is a far more competitive level. But Mumme had at least two things in his favor: 1) strong recommendations from respected coaches and 2) his vow, which he has kept, to make the pass a key part of the Cats' offense, something fans have dreamed of for years. Quarterback Tim Couch, who had an outstanding high school career in Kentucky and has been ranked as one of the nation's best passers, as well as a Heisman finalist in 1998, has played a major role in this transition.

Mumme took the helm from Bill Curry, who coached the Wildcats to a 26-52 record in seven seasons. Curry was notified with four games left in the 1996 season that his contract would be terminated at the end of the season. The team rebounded to win three straight before losing its finale to Tennessee, finishing with a 4-7 record, but it was too late to save the coach's job.

In one sense, it was a shame to lose Curry, a genuinely nice guy who ran a football program that was at least marked by integrity if not by inspiring performances. But the fact

remains that football coaches are paid to win games. Fast forwarding a bit, in 1998 "Mumme-ball" became a household word, and the Wildcats went 7-4 and landed a New Year's Day game at the Outback Bowl, the team's first appearance at a New Year's Day game since 1952. Fans were ecstatic. Football fervor is making a comeback.

Not surprisingly, on the eve of the 1998 bowl game, Mumme landed a new five-year contract worth $4 million, placing him among the highest-paid coaches in the Southeastern Conference.

Commonwealth Stadium
Cooper Dr., University of Kentucky campus • 257-1818 for tickets

While there hasn't been a whole lot to cheer about when watching the football Wildcats, the team nevertheless continues to draw respectable crowds at 58,000-seat Commonwealth Stadium. Of course, this stadium seats 2½ times the capacity of Rupp Arena, so getting a ticket isn't all that difficult, even on game day. Just stand outside the stadium and, as kickoff approaches, the prices from those with tickets to sell will generally come down.

We'd like to remind you that ticket scalping is illegal in Kentucky. In addition, paying scalper's prices for UK football tickets, at least at this point, might be considered criminally stupid.

Cincinnati Bengals
Riverfront Stadium, Pete Rose Way, Cincinnati • (513) 621-3550 for tickets

National Football League fans in Greater Lexington can catch the Cincinnati Bengals about 80 miles away in Riverfront Stadium. But those interested in seeing them gear up for the season don't have to drive nearly that far since the Bengals moved their summer training camp to Georgetown, Kentucky, from Wilmington, Ohio.

In 1997 Georgetown College built a $15 million Rawlings stadium and sports-training facility to lure the Bengals. When the Bengals

When you're looking for sports action, don't forget the local college and university teams.

aren't in town, the complex will also be used by Georgetown's Tigers. Scott County High School will also play its games at Rawlings Stadium, which has permanent seating for 5,000 and can be expanded to accommodate as many as 20,000. Under a seven-year agreement with the college, the NFL team will hold its four-week summer training camp in Georgetown until 2003.

The Bengals' 1997-98 season was the first full season under Bruce Coslet, who took over midway through the previous season when Dave Shula was fired. The team, 1-6 at the time of the firing, won seven of its last nine games to finish with an 8-8 record, just missing the playoffs.

Hockey

Hockey is a relative newcomer to the Bluegrass, but its popularity is growing rapidly, especially since the 1997 arrival of a pro team, the Kentucky Thoroughblades.

Kentucky Thoroughblades
Rupp Arena, 430 W. Vine St.
• **233-3565 for tickets**

The Ice Age has come to Lexington, to quote an advertisement used to promote the inaugural 1996-97 season of the Kentucky Thoroughblades, our professional hockey franchise. The Thoroughblades have proved that people will flock to Rupp Arena for more than basketball, concerts and tractor pulls. In the process they introduced phrases such as "icing," "face-off," "body check" and "power play" into the lexicon of many sports fans in Lexington and throughout the state.

The Thoroughblades, who play in the Mid-Atlantic Division of the 18-team American Hockey League, are an affiliate of the National Hockey League's San Jose Sharks. They are essentially the equivalent of a AAA baseball team, and throughout their first season, many of the T-blades' top players graduated to the majors. Even so, the team, coached by Jim Wiley, finished the regular season with a 36-35-9 record before losing three games to one to their archrivals, the Hershey (Pennsylvania) Bears in the first round of their Calder Cup playoff series.

The team nickname was chosen from a contest that drew 5,000 entries, and 1,700 different names; the mascot, appropriately, is Lucky, an upright thoroughbred horse on ice skates. Lucky is popular with the little ones and is just one way that the Thoroughblade organization is seeking to make games fun for the whole family. Games are events, featuring music and entertainment, contests, an indoor blimp and other promotions. It all seems to be working, as the team sold 304,349 tickets during its first regular season, with an average attendance of 7,608 at home games, the second-highest average in the league. And fans spent thousands and thousands of dollars on T-shirts, sweat shirts, pennants, pucks and other merchandise featuring the green-and-purple Thoroughblade logo.

Soccer

Bluegrass Bandits
• **266-5288**

The Bluegrass Bandits, formed in 1993, play in the 52-team U.S. Interregional Soccer League. The Bandits, who began as an amateur team but are now semiprofessional, played their 1997 home games at Henry Clay High School. The 18-game season runs from April through August. Tickets are $5 for adults, $3 for children. Call for more information.

Collegiate Sports Programs

University of Kentucky
• **257-3838 sports communications**

In addition to its more high-profile sports, UK also participates in intercollegiate competition in men's golf, soccer, swimming, tennis and track/cross country, and women's golf, gymnastics, soccer, softball, swimming, tennis, track/cross country and volleyball.

Gymnast Jenny Hansen, who graduated in 1996, became the top gymnast in college history by winning eight titles, including three overall NCAA titles. There is also a coed rifle team.

Horse Country

"You were a lord if you had a horse," wrote D.H. Lawrence in 1931. "Far back, far back in our dark soul the horse prances. . . . The horse, the horse! The symbol of surging potency and power of movement, of action, in man."

Lawrence's words seem appropriate to introduce this section on Kentucky's most prized animal. Lexington and its surrounding areas comprise the most renowned and most concentrated horse-breeding grounds in the world. Kentucky each year is responsible for the production of more thoroughbreds than any other state, and Lexington itself is Thoroughbred Central. Visitors from all over flock to the Bluegrass to drive past rolling, picturesque horse farms, visit the Kentucky Horse Park, bet on races and enjoy other equine attractions.

The horse has a long and glorious history within the state's borders, having been brought by settlers in the late 18th century. A Fayette County census in 1789 recorded an equine population of 9,607, compared with a human population of only 9,000. Even back then, horses were used for racing as well as for more mundane tasks, such as farm work and war. There is historical record of three-day race meetings being held in 1791. The first Jockey Club in the state was formed at a local tavern in 1797.

The glamorous thoroughbred, star of the most spectacular and most hyped 2 minutes in sports, gets most of the attention. But, however much we associate this sleek horse with the Bluegrass, it was developed more than 300 years ago by Europeans who bred their own horses with a trio of Arabian stallions. The only breed of horse native to Kentucky is the American saddle horse, a sturdy and spirited breed that originated in the 19th century as a direct descendant of a horse named Denmark, a thoroughbred who was in Confederate Gen. John Hunt Morgan's cavalry.

You might be surprised to find that the thoroughbred is not the most abundant horse in Kentucky. An equine census conducted by The American Horse Council Foundation in 1987 found 36,000 quarter horses to 32,000 thoroughbreds. Next, in descending order, came Arabians, saddlebreds and standardbreds. While those numbers, the most recent available, have undoubtedly changed, a 1996 study prepared for the foundation sheds additional light on the horse industry in Kentucky. That study, "The Economic Impact of the Horse Industry in the United States," found that out of 150,000 active horses in the state, 67,000 were used for racing, 37,000 for recreation, 32,000 for showing and 15,000 for other uses. Additionally, the study found, the state horse industry produces $1.2 billion in annual goods and services and involves 128,800 Kentuckians as horse owners, service providers, employees and volunteers. This figure includes 16,600 full-time equivalent jobs.

Even without the presence of the thoroughbred, horses would play a highly visible role in Lexington's economy, its culture and its day-to-day life.

For example, in Lexington you can:

• Bet on standardbreds at The Red Mile, the fastest harness racing track in the world.

• Take a romantic horse-drawn carriage tour through the center of town.

• Go horseback riding.

• Watch or participate in steeplechases, polo matches, Three Day Events and horse shows.

• See mounted police patrolling downtown streets.

Other locally prominent breeds of horses are the Morgan, the Tennessee walking horse, the Appaloosa and a variety of show horses, work horses and ponies. At the Kentucky Horse Park, you're likely to see, depending on the occasion, such diverse breeds as Lipizanners and miniature horses.

But, without a doubt, it is the thoroughbreds — and the farms where they are bred and raised — that most visitors have come here to see. They are the horses that bring the big money into town. Should you and your bank account be so inclined, you might plunk down several million dollars for a horse as some of the richest and most glamorous people in the Bluegrass, the world (Sheik Mohammed bin Rashid al Maktoum and his brothers from oil-rich Dubai) and even the galaxy (*Star Trek* star William Shatner, who owns a farm in Woodford County) look on.

The Bluegrass thoroughbred is recognized and cherished worldwide for its beauty, speed and stamina. The plentiful calcium and phosphorous in the limestone deposits that feed the soil apparently help the horses develop strong skeletons perfectly suited for the strenuous sport of racing. The land itself — rolling, firm, well-drained — is ideal for training. As producing fine wines seems to come naturally to the people of France, so it is with breeding fine thoroughbreds for the people in and around Lexington. There must be something in the water indeed.

No wonder those with the wherewithal to do so are willing to pay dearly for these animals. Shakespeare, taken out of context, might have been referring to the Keeneland or Fasig-Tipton thoroughbred auctions when he wrote in King Richard III: "A horse! a horse! my kingdom for a horse!" When you look at the top thoroughbred prices, including a world record $13.1 million paid for a son of Nijinsky II and My Charmer in 1985, you begin to think that many kingdoms probably have been exchanged for the opportunity to achieve track immortality with one of these regal beasts.

When your horses are worth that much, you do whatever you can to keep them healthy. To that end, the Maxwell H. Gluck Equine Research Center was opened on the University of Kentucky campus in 1987. This center, acknowledged as the finest equine research facility in the country, has resulted in a number of discoveries related to vaccination and disease control, blood testing and breeding efficiency.

Look up "Horse Farms" in the Lexington Yellow Pages, and you will find more than 150 entries, thoroughbred as well as standardbred and saddlebred. The names of the famous ones, of which there are many, trip off the tongue. Calumet (ever notice how much that sounds like Camelot?), the first horse farm that people generally see when they fly into Lexington. Airdrie Stud. Castleton. Claiborne. Darby Dan. Domino Stud. Elmendorf. Gainesway. Hamburg Place, long known for its horses as well as its extravagant pre-Derby parties. Lane's End, where Queen Elizabeth II stays when she visits Central Kentucky. Overbrook. Stoner Creek Stud. Taylor Made. Three Chimneys. Walmac International. The list goes on and on.

Calumet, which in 1991 was bankrupt and at risk of being auctioned off in parcels, was rescued from such an inglorious fate by Henryk de Kwiatkowski, a Polish-born aviation executive. De Kwiatkowski — who paid $17 million for the farm plus $250,000 for the right to use the name and logo — vowed not only to refrain from changing the character of the storied farm but also to return Calumet to its glory days. This is a farm, after all, that has bred nine Kentucky Derby winners, including Whirlaway (1941), Citation (1948) and Strike the Gold (1991); eight of them were foaled in the same barn.

Seventy-five percent — 92 out of 123 — of the Kentucky Derby winners have been foaled in Kentucky. So were the first six winners — and eight of 11 total — of the elusive Triple Crown, which consists of the Derby, the Preakness and the Belmont Stakes. In light of such impressive pedigrees, it's only natural that Lexington be entrusted with the sacred American Stud Book, a register of all thoroughbreds foaled in the United States, Canada and Puerto Rico. The computerized database, maintained by the Lexington office of The Jockey Club, contains the names of more than 2 million horses tracing back to the late 1800s. It also contains results of every thoroughbred race in North America, plus pedigree and racing data from around the world.

For years, during the 1930s, the *Lexington*

> # FYI
>
> If no area code is given, it's a local call from Lexington-Fayette County. If an area code is given, whether it's 606 or 502, it's a long-distance call: dial 1, the area code and the number. See the How To Use This Book chapter for detailed information on calling.

Herald had a standing offer to give subscribers free papers on any day that no horse bred within a 50-mile radius of Lexington won a race at any major track. At that time, there would be periods during the year when only one track in the country would be running, which greatly increased the odds that no Kentucky horse would win on a particular day. But no one can remember it ever happening.

That a newspaper would even make such an offer is indicative of the pride many Central Kentuckians feel in being able to live in such a special place. You don't have to be involved in the horse industry to feel it.

Of course, lots of people are attracted to the racing scene simply because it provides a fabulous excuse for a party. In the Bluegrass you will find, especially around Derby time, some of the most extravagant parties anywhere, where beautiful people in tuxedos and glittering evening gowns mingle and champagne flows freely. Anita Madden's annual Derby Eve blowout at Hamburg Place in Lexington is perhaps the grandest of them all. Should you rate as a "somebody" important enough to merit an invitation to one of these gala events (so far, we haven't), you may find yourself rubbing elbows with famous actors and actresses, rock stars, sports legends or perhaps even a president or two.

Elsewhere, we "regular" people hold our own Derby celebrations, which, while substantially less stylish, are characterized by no less enthusiasm. Most of us tend to steer clear of Churchill Downs itself on the first Saturday in May, but we can make a day-long party out of the 2-minute race on our televisions.

Then there are the brave souls who do travel to Louisville to experience the Derby amid that strange world known as the infield. On the big day, the area inside the track is packed with humans, a sizable percentage of whom are of the "party animal" species. They

will tell you that it is entirely possible to attend the Run for the Roses without ever seeing an actual horse. Some have their vision obscured simply because they are surrounded by taller people and are a prohibitive distance from the action on the track. Others have theirs obscured by perhaps a few too many mint juleps. This is not advisable.

If you would like to see, feel, ride or learn about the many varieties of horses in the Bluegrass, there are numerous places and events in Greater Lexington that will allow you to do so.

Racecourses

Lexington

Keeneland
4201 Versailles Rd. • 254-3412

With its manicured, meticulously landscaped grounds, its paddock shaded by dogwood and many other colorful trees, and its historic setting, Keeneland has been called the most beautiful racecourse in the world. And until recently, it was also one of the quietest. But the spring 1997 racing season saw Keeneland end its long-standing tradition of no public-address announcer. With or without an announcer, and with just six weeks of racing each year (three in April and three in October) the track has long made a big noise in the racing world. The Blue Grass Stakes, for example, is one of the major pre-Derby races for 3 year olds. The $11/_{16}$-mile course, which opened in 1936, also features a 7½-furlong turf course.

On Saturday afternoons during the racing season, Keeneland is the place to be seen, a social occasion even for those who think the Daily Double is a drink served during happy hour in the clubhouse. Keeneland is also the

---

INSIDERS' TIP

A thoroughbred stallion named Lexington won six of seven races during a brief but impressive 19th-century career, then became even more productive as a stud. Lexington was the nation's top sire for a record-breaking 16 years, producing 84 stakes winners and 11 champions.

only American track where the races have been attended by Queen Elizabeth II.

Keeneland's influence continues to be felt when horses aren't racing there. No fewer than 12 future Derby winners have been acquired through Keeneland's July and September yearling sales, which also were the occasion for the record $13.1 million sale in 1985. The training facilities are open year round. If you haven't been to Keeneland, a National Historic Landmark, then you haven't really been to Lexington.

The spring racing season typically opens the second Friday in April and runs for three weeks. The fall season typically opens the second Saturday in October and runs for three weeks. Post time is at 1:10 PM.

The prices for admission and parking in 1998 were: general admission $2.50, preferred parking $1 and free parking available for those who don't mind walking. For $3 more, or $5 more on weekends, you can get a reserved seat in the grandstand — but, frankly, the rails and the paddock area are better if you're into the sport of people-watching. Availability of reserved tickets varies: During the week, you can generally get them at the gate, but on weekends and for major stakes races, you'll probably have to order them in advance. Incidentally, if you want to eat at the Keeneland restaurant, you should make your reservations as far in advance as possible. You can also enjoy Keeneland during the off-season of racing. Public workouts are held from 6-10 am on the main track from mid-March to late November. While you're there, be sure and have a country style buffet breakfast at the Track Kitchen (open from 6-11 am daily).

Incidentally, if you're interested in researching thoroughbred history, you're in the right place. Keeneland's library is acclaimed as one of the world's finest thoroughbred research facilities. It's open to the public from 8:30 AM to 4:30 PM Monday through Friday.

Before you leave Keeneland, be sure to visit its unique gift shop (see our Shopping and Antiques chapter).

The Red Mile
1200 Red Mile Rd.
• 255-0752

The Red Mile is the fastest harness track in the world, and the oldest existing racecourse in Lexington. Compared with Keeneland, this track — named for its red soil — is a horse of a different color. Harness racing is naturally slower than thoroughbred racing, but it's just as exciting to watch the trotters head into the stretch, drivers perched precariously (so it seems) behind them in their two-wheel sulkies. The track, the oldest stop on the Grand Circuit race series, is also host of the Kentucky Futurity, which, with the Hambletonian and the Yonkers Trots, makes up the Triple Crown of trotting.

The original version of The Red Mile opened in Lexington in 1875. It is now on its third grandstand, but it retains much of its old-fashioned flavor. In the grandstand and along the rail, the atmosphere is casual. A clubhouse allows more formal dining while watching the races. The Paddock Park area is used for concerts, and the infield is the site of the annual Memorial Stakes Day and other events.

The Red Mile's operations also include the Tattersalls standardbred auctions three times a year. The tentative racing schedule as of 1997 was 24 nights for the spring season, from late April through June, and 9 days for the fall Grand Circuit meet, in late September and early October. Post time varies. Schedules are subject to change, so it's wise to call first or

www.insiders.com

See this and many other
Insiders' Guide®
destinations online.

Visit us today!

Photo: Jeff Rogers, courtesy of the Lexington Convention and Visitors Bureau

Real horses have been reportedly spooked by this statue at Thoroughbred Park.

check out the billboard at South Broadway and Red Mile Road. Admission, which also is subject to change, is likely to be $2 for grandstand entry, with a $3 fee for the clubhouse.

Louisville

Churchill Downs
700 Central Ave., Louisville
• (502) 636-4400

Lexington has the horses, but Louisville has the home of the greatest — or at least the most famous — two minutes in horse racing. The Kentucky Derby, which first ran in 1875 and offered a purse of $2,850, now attracts more than 100,000 fans every year to Churchill Downs, and millions more watch the race on television. The Breeders' Cup, held in November, is a full day of stakes races billed as the richest day in racing. No wonder the track's twin spires adorn the Kentucky license plate and are recognized all over the world.

There is a long waiting list for Derby tickets, but you can be part of the mass of humanity that packs into the infield. If you really want to enjoy Churchill Downs, however,

you're much better off going at a more sane time than the first Saturday in May.

Churchill's spring meet typically runs from late April through the end of June; the fall meet runs during November. Post times vary. Admission is $3.50 for the clubhouse, $2 for the grandstand. Reserved seats are $2 extra. Parking is $2.

Other Equine Attractions

Kentucky Horse Park
4089 Iron Works Pike • 233-4303

The Kentucky Horse Park, which opened in 1987 at a cost of $35 million, is the only equestrian theme park in the world. Its lush, rolling 1,032 acres provide a comprehensive look at the importance of the horse in Kentucky and the rest of the world. The legendary Man o' War, who lost only one race in his career, is buried beneath a statue of himself at the park entrance. After viewing the widescreen films *All the King's Horses* and *Thou Shalt Fly Without Wings* in the information center, visitors can tour the park on foot, aboard shuttle or horse-drawn carriage or on horse-

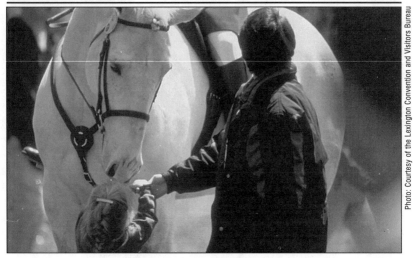

A resident of Kentucky Horse Park gets a pat on the nose.

Photo: Courtesy of the Lexington Convention and Visitors Bureau

back. They also can witness day-to-day operations of a working horse farm, see representatives of more than 30 breeds of horses in the Breeds Barn and the Parade of Breeds, and pay tribute to racing and show greats in the Hall of Champions.

The Horse Park, which includes a 3,500-seat arena, is the site of many world championship equestrian events each year, including the annual Rolex Three Day Event, the High Hope Steeplechase and the U.S. Open Polo Championships. Other horse shows and polo matches are held regularly on the grounds. The International Museum of the Horse, contained within the Horse Park, traces the history of the horse and also features the huge Calumet Farm Trophy Collection. A camping resort area includes swimming pool and tennis facilities.

The Kentucky Horse Park is open from 9 AM to 5 PM daily except from November 1 through March 31, when it is closed Monday and Tuesday. One-day general admission is $9.95 for adults and $4.95 for children ages 7 through 12. A combination ticket, $12.20 for adults and $6.20 for children, also includes admission to The American Saddle Horse Museum (see below). A 50-minute guided trail ride on the outskirts of the park is $12 per person.

The park also has a number of horse shows and special events throughout the year. Call for details.

The American Saddle Horse Museum
4093 Iron Works Pike • 259-2746

Kentucky's only native breed is also the oldest registered American breed of horse. Saddlebreds, the result of breeding thoroughbred stallions with a number of other breeds, are used for a variety of purposes in addition to their main purpose of show horses. Museum officials like to point out, for example, that Gen. Robert E. Lee rode a saddlebred and that Mr. Ed was one. The museum offers a variety of permanent and changing exhibits (some of them hands-on) and an award-winning multi-image theater show. One exhibit allows visitors to see themselves riding American saddlebreds through a reverse-screen projection illusion. There's also a gift shop.

The American Saddle Horse Museum is open 9 AM to 6 PM Memorial Day through Labor Day and 9 AM to 5 PM September through May. It's closed Mondays and Tuesdays from November through mid-March. Admission is $3 for adults, $2.50 for senior citizens and $2 for children ages 7 through 12 (see above for information on combination tickets with Horse Park admission).

Kentucky Horse Center
3380 Paris Pike • 293-1853

Two training tracks — a $5/8$-mile covered track and a $7/8$-mile open track — and a 900-seat sales pavilion are the highlights of this working thoroughbred training complex, which has room for 1,100 racehorses in training. A 1½-hour tour gives visitors a behind-the-scenes look at the industry. Tours are offered at 9 and 10:30 AM and at 1 PM Monday through Friday, as well as at 9 and 10:30 AM Saturday, from April 1 through October 31. Schedules vary during the rest of year, so call first. Cost is $10 for those 12 and over, $5 for children younger than 12.

Masterson Station Park
Indoor Arena Complex
3051 Leestown Rd. • 253-0328

This indoor arena, operated and maintained by the Division of Parks and Recreation, provides opportunities for riding lessons, shows, seminars and clinics. It features a 20-by-60-meter arena that seats 200 people, a judges stand, and a 32-stall attached barn. Groups can also rent the facility for their own equestrian events. Hourly rentals, available November 1 through March 31, must be made at least 48 hours and no more than seven days in advance. Exclusive use of the arena complex is $25 an hour; time share, with three horses maximum, is $10 an hour.

Lexington Livery Company
171 Saunier Ave. • 259-0000

The Lexington Livery Co. offers horse-drawn carriage tours. For $25, up to four people can enjoy a 25- to 30-minute ride through the streets of historic downtown Lexington. This makes a romantic addition to any evening, or it can be part of an enjoyable and relaxing night out with the family. You can make reservations in advance, or simply catch one of the carriages in front of the Radisson after 7:30 PM.

Thoroughbred Park
Main St. and Midland Ave.

The newest of Lexington's downtown parks is a tribute to the spirit of the thoroughbreds and their jockeys. The focal point is a life-size freeze-frame of a race in action, seven bronze horses streaking toward the finish line. Their jockeys are seven of the greats: Randy Romero, Pat Day, Bill Shoemaker, Jerry Bailey, Don Brumfield, Chris McCarron and Craig Perret. Lexington sculptor Gwen Reardon took three years to sculpt the richly detailed figures. In a grassy meadow above the "track," six more horses "graze": brood mares, foals and, in the center, the stallion Lexington. Fountains and a still pool complete the $8 million park, which was dedicated in April 1992. Four of the jockeys who later visited the park were impressed with its realism. More telling, however, is the report that real horses have seen the statues and been spooked.

Horse Farm Tours

Horse farm visitation policies differ from farm to farm. Many are not open to tours, while others permit visitors at selected times. Because of the uncertain and often hectic nature of the business, policies are subject to change from day to day. We have listed a few of the farms that are open to the public, as well as some companies and individuals that provide tours. If you are interested in other farms, call them and ask whether visitors are allowed. In fact, to avoid disappointment, you should call any horse farm before visiting.

Claiborne Farm
Winchester Rd., Paris • 233-4252

The great Secretariat, who won the Triple Crown in 1973 and whose world record of 2:24 for 1½ mile has yet to be matched, is buried at this farm where he was retired to stud and

Lexington Gets Cultural with Sister Cities

Question: What does Lexington, Kentucky, have in common with Deauville, France; County Kildare, Ireland; and Shizunai, Japan?

Answer: For one thing, all four cities are thoroughbred capitals of their respective countries. More important, Lexington has "twinned" with its French, Irish and Japanese counterparts through Sister Cities International, a program created by President Eisenhower in 1956 and based in Alexandria, Virginia. Lexington became one of the first U.S. cities to participate in the program when it established a relationship with Deauville in 1957; this relationship was renewed on its 40th anniversary in August 1997.

Student exchanges, university scholarships, organized group tours and trainee exchanges in such areas as business, hospitality, travel, sports and the horse industry are among the opportunities that our Sister Cities relationships provide. Over the years, Lexington residents have developed lasting friendships with residents from our twin communities.

Deauville, France

Deauville is a luxurious seaside resort on the coast of the English Channel near the port of Le Havre and 100 miles northwest of Paris. Its population, just 8,000 during the winter, swells to 100,000 during vacation season, with visitors enjoying the beach, horse racing, a casino, the American Film Festival and other activities.

High school student exchanges between Lexington and Deauville have taken place each year since 1975. The University of Kentucky and the University of Caen, near Deauville, began an exchange program offering one-year scholarships in 1977. In addition, adults from both communities have held organized group tours since 1976. Other programs include the placement of young people as tourism and business trainees in both cities.

County Kildare, Ireland

The Sister City relationship that Lexington and County Kildare instituted in November 1984 was a natural one, as the two communities already had a history of equine-related contact. County Kildare, just west of Dublin, is the center of Ireland's thoroughbred industry and home of the Irish National Stud, the country's top breeding facility.

In addition to the medieval castles and rolling hills that characterize much of Ireland, Kildare County is home to the famous Irish Derby and to world-renowned golf courses, museums and parks.

Lexington and County Kildare have operated a successful and widespread trainee exchange program since 1987. Through

Photo: Sister Cities Commission

Lexington Mayor Pam Miller checks out a sign in Deanville, France, marking the distance to Lexington.

special arrangements with the University of Kentucky's College of Business and Economics and St. Patrick's College, Maynooth, a summer school program began in the summer of 1991 in County Kildare. Students study courses in accounting, finance, Irish studies and equine management.

Shizunai, Japan

Lexington and Shizunai officially established their Sister City relationship in July 1988 during the Sister Cities International Conference in Lexington. Shizunai, population 26,000 is on Hokkaido, the northern island of Japan.

Known as "Heart of the Horse Industry" in Japan, Shizunai is surrounded by thoroughbred farms, where the country's top stallions stand at stud, and home to Japan's largest horse sales pavilion. Vistas of the Hidaka mountain range, the Pacific Ocean, rolling meadows, lakes and cherry blossoms in spring make Shizunai a beautiful place to visit.

The first exchange between the two cities came in March 1989 when a language instructor went to Shizunai to teach English. The Lexington-Shizunai program has included successful student and practical trainee exchanges, cultural exchanges and opportunities for foreign trade and tourism activities.

sired more than 300 sons and daughters. Other top horses who have made their homes here include Kelso, Buckpasser, Bold Ruler, Swale, Danzig, Forty Niner and Mr. Prospector. Times for Claiborne Farm tours vary, and you must call in advance to arrange an appointment.

Three Chimneys Farm
Old Frankfort Pike • 873-7053

The 11 stallions who stand at stud at picturesque Three Chimneys include 1977 Triple Crown winner Seattle Slew and two of his sons: Slew o' Gold and Capote. Thousands of people visit Three Chimneys each year, but appointments are absolutely required, so call first. No tours are offered during December and January.

Vinery
Weisenberger Mill Rd., Midway • 846-5214

Although it's not one of the better-known Bluegrass farms, Vinery is home to 1991 Derby victor Strike the Gold, 1992 "Horse of the Year" Black Tie Affair and Dare And Go, who broke

Cigar's 16-win streak in 1996. More than 30 stallions stand at stud here, and if you call in advance, the farm owners will make an effort to let you see many of these horses up close.

Blue Grass Tours
1116 Manchester St. • 233-2152

Blue Grass Tours, Lexington's oldest tour and charter company, offers two daily tours, at 9 AM and 1:30 PM, March through October, by appointment the rest of the year. Each tour includes a stop at a working horse farm; a stop at Keeneland, The Red Mile or both; a driving tour of other area horse farms; and a tour through the historic downtown area, including Thoroughbred Park. Tours are $20 a person. Senior citizens and AAA members get a $2 discount, and children younger than 6 pay $10. The Marriott's Griffin Gate Resort is the main departure point, but the bus will pick up passengers at any Lexington hotel for no additional charge. Blue Grass Tours also provides step-on guides and tours for convention or large groups. UK basketball fans might be

INSIDERS' TIP

The 1973 Triple Crown winner Secretariat was bred in Virginia but was retired to stud at Claiborne Farm near Paris, where he sired more than 300 sons and daughters. He is buried at Claiborne Farm.

The Red Mile was named for the color of its soil.

interested in knowing that Blue Grass Tours is owned by former Wildcat star Wallace "Wah Wah" Jones.

Historic & Horse Farm Tours
3429 Montavesta Dr. • 268-2906

This tour company has a monopoly on Calumet, the farm distinguished by its track record of nine Derby winners and for its white barns trimmed in red. Several other well-known Bluegrass horse farms also can be visited through this company. Tours of three to 3½ hours are offered seven days a week, with the agenda changing daily. The normal tour drives by Calumet (you'll just see it from the road), then visits Keeneland, a brood mare farm and a stallion complex. To actually visit Calumet, take the tour on Monday morning, Thursday afternoon or Saturday morning. Reservations are necessary. The tour van picks up visitors at most hotels and motels in the Lexington area. Locals can catch the van at a designated hotel or motel. Two tours a day, at 8:30 AM and 1:30 PM, are offered. The cost is $23. A caution: There is sometimes a two- to three-week wait for Calumet tours.

Karen Edelstein
• 266-5465

Karen Edelstein has been involved in the horse industry for a number of years and was a hostess at Calumet for several years. Now she offers customized private "step-on" tours. You drive your own car and she talks. You'll pick up a wealth of fascinating information about breeding, training, racing and more during her friendly, conversational tour. You'll probably get a chance to meet a legendary racehorse and stallion and talk with a trainer or groom. Edelstein's basic rates, which include a glossary of horse terms and additional printed material, are $65 for a minimum of 2 hours for up to four people and $10 an hour after that. Rates are slightly higher for groups larger than four people. Take a few extra dollars and enjoy breakfast in the Keeneland Track Kitchen.

Suburban Women's Club Open Horse Farm Tour
• 254-3959

This opportunity comes only once a year, and people have been known to plan their vacations around it. The Open Horse Farm Tour, usually held the second weekend in June, attracts 800 to 1,000 people over two days. The farm changes from year to year, but it's always a well-known thoroughbred operation and usually includes a look at every phase of the business: stallion complex, yearling and brood mare complex, farm house and more. The tour, which lasts four to 4½ hours, costs about $25.

Riding and Instruction

Lexington

Champagne Run
5991 Old Richmond Rd. • 263-4638

A variety of training, including dressage, eventing and hunter-jumper, is available. Champagne Run has indoor and outdoor arenas, as well as a cross-country course with fields and jumps. Private lessons are $28 for a half-hour, semiprivate (two people) lessons are $25 for 40 minutes, and instruction for groups of three to six is $20 for an hour.

Kentucky Belle Stables
Spurlock Ln. • 272-2611

Kentucky Belle, actually just inside Jessamine County past Lexington's Hartland subdivision, offers private lessons for beginning, intermediate and advanced riders, with horse care emphasized. Advanced lessons are given on American saddlebred show horses. Western-style training is available, but most lessons are for English-style riding. The facility has an indoor and an outdoor arena; trails are available for students only. Individual one-hour lessons are $27, or you can get 10 one-hour lessons for $250. Take Tates Creek Road south to Ashgrove Pike, then follow Ashgrove 1 mile to Spurlock Lane.

Central Kentucky Riding for the Handicapped
4089 Iron Works Pike • 231-7066

This nonprofit organization, with the motto "Ability . . . not disability," provides lessons at the Kentucky Horse Park. Chieftain, a 29-year-old Appaloosa, is one of the stars of the

Keeneland comes alive with a thunderous pounding of hooves for three weeks in April and three weeks in October.

program, which is open to any interested rider, subject to availability. The program, which is totally dependent on volunteers and contributions, is growing in popularity and is frequently overbooked. Scholarships are available.

Gold Spring Farm
3065 Spurr Rd. • 252-5650

Gold Spring Farm, ¼ mile from Masterson Station Park, is a full-board facility offering horse training, sales and private riding lessons in an outdoor sand arena. Lessons, from beginner through advanced, start at $25 an hour.

Robert Murphy Stables
5531 Parkers Mill Rd. • 255-3422

This facility boards and trains hunter-jumpers and also offers lessons for children and adults, from beginners to advanced, at $20 an hour. There are outdoor and indoor rings.

Richmond

Deer Run Stables
2001 River Circle Dr., Richmond
• (606) 527-6339

Surprisingly, this is about the only place we know of in the area where you can just go rent a horse and ride for a while on your own. The reason, instructors say, is rising overhead and insurance costs. Deer Run offers unguided or guided 3-mile tours along a gorgeous, varied trail that takes you up and down hills, through woods and along a creek. The ride generally takes about 45 minutes. Horses, which are available to accommodate all levels of experience, range from docile to more spirited. Riders must be at least 6 years old. The cost is $10 a person.

To get to Deer Run Stables, take I-75 S. from Lexington to Exit 97, then follow the winding, scenic two-lane road east about 4.5 miles, keeping your eyes peeled for signs in residents' yards. As one rider says, "It's a little hard to find, but it's well worth the trouble."

Nicholasville

Sugar Creek Resort/ Wildwood Stables
5800 Sugar Creek Pk., Nicholasville
• 885-9359

Wildwood Stables moved in May 1995 from Richmond to Nicholasville and greatly increased their offerings in the process. In summer 1997 an entire outdoor complex was in the works; thus the expanded name. The resort was to include a conference center, store and much more, including river frontage for fishing. Riders can choose from one-hour, two-hour and four-hour rides. "Lunch box" rides, which run for four hours and include lunch on the trail, are also available, as are moonlight rides three nights each month.

Prices vary from $15 for the one-hour ride to $60 for the lunch box ride. Reservations are required, and be sure to arrive about 15 minutes early. Wildwood also makes its trails available, for $5 a rider, to those who own their horses. Take Nicholasville Road south from Lexington to Ky. Highway 1268 east to Sugar Creek Pike.

Equine Annual Events

Blessing of the Hounds
Grimes Mill Rd. • 263-5482
The Blessing of the Hounds, a tradition harking back to the gentry's fox hunts of old, is held the first Saturday in November at the Iroquois Hunt Club's clubhouse. Nature's colors combine with the riders' scarlet coats to create a truly colorful event that is also filled with pageantry and music. And you'll enjoy the ride on beautiful old Grimes Mill Road, which, unlike many of Lexington's mill roads, still has a mill, which serves as the hunt's clubhouse.

EquiFestival
This October event, started in 1991, revolves around the opening weekend of Keeneland's fall racing season. Highlights over

a period of several days include a Parade of Breeds in downtown Lexington, a foot race through horse farm country and a family breakfast at Keeneland.

Lexington Junior League Horse Show
200 Market St. • 252-1893
The American saddle horse is the star of this weeklong show, the largest outdoor horse show in the country. Each July the Junior League Horse Show, first held in 1937, features the world's finest specimens of Kentucky's only native breed. The event is held at The Red Mile.

Festival of the Horse
Georgetown • 863-2547
The annual Festival of the Horse is held the third full weekend each September in downtown Georgetown. Its three days of events honoring the horse industry include food and craft booths, free entertainment and carriage rides, a tennis tournament, children's games, a parade with more than 200 horses and two horse shows.

Rolex 3-day Event
4089 Iron Works Pike, Kentucky Horse Park • 233-2362
This fantastic annual equestrian competition is written up in detail in our Annual Events chapter. See write-up in the "April" section.

Suburban Women's Club Open Horse Farm Tour
• 254-3959
See our write-up in this chapter under Horse Farm Tours.

The historic
architectural resources
of the area are
abundant, well
preserved and, in many
cases, open to the
public either daily or by
appointment.

Attractions

Rub elbows with some friendly old ghosts in a historic house; visit a Civil War battle site; marvel at beautiful native Kentucky plants and breathtaking river vistas; study animals in the wild; witness the creation of (and, if you like, purchase) handcrafted pottery, weavings and other arts and crafts; sample local delicacies; and travel to another planet (OK, it's really a planetarium, but a darn good one). These are just a few of the activities awaiting you at Greater Lexington's many attractions. Venture a little outside the immediate area and you can ride an awesome roller coaster called Chang or visit a major zoo.

This chapter covers general attractions in Lexington and surrounding counties (with a couple of "outside" exceptions), but there are plenty of additional activities in our other chapters. Be sure to check out the Kidstuff and Arts chapters and take a look at what's going on month by month in the Events and Festivals chapter.

If you're looking for something "horsey" to do (come on, you know you've always wanted to ride a horse!), trot on over to the Horse Country chapter.

We've divided attractions into categories —which we've, in turn, subdivided geographically. Our categories are: Oldies But Goodies (historic sites); History in the Making (still-in-use "political" buildings); Our Checkered Past (historical museums); Gone But Not Forgotten (cemeteries and a memorial); Natural Wonders; Wild Things (zoos and a wildlife sanctuary); Thrills, Chills and Spills (amusement parks); Crafted With Pride (handmade arts and crafts); River Crossing (bridges and a ferry); Planes, Trains and Automobiles; Sweet Stuff (candy and soft drink makers); and Seeing Stars (a somewhat whimsical combination of a planetarium and two performing arts centers). Enjoy!

Oldies but Goodies

Fayette County

Lexington is fortunate both in that it is rich in history dating back to pioneer days and that most of its important historic sites were left relatively unscathed by fighting during the Civil War. The historic architectural resources of the area are abundant, well preserved and, in many cases, open to the public either daily or by appointment.

One of the most pleasant ways to experience much of Lexington's historic architecture is to embark on the Lexington Walk, a picturesque walking tour that hits many of the high points of Lexington's historic places. Maps of the tour, which include one for the Bluegrass Driving Tour as well, are available at the Lexington Convention and Visitors Bureau at 301 Vine Street, Lexington, KY 40507. If you can't get downtown to the visitors bureau, call 233-1221 in Lexington or (800) 84-LEX-KY.

The Lexington Walk is about 2 miles long, but there are plenty of pleasant places to stop and rest or maybe even chat awhile. It incorporates some of downtown Lexington's nicest parks and most unique shopping areas. Triangle Park on Main Street is highlighted by pretty fountains and flowering pear trees. Gratz Park, a few blocks up N. Mill Street from Main Street, was originally the campus lawn of adjacent Transylvania University. It was at one time the focal point of one of Lexington's most prominent and wealthiest neighborhoods. Both the Bodley-Bullock House (used as a Union headquarters during the Civil War) and the Hunt-Morgan House (onetime home of a famous Confederate Civil War general) face Gratz Park.

The walking tour also takes you past Henry Clay's law office on N. Mill Street, the Lexington Children's Museum, Victorian Square shopping area, Transylvania University and the Opera House.

Several of the following historic sites are included in the walking tour, but you'll probably have to drive to the others. Oh, and don't forget to take special note of the statue of Confederate Gen. John Hunt Morgan (whose family home is in Gratz Park) astride a stallion instead of his most well-known mount, Black Bess, on the lawn of the Fayette County Courthouse. As to how this horse ended up anatomically incorrect — well, your guess is as good as ours.

Ashland (Henry Clay Estate)
120 Sycamore Rd., Lexington • 266-8581

Ashland was the estate of the Great Compromiser, Henry Clay, from 1811 until his death in 1852. Clay, a Lexington lawyer, played a prominent role in U.S. politics throughout his lengthy career, serving as U.S. senator, speaker of the House, secretary of state and three-time presidential candidate.

One of the nicest features about a visit to Ashland, at the corner of Richmond and Sycamore roads, is exploring the beautiful grounds and gardens around the house. The 20 acres of the Henry Clay estate are filled with ancient and unusual trees, including a ginkgo tree (a species that Clay imported to Kentucky) near the house's entrance. There are also several original outbuildings, including a pair of 19th-century round icehouses and a smokehouse. A real bonus is the Ginkgo Tree Cafe, serving lunch April through December.

Ashland is open Tuesday through Saturday 10 AM to 4:30 PM and Sunday 1 to 4:30

FYI
If no area code is given, it's a local call from Lexington-Fayette County. If an area code is given, whether it's 606 or 502, it's a long-distance call: dial 1, the area code and the number. See the How To Use This Book chapter for detailed information on calling.

PM, with tours of the home starting on the hour. Admission is $6 ($3 for students, $2 for children ages 6 to 12 and free for children younger than 6). Group rates are available. The house is closed during January.

Bodley-Bullock House
200 Market St., Lexington • 259-1266

One of the most stunning features of the Bodley-Bullock House is its grand staircase, one of the few cantilevered staircases left in the state. This Kentucky Federal-style house was built around 1814 for Lexington Mayor Thomas Pindell. Pindell in turn sold the house to Gen. Thomas Bodley, a hero of the War of 1812. The house was used as Union headquarters during the Civil War, and one popular story has it that Union troops painted one of the beautiful hardwood floors red, white and blue in celebration of a victory.

While the Bodley-Bullock House is open by appointment for tours Monday through Friday 9 AM to 1 PM (admission $4 for adults, $1.50 for kids older than 5), one of its most popular uses is as a rental space for parties, weddings, receptions and board meetings. Lovely and ornate gardens, as well as a beautifully restored interior, make the house a favorite in Lexington. The Bodley-Bullock House is also the current headquarters of the Lexington Junior League. Be sure to see the unusual snuffbox collection.

Hopemont (Hunt-Morgan House)
201 N. Mill St., Lexington • 253-0362

This Federal-style house in historic Gratz Park was built in 1814 by John Wesley Hunt, the first millionaire west of the Alleghenies. Prominent Hunt family members include John

Hunt Morgan, the Thunderbolt of the Confederacy, and 1933 Nobel Prize-winner Thomas Hunt Morgan.

The house and gardens are open to the public, and a Civil War museum inside the house opened in the summer of 1994. Guided tours are offered March 1 through December 22, Tuesday through Saturday 10 AM to 4 PM and Sunday 2 to 5 PM. Admission is $4 for adults, $2 for ages 6 to 12. Group rates are available.

Mary Todd Lincoln House
578 W. Main St., Lexington • 233-9999

As the first site restored in America to honor a First Lady, Lexington's Mary Todd Lincoln House offers a unique glimpse into the early years of the life of this wife of America's 16th president, Abraham Lincoln. The house was originally a brick tavern constructed in 1803. Mary's father, Robert Todd, renovated the tavern into a family dwelling in the 1830s, and the family moved there in 1832.

This cheerful house contains many fine period furnishings, as well as a collection of Mary's personal belongings. Public tours of the home are offered April 1 through December 15, Tuesday through Saturday 10 AM to 4 PM. Admission is $4 for adults, $1 for ages 6 to 12.

Loudoun House
209 Castlewood Dr., Lexington
• 254-7024

Loudoun House, one of five remaining castellated Gothic villas designed by architect A.J. Davis in the United States, is currently home to the Lexington Art League. It was built in 1852.

Loudoun House features rotating exhibits and artist studio tours. It is open free to the public Tuesday through Friday noon to 4 PM and Saturday and Sunday 1 to 4 PM. To get there from downtown, go north on Broadway, turn east on Loudoun Avenue, left at the "V" in the road and right on Castlewood Drive.

Pope House
326 Grosvenor St., Lexington • 253-0362

The John Pope House is one of Lexington's most recently opened historic homes. It is one of three surviving houses by early 19th-century architect Benjamin Henry Latrobe. Latrobe immigrated to the United States from England in the late 18th century. After befriending many of America's founding fathers, he was appointed architect of the U.S. Capitol by Thomas Jefferson, in which position he created such impressive neoclassical spaces as the old Senate Chamber and the House Chamber, which is now Statuary Hall in Washington, D.C.

One of the most interesting architectural features of the Pope House is the rotunda set in the middle of the square house plan. While the house is still in the process of restoration, exhibits focus on ongoing conservation work as well as on Latrobe and Sen. John Pope, the house's first owner.

The Pope House is open to the public for tours Saturday 10 AM to 4 PM; admission is $4.

Waveland State Historic Site
225 Higbee Mill Rd., Lexington
• 272-3611

This Greek Revival mansion built in 1847 by Joseph Bryan, a relative of Daniel Boone, is a good example of the lifestyle of the landed gentry in antebellum Kentucky.

Waveland is open to the public March through December, Tuesday through Saturday 10 AM to 4 PM and Sunday 2 to 5 PM. Guided tours of the home and grounds are offered throughout the day, but make sure you arrive no later than one hour before closing for a tour. To get to Waveland, drive south on Nicholasville Road past Man o' War Boulevard and take the next right onto Old Higbee Mill Road. Admission is $5 for adults, $4 for seniors and $2 for students and children.

Madison County

Battle of Richmond Driving Tour
351 W. Main St., City Hall, Richmond
• (606) 626-8474, Ext. 210

Follow the paths of Union and Confederate troops during one of the earliest and bloodiest military engagements of the Civil War in Kentucky. The self-guided driving tour of the Battle of Richmond gives you the opportunity to visit the high points of this battle that spelled a rousing victory for Confederate troops.

Maps of the tour route, as well as audiocassettes detailing the history of the stations along the tour, are available at the Richmond Tourism office in City Hall. The tour takes about two hours.

Fort Boonesborough State Park
Ky. Hwy. 627, Richmond
• (606) 527-3131

In addition to its historical significance as Kentucky's second settlement, built by Daniel Boone and his company of explorers in 1775, Fort Boonesborough is a popular recreational tourist spot, attracting thousands of visitors each year in its role as part of the Kentucky State Parks system.

A new public swimming pool is the latest addition to the park's camping and visitor facilities, which include 167 camping sites with electricity and water hookups (as well as primitive sites), tours of the reconstructed fort and museum, boating and fishing on the adjacent Kentucky River, an 18-hole miniature golf course, picnic areas and playgrounds.

The fort and museum are open from April through October Wednesday through Sunday 9 AM to 5:30 PM and from November through March from 10 am to 4 pm. Admission is $4.50 for adults and $3 for children ages 6 to 12. During the winter season admission is $2 for adults and $1 for children during the winter.

To get to Fort Boonesborough, take the Winchester Exit off I-64 or Exit 95 off I-75. It's about 10 miles from Winchester and 15 miles from Lexington.

White Hall State Historic Site
500 White Hall Shrine Rd., Richmond
• (606) 623-9178

Visiting the beautiful Italianate mansion of outspoken abolitionist Cassius Marcellus Clay in the northern part of Madison County is a true aesthetic and historical delight. The ex-tensive grounds are well-maintained, and the restored home is filled with gorgeous examples of period furnishings, many of which are from the original home.

White Hall is open daily April through Labor Day from 9 AM to 5 PM. It's closed Monday and Tuesday through October and every day in November. A small admission is charged for tours, but you receive a discount when buying admission tickets for both White Hall and Fort Boonesborough at the same time. A combination ticket costs $6.

To get to White Hall, take Exit 95 off I-75 and follow the signs.

Woodford County

Jouett House
255 Craigs Creek Rd., 5.5 miles west of Versailles • 873-7902

This is the former residence of Jack Jouett, a Virginia-born Revolutionary War captain who became known as the Paul Revere of the South. In June 1781 he made a heroic ride through the Virginia backwoods to warn Gov. Thomas Jefferson, Patrick Henry and other members of the Virginia General Assembly of an impending British attack. Jouett was also the father of antebellum portrait artist Matthew Jouett. The house is open for free tours from April 1 to October 31.

Pisgah Church
710 Pisgah Pike, Versailles • 873-4161

In the Bible, Pisgah was the mountain from which Moses first beheld the Promised Land. In Woodford County, it's a beautiful little stone country church in the wildwood, and it's almost equally capable of evoking a spiritual experience. In 1784 a group of Presbyterians settled in the area, founding the first

---

INSIDERS' TIP

Madison County was named after James Madison, the fourth president of the United States.

Photo: Ken Colebank

Don't limit your visit to just the house at Ashland. The 20 acres of grounds and gardens that surround it are breathtaking.

Presbyterian church west of the Alleghenies. They built a log church in 1794, which was renovated in the Gothic style in 1868. The church, which still has an active congregation of about 120, has magnificent stained-glass windows with scenes of native wildflowers.

Pisgah Church lies at the heart of the picturesque Pisgah Historic District. This area, truly a "must-see," has roads lined with 200-year-old osage orange trees and dozens of old farms with stone fences. The small building behind the church, opened by the Presbyterians in 1794 as the Kentucky Academy, was used for other church functions after the school merged with Transylvania University in 1798. Tennis courts on the church grounds are the site of the weeklong Pisgah Invitational Tournament held each August.

Take Pisgah Pike (Ky. Highway 1967 N.), the first road past the castle as you head out Versailles Road from Lexington. The church is less than a mile up the road on your right. Former governor Happy Chandler is buried in the church cemetery.

Franklin County

Liberty Hall Historic Site
218 Wilkinson St., Frankfort
• (502) 227-2560

Liberty Hall, begun in 1796 and completed in 1801 by John Brown, Kentucky's first U.S. senator, also served as the site of the first Sunday School west of the Alleghenies. According to some accounts (including that of the caretakers), Liberty Hall is haunted by at least two ghosts: a relative of John Brown's wife and a Spanish opera singer. The Orlando Brown House, home of the senator's son, is also included on the approximately one-hour tour, as are the landscaped grounds and a formal garden.

Four daily tours are offered Tuesday through Saturday: 10:30 AM, noon, 1:30 PM and 3 PM. There are two Sunday tours, at 1:30 PM and 3 PM. Cost is $4.50 for adults, $4 for seniors and $1 for ages 6 through 16. Group discounts are also available. Groups must call in advance. Liberty Hall and the Orlando Brown House are closed in January and February.

Old State Capitol
300 Broadway, Frankfort
• (502) 564-3016

This 1831 Greek Revival structure was Kentucky's fourth capitol building. Take note of the self-supporting staircase. Free tours are offered from 9 AM to 4 PM Monday through Saturday, noon to 4 PM Sunday.

Zeigler House
509 Shelby St., Frankfort
• (502) 227-7164

The Zeigler House, built in 1910, is the state's only building designed by Frank Lloyd Wright. Its design, created in Wright's famous prairie style, was advertised in 1907 in *Ladies' Home Journal* as the "$5,000 fireproof house." A few modifications were made for the Frankfort version, originally owned by the Rev. Jesse R. Zeigler and his family.

Wright fanatics Jim and Jane Brockman, who had visited 300 Wright structures and dreamed of owning one, moved from Western Kentucky in 1991 to buy and restore Zeigler House. Now the house, which is on the National Register of Historic Places, looks much as it did in 1910. Its lighted, stained-glass case over the fireplace and other features are of museum quality.

Please note that this is now a private residence — the Brockmans live here — and that tours are available by appointment only. The minimum cost for a tour is $20 for four people.

Scott County

Cardome
U.S. Hwy. 25, Georgetown • 863-1575

This property, where James Fisher Robinson lived before becoming governor in 1862, also served as a monastery and acad-

emy for the Roman Catholic Sisters of the Visitation. The name, coined by Robinson, comes from the Latin *carus domus*, or "dear home." Now the site holds a community center with the Scott County Museum for Local History. Free tours are available; call for times.

Royal Spring Park
S. Water St., Georgetown • 863-2547

The site of Georgetown's birth, and possibly bourbon's birth as well, Royal Spring Park features a small local history museum and an 1874 cabin built by a freed slave. The park, which also contains a deck, benches and picnic area, is open year round; the cabin is open April through September.

Bourbon County

Cane Ridge Meetinghouse
Ky. Hwy. 537, Paris • (606) 987-5350

Cane Ridge Meetinghouse, built in 1791, is the site of the origination of the Christian Church and Christian (Disciples of Christ) denominations during the Great Revival of 1801. That summer, more than 20 Presbyterian, Baptist and Methodist preachers met at the Cane Ridge Presbyterian meeting house, preaching throughout the days and nights from wagon beds and tree stumps to congregations of more than 20,000.

Thought to be the largest one-room log structure in the country, Cane Ridge Meetinghouse and Museum is open free to the public April through October, 9 AM to 5 PM Monday through Saturday and 1 to 5 PM Sunday. To get to the Meetinghouse (which is 7 miles east of Paris), take U.S. Highway 460 to Ky. Hwy. 537.

Duncan Tavern
323 High St., Paris • (606) 987-1788

Historic Duncan Tavern, built by Maj. Joseph Duncan in 1788, is the Kentucky headquarters for the Daughters of the American

INSIDERS' TIP

Georgetown's Toyota plant is the first North American manufacturing facility to produce two different types of vehicles on the same assembly line.

Revolution. It has been host to such famous historic figures as Simon Kenton and Daniel Boone. Located in downtown Paris, Duncan Tavern is open to the public Tuesday through Saturday, 10 AM to noon and 1 to 4 PM. John Fox Jr.'s library is located in one of the Tavern's 20 rooms. Duncan Tavern is furnished with Kentucky antiques and the library contains original manuscripts of several of his novels dealing with life in the mountains of eastern Kentucky, including *The Little Shepherd of Kingdom Come*, which was the first American novel to sell a million copies in the early 1900s. In the summer of 1997 the tavern began experimenting with serving Sunday brunch once a month (call for details). Admission is $4 for adults, $1.50 for children.

Clark County

Old Stone Church
Old Stone Church Rd., Winchester

Built in 1792, the quaint structure is considered to be one of the oldest established church west of the Alleghenies. Daniel and Rebecca Boone even attended services here. Old Stone Church Road is off Boonesboro Road about 2 miles outside Winchester. Services are no longer held here but you can call the Winchester-Clark County Chamber of Commerce, (606) 744-6420, for information about seeing the inside of the church.

History in the Making

Franklin County

Executive Mansion
Just east of the Capitol, Frankfort
• (502) 564-3449

This mansion, the official governor's residence since 1914, overlooks the Kentucky River. It was built of Kentucky limestone and reportedly was modeled after Marie Antoinette's summer villa. Free guided tours, which include the state dining room, ballroom, reception room and formal salon, are offered Tuesday and Thursday from 9 AM to 11 AM.

Kentucky State Capitol
Capital Ave., Frankfort • (502) 564-3449

Today's Capitol building, Kentucky's fifth, is a beautiful, domed, French Renaissance-style building that invites many comparisons to the U.S. Capitol. The imposing structure was begun in 1905 and completed in 1910 at a cost of $1.75 million. The Capitol Annex, a near replica of the statehouse without a dome, was finished in 1952. The ground floor of the Capitol features a variety of changing historical and cultural exhibits.

The highlight of the Capitol grounds is the Floral Clock, a working timepiece 34 feet in diameter with thousands of colorful flowers covering its face.

Free Capitol tours are offered from 8 AM to 4:30 PM Monday through Friday, 8:30 AM to 4:30 PM Saturday and 1 to 4:30 PM Sunday. Reservations are suggested for groups.

Lieutenant Governor's Mansion
420 High St., Frankfort • (502) 564-3449

Here's where the Kentucky governor lived until 1914, when he got new digs and the lieutenant governor moved into the old ones. This federal mansion, completed in 1798, is the oldest official executive residence still in use in the United States. Free tours are available from 1:30 PM to 3:30 PM Tuesday and Thursday.

Our Checkered Past

Franklin County

Kentucky Military History Museum
E. Main St. at Capital Ave., Frankfort
• (502) 564-3265

The Kentucky Historical Society operates this museum, appropriately located in the Old State Arsenal building. The state's military history is traced through photographs and displays of weapons, flags and other artifacts. The Kentucky National Guard and militia and the Civil War are especially emphasized. The tour is free, but large groups should make reservations. The museum is open from 9 AM to 4 PM Monday through Saturday and from noon to 4 PM Sunday.

Bourbon County

Hopewell Museum
800 Pleasant St., Paris • (606) 987-7274

The citizens of Bourbon County opened Hopewell Museum in 1995 to present the rich historical story of one of Kentucky's oldest counties and to provide a showcase for Kentucky arts. The pretty beaux arts building which houses the museum is an attraction in itself. The structure was built in 1909 as the town's post office building. The museum is open from noon to 5 PM Thursday, Friday and Saturday; 2 to 4 PM Sunday; and by appointment. Admission is $2.

Clark County

Pioneer Telephone Museum
203 Forest Ave., Winchester
• (606) 745-5400

This one-room museum features switchboards, booths and phones from as early as 1877. It is open free to the public on Monday, 1 to 4 PM.

Gone but Not Forgotten

Fayette County

Lexington Cemetery
833 W. Main St., Lexington • 255-5522

The Lexington Cemetery, chartered in 1848, is perhaps best-known nationally as an arboretum. More than 200 varieties of trees grow in the cemetery, including the country's second-largest known linden tree. In addition to the many unusual memorials and the more than 60 pieces of statuary on family graves, the Lexington Cemetery is home to nearly 180 species of birds.

Among the famous people buried in its 173 acres are Henry Clay, Gen. John Hunt Morgan, members of Mary Todd Lincoln's family, U.S. Vice President John Cabell Breckinridge, author James Lane Allen and basketball coach Adolph Rupp.

The Lexington Cemetery is open free to the public from 8 AM to 5 PM. Be sure to observe the time rules, since the gates are closed and locked at 5 PM, and it is easy to lose track of time in this beautiful location. During office hours (8 AM to 4 PM weekdays, 8 AM to noon Saturday) you can pick up a free brochure that will guide you to the graves of famous Lexingtonians.

FYI

If no area code is given, it's a local call from Lexington-Fayette County. If an area code is given, whether it's 606 or 502, it's a long-distance call: dial 1, the area code and the number. See the How To Use This Book chapter for detailed information on calling.

Franklin County

Frankfort Cemetery
215 E. Main St., Frankfort
• (502) 227-2403

The highlight of this peaceful, well-shaded cemetery is the grave site of Daniel and Rebecca Boone. Although the Boones were originally buried in Missouri, where they had lived the last years of their lives, their remains were moved to Kentucky in 1845; a monument was placed over their graves in 1862. From the grave site, perched on the edge of a hill, visitors can gaze down upon the Kentucky River and the state Capitol.

Native artist Paul Sawyier is also buried

INSIDERS' TIP

Thousands of people from Central Kentucky flock to the Living Christmas Tree musical program at Jessamine County's Southland Christian Church each December. The enormous tree, which reaches the ceiling of the huge church, is made up of choir members who form the "branches."

Henry Clay is buried in Lexington Cemetery.

Spend a few hours at the Henry Clay Estate and soak in the ambiance that surrounded the great statesman.

here, as are sculptor Joel Tanner Hart, whose poem "The Bivouac of the Dead" is inscribed in part at the gate to Arlington National Cemetery; and Richard M. Johnson, vice president under Martin Van Buren. Frankfort Cemetery is open from 7 AM to 8:30 PM during the summer and 8 AM to 5:30 PM during the winter.

Kentucky Vietnam Veterans Memorial
Coffee Tree Rd., Frankfort

This strikingly unusual memorial, honoring those Kentucky natives who died in Vietnam, resulted from a push by surviving veterans. A looming sundial is designed so that the point of its shadow touches the name of each veteran, etched on the ground in granite, on the anniversary of his death. The memorial, on the grounds of the State Library and Archives, is open daily until dusk.

Natural Wonders

Fayette County

University of Kentucky Arboretum
Alumni Dr., Lexington

If you just want to wind down and meander through pretty gardens and native Kentucky plants, you'll enjoy this rather young display of flowers and trees. The first phase of the arboretum was started in 1991; in the spring of 1996 more than 1,500 trees and shrubs were planted, and there are plans for a 2.1-mile Walk Across Kentucky with plants native to the geophysical region. You can relax on benches and watch the butterflies, meditate by the fountains, get ideas from the herb and knot gardens or take a walk into the natural woods at the back of the property. The Arboretum is open from dawn to dusk all year. It's located across from Commonwealth Stadium.

Jessamine County

Jessamine Creek Gorge Preserve
Information, The Nature Conservancy
• 259-9655

This may be the closest thing to a virgin forest you can find in this part of the country. The international Nature Conservancy has identified more than 350 species of plants and 25 species of animals in the gorge, which also has, among its cliffs and crevices, two caves with rare bat populations. The gorge is also largely inaccessible and on private land; to visit it, you'll have to arrange a private guided tour by calling the Nature Conservancy. Only three or four tours are offered each year, at a cost of $10 a person.

Kentucky River Palisades
Scenic stops on U.S. Hwy. 68, U.S. Hwy. 27 and Ky. Hwy. 29

For a breathtaking view of the river, try looking down from sheer limestone cliffs towering 300 feet above the banks. These rugged gray cliffs, which stretch for 75 miles, were cut by the river as it stubbornly plotted its course millions of years ago. Watch for signs to the scenic stops along the highway. Hikers at nearby Raven Run Nature Sanctuary — see The Great Outdoors chapter — can trek to the palisades, sit on a big rock and marvel.

Wild Things

Jessamine County

Wolf Run Zoo and Education Center
7376 Old U.S. Highway 27, Nicholasville • 887-2256

Lions, monkeys and other wild creatures, as well as farm animals, reside at Wolf Run Zoo, which doubles as an animal refuge for injured or abandoned critters. For more information, see Kidstuff.

Woodford County

Buckley Wildlife Sanctuary
1305 Germany Rd., 6 miles off U.S. Hwy. 60 in rural Woodford County • 873-5711

This 275-acre sanctuary, operated by the National Audubon Society, is a sanctuary to deer, birds, 'possum (Kentuckians say it without the "o") and the occasional skunk. Hard telling what you'll see on a given visit, but you'll always find nature trails, a nature center, great birdwatching and plenty of wildflowers in spring and summer. Sometimes workshops and other special events are scheduled.

Buckley Wildlife Sanctuary, which lies about a half-mile from the Franklin County line and has a Frankfort mailing address, is open from 9 AM to 5 PM Wednesday through Friday and 9 AM to 6 PM Saturday and Sunday. The nature center is open from 1 PM to 6 PM Saturday and Sunday. Admission is $2 for adults, $1 for children ages 16 and younger.

Not Too Far Away

Both of these regional zoos are less than a 90-minute drive from Lexington.

Cincinnati Zoo and Botanical Garden
3400 Vine St., Cincinnati, Ohio • (513) 281-4700

This zoo, long known for its outdoor gorillas, also has two white tigers and an okapi, a rare hooved animal that resembles (but is not) a cross between a giraffe and a shorter-necked zebra. The insectarium is the only one of its kind in the country, and the zoo also has a fabulous Asian and African rain forest exhibit and a new birdhouse.

Cincinnati Zoo also features "Jazzoo at the Zoo," a summertime series of musical concerts by nationally known stars. The gates are open every day of the year, rain or shine, from 9 AM to 6 PM; once inside, you can stay until 8 PM, though some exhibits close earlier. Admission is $10 for adults, $5 for children ages 2 through 12, $8 for senior citizens and free for those younger than 2. Parking is $5.

Louisville Zoo
1100 Trevilian Way, Louisville • (502) 459-2181

The Louisville Zoo has more than 1,200 animals, about a third of which are endangered species. Highlights include a realistic indoor re-creation of a tropical rain forest —

INSIDERS' TIP

Lexington Cemetery is as noted for its flowering plants as it is for the famous people who are buried there.

complete with real snakes and other jungle flora and fauna. Live shows daily feature zoo inhabitants in sessions that are informative, entertaining and often eye-opening. All your favorites, such as lions and tigers and bears (oh, my!) are there.

The Louisville Zoo is open year round. Hours from April through Labor Day are 10 AM to 6 PM, with extended hours until 8 PM on Wednesday through Friday from June through August. The rest of the year it is open from 10 AM to 5 PM. (Gates close one hour earlier than closing time.) Admission is $7.95 for ages 12 through 59, $5.95 for senior citizens (60 and older), $4.95 for ages 3 to 11 and free for those 2 and younger.

Thrills, Chills and Spills

Both of these amusement parks are less than a two-hour drive from Lexington.

Kentucky Kingdom
at the Kentucky Fair
and Exposition Center
Louisville • (800) SCREAMS

This park at the Kentucky Fair and Exposition Center in Louisville opened briefly in 1986 and closed the same year. When new owners reopened it in 1990, it was vastly improved, and it has continued to improve on an almost yearly basis.

Kentucky Kingdom, about 75 miles from Lexington, is home to a number of thrilling rides, including Chang, a $12 million roller coaster added in 1997. Chang, at 154 feet high, is the world's tallest, fastest and longest stand-up coaster. It takes almost three minutes to complete the journey through 4,100 feet of track.

Other thrillers include the Hellevator, a 15-story free-fall ride; a wooden roller coaster, Thunder Run, that *Amusement Business* magazine called the most terrifying in North America;

T2, a $7 million suspended looping roller coaster billed as the first of its kind in North America when it made its debut in the summer of 1995; and the twisting, looping steel coaster known as The Vampire. The Mile High Falls spill ride plunges you nine stories into a 300,000-gallon landing pool, guaranteeing that you'll be soaked when it's all over.

You'll also find a 15-story Ferris wheel; the tropical-themed Hurricane Bay water park, which features slides, children's activity area and a sometimes ferocious wave pool; a section filled with kid-size rides; and a variety of stage shows.

General admission is $27, with seniors and children shorter than 54 inches tall getting in for $15 and no charge for ages 3 and younger. During the regular season, gates open at 10 AM and the rides start at 11; Kentucky Kingdom stays open until 9 PM Sunday through Thursday and until 11 PM Friday and Saturday. The park is also open on weekends in April and May and in September and October; hours vary. (The prices and hours above are from 1997 and are subject to change.)

To get to Kentucky Kingdom from Lexington, take I-64 W., exit on I-264 W. and follow the signs to the Fair and Exposition Center.

Paramount's Kings Island
Off I-71, Kings Mills, Ohio
• (800) 288-0808

A little farther away — 24 miles north of Cincinnati — lies a longtime regional favorite. This 185-acre park, known for its Hanna-Barbera cartoon characters and its Beast roller coaster, was bought in 1992 by the Paramount movie studio. In addition to The Beast, one of the longest and best wooden roller coasters in the United States, the park has several other coasters and thrill rides. The Hollywood connection resulted in a Top Gun ride for 1993, and a Days of Thunder racing ride in 1994. There's also a thrilling stand-up coaster, King Cobra; the twisting and looping Vortex coaster;

INSIDERS' TIP

For a cheap but memorable close to a summer date, take that special someone to Triangle Park and watch the water from lighted fountains cascade down the steps.

Photo: Kentucky Department of Parks

The Greek Revival architectural style of Waveland was popular
in the area in the mid-19th Century.

the Amazon Falls log-flume ride; and The Outer Limits: Flight of Fear indoor coaster.

Milder rides include the enchanting, air-conditioned Smurf's Voyage for all ages. Kings Island also offers a "safari" monorail ride, a petting zoo and, at no extra charge, the adjoining WaterWorks water park. Kids will go wild (and probably get slimy) at Nickelodeon's Splat City area. All in good fun, of course.

And let's not forget International Street with its one-third-scale model of the Eiffel Tower. Be sure to stick around for the spectacular fireworks show at the end of the day, too.

In addition to live shows throughout the park, Kings Island also has an amphitheater that regularly features concerts by popular national acts.

General admission is $32.95, senior citizens and children shorter than 48 inches get in for $18.95, and those 2 and younger get in free. The park is open Memorial Day through August 24, as well as selected weekends in April, May, September and October. Gates open at 9 AM; rides and attractions start at 10.

The park is generally open until 10 PM, though closing hours do vary some — for example, it's open until 11 PM on summer Saturdays. WaterWorks is open on operating days from mid-May through September 1. (The prices and hours above are from 1998 and are subject to change.)

River Crossings

Jessamine County

High Bridge
Ky. Hwy. 29, Wilmore

At 275 feet above the Kentucky River, this is the nation's highest railroad bridge over a navigable stream. The original High Bridge, built near Wilmore in 1877 for the Cincinnati Southern Railroad and dedicated by President Rutherford B. Hayes, was also the first cantilever bridge in North America. It was replaced in 1911.

Valley View Ferry
Tates Creek Rd. at Kentucky River

The river isn't wide at this point, where it separates Jessamine County from Madison County, but the $2.50 ride on a paddle-wheel-powered ferry is worth the price for historical value alone. The Valley View Ferry is officially the state's oldest continuously operated business, having been granted its title by the Virginia General Assembly in 1785, seven years before Kentucky became a state. (In reality, it has been closed a few times by flooding or business changes, but let's not get technical.)

The short trip across the river is sure to be a treat for the kids, especially ones who have never experienced a ferry. Catch it before 7 PM Monday through Saturday and before 6 PM Sunday.

Bourbon County

Colville Covered Bridge
Colville Rd., 3 miles south of Ky. Highway 32 near the Bourbon-Harrison county line

The Colville Covered Bridge, 4 miles northwest of Millersburg on Hinkston Creek, is one of a handful of functioning covered bridges in Kentucky. Built in 1877, Colville Covered Bridge is 124 feet long and 18 feet wide. It is a single span of bur oak truss construction and is on the National Historic Register.

Planes, Trains and Automobiles

Fayette County

Aviation Museum of Kentucky
4000 Versailles Rd., Lexington • 231-1219

More than a dozen vintage airplanes and a flight simulator are among the highlights at this museum, which is actually off Airport Drive on Hangar Drive near the Bluegrass Airport. It's open Tuesday and Thursday through Saturday from 10 AM to 5 PM and Sunday from 1 PM to 5 PM. For more information, see Kidstuff.

Woodford County

Bluegrass Scenic Railroad & Bluegrass Railroad Museum
U.S. Hwy. 62 W. at Beasley Rd., Versailles • 873-2476

The Bluegrass Scenic Railroad takes passengers on a 90-minute old-fashioned train ride through pastoral Woodford County farmland, with an optional side trip by foot to Young's High Bridge, a c. 1888 railroad trestle spanning 1,658 feet across and 280 feet above the Kentucky River. Special events are held throughout the year, including re-enacted train robberies, a Halloween "ghost train" ride and the Santa Claus Special.

The Bluegrass Railroad Museum, a non-profit volunteer organization devoted to railroad restoration, displays a variety of railroad artifacts, including a 1960s caboose used by the Louisville & Nashville Railroad and a restored steam engine. The museum is open weekends from early May through October. Train rides are offered at 10:30 AM, 1:30 PM and 3:30 PM Saturday and at 1:30 PM and 3:30 PM Sunday in season. Standard prices are $7 for adults, $6 for seniors (62 and older) and $4 for children ages 2 through 12. Group discounts are available for groups of 20 or more with advance purchase.

Nostalgia Station Toy & Train Museum
279 Depot St., Versailles • 873-2497

This former L&N depot is stocked with a number of working electric trains, along with other toys and railroad memorabilia. Nostalgia Station is open from 10 AM to 5 PM Wednesday through Saturday and from 1 to 5 PM Sunday. Admission is $3 for adults, $2.50 for seniors, $1.50 for children and free for those 5 and younger.

Scott County

Toyota Motor Manufacturing USA
Cherry Blossom Way (I-75, Exit 26), Georgetown • 868-3027, (800) TMM-4485

The Toyota plant, the Japanese company's first wholly owned U.S. manufacturing facility, added the Sienna minivan to its lineup in August 1997, making it the first North American manufacturing plant to produce two different types of vehicles on the same assembly line. The Sienna uses the same vehicle platform as Toyota's highly popular Camry, the first automobile produced at the plant. The Avalon is also produced here.

Toyota offers free tours Tuesday and Thursday at 8:30 AM, 10 AM, noon, 2 PM and 6 PM; and Wednesday and Friday at noon and 2 PM. Reservations are required, so call in advance. No shorts, cameras or children younger than 8 are allowed on the tour. The Toyota visitors center is open Monday, Wednesday and Friday from 10 AM to 4 PM and Tuesday and Thursday from 8 AM to 7 PM.

Crafted with Pride

Madison County

Bybee Pottery
Ky. Hwy. 52 E. (Irvine Rd.), Richmond • (606) 369-5350

The Cornelison family has been making pottery at this site, which is the oldest existing pottery west of the Alleghenies, since 1809. Bybee Pottery, east of Richmond, is one of those don't-miss-it-or-you'll-really-regret-it experiences that even native Madison Countians never seem to tire of. And it's hard to explain exactly why: The building itself is a place you would likely overlook just driving by, and it's not a big operation. But there's just something incredibly appealing about the approximately 125,000 pieces of primitive pottery produced from native clay at Bybee Pottery each year that keep collectors flocking back for more.

Admission to the pottery is free, and it's open Monday through Friday from 8 AM to noon and 12:30 to 4 PM. But unless you get there long before the doors open at 8 AM on Monday, Wednesday and Friday, don't count on getting much pottery. Those are the days the family stocks the shelves, and die-hard Bybee buffs gather before dawn — in rain, snow or sleet — to stake out a place in the lines that form at the front and back doors of the pottery. (Hint: Friday is the best day to go.) When the doors open, it's every person for himself or herself, with the showroom usually cleared in 10 to 15 minutes.

To get to Bybee Pottery, take Exit 87 off I-75 into Richmond. Follow the road you are on (Ky. Highway 876) until it dead ends. Turn right onto Irvine Road. Bybee is 8 miles from town on the left.

Churchill Weavers
Lorraine Ct., Berea • (606) 986-3126

Founded in 1922 by former missionaries Eleanor and Carroll Churchill, Churchill Weavers became Berea's first non-college industry. Today, it is one of the nation's premier handweaving studios, and signature Churchill Weavers ties, baby throws and blankets are sold throughout the world.

Self-guided tours of the loomhouse, where you'll see the process from warping to weaving and finishing, are offered Monday through Friday, 9 AM to noon and 1 to 4 PM, although hours may vary seasonally. Call ahead to be sure the loomhouse is open. A gift shop and outlet at the loomhouse is open Monday through Saturday 9 AM to 6 PM and Sunday noon to 6 PM.

To get to Churchill Weavers, take Exit 76 or Exit 77 off I-75 into Berea and follow U.S. Highway 25 N. to Ky. Highway 1016. It's not as complicated as it sounds. There are lots of signs and very friendly people around if you have any trouble finding it.

Berea College Crafts
Log House Craft Gallery, Estill St. and U.S. Hwy. 25, Berea • (606) 986-9341, Ext. 522; (800) 347-3892

Since 1893, Berea College students and master craftspeople from the Appalachian

---

INSIDERS' TIP

Indians occupied Kentucky for at least 10,000 years before English-speaking explorers ever saw the state.

region have collaborated in the production of fine traditional art and crafts. Today, more than 150 students work and learn through the Berea College Crafts program.

In addition to showrooms in the Log House Craft Gallery and other locations around the state, including the Civic Center Shops on Main Street in Lexington, the Berea College Crafts program has several working studios around the Berea College campus where visitors can see fine, indigenous woodcraft, weaving, ceramics, broom-making and wrought-iron work in the process of being made. For more information, call one of the above numbers for a copy of the "Guide to College Crafts."

Sweet Stuff

Franklin County

Rebecca-Ruth Candies
112 E. Second St., Frankfort
• (502) 223-7475, (800) 444-3766

Combine pecans, powdered sugar and 100-proof bourbon, then dip the whole concoction in rich chocolate, and what do you get? You get an intoxicating treat that before 1986 was technically a federal offense to mail beyond Kentucky's borders — and you get the biggest claim to fame for this candy-maker founded in 1919. Schoolteachers Rebecca Gooch and Ruth Hanly are credited with inventing bourbon balls, the popularity of which has spread far beyond Kentucky's borders. Rebecca-Ruth Candies also makes a wide range of other liquor-filled candies — rum, Scotch, cognac, mint julep and Irish coffee — plus pulled cream candy, peanut brittle and many other delicacies that your dentist really doesn't need to know about.

The sales room is open from 8 AM to 5:30 PM Monday through Friday and from 9 AM to 5:30 PM Saturday. Free factory tours are offered from 9 AM to 4:30 PM Monday through Thursday, January through October. No tours are available in November and December because everyone is too busy filling holiday orders. Rebecca-Ruth, which ships candy year

round across the country, Canada and Europe, will send you a mail-order catalog if you call the toll-free number and request one.

Clark County

Ale-8-One Bottling Plant
25 Carol Rd., Winchester • 744-3484

If there's one thing Clark County natives are serious about, it's their local drink in the bright green bottle called Ale-8-One. It's a little gingery, only more subtle, with quite a caffeine kick, and so far, there's no diet version! Since 1926 the drink has been bottled in Winchester, and in 1965 the company built a new modern plant. Tours of the plant are offered Monday through Friday from 8:30 AM to 4:30 PM, and visitors are asked to call in advance. It's really cool to have an Ale-8-One ball hat, and you can buy one at the boutique which is open the same hours. See Lexington's Neighbors chapter for more information about the plant.

Seeing Stars

Fayette County

University of Kentucky Basketball Museum
410 West Vine Street . (800) 269-1953, (606) 225-5670

This $5.5 million interactive museum is filled with exhibits and activities of "hoop stars" from the early 1900's to the present. For more information, see the Big Blue Basketball and Spectator Sports Chapters.

The Opera House
401 W. Short St., Lexington • 233-4567

Dubbed "the best one-night stand in America" after its opening in 1887, the Opera House has welcomed such legendary performing stars as Al Jolson, Will Rogers, Fanny Brice, Lillian Russell and the Barrymores. It still plays host to nationally touring musicals and other productions. For more information, see the Nightlife chapter.

Madison County

Clark County

Hummel Planetarium
and Space Theatre
Kit Carson Dr., EKU campus, Richmond
• **(606) 622-1547**

The Hummel Planetarium, on the campus of Eastern Kentucky University, is the 11th-largest planetarium in the nation. State-of-the-art star show equipment takes you billions of miles out into space on a journey of science and fantasy. The Hummel Planetarium and Space Theatre also features large-format films and a unique gift shop, all geared toward kids.

The star shows and films are shown Thursday through Sunday at 7:30 PM and Saturday and Sunday at 3:30 PM. Admission is $3.50 for adults, $3 for students and senior citizens and $2.75 for children 12 and younger.

To get there, take Exit 87 off I-75 and turn left. Kit Carson Drive turns off the main road from the exit (the Eastern By-Pass).

Leeds Theatre
37 N. Main St., Winchester
• **(606) 744-6437**

This art deco theater, built in 1925, quickly became one of Winchester's most popular entertainment venues. It was closed in 1986 and was later purchased and renovated by the Winchester Council for the Arts. It opened as the Leeds Theatre and Performing Arts Center in 1990 and is now used for local arts productions — featuring, perhaps, the stars of tomorrow.

Getting to Winchester from Lexington is fairly straightforward. Your two basic options are either to take U.S. Highway 60 (Winchester Road) out of Lexington, which is the more scenic route, or I-64 W. off I-75 as it passes Lexington — the more direct route. There are two main Winchester exits off I-64.

For a relatively small city, Lexington has a huge arts community.

The Arts

For a relatively small city, Lexington has a big arts community that is thriving and growing even in the midst of the economic slowdown following the boom years of the 1980s. From poetry readings, shape note singing and flamenco dance to chamber music, painting and live theater, most interests you may have in the way of the arts can usually be fulfilled by one of the arts groups in Lexington.

Arts events fill the calendar year, although many groups try to stage their performances during times in which the local universities are in session, roughly from January to May and September to December. Productions are staged at a number of performance halls, and many groups have their own performance space as well. Most of the concert halls, theaters and galleries are concentrated in the downtown area between the University of Kentucky to the south of the Main Street corridor and Transylvania University to the north.

The Lexington Children's theater celebrated a gala year in 1998 with the opening of its new $3.3 million home on Short Street. Other major performance space includes ArtsPlace, home to several arts groups including the Lexington Arts & Cultural Council; the Lexington Opera House, on the corner of Short Street and Broadway; the Singletary Center for the Arts, which houses a concert hall, recital hall and the UK Art Museum; and the Mitchell Fine Arts Center, on the Transylvania University campus. Other smaller events are often held in the performance space at the Carnegie Center for Literacy and Learning, 251 W. Second Street, and the Central Library Theatre on E. Main Street.

The following list of arts organizations and performing groups includes some of the better known ones — and some new or lesser known ones — but there are dozens of others. For a more inclusive list contact the Lexington Arts and Cultural Council, Inc., 255-2951. (See our separate write-up in this chapter about LACC.)

For even more arts events that are about an hour's drive away check out *The Insiders' Guide® to Louisville*.

Organizations

Lexington Arts & Cultural Council
ArtsPlace, 161 N. Mill St.
• **233-1469, 255-2951**

Created in 1986 by a merger of the Lexington Council for the Arts and the Lexington Fund for the Arts, the Lexington Arts and Cultural Council is a cultural planning organization that focuses its efforts on fund-raising for and advocacy of the arts in the Lexington community. Housed in ArtsPlace, a 1904 Beaux-Arts building downtown, the LACC raises about a half-million dollars each year to fund local arts organizations and activities. Dozens of organizations are members of LACC, and there's a published list of those members available free for anyone interested.

The Kentucky Guild of Artists and Craftsmen
P.O. Box 291, Berea KY 40403
• **(606) 986-3192**

Since it began in 1961, the Kentucky Guild of Artists and Craftsmen has dedicated itself to educating the public and developing viable markets for members' work. One of the guild's original purposes was to help the economically depressed people of the state, particularly in the eastern region, which is rich with traditional art forms. The guild created an opportunity to raise the standard of living by allowing individuals to market baskets, quilts, wood carvings and other indigenous arts and crafts.

Through the ensuing years, the membership of the guild has expanded with the addition of professional artists and craftspeople and contemporary art and crafts.

Each year, the guild sponsors a Fall and Spring Fair in Berea, featuring the works of more than 100 juried artists. (See the Close-up in this chapter.)

Lexington Art League
209 Castlewood Dr.,
Loudoun House
• 254-7024

Started in 1957 by a group of friends united by the common bond of their love of art, the Lexington Art League was officially incorporated as a nonprofit organization in 1976. In 1984 the League moved into its present location, the historic Loudoun House, a restored Gothic villa built in 1852.

Now 450 members strong, the Lexington Art League is an active force in the local cultural arena, sponsoring numerous exhibits in public spaces around Lexington in addition to its own rotating Loudoun House exhibits. (For more information see the write-up in this chapter under Visual Arts.)

Music

Spotlight Jazz Series
Various UK auditoriums • 257-8427

A University of Kentucky project, the Spotlight Jazz series has featured some of the greatest jazz musicians in America over its 18 years of operation, including scheduled appearances in 1997-98 by Wayne Shorter, Herbie Hancock, Richard Davis, T.S. Monk, James Carter and Christian McBride. Tickets usually run about $10 to $15.

Lexington Philharmonic Orchestra
161 N. Mill St. • 233-4226

Under the longtime direction of George Zack, the Lexington Philharmonic Orchestra has pursued its mission of presenting high-quality orchestral and chamber music to Central Kentuckians. From its subscription series concerts to full-scale productions for school-

FYI

If no area code is given, it's a local call from Lexington-Fayette County. If an area code is given, whether it's 606 or 502, it's a long-distance call: dial 1, the area code and the number. See the How To Use This Book chapter for detailed information on calling.

age youngsters, the LPO strives to provide musical enrichment to all areas of the community.

Performances include the Master Classics Series at UK Singletary Center for the Arts, the Unplugged and Untied Series at the Opera House, the Family Series at the Singletary Center, and Coffee Concerts at local restaurants. These performances are held throughout the year. Ticket prices range from $5 to $26 depending on the series. Another especially popular event is the Picnic with the Pops at the Kentucky Horse Park. (See our Annual Events and Festivals chapter).

University Artist Series
University of Kentucky
College of Fine Arts, 105 Fine Arts Building • 257-4929

For the past 17 years, the University Artist Series has been providing Lexingtonians with an outstanding series of distinguished classical music concerts. Past performers have included Isaac Stern, Leontyne Price and the Montreal Symphony Orchestra. Ticket prices vary. Season subscribers save as much as 30 percent off individual ticket prices. All performances are at the Singletary Center for the Arts on the corner of Rose Street and Euclid Avenue.

Sweet Adelines
• 224-3550

With about 30 women on its membership roster, the Lexington Chapter of Sweet Adelines International teaches and trains its members to sing in four-part harmony, barbershop style. The group's annual concerts at the Opera House are just good fun. Tickets to the annual October performance are $8.

The group can also be enlisted to play for special occasions; call for more information.

Lexington Shape Note Singers
3534 Tates Creek Rd., Chapel Hill
Presbyterian Church • (606) 527-3536

Anyone who enjoys vigorous singing with a bit of a "frontier roughage" is invited to come and participate in this old English tradition of choral singing. Originally taught in singing schools to help educate early American pioneers, shape note songbooks use squares, diamonds, circles and triangles instead of musical notes because it was easier for the pioneers to read. Join in on the second Sunday of each month from 3 to 5 PM.

Central Kentucky Youth Orchestras
161 N. Mill St. • 254-0796

For more than four decades, the Central Kentucky Youth Orchestras have been providing a training ground for serious young musicians in the Central Kentucky region. There are now two separate full orchestras with about 70 members in each: the Symphony Orchestra (high school age) and the Concert Orchestra (middle school age). The orchestras comprise 136 youngsters from 34 schools in 11 counties. They perform about 10 concerts each season. Membership is by audition each August.

Central Kentucky Concert Band
• 873-0633

For 19 years this adult community band, whose members include lawyers, homemakers, teachers and factory workers, has provided Lexington with both the opportunity for amateur musicians to share their love of playing music and for audiences to enjoy the efforts of their friends, neighbors and coworkers. The band gives three major concerts each year as well as performing for community events.

Center for Old Music in the New World
161 N. Mill St. • 269-2908

Early music from the Medieval, Renaissance and Baroque periods is the primary area of interest for the Center for Old Music in the New World. The center's goals are to hear, share and present music from these eras that is both historical and beautiful. Founded in 1977, the Center's unique concerts, which have included such programs as "Six Centuries of Music by Women Composers" and "Old Music for the Amorous Season," have become popular additions to the Lexington cultural scene.

The center's programs are presented at Lexington locations including historic downtown churches and the campuses of both

Photo: Lee Thomas

Charlotte's Web was one of the five plays the Lexington Children's Theatre presented in 1996.

Transylvania University and the University of Kentucky. Member musicians offer lessons or can recommend teachers in historic instruments such as lute, recorder and harpsichord. Tickets are $2 to $10, depending on size of concert and where it's held.

Chamber Music Society of Central Kentucky
University of Kentucky College of Fine Arts, 105 Fine Arts Building • 257-3575

The Chamber Music Society of Central Kentucky brings nationally acclaimed small ensembles to perform in Lexington. Subscriptions are available to the five annual concerts that are usually at 8 PM on scheduled Sunday nights at the UK Singletary Center for the Arts Recital Hall. Prices vary by program. Recent appearances include the Alexander String Quartet, Amernet String Quartet, Parisii Quartet and the Quink Vocal Quintet.

Lexington Community Orchestra
• 858-0816

Formed to meet a need in the community for musicians who were not members of the Lexington Philharmonic Orchestra to have an opportunity to perform, the Lexington Community Orchestra held its first concert in April 1990. Since then the orchestra has performed a wide range of music for many local events and at locations throughout Lexington. There are about 50 members and auditions are not required. All performances are free and open to the public.

Lexington Men's Chorus
P.O. Box 1913, Lexington, KY 40593
• 266-9175

Now in its sixth season, the Lexington Men's Chorus, 40 members strong, has become one of Lexington's favorite performing arts organizations. A member of the International Gay and Lesbian Association of Choruses, the group usually performs two or three concerts a year at the UK Singletary Center for the Arts, with tickets priced at about $10. There is no audition necessary to join this gay men's chorus, and a person does not have to be gay to become a member.

The Lexington Chapter of the Society for the Preservation and Encouragement of Barbershop Quartet Singing in America
245 La Somme Dr. • 299-0154

The Lexington Chapter of the SPEBQSA's mission is incorporated in its name. The group typically performs more than 75 programs reaching 23,000 people at area events, hospitals, churches and nursing homes. Several large-scale performances are held each year at the Lexington Opera House, and ticket prices usually range from $5 to $10.

Lexington Singers
P.O. Box 23002, Lexington, KY 40523
• 323-5511

For 37 years, the Lexington Singers have offered Central Kentuckians both the opportunity to participate in the performance of and to enjoy the performance of good choral music.

The Lexington Singers present several concerts a year at the Singletary Center for the Arts and Rupp Arena (for the Kentucky Christmas Chorus), including joining the Lexington Philharmonic Orchestra for performances of Handel's *Messiah*. Their spring pops concert is also a popular event. Auditions are held in January and September. Ticket prices vary.

Dance

After a big (and much publicized) financial crisis in 1998, the board of directors of the 25-year old Lexington Ballet decided to dissolve the professional dance company but keep the school - which, of course, meant major cutbacks. Some of the fired dancers re-grouped and formed the Ballet Theatre of Lexington. In the long run, the community actually benefited from the rift because now we have productions from two good companies to look forward to.

Both groups presented successful performances of The Nutcracker in December of 1998, and are ambitiously moving on to other projects with much community support and loyalty (a bit divided, of course, as you might expect).

Stay tuned for new productions - and maybe even some surprises - in 1999. Call for information about upcoming performances.

Lexington Ballet
161 N. Mill St. * 233-3925

Now celebrating its 25th season, the Lexington Ballet continues to inspire interest in and appreciation for classical ballet, even though it teetered through serious financial problems and cuts in staff in 1998. Through performances by its professional company of dancers and through its ballet school, where students can begin as young as 3 years old, this company continues to bring classical ballet into the lives of Lexingtonians throughout

---

INSIDERS' TIP

Bring the kids, the dog and a picnic to the arboretum on Alumni Drive in July to enjoy productions of Shakespeare in the Park and the Renaissance carnival atmosphere.

The Kentucky Guild of Artists and Craftsmen's Fair

Over 100 artists — painters to potters to weavers to woodturners — exhibit and demonstrate their work at the Kentucky Guild of Artists and Craftsmen's (KGAC) Fair that's set in the foothills of the Appalachian Mountains, at the peaceful wooded Indian Fort Theater just outside of Berea. For more than three decades, thousands of Kentuckians and out-of-towners have made the pilgrimage to the KGAC's Fairs which are free and held the second or third weekends in October and May.

"I've been here since 1991 and we have three unrelated families from California who call every year, a year ahead of time, to find out the dates of the fair so they can make plane reservations," said Guild director Ann Reiss. "A lot of people arrange their vacations around the fairs because this area is so beautiful in the fall and spring." In fact, it almost seems like Mother Nature is a co-sponsor of the fall and spring fairs. Invariably, she puts on a show — flourishing the landscape with her palette of rustic fall colors or a profusion of spring greens. (Sometimes, she gets carried away and brings rain, too, but all the exhibitors are under tents, so the show goes on.)

Spend a peaceful but stimulating day in the woods browsing through booths filled with fine arts and fine crafts. Meet the artists, have a bite to eat and enjoy lively fiddling or soothing dulcimer music — or maybe a little jazz or blues — performed by local musicians. Be sure to bring the kids because there are plenty of creative hands-on activities for artists and craftspeople of tomorrow. Kids can participate in things such as making magic wands, sculpting with clay, spinning, weaving or listening to storytellers. Expect to thoroughly enjoy yourself and expect high quality work. "What makes our fairs unique is that everything really is handmade," said Reiss. "There are so many fairs around the country that display what we could call country crafts, the public has gotten jaded. They forget what fine arts and crafts passed down through the generations really

— continued on next page

Photo: Kentucky Dept. of Travel Development

You can see the handwork of more than 100 artists at the fair.

are," she explained. Many visitors don't realize that exhibitors at the Guild fairs must go through a strict jurying process before they are admitted.

The KGAC was chartered in 1961 to help talented artisans in the remote Appalachian Mountains market their crafts and supplement their incomes. Today about 50 percent of Guild members still are from the Appalachian region. "At the fairs you might talk to some of the people who have voluntarily given up traditional jobs and lifestyles to go off and live a simple life, maybe even in the woods without electricity, to be self sufficient and pursue their craft full-time," said Reiss. "It's a lifestyle that's fascinating to a lot of people and, in a way, when you meet the artist or craftperson and buy a piece of their work, it's like buying a piece of their lifestyle," she said. "Each time you look at the object, you think about that person. It's like taking home a friend."

Lara Carter, a resident of nearby Richmond and a faithful fair-goer said she loves getting out in the natural surroundings of the woods and watching the artists at work. "There's such a variety of colors and textures and sounds," she said. "It's absolutely a feast for the senses."

For more information about the spring and fall fairs see our chapter on Events and Festivals.

the year. Dance instruction is conducted at ArtsPlace and ballet performances are at the Opera House.

Ballet Theatre of Lexington
736 National Avenue * 252-5245

After forming in 1998, Ballet Theatre of Lexington successfully presented its first major performance, The Nutcracker, to good reviews at Transylvania University's Haggin Auditorium. Instruction at Ballet Theatre's academy includes not only classical ballet for children and adults, but also flamenco, swing, ballroom, Tai Chi movement, Pilates method and musical dance of South Africa.

Folk and Traditional Dance Organizations

Folk and traditional dance groups are very popular in Lexington and the surrounding region. These groups are usually participatory more than presenting, although they do perform at many events and productions in the area throughout the year. Most of these groups are aimed at providing an opportunity for folks to get together and dance in a fun and relaxed environment. Beginners are almost always welcome, since those who practice these traditional dance forms are always glad to share them with others.

Listed below are some of the more established dance groups in the area.

• **International Folk Dancers**, 887-1250, focuses on Eastern European and Mediterranean dances.

• **Lexington Scottish Dance Society**, 277-7710.

• **Lexington Vintage Dance Society**, 277-0422.

• **Oh Contraire**, (606) 986-2558, lively contra and square dancing.

• **Traditional Dance Association of Lexington**, 269-2542, focuses on English dance forms.

Theater

Broadway Live at the Opera House
401 W. Short St. • 233-3565

The Broadway Live at the Opera House series presents international touring professional theater performances to Central Kentucky audiences throughout the year. Recent productions include *Ain't Misbehavin'*, *Hello Dolly* and *Smoky Joe's Cafe*. Ticket prices vary according to the performance and location of seats.

Actors' Guild of Lexington
139 W. Short St. • 233-7330

Now in its 14th season, Actors' Guild of Lexington has produced more than 80 plays since it started. The mission of the theater group is "to create and present compelling contemporary theatre for the region." The non-profit group moved into its own space in 1992. Recent popular presentations have included *Times Square Angel*, *Keely and Du* and *Jeffrey*.

All actors are paid, and you can call the number listed above to read the scripts before auditions are held for upcoming parts. Actors' Guild also offers a variety of acting, directing and stage-building classes throughout the year. Tickets are $12 and $14.

Studio Players
545 Sayre Ave., Carriage House, Bell Court • 253-2512

This all-volunteer theater group has been staging plays in Lexington for the past 42 years. Each season includes works by well-known and lesser-known playwrights in drama and comedy. Performances are usually at 8 PM on scheduled Thursdays, Fridays and Saturdays and at 2:30 PM on Sundays at the Carriage House, Bell Court. Prices vary. Tickets are $6 for students and $10 for general admission.

Lexington Children's Theatre
418 West Short St.

The Lexington Children's Theatre has provided nearly 60 years of professional theater and classes for young audiences. Each season, this adult professional acting company presents more than 200 performances reaching 100,000 young people in the area. Recent productions have included *The Three Musketeers*, *The Secret Garden*, *Winnie the Pooh* and *Really Rosie*.

Performances are presented at schools and at the new building they moved into in the summer of 1998. Tickets range from $4 to $8 depending on how large the production is.

Kentucky Horse Center
Theatre for Children
3380 Paris Pike • 293-1853

Performances by professional acting troupes are at 10 AM and 12:30 PM on various weekdays for schools and groups and at 11 AM Saturdays or 4 PM Sundays for the general public at the Kentucky Horse Center. Admission is $8 for a single ticket; $4.75 for a

Photo: Kentucky Department of Parks

A performance of *Stephen Foster—The Musical,* formerly *The Stephen Foster Story,* at My Old Kentucky Home State Park is a foray into the Old South.

The Lexington Ballet's annual performances of *The Nutcracker* inspire the holiday spirit in all who see them.

group of 10 or more. The 1997-98 schedule includes *The Lion, the Witch and the Wardrobe*, *The Wizard of Oz*, *Swiss Family Robinson*, *Jungle Book* and *The Prince and the Pauper*.

Outdoor Drama

Summer in Central Kentucky brings many beautiful, sunny, warm (all right, sometimes hot) evenings that are just perfect for the production of outdoor drama. The region's temperate climate and beautiful landscape that is, for the most part, free from the noisy hustle and bustle of major metropolitan areas, combine to create ideal conditions for the staging of outdoor theater. Here is a listing of major annual outdoor events. However, many smaller productions come up during each season, so keep your eyes out for other opportunities to enjoy fine theater in the good old summertime in the great outdoors.

Shakespeare in the Park
The arboretum on Alumni Dr. • 288-2900

For the past 14 summers, the Shakespeare Festival Commission and the Lexington Parks Department have combined forces to present one of Lexington's most popular and well-attended outdoor events. In 1996 the event moved from Woodland Park to the more open, less congested arboretum across from Commonwealth Stadium on Alumni Drive where organizers hope to regain an audience that reached 28,000 in past years.

Usually three plays are presented. Most people bring dinner or snacks, pets and kids. Unless you want to sit on the grass, you should also bring lawn chairs or blankets. The 1997 summer plays cost $2 except for Sunday performances, which were free; seats can be reserved for $5 to $10.

While the shows don't start until 8:45 PM, pre-show entertainment gets in swing around

8 PM. Get there early to stake out your spot, since the plays usually attract huge audiences, especially on the not-too-hot evenings.

The Stephen Foster Story
My Old Kentucky Home State Park, Bardstown • (800) 626-1563

After 40 years *The Stephen Foster Story* has been updated and rewritten as *Stephen Foster — The Musical*. The show delights audiences of all ages with its grand, colorful depiction of one of America's most beloved songwriters. Staged under the stars on the grounds of My Old Kentucky Home (the antebellum mansion that inspired the song by the same name) in Bardstown, *Stephen Foster — The Musical* transports you more than 100 years in the past to the grace and hospitality of the old South in a romantic, heartwarming comedy. The show features dozens of his most famous songs, from "Oh! Susanna" to "Camptown Races."

The show runs from early June to the end of August nightly except Monday at 8:30 PM, with an indoor Saturday matinee at 2 PM. Tickets are $15 for adults, $5 for kids 7 to 12 and free for children 6 and younger.

Jenny Wiley Theatre
29 Jenny Wiley Rd., Jenny Wiley State Resort Park, Prestonsburg • (606) 886-9274

One of the oldest outdoor summer musical theaters in the country, Jenny Wiley Theatre has been providing a season of superb musical theater, apprentice program and arts workshops since 1965. It is one of the few rotating repertory theaters in existence. What is unusual about this is that when the season is in full swing, you can see as many as four Broadway musicals in as many days.

Over the past 29 years, Jenny Wiley has presented nearly 100 musicals to audiences totaling more than 400,000 by 1,000 actors, singers, dancers, musicians and technicians.

Plays are staged June through August, and performance times vary. Tickets are $13 for adults, $12 for senior citizens and $7 for students; group rates are also available. Some shows include a dinner buffet that starts at 6:45 PM. Call for information about when these dinner or luncheon packages are available.

Someday Outdoor Drama
Rt. 7 Grayson, Lake State Park, Grayson • (606) 286-4522

This beautiful outdoor musical drama depicts a love story set in the hills of Eastern Kentucky during the Civil War. Through the course of the drama, which has been performed for the past three summers, the characters explore many of the conflicts, especially in Kentucky as a border state, of that turbulent time in American history.

Shows are staged June through mid-July on weekends at 8:30 PM. Reserved tickets are $7 for adults and $4 for kids younger than 10. Tickets at the gate are $9 for adults and $5 for kids. For groups of 10 or more, the discount price is $6 a person. Call for specific show dates. Reservations are recommended.

Pioneer Playhouse
840 Stanford Rd., Danville • (606) 236-2747

With a list of alums that includes John Travolta, Lee Majors and Jim Varney, Pioneer Playhouse has made its mark in show business history as a training ground for aspiring actors and theater technicians during its 47 seasons of operation. All in all, more than 3,000 up-and-coming actors have appeared in productions at the Pioneer Playhouse.

Shows are produced June through mid-August Tuesdays through Saturdays. Dinner is served at 7:30 PM. Adult tickets are $18.50 for the play and dinner or $10.50 for the play only; tickets for children younger than 6 are $6.50 for the dinner and the play or $3.50 for the play only.

INSIDERS' TIP

Poetry readings by The Working Class Kitchen are well attended at Alfalfa Restaurant on Limestone Street.

Pine Knob Outdoor Theatre
2250 Pine Knob Rd., Caneyville
• (502) 879-8190

Each summer, Pine Knob Outdoor Theatre presents an exciting series of plays that centers on early life in the Pine Knob region. Filled with music, comedy and adventure, these grand-scale outdoor dramas are staged June through September on Friday and Saturday at 8:30 PM. Different plays are produced on different nights, so call for specific show information. Tickets are $8, and the management recommends that children who attend be older than 5. There are no shows on the Labor Day weekend.

Visual Arts

Lexington Gallery Hop
161 N. Mill St., Lexington Arts and Cultural Council • 255-2951

When you're thinking about art, be sure and put the Lexington Gallery Hop dates on your calendar. This fun, festive annual event highlights more than 20 art galleries and shops that are open on scheduled Friday nights from 5 to 8 PM throughout the year. Sponsored by the Lexington Arts and Cultural Council, the popular free event is "a big arts get together" with many of the galleries offering refreshment and entertainment. A good place to start and to pick up a map is at ArtsPlace, 161 North Mill Street.

University of Kentucky Art Museum
Singletary Center for the Arts, Rose St. and Euclid Ave. • 257-5716

One of the largest art museums in the area, the University of Kentucky Art Museum displays two or three special exhibits in addition to its permanent collection. A recent popular exhibit featured the art and fashion of Countess Mona Von Bismarck (she was born in Louisville and has been labeled "the most elegant woman in the world"), including her portrait by Salvatore Dali. The museum's permanent collection features many fine examples of European and American paintings, including Francisco Goya's *Portrait of a Bullfighter* and El Greco's *Boy Lighting a Candle*. A favorite with locals is Julien Dupre's *In the Pasture*, a 6-foot-wide painting of a young girl in wooden shoes and kerchief trying to hold on to a big black-and-white cow. (A tip: You can purchase a poster-size version of this painting for $12 at the museum.) Hours are noon to 5 PM Tuesday through Sunday. It's closed Monday and on University of Kentucky holidays. Admission is free.

Lexington Art League
209 Castlewood Dr. • 254-7024

The 450-member Lexington Art League sponsors a number of community art displays in various locations around town in addition to its main revolving shows at Loudoun House on Castlewood Drive (where the league's offices are located). The Annual Nude Show (see our Annual Events and Festivals chapter) is among the biggest and most interesting of these shows, and it takes place at the beginning of each new year. In addition, the organization sponsors classes, seminars, weekend and weeklong workshops. One of its most popular features is Masterpiece Meals held on the first Thursday of each month at the University of Kentucky Boone Faculty Club. The evening includes a guest speaker (always a prominent local or regional artist), a question and answer session and a sumptuous dinner, all for $18. Call the number above for reservations.

The league also sponsors art trips that recently included a Monet exhibit in Chicago and a Cezanne exhibit in Philadelphia. In 1998 the Art League plans to add a European trip.

Other Lexington locations where the Art League sponsors shows are the Blue Grass Airport Gallery at the Blue Grass Airport, 4000 Versailles Road (open 24 hours a day); the Opera House Gallery, 401 W. Short Street (open during Opera House events only); and

---

INSIDERS' TIP

Take a brown-bag lunch to the Lunch with the Arts series at Phoenix Park on Main Street every Thursday from noon to 1 PM.

the MetroLex Gallery at National City Bank, 301 East Main Street, open 7:30 AM to 6:30 PM Monday through Friday, 8 AM to 1 PM Saturday.

Artists' Attic
Victorian Square, 401 W. Main • 254-5501

This unusual studio offers Lexingtonians a chance to see local artists at work. About 15 artists have small studios in Victorian Square and spend at least 15 hours a week working there. Members of the public are invited to watch, browse and ask questions. Hours are 10 AM to 4 PM Monday through Saturday; and 1 to 4 PM Saturday and Sunday or by appointment.

ArtsPlace
161 N. Mill St. • 255-2951

A number of unusual exhibits by Kentucky's finest artists are on display in the ArtsPlace Gallery throughout the year and are open free to the public. One of the more unique recent exhibits was "Beyond Sight," designed for the special needs of visually impaired audiences. Hours are 9 AM to 4:30 PM Monday through Friday and 10 AM to 2 PM Saturday.

Headley-Whitney Museum
4435 Old Frankfort Pike • 255-6653

A true treasure in the Lexington cultural milieu, the Headley-Whitney Museum houses an eclectic collection of some of the most beautiful and unusual fine art objects in Kentucky. For instance, the Jewel Room contains a dazzling collection of bibelots (small objects of rarity or beauty). These bibelots are miniature plants, animals, gods and goddesses made of gold, ivory, coral, amber and lapis lazuli and studded with precious gemstones. This is the only contemporary collection of its kind open to the public.

Other parts of the museum include the Shell Grotto and the Oriental Gallery featuring Chinese robes embroidered with the "forbidden stitch," so named because the stitch was outlawed in the 19th century since many seamstresses went blind using it. Hours are 10 AM to 5 PM Tuesday through Friday and noon to 5 PM Saturday and Sunday.

Kentucky Gallery of Fine Crafts and Art
139 W. Short St. • 281-1166

Contemporary art, functional crafts and folk art can all be found in this delightful downtown gallery. Featuring the work of Kentucky's finest artists and craftspeople, Kentucky Gallery has paintings, photographs, pottery, jewelry, quilts, weavings, sculpture, furniture, blown glass, folk art and woodcuts. Services include a bridal registry, interior design, custom framing and Kentucky gift baskets. Hours are 10 AM to 5:30 PM Monday through Saturday and during Actors' Guild performances.

In addition to the above galleries, rotating small exhibits by local and other artists are displayed in many Lexington businesses and public buildings. Exhibits range from art with an international theme by local elementary students to some of the works of the area's most promising up-and-coming young artists.

A few more places that exhibit art are the Carnegie Center for Literacy and Learning, 251 W. Second St.; Central Bank Galleries, second and third floors of the Kincaid Tower, 300 W. Vine St.; Central Library Gallery, 140 E. Main St.

Writing

The Working Class Kitchen
• 278-4107

The Working Class Kitchen was started by Lexington poet Laverne Zabielski in 1990 to provide a forum in which emerging writers in the region could have an opportunity to read their work in public.

Since that time, the organization has grown to encompass a variety of community poetry and prose readings, a series of small writing groups for emerging writers and the publication of chapbooks of the works of local poets. The main series of readings is held the third Sunday of each month in the spring and fall at Alfalfa Restaurant on Limestone Street from 6 to 8 PM. A $3 donation includes dessert. Call if you are interested in reading your work.

Each year's calendar of events is chock-full of exhibits, festivals, shows and celebrations.

Annual Events and Festivals

NCAA basketball, thoroughbred horse racing, craft festivals, clogging competitions, and even a weekend festival celebrating a caterpillar — if you're looking for something fun and interesting to do in the Greater Lexington area, you won't be looking long.

Each year's calendar of events is chock-full of exhibits, festivals, shows and celebrations. We've chosen many of them to include in this chapter, and we hope this will entice you to go out and experience many of them for yourself!

January

Excite Nite '98
University of Kentucky, Memorial Coliseum, Avenue of Champions, Lexington • 257-3838

Thousands of fans come to see the UK gymnastics team perform at this exhilarating event, which includes door prizes and special guest characters for kids. There's always a theme, such as "Swing Music" in 1999. It's usually held in mid-January.

"The Nude" Exhibit
209 Castlewood Dr., Loudoun House, Lexington • 254-7024

This annual juried exhibit devoted to artistic depictions of the nude human figure has become the Lexington Art League's biggest show of the year. Now in its ninth year, "The Nude" draws the submission of work from about 100 artists annually from across the United States. The show is open to the public throughout most of the month.

February

Abraham Lincoln Birthday Commemoration
2995 Lincoln Farm Rd., Hodgenville • (502) 358-3137

This annual event commemorating the birth of President Abraham Lincoln is held at the Abraham Lincoln Birthplace National Historic Site. There's always a day of celebrating, plus a wreath-laying ceremony on Lincoln's symbolic cabin at 1:30 PM followed by cake and punch. It's always held on February 12, Lincoln's birthday.

March

Sweet 16 Boys High School Basketball Championship
430 W. Vine St., Rupp Arena • 299-5472

This is the highlight of the high school boys basketball competition each year. Sixteen of the best teams from across the state travel to the tournament, which will be held in Lexington through 1999. It's a week of triumph and tears as teams are one by one eliminated. The tournament is usually the second week in March.

Sweet 16 Girls High School Basketball Championship
Eastern Kentucky University Alumni Coliseum, Richmond • 299-5472

This tournament has the same format as the boys' tournament, but it's held in different locations each year. It's usually the second week in March.

St. Patrick's Day Parade
Main St., Lexington • 278-7349

Check the weather, don your green and get out early to enjoy the annual St. Patrick's Day parade that runs down Main Street about 1 PM. It's usually the Saturday before St. Patrick's Day.

Lexington Antiques and Garden Show
Keene Barn, Keeneland Race Course, 4201 Versailles Road, • 253-0362

Benefitting the Bluegrass Trust for Historic Preservation, this festive event features about 40 antique dealers and garden specialists with beautiful displays. There's a luncheon, special lectures, and it's usually the second weekend in March.

April

Keeneland Spring Racing
4201 Versailles Rd., Lexington • 254-3412, (800) 456-3412

The spring race meet at Keeneland, one of the most heralded events of the season, runs through the month with daily racing except on Monday, Tuesday and Easter Sunday. General admission is $2.50, reserved seats are $5.50 ($7.50 on weekends), except on Blue Grass Stakes Day when admission is $10. Post time is 1:10 PM.

Rolex 3-Day Event
4089 Iron Works Pike, Kentucky Horse Park, Lexington • 233-2362

This thrilling internationally recognized competition held each year at the Kentucky Horse Park showcases the best in equestrian competition, from the intricate schooling of dressage to the majestic athletic feats of stadium jumping. In 1998 the event became the nation's first annual four-star, three-day event outside of England. (Just to give you an idea how big this is, the Olympics is also a four-star competition.) The 1999 event will hold the same prestige.

Tickets bought in advance are $20 for a pass to the entire event or $5 to $10 per day for an adult, depending on the events. A big highlight is the Lexington Trade Fair, held in conjunction with the Rolex, which features retail booths with everything from art to jewelry to horse supplies. The 1999 Rolex is April 22-25.

Mountain Mushroom Festival
142 Broadway, Irvine • (606) 723-2554

For the fungally inclined, this unique annual festival includes everything from a street dance to a mushroom cook-off and the Fungus 5K race. Other events throughout the weekend include an antique car show, parade and gospel music festival. It's usually the last weekend in April.

May

Kentucky Derby
700 Central Ave., Churchill Downs, Louisville • (502) 636-4400

This first and most prestigious leg of thoroughbred racing's Triple Crown competition is held the first Saturday in May. Post time for the first pre-Derby race is 11:30 AM. The last race of the day, the exclusive Derby race, is for 3-year-olds and is 1¼ miles in length (see our Horse Country chapter).

INSIDERS' TIP

Lexingtonians enjoy going to The Red Mile in May for Memorial Stakes Day, when the highlights are chili, live music, chili, beer and chili.

Kentucky Mountain Laurel Festival
1050 State Park Rd., Pineville
• (606) 337-6103

For 65 years, not a May has gone by without this festive weekend celebration that includes everything from the coronation of a festival queen to picnics, fireworks, parades, golf tournaments and hiking at Pine Mountain State Park. It is the second-biggest annual event in Kentucky, just behind Louisville's Kentucky Derby Festival. It's always the last weekend in May, and most events are free and open to the public.

Memorial Stakes Day
1200 Red Mile Dr., The Red Mile,
Lexington • 255-0752

If you're looking for a fun way to celebrate your Memorial Day weekend, then come to The Red Mile for live entertainment, music and a to-die-for chili cook-off where you can eat all you can for $3, with proceeds benefiting the American Cancer Society. Admission to the Memorial Stakes Day itself is $5.

Kentucky Guild of Artists and Craftsmen Spring Fair
U.S. Hwy. 21 E., Indian Fort Theatre,
Berea • (606) 986-2540

For 30 years, artists and craftspeople from across the commonwealth and surrounding region have brought the fruits of their labor to Berea's Indian Fort Theatre to showcase and sell. More than 100 juried exhibitors attend this outdoor weekend event, including glass blowers, potters, weavers, silversmiths, photographers and basket makers. Friday and Sunday hours are 10 AM to 5 PM, and the fair is open 10 AM to 6 PM on Saturday. Admission is about $4 for adults and $1 for kids ages 6 to 12. See our Close-Up in the Arts chapter.

The Walk for Life
152 W. Zandale Dr., Lexington
• 254-AVOL

The annual AIDS Volunteers of Lexington's Walk for Life is held each year the Sunday before the Kentucky Derby. The walk is usually in May, but sometimes occurs the end of April. In 1997, some 2,000 people participated in the 5K walk at UK's Commonwealth Stadium to raise money to help with the medical needs of HIV/AIDS patients in the area.

June

Lexington Lions Bluegrass Fair
Leestown Rd., Masterson Station Park,
Lexington • 266-8727

This is the major annual fund-raising event for the Lexington Lions Club. It is a big summer carnival featuring rides, food, games, display tents and entertainment. A small admission is charged (usually $2 to $3). You buy tickets for the rides or you can pay more for an all-you-can-ride pass.

Great American Brass Band Festival and Balloon Race
Centre College campus, Danville
• (606) 236-7794

Imagine the best brass bands from around the world all gathered together in one spot for a weekend musical festival. Then add a Friday night balloon race with 28 balloons and about 30,000 people turning out for the festivities and you have one of the area's most popular summer events. Bands have included Dallas Brass, Canadian Brass and the Salvation Army Band. Admission is free but you need to go prepared with chairs or blankets for seating. It's usually mid-May.

Festival of the Bluegrass
4089 Ironworks Pike, Kentucky Horse
Park Campground, Lexington • 846-4995

This annual bluegrass and gospel extravaganza has become legendary in Lexington for presenting some of the very best bands and performers in the country. This huge weekend event is a family affair with hands-on activities for children (everything from playing acoustical instruments to a giant bubble-blowing table) and workshops for adults. Ticket prices range from $40 for the weekend or about $10 to $25 for a day, depending on the scheduled bands. The entertainment roster has included such greats as Alison Krauss and Union Station, Ricky Skaggs, The Seldom Scene, IIIrd Tyme Out, and J.D. Crowe and the New South. It's the second weekend in June, and people with campers can make reservations for both camping and the festival by calling the number above.

Annual Egyptian Event
4089 Ironworks Pike, Kentucky Horse Park, Lexington • 231-0771

The Annual Egyptian Event highlights this rare breed that traces its pedigree back to the time of the pharaohs. Featured in this weekend event are show classes, demonstrations and sales, art exhibits, a film festival and a commercial bazaar. It's usually the second weekend in June.

Seedtime on the Cumberland
306 Madison St., Whitesburg • (606) 633-0108

Appalshop's annual festival of traditional mountain arts, Seedtime on the Cumberland celebrates the exciting diversity of Appalachian music. From old-time fiddle and banjo tunes to bluegrass, blues, gospel and labor songs, you'll find plenty to please any musical palate. This popular weekend event also features regional crafts, theater and screenings of Appalshop films and videos. Ticket prices for evening concerts and theater presentations vary and the festival is usually the first weekend in June. Reservations are recommended.

Country Fair
1750 Summerhill Dr., St. Elizabeth Ann Seton Church, Lexington • 276-7103

A fun-for-the-whole-family annual summer event, this big Country Fair runs Thursday through Saturday with a midway, petting zoo, game booths, a bingo tent, lots of food and live entertainment. It's the first weekend in June in 1998.

July

Lexington Junior League Horse Show
1200 Red Mile Rd., Lexington • 252-1893

The world's largest outdoor American Saddlebred show, this event has been held in Lexington since 1937. Since it started, hundreds of thousands of visitors and competitors have come from across the United States

and Canada to participate in this prestigious equestrian event. In 1999 the show is July 12-17. Tickets are $3-$5.

Bluegrass State Games
Various sites in Lexington • 255-0336, (800) 722-BGSG

Any Kentucky resident of any age or skill level can compete in this major sporting event, which includes competitions in the Olympic tradition. The Games, started in August 1985, are the state's largest amateur sporting event with thousands of competitors. Usually held during the second and third weekends of the month, the Games take place at various locations in Lexington and surrounding counties. Recently, a smaller winter version of the games was added in January.

Berea Craft Festival
U.S. Hwy. 21 E., Indian Fort Theatre, Berea • (606)986-2540

Since 1896 Berea has hosted regional craft gatherings. The Berea Craft Festival has been held outdoors at Berea's Indian Fort Theatre since 1982. More than 100 exhibitors representing 20 states are featured each summer. Craft demonstrations, food and live entertainment round out the weekend event. Admission is about $4. It's usually held mid-May. See our Close-Up in the Arts chapter.

Bluegrass 10,000
545 N. Upper St., Lexington • 288-2900

The Bluegrass 10,000 foot race, sponsored by Parks and Recreation in conjunction with the Lexington Herald-Leader, is held every July 4 and is open to all ages (see the Parks and Recreation chapter). Watch the newspaper for details at the date approaches.

Shakespeare Festival
Alumni Dr., UK Arboretum, Lexington • 253-7755

Thousands of people flock to see this theatrical festival, which usually consists of three plays with local actors cast as Shakespearean characters. Most people bring picnics, kids and chairs or blankets for seating. Reserved chairs cost $5; reserved blanket seating is $10 for four people; general admission is $2

Competitions at the Rolex 3-day event range from dressage to stadium jumping.

Wednesday through Saturday night; Sunday nights are free. It's usually in late July.

Old Joe Clark Bluegrass Festival
U.S. Hwy. 25, Renfro Valley
• (800) 765-7464

This huge weekend event held at the Renfro Valley Country Music Center is for serious bluegrass, gospel and traditional music fans. Some of the best in the business can be seen on stage in this marathon musical event. Bring your family, food and lawn chairs and be prepared to settle down and enjoy. The cost is $15 for one day, $25 for two days, $32 for three days, and it's held the July 4th weekend.

August

Big Hill Mountain Bluegrass Festival
Big Hill • (800) 598-5263

Each year, bluegrass and gospel aficiona-dos flock to Big Hill (just south of Berea) for this huge, bring-the-whole-family event. Headliners in the past have included John Cosby and the Bluegrass Drifters and Ralph Stanley and the Clinch Mountain Boys.

A pig roast, band contest, arts and crafts exhibits and open stage jam sessions round out the action-packed weekend. Ticket prices range from $8 to $12 at the gate. Children younger than 13 are admitted free with parents.

Midsummer Night's Run
Vine St., Lexington • 275-6665

This is one of Lexington's premier fun and fitness events. Actually, the Midsummer Night's Run is a whole group of events involving the entire family. Now in its 12th year, the Midsummer Night's Run events include a 1-mile family walk/run, the Fastest Kid in Town race and the 5K run through downtown. All kinds of local celebrities participate, and there's a Midsummer Health Affaire during the afternoon with free health screenings and information

Christmas and equestrian themes combine for an illuminating display for The Southern Lights Holiday Festival.

and lots of activities for kids. It's usually the second weekend in August. The events are sponsored by Central Baptist Hospital.

Kentucky Hunter/Jumper Association Annual Show
4089 Iron Works Pike, Kentucky Horse Park, Lexington • 266-6937

This popular five-day horse show at the Kentucky Horse Park offers $25,000 in prize money. The final night of competition features a Grand Prix when riders are judged on both time and number of faults over a strenuous indoor jumping course. This final competition provides some real edge-of-the seat excitement. It's usually held mid-June.

Kentucky State Fair
Kentucky State Fair and Exposition Center, junction of I-65 and I-264, Louisville • (502) 367-5002

The Kentucky State Fair is 10 days of some of the best summer fun and entertainment in the commonwealth. In addition to traditional state fair activities like livestock judging, baked goods competitions and a huge midway, the Kentucky State Fair is loaded with special events such as the World's Championship Horse Show and concerts by some of the biggest names in popular music. Bands and performers who have appeared at the fair in the past include Garth Brooks, Michael Bolton, Vince Gill, Kris Kross, Clint Black and Wynonna. General admission is $6 for adults and $4 for kids 12 and younger and $2 for those 55 and older. Some concerts are free, but others are extra and range from about $15 to $25, depending on the act. It usually begins mid-month.

World's Longest Outdoor Sale
U.S. Hwy. 127 • (800) 327-3945

It's called the "world's longest yard sale." Each August, vendors, businesses and other folks set up along a 450-mile stretch of U.S. Highway 127 covering nine Kentucky counties stretching into Tennessee. Usually held the third weekend in August, the sale is open from sunrise to sunset Thursday through Sunday. About 80,000 people attend each year.

Picnic with the Pops
4089 Iron Works Pike, Kentucky Horse Park, Lexington • 233-3565

An evening under the stars with the heavenly music of the Lexington Philharmonic Orchestra, good food (that you bring) and good friends and neighbors make the annual Picnic with the Pops a favorite Lexington summertime event. General admission is $7.50, and you can also purchase table seats for you and a group of friends for $120 to $160. People go all-out decorating tables — which are judged, by the way — and the decorations range from the beautiful to the bizarre! So an added attraction is to walk around and admire the tables, and maybe even get ideas for your own table for the next year. It's usually the third weekend in August.

Central Kentucky Steam & Gas Engine Show
Main St., Bourbon County Park, Paris • (606) 987-4757

Held the first weekend in August, the Central Kentucky Steam & Gas Engine Show features working displays of antique farm and industrial machines, a tractor pull, a gristmill and tours of the old Paris power plant. The festivities include an old-fashioned pie dinner on Friday night and a country band on Saturday night. Admission is about $3.

Pops at the Park
500 White Hall Shrine Dr., White Hall State Historic Site, Richmond • (606) 623-1720

This concert is similar to the Picnic with the Pops in Lexington. It is held on the grounds of Cassius Marcellus Clay's stately Madison County mansion, with music provided by the Lexington Philharmonic Orchestra. Blanket seats are $8, and preferred and general tables are available, although they sell out quickly each year. It's held mid-August.

Ballet under the Stars
High St., Woodland Park, Lexington

Woodland Park is the site of many interesting summer arts events. Ballet Under the Stars is a festival of dance featuring excerpts from popular and well-known ballets performed by the Lexington Ballet Company. It's usually held the first week and weekend in August and is free and open to the public.

September

Roots & Heritage Festival
Rose St., Lexington • 258-3014

This annual street fair, which has grown to encompass a week of events culminating in a weekend festival, celebrates African-American heritage and culture in Lexington and around the world. Theater, music, lectures, poetry readings and art exhibits are held during the week preceding the weekend festival. Weekend attractions include everything from vendors selling jewelry, T-shirts, music, arts and crafts and lots of food to gymnastics exhibitions, live music, karate demonstrations, dance and fashion shows. The event is free and open to the public. It's usually the second weekend in September.

Historic Constitution Square Festival
Main St., Danville • (606) 236-9690, (606) 236-5089

Historical re-enactments, living history presentations, live entertainment, lots of food, arts and crafts from more than 80 artists and craftspeople and museum tours round out the schedule of events that fill the weekend of this free commemorative event celebrating Kentucky's statehood.

Kentucky Athletic Club's Charity "Bash"
1200 Red Mile Rd., The Red Mile, Lexington • 233-0814

For the past 24 years, this annual charity ball at the Red Mile has generated thousands of dollars for local charities and kicks off the University of Kentucky's football season. Food, drink and dancing to music by such popular bands as The Association and the Trendells make it an event to remember. Coaches and members of the UK football and basketball teams make appearances. Admission is $25 to $30. It's after the first UK football game which is usually the first Saturday in September.

Kentucky Bourbon Festival
107 E. Stephen Foster Ave., My Old Kentucky Home State Park, Bardstown
• (502) 348-4877, (800) 638-4877

Perhaps the only bourbon festival in the world, this annual event features a variety of bourbon-related activities including bourbon tasting, a music festival, tours of local distilleries, a golf tournament and My Old Kentucky Dinner Train Bourbon Excursion. This event is usually in mid-September.

World Chicken Festival
Downtown London • (800) 348-0095

This "fowl" event is held each year in downtown London, but in case you're wondering why, London is the home of the first Col. Harland Sanders Kentucky Fried Chicken restaurant. Held the last weekend of each September, the fun includes carnival rides, games and live entertainment. If you're looking to increase your flock, you won't find any live chickens, but you'll sure find some good things like local sorghum molasses, and items like those rustic wooden boards with the carved-out letters of your farm name to nail up on the front fence.

Festival of the Horse
Downtown Georgetown • 863-2547

The third full weekend each September is set aside for events honoring the horse industry. Food and craft booths, free entertainment and carriage rides, a tennis tournament, children's games, a parade with more than 200 horses and two horse shows provide three days of fun for all ages.

Admirals Day Parade
4375 Boonesboro Rd., Fort Boonesborough • (606) 527-3131

A warm summer day, colorfully decorated boats, a wide, lazy river — these are the ingredients that make up the annual Admirals Day Parade on the Kentucky River. People bring lawn chairs, picnics and the kids to enjoy the live entertainment, boat rides and the parade of boats on the river. It's always on Labor Day, and it's free.

October

Kentucky Guild of Artists and Craftsmen Fall Fair
Indian Fort Theatre, Berea
• (606) 986-2540

This is the fall equivalent of the spring fair. See the previous under entry under "May" for more details.

Forkland Festival
Forkland Community Center, Gravel Switch • (502) 692-3993

Anybody who likes old-timey bean suppers (complete with a "drama" put on by the local residents), hayrides, country and gospel music, animal husbandry, quilting, spinning and sorghum makin' ought to put this weekend event on the calendar. Admission is $1 for the festival. Tickets for the bean supper (including drama) are $8.

Forkland Festival boasts that it hasn't changed a thing in the past 27 years. It's usually in early October.

Celebration of Traditional Music
Berea College Campus, Berea
• (606) 986-9341, ext. 5103

Some 800 people from across the country attend this annual event celebrating the best of old-time and folk-art musical forms that predate bluegrass and country. Performances of ballads and duets, string band music, workshops by participating artists and nightly dances are some of the highlights of this exciting celebration. The events are at various buildings on campus, usually the last weekend in October. Some are free, and there is a charge for others (no more than $5 for any performance.)

INSIDERS' TIP

Two good places to watch **Fourth of July** fireworks are **The Red Mile** and **Masterson Station Park**.

Performances of *A Christmas Carol* by the Lexington Children's Theatre are an annual favorite.

Perryville Battlefield Commemoration and Re-enactment
1825 Battlefield Rd., Perryville
Battlefield, Lexington • (606) 332-8631

Military drills and parades, a flea market, a street dance, activities for kids and walking tours are all part of this historic weekend event commemorating a significant Civil War battle in Kentucky (see our Daytrips chapter for more details on the actual re-enactment). It's always the weekend closest to September 8.

Keeneland Fall Racing
4201 Versailles Rd., Lexington
• 254-3412

It wouldn't be fall without three weeks of racing at Keeneland. The fall foliage and aroma of burgoo combine with the thrill of some of the best horse racing in the country for a thoroughly satisfying time. The fall season typically opens the second Saturday in October and runs for three weeks, with no racing on Monday or Tuesday. General admission is $2.50. Reserved seats are $5.50, $7.50 on weekends.

Woolly Worm Festival
Main St., Beattyville • (606) 464-2888

Where can you rent a caterpillar to race for a quarter while you find out what the weather will be like for the next few months? At the annual Woolly Worm Festival, of course. Each October, the small town of Beattyville (population about 1,100) is crowded with thousands of visitors who come to hear the weather predictions of Rosemary Kilduff from her annual Woolly Worm survey. It's not exactly scientific, but Rosemary's usually right. This weekend festival has arts and crafts booths, a flea market, food booths, live entertainment, a car show and a beauty pageant. It's always the Friday after the third Monday in October.

Walk for Hunger
104 S. Forbes Rd., Lexington • 259-2308

Each year, volunteers collect pledges from the community then walk a 5K or 10K course to raise money for God's Pantry, a Lexington food bank. The race starts at UK's Commonwealth Stadium, and the goal is to raise about $45,000. It's usually held during the last week in September.

Alzheimer's Memory Walk
801 S. Limestone, Lexington • 252-6282

This 5K walk starts at Commonwealth Stadium. It's the main fund-raiser of the Lexington-Bluegrass Chapter of Alzheimer's Association, and it's held the first Sunday in October.

Court Days
Downtown Mount Sterling
• (606)498-5343

It's big. Real big. About 2,000 vendors and tens of thousands of visitors crowd into downtown Mount Sterling each year for Court Days festivities. You can buy everything from a Barney T-shirt to rifles (lots of rifles), tools, crafts, jewelry, elephant ears and Polish sausage. It's always the Saturday and Sunday before the third Monday in September.

Iroquois Hunt Club Horse Show and Barbeque
Athens-Boonesboro Rd., Lexington
• 263-5482

This annual, daylong event in the country is usually held the last Sunday in September, rain or shine. The colorful parade of Iroquois hounds after lunch is a real highlight. The horse show competition throughout the day is complemented by some "real" barbecue, which is smoked in pits on the show grounds, plus all the fixins. There is no admission charge for the show, but lunch costs about $6. The show is held in a big, open field — which makes for a great day out — and there are always plenty of direction signs.

November

Kentucky Book Fair
400 E. Main St., William Exum Bldg.,
Kentucky State University, Frankfort
• (606) 873-8989

Imagine dozens of your favorite authors all under one roof. Each year for the past 15 years, the Kentucky Book Fair in Frankfort has done just that — gathered dozens of authors from across the state and the country to the state capital to sell and sign their books. An added bonus is that profits from the book sales are given to public libraries and school libraries around the state to purchase books. Thousands of people regularly attend the fair, many with Christmas shopping in mind because the books are sold at a 20 percent discount. Well-known authors from the past few years include Howard K. Smith, Eleanor Clift, Wendell Barry, Bobbie Ann Mason, James Still, Dr. Thomas Clark, Nick Clooney and George Ella Lyon.

December

Southern Lights
4089 Iron Works Rd., Kentucky Horse Park, Lexington • 233-4303

This dazzling light show which started in 1994 attracts thousands of people in cars, vans and buses who drive through this 2.5 mile display of configurations outlined in glowing lights, many of them with an equine theme. The display includes horses "racing" as a crowd cheers them on, foals and mares "grazing" in a glittering field. Elves, snowflakes, stars, a moving train, fairy tale displays and Christmas figures complete the show. Admission is $10 and up, depending on the size of your vehicle, but, of course, the idea is to fill up your vehicle with as many people as possible. The show usually opens about the third week in November and runs through December 31 from 5:30 to 10 PM nightly.

Annual Christmas Parade
Main St., Lexington • 231-7335

Usually held the first weekend in December in the early afternoon, Lexington's Annual Christmas Parade ushers in the holiday season with a colorful display of about 115 floats and entries that include some of the top Central Kentucky marching bands. The parade route typically runs down Main Street between Midland and Broadway.

Kentucky Christmas Chorus
430 W. Vine St., Rupp Arena, Lexington • 258-3112

This uplifting choral extravaganza features the singing talents of more than 80 choirs and choral groups, plus the music of the Lexington Philharmonic. Some 7,000 people typically attend this festive evening yuletide event. People who attend say if you don't have the Christmas spirit when you go, you'll certainly have it when you leave. It's free and is held around the second week in December.

Annual Christmas Candlelight Tour
225 Waveland Museum Ln., Waveland State Historic Site, Lexington • 272-3611

Step back in time to Christmas in the old Bluegrass as you tour this pre-Civil War mansion by candlelight. Refreshments, character re-enactments and live music complement the festive atmosphere. This special weeklong tour is in mid-December, and a small admission fee of $5 ($2 for children and $4 for seniors) is charged.

A Victorian Christmas
500 White Hall Shrine Rd., White Hall State Historic Site, Richmond • (606) 623-9178

Experience a Victorian Christmas on a tour of the stately Italianate mansion that belonged to the abolitionist Cassius Marcellus Clay. Many of the furnishings are from Clay's family, and Christmas decorations last year included a tree decorated with dried roses from the garden. It's usually mid-December, and there's a small admission charge of $4.

Many other historic houses and towns have candlelight tours. For information about those tours and other special Christmas events, call (800) 225-TRIP.

Amusement parks, major metropolitan areas, spectacular state parks, fabulous fishing and boating areas, zoos, planetariums, art museums and national historic sites are all easily accessible from Lexington.

Daytrips and Weekend Getaways

If you spend any time at all in Lexington, you'll soon find out that one of the best things about it is its central location in the state. Just about anywhere you want to go in Kentucky is within a half-day's drive from Lexington.

Amusement parks, major metropolitan areas, spectacular state parks, fabulous fishing and boating areas, zoos, planetariums, art museums and national historic sites are easily accessible from Lexington.

There are, at the very least, hundreds of possible daytrips from Lexington. In this section, however, we will take an in-depth look at a few of our favorites: Louisville, Cincinnati and Covington, Ashland, Bardstown, Danville/Perryville, Renfro Valley, Shaker Village of Pleasant Hill and Big South Fork National River and Recreation Area.

"Daytrip," in the cases of these listed above, is really a misnomer. While you could go and come back to Lexington within a day, once you get there, you're likely to find you want to stay at least overnight. This is by no means a complete listing of the wonderful daytrips from Lexington. The sections that follow list some of the high points and attractions of each daytrip destination. For more detailed information about lodging and restaurants, call the number given at the beginning of the section. And if you have ski slopes in mind, see our Parks and Recreation Chapter because there are several just a couple of hours drive from Lexington.

Don't forget our state parks. They make great trips for the whole family. For more information on specific parks, see Parks and Recreation and Campgrounds chapters or call (800) 225-TRIP.

Louisville

Louisville Convention & Visitors Bureau
400 S. First St., Louisville
• (800) 626-5646,
(800) 633-3384 in Kentucky

The annual Run for the Roses, famous baseball bats and one of the world's greatest heavyweight champions of all time, Muhammad Ali, are just a few of the things that have helped secure Louisville's place in American history.

On the banks of the Ohio River, Kentucky's largest city is a veritable cornucopia of great things to see, do and experience. If you think "veritable cornucopia" is hard to spit out, though, just wait 'til you try to pronounce the name of this river city as a native would. To prepare to get just the right accent, fill your mouth up with crackers or a big wad of bubble gum, then say it real fast. If it comes out something like "loo-a-vul," you're on the right track. If you can't pronounce it like a native, however, it's best to stick to the acceptable "looey-ville." But whatever you do, never say "looisville."

Louisville, a little more than one hour west of Lexington on Interstate 64, is a great mix of history and modern big-city activities. Thousands of visitors from around the world flock to Louisville each May for the Kentucky Derby. The 15-day Kentucky Derby Festival is the country's largest civic celebration.

The West Main Street Historic, Cultural and Arts District, between the 500 and 900 blocks downtown, features the largest collection of

19th-century cast-iron storefronts outside of Soho in New York City. Tour maps are available at the Preservation Alliance, (502) 583-8622.

A leisurely walk on the Belvedere along the Ohio River will give you a great view of the city, as well as the world's tallest computerized floating fountain — Falls Fountain — in all its colorful splendor.

If you head across the river to Clarksville, Indiana, you can go back in time some 350 million years: Walk out onto the Falls of the Ohio where the largest exposed fossil bed in the world is located.

Contact the Louisville Convention & Visitors Bureau for more information. And for a thorough guide to this area, look in your favorite bookstore for our sister publication, *The Insiders' Guide to Greater Louisville*. Following are some of the great things to do during your daytrip to Louisville.

Churchill Downs
700 Central Ave., Louisville
• **(502) 636-4400**

Made famous by the first leg of thoroughbred racing's Triple Crown — the Kentucky Derby, run the first Saturday in May — Churchill Downs is also one of Louisville's historic landmarks. The Kentucky Derby has been run on this same course since 1875. Racing is scheduled here from the last week in April to the first week in July and from the end of October to the end of November. For more information, see our Horse Country chapter.

The Kentucky Derby Museum
700 Central Ave., Louisville
• **(502) 637-1111**

The highlight of this museum at Churchill Downs is a unique movie of an exciting Derby race that's projected on a 360-degree screeen in the shape of the track. It has all kinds of unusual images (such as surrounding viewers with the Derby winner's rose) and action shots. Upstairs in the museum are exhibits focusing on thoroughbreds: African Ameri-

cans' involvement in thoroughbred racing, interactive videos where you can pick the winners of a race, exhibits on pedigrees and confirmation, and even a chance to see how it feels to sit in the jockey's saddle. Admission is $6 for adults, $5 for seniors and $2 for children ages 5 to 12.

FYI

If no area code is given, it's a local call from Lexington-Fayette County. If an area code is given, whether it's 606 or 502, it's a long-distance call: dial 1, the area code and the number. See the How To Use This Book chapter for detailed information on calling.

Kentucky Center for the Arts
Main St. between Fifth and Sixth Sts., Louisville
• **(502) 562-0100**

Plays, music, dance — the Kentucky Center for the Arts has just about everything you'd want to experience in the arts. The center has three stages and a magnificent sculpture collection.

Prices vary according to performance. Tours can be arranged by appointment.

Kentucky Kingdom Amusement Park
937 Phillips Ln., Kentucky Fair and Exposition Center, Louisville
• **(502) 366-0033, (800) SCREAMS**

The fourth-largest wooden roller coaster in the world and the second-largest wave pool in the country are only two of the more than 60 rides, games and attractions at this Kentucky amusement park (see the Kidstuff chapter for more information). The park which is on the grounds of the Kentucky Fair and Exposition Center. The park is open from the first week in April until November 2, and different parts of the park open and close at different times, depending on the time of year. It's best to call the toll-free number before you go.

Admission is $27 for adults, $15 for senior citizens and children shorter that 54 inches. Admission is free for children younger than 3. There's a special $9.95 twilight charge if you go after 5 PM.

Louisville Slugger Tour/Hillerich & Bradsby Company
800 W. Main St., Louisville
• **(502) 585-5229, ext. 227**

Guided tours of Hillerich & Bradsby's baseball bat and golf clubs manufacturing plant —

the company also makes PowerBilt clubs — include a stop in a museum featuring a bat used by Babe Ruth and souvenir miniature bats.

The plant is open to the public Monday through Friday, with tours every 20 minutes, starting at 9 AM. The last tour is at 4 PM. Cost is $4 for adults and $3.50 for children.

Other places of interest you might want to check out while touring Louisville include the following.

Farmington
3033 Bardstown Rd., Louisville
• **(502) 452-9920**

Built by John and Lucy Speed in 1810 and designed by Thomas Jefferson, Farmington is a step back in history. Abraham Lincoln was among the famous visitors to the home.

Judge John Speed and his wife Lucy built Farmington in 1810 from plans given to them by amateur architect Thomas Jefferson as a wedding gift. The house is built in the Adam style that was popular around the Eastern seaboard cities at the time. Architectural details such as the fanlights between the front and back halls, and two octogonal rooms in the center of the house, are highlights. Farmington was first opened to the public in 1959 and was the city's first historic house museum. Visitors can enjoy a formal garden on the grounds, as well as a blacksmith shop, a stone springhouse and an orchard.

The site is open Monday through Saturday 10 AM to 4:30 and Sunday 1:30 PM until 4:30. Admission is $3 for adults, $1 for children younger than 16 and free for kids younger than 6.

Filson Club
1310 S. Third, Louisville
• **(502) 635-5083**

Filson Club is the museum of the historical society. It's named for Kentucky's first historian. There is an outstanding history and genealogy library on site. The museum has a collection of Kentucky artifacts. However, many people come just to see the historic Beaux Arts-style house where the Filson Club is located. Others come for its outstanding collection of paintings, all with a Kentucky connection. The museum is open free to the public Monday through Friday from 9 AM until 5 PM

and Saturday 9 AM to noon. There is a $2 admission charge to go into the library.

Hours are Monday through Friday from 8 AM until 5 PM.

Kentucky Art and Craft Gallery
609 W. Main St., Louisville
• **(502) 589-0102**

You'll find many examples of the rich craft tradition of this region at the gallery. Look for painted gourds, pottery, sculpture, jewelry and lots of folk art. Admission is free and it's open Monday through Saturday from 10 AM to 4 PM.

Locust Grove
561 Blankenbaker Ln., Louisville
• **(502) 897-9845**

Built in 1790, this beautiful Georgian home was the last residence of Louisville's founder, George Rogers Clark. The home is open Monday through Saturday from 10 AM to 4:30 PM and Sunday from 1:30 PM to 4:30 PM. Admission is $3, $2.50 for senior citizens.

Belle of Louisville
Fourth St. and River Rd.
• **(502) 574-2992**

After a short (and much-publicized) hiatus in 1998 from a valve problem which caused this grand old sternwheeler to "take on water," she's back in fine form in 1999, ready to shuttle passengers on the Mississippi River system.

The "Belle" is one of only six sternwheel steamboats operating in the U.S. today and, to top it all, she's one of the oldest (built in 1914) and most authentic.

This "grand dame" of the river runs public cruises throughout the summer and can be reserved for private functions during the winter months.

Cruises are offered Tuesday through Saturday from Memorial Day to Labor Day. Afternoon cruises run 2 to 4 PM, boarding at 1 PM. Sunset cruises on Tuesday and Thursday board at 6 PM and run 7 to 9 PM with live entertainment. There is also an adult dance night from 8:30 to 11:30 PM, boarding at 7:30 PM.

Admission is $12 for the dance cruise. For all other public cruises, tickets are $8 for adults, $7 for seniors, $4 for kids. Discounts are available for large groups.

The Star of Louisville
151 W. River Rd., Louisville
• **(800) 289-7245**

Enjoy buffet dining, live entertainment and dancing while cruising the Ohio River on this 130-foot ship. Lunch, dinner and moonlight cruises are offered Monday through Thursday at noon and 7 PM, Friday and Saturday at noon, 7:30 PM and 11:30 PM and Sunday at 1 and 7 PM. Prices range from $23.25 to $47.00.

Water Tower/Louisville Visual Art Association
River Rd. and Zorn Ave., Louisville
• **(502) 896-2146**

Travelling exhibits are showcased in the oldest water tower in America. This cast iron structure is a Louisville landmark. It's open free to the public Monday through Friday from 9 AM to 5 PM, Saturday 9 AM to 3 PM and Sunday noon to 4 PM.

www.insiders.com

See this and many other **Insiders' Guide®** destinations online.

Visit us today!

Antiques

If you love browsing through antiques shops, you can spend several days — weeks even — in Louisville's dozens of shops and malls. For a complete list call the Louisville and Jefferson County Convention and Visitors' Bureau at (800) 633-3384. In the meantime, here are a few good ones just to get you started.

Louisville Antique Mall
900 Goss Ave., Louisville
• **(502) 635-2852**

Located in an old cotton mill, this mall has 400 displays in 70,000 square feet, with everything from Victorian to rustic country furniture and accessories.

Swan Street Antique Mall
947 E. Breckinridge St., Louisville
• **(502) 584-6255**

Browse through 100 booths in 30,000 square feet of space. Collectibles and small antiques are the specialty, along with old guns, toys, art deco and '50s items.

Joe Ley Antiques Inc.
615 E. Market St., Louisville,
• **(502) 583-4014**

It's been called "a carnival, a museum, a treasure hunt, a trip through time three stories tall," which just about says it all. This place is a ball — with everything from old doors and stained-glass windows to carousel horses and crystal chandeliers. There's also plenty of furniture, old china, silver, toys and garden accessories.

Covington and Northern Kentucky

A trip to the Covington area of northern Kentucky will most likely fill up more than a day since it'll most likely include Cincinnati, one of Ohio's largest cities. Luckily, it's only about 70 miles from Lexington up Interstate 75, so you can plan to visit different areas on different daytrips.

You might want to plan a couple of your trips to coincide with a baseball or football game (Cincinnati is home to two major ball clubs, the Cincinnati Bengals and the Cincinnati Reds) or a major concert — Riverbend hosts numerous national music acts (perhaps best-known to all you Parrotheads are Jimmy Buffett's annual late-summer sell-out concerts). For more information about the Reds and Bengals, see our Big Blue Basketball and Other Spectator Sports chapter. For more information about Riverbend, see our Nightlife chapter.

You may want to plan a trip centered on the many beautiful and historic churches and cathedrals in Covington and Cincinnati, several of which are detailed below. You can go to the races at Turfway Park, or plan a whole day of shopping at Covington and Florence's many great malls and retail centers.

For the sake of brevity, only Covington area attractions are detailed here. For more information, contact the Northern Kentucky Convention and Visitors Bureau. To receive more information on Cincinnati activities and attractions, call the Cincinnati Visitor's Information at (800) 344-3445.

MainStrasse Village
Main St., Covington • (606) 491-0458

This five-block-long restored 19th-century German village houses more than 40 unique shops, restaurants and businesses between 5th and 7th streets. The renovated buildings that make up the village are connected by cobblestone walkways, giving the area old-world charm.

Two architectural highlights of the village are the Carroll Chimes Bell Tower, a German Gothic structure featuring a 43-bell carillon that plays hourly, and the Goose Girl Fountain, commissioned by the Northern Kentucky Convention and Visitors Bureau and constructed by noted Greek sculptor Eleftherios Karkadoulias.

MainStrasse Village is host to a number of festivals and special events throughout the year, including The World's Largest Outdoor Sale the third weekend in August and Oktoberfest held on the weekend following Labor Day.

Behringer-Crawford Museum
1600 Montague Ave., Covington
• (606) 491-4003

The Behringer-Crawford Museum features items illustrating the area's cultural and natural history. Displays cover a wide range of areas, from paleontology and wildlife to the arts. The museum is open Tuesday through Friday 10 AM to 5 PM and Saturday and Sunday 1 to 5 PM. To get there, take the Fifth Street Exit off I-75 to Montague Avenue in Devou Park.

Admission costs $3 for adults, $2 for children ages 3 to 18 and seniors.

Covington Landing
Madison Ave., Covington
• (606) 291-5410

One of the largest floating restaurant/entertainment centers on the nation's inland waterways, Covington Landing is an extravaganza of shopping, dining and recreation. It is located on the Ohio River next to the Roebling Suspension Bridge, the prototype for the Brooklyn Bridge in New York and one of the nation's first suspension bridges.

Covington Landing is open 10 AM to 2 AM, Monday through Saturday; call for Sunday hours. To get there, take the Fifth Street Exit off I-75.

Mimosa House
412 E. Second St., Covington
• (606) 261-9000

Historic Mimosa House, built in the mid-1850s, is the largest single-family home in the area. Its 22 rooms, with 14 fireplaces and the original gas lighting system, feature Rococo Revival furniture designed by Belter, Baudouine and Meeks. The house is open for tours Saturday and Sunday 1 to 6 PM, with Christmas tours December through mid-January on Saturday and Sunday, 1 to 8 PM. Admission (which includes a tour) is $4.

Cathedral Basilica of the Assumption
1140 Madison Ave., Covington
• (606) 431-2060

Modeled after the Notre Dame cathedral in Paris, France, Cathedral Basilica of the Assumption, completed in 1901, features a spectacular display of 82 stained-glass windows, including the largest stained-glass church window in the world.

The cathedral is open for self-guided tours Monday through Friday 8 AM until 4:30 PM and Saturdays and Sundays 8 AM to 6:30 PM. Guided tours are conducted at 2 PM on Sundays, June through August.

Monte Casino
Turkeyfoot Rd., Crestview Hills
• (606) 341-5800

Constructed of fieldstone from the area, this tiny chapel at Thomas More College is

---

INSIDERS' TIP

Watch for Kentucky Scenic Byway signs on country roads. They are always a clue that the road is an especially pretty drive.

said to be the smallest house of worship in the world. No more than four people can fit in at one time. It is free to the public and open from dawn to dusk every day. Take Interstate 275 to Turkeyfoot Road south. Monte Casino is in Cresview Hills.

Mother of God Church
119 W. Sixth St., Covington
• (606) 291-2288

Constructed around 1870, the Mother of God Church is an ecclesiastical art lover's dream come true. Among the treasures on display here are five large murals by Vatican artist Johann Schmitt, 200-foot twin Renaissance towers, stained glass and inlaid tile. You can visit by appointment.

Ashland and Eastern Kentucky

Ashland Area Convention and Visitors Bureau
728 Greenup Ave., Ashland
• (606) 329-1007, (800) 377-6249

Ashland, a steelmaking and petroleum-refining Ohio River town of about 25,000 people, is the largest city in Eastern Kentucky. With neighbors Huntington, West Virginia, and Ironton, Ohio, it forms a metropolitan Tri-State area with more than 300,000 people — and more than a few opportunities for recreation, sightseeing, shopping and entertainment. When you expand your quest into the surrounding Appalachian region, your opportunities multiply significantly. We have chosen to focus primarily on Ashland and Boyd County, including a few sites of interest in nearby Eastern Kentucky counties.

Ashland, named after the Lexington estate of famed statesman Henry Clay, is an easy and scenic two-hour drive from Lexington by I-64. Once you get into Boyd County, you have a trio of choices on how to enter Ashland. You can approach the city from the southwest by taking Exit 181 onto "old" U.S. Highway 60 (two lanes), then turning left when you hit the "new" U.S. 60 and driving on into Ashland — or, to skip the two-lane route segment, drive on up to Exit 185, get on U.S. 60 from there. Or you can come in from the southeast by staying on I-64 for six more miles until you hit Exit 191, which will put you on U.S. Highway 23 near the Ashland Inc. refinery. The latter approach will first take you through the small town of Catlettsburg, the county seat.

Although the surrounding areas of Boyd County are mostly rural and agricultural, Ashland itself is an industrial town. If you travel south from Ashland on U.S. 23, you'll soon

Photo: Kentucky Department of Parks

Federal Hill was completed in 1818.

find yourself deep in coal country. Kentucky is the nation's second-leading coal producer, after Wyoming, and much of the state's output is mined in the eastern Appalachian counties. The hard-working Ashland area has a strong sense of history that comes through in many of the region's attractions.

All attractions detailed below are in Ashland unless otherwise noted.

Ashland Area Art Gallery
1516 Winchester Ave., Ashland
• **(606) 329-1826**

Regional artists showcase their work at this downtown gallery with more than 2,000 square feet of display space, including an Artist's Market. Executive director Brenda Keithley heads the 18-member board, overseeing exhibits that change about every two months. Sometimes a single artist will be in the spotlight; other times it might be a collection of contemporary works by various artists, or even a juried show. Works on display are available for purchase. Media run the gamut from watercolor and oil paintings to sculpture, pottery and stained glass. A woodcarvers club meets in the gallery once a month, offering demonstrations and classes. Hours are 10 AM to 4 PM Monday through Saturday. Admission is free, though donations are appreciated.

Kentucky Highlands Museum
1620 Winchester Ave., Ashland
• **(606) 329-8888**

The Kentucky Highlands Museum, which opened in 1984, moved a few years ago from its original home in Ashland's Mayo Mansion. From its current location in another local landmark — the former site of the C.H. Parsons department store — it continues to offer, through its collection of artifacts and information, a tangible view of the region's history and culture. It occupies the first floor and mezzanine of the old store. The museum's most prized asset is its antique clothing collection, which dates from the 1800s and is valued at more than $400,000. This display changes every three months. Another treasure is part of the collection of the late Jean Thomas, "The Traipsin' Woman," an Ashland native who devoted her life to promoting folk music and Appalachian folklore.

The Country Music Highway exhibit is being developed in an ongoing process that is expected to take nearly a decade. It will eventually honor all of the singing stars whose names have been affixed to the sections of U.S. 23 where they had their origins. Naomi and Wynonna Judd were the first to be included in the exhibit, which, when completed, will also include native sons and daughters Billy Ray Cyrus, Patty Loveless, Tom T. Hall, Keith Whitley, Dwight Yoakam, Loretta Lynn, Crystal Gayle, Ricky Skaggs and Hylo Brown. (The Country Music Highway quickly links South Shore, north of Ashland in Greenup County, to Pike County in far Eastern Kentucky.)

A children's museum, focusing largely on the history of transportation in the area, is also an ongoing process. It now includes a tugboat pilothouse and will eventually include an airplane and a locomotive engine. Other exhibits include Adena Indian arrowheads, two replicas of American Indian villages, World War II memorabilia, early communications equipment and a Boy Scout collection.

The Kentucky Highlands Museum and its gift shop are open 10 AM to 4 PM Tuesday through Saturday. Group tours are welcome. Admission is $2 for adults, $1 for children and seniors.

Paramount Arts Center
1300 Winchester Ave., Ashland
• **(606) 324-3175**

When it first opened in 1931, the Paramount was one of the first places in the region to view "talking pictures." Now it is a quarter-century into its second life, as a performing arts center. The Paramount was reopened in 1972 and placed on the National Register of Historic Places in 1975. The renovation is ongoing, with improvements each year ranging from new seats to new carpet. The arts center, a nonprofit organization, has taken care to preserve its art deco roots: brass and aluminum fixtures, gold leafing, red velvet curtains between the lobby and theater. In 1996, artist and preservation specialist David Musselman was brought in to restore the classic commedia dell'arte murals decorating the walls to their original beauty. The most recent renovation, also in 1996, was the opening of the Marquee

Room, a concession and meeting area adjacent to theater.

The video for "Achy Breaky Heart," the song that catapulted local boy Billy Ray Cyrus to stardom, was filmed at the Paramount. In recent years, the center has been host to a wide range of performers, including Ray Charles, Tony Bennett, Ben Vereen, Trisha Yearwood, Ricky Skaggs, Steve Earle and comedian Gallagher. The acclaimed Troubadour Concert Series, which uses Lexington's Kentucky Theatre as its home base, brings many of the same acts to the Paramount. Dance and theater productions also visit.

The center, which offers theater tours and a gift shop, is open 9 AM through 4 PM Monday through Friday. Guided tours are available by appointment.

Central Park
17th St. and Central Ave., Ashland
• (606) 327-2046

Ashland's 47-acre Central Park can't compare in size with its New York City namesake, but it has something that the other one doesn't: several ancient Indian burial mounds that are said to date from the Adena period (800 B.C. to A.D. 800) A few years ago, city officials roped them off to put an end to a politically incorrect but innocent practice that generations of Ashland children had enjoyed: riding their bikes over the mounds. Biking's loss is historical awareness's gain. But there's much more to Central Park than just the mounds: tennis courts, softball and baseball diamonds, a volleyball court, assorted playgrounds and picnic areas, a concession stand, walking and jogging trails and a gazebo that is often used for concerts.

Ashland Historical Tour

Ashland is filled with elegant and historic homes, churches and businesses. You can see many of these on the Ashland Historical Tour, a 2-mile walk through the downtown area, including Central Park. Just pick up a self-guided tour map at the Ashland Area Convention and Visitors Bureau; or, if you prefer, you can arrange a guided tour through the bureau. The bureau is at 728 Greenup Avenue; phone numbers are (606) 329-1007 and (800) 377-6249.

Armco Park
U.S. 60 and Ky. Hwy. 716, Summit
• (606) 739-4134

Armco Park, a popular site for family reunions, picnics and other get-togethers, offers shelter houses, playgrounds and a picnic area. It is open from May through late fall. Call to reserve shelters for your event.

Irish Acres Antiques
24203 Jack's Fork, Rush
• (606) 928-8502

If you're familiar with Irish Acres Gallery of Antiques, near Lexington in Woodford County, then all you need to know is that this similarly named Boyd County shop is where the whole thing started. If you're not familiar with Irish Acres, ask someone who is.

You'll discover that the two-store, family-run business is worthy of its name, as it seemingly does have acres of antiques and collectibles.

The "Irish" part of the name comes from Bonnie and Arch Hannigan, the husband-and-wife team who opened the original shop in 1976. Their two daughters are also involved, helping to run both operations. (The Woodford County shop, which includes The Glitz restaurant, came along in 1987; for information on it, see the Shopping and Antiques chapter.) The Boyd County shop, which lies on a farm 12 miles south of the Cannonsburg exit of I-64, features 16,000 square feet of antiques in 26 showrooms.

Furniture displays are arranged according to styles including French, English and Early American, and there's also a "bargain barn." Irish Acres is open 10 AM to 5 PM Monday through Saturday.

Greenup Locks and Dam
off U.S. 23, Greenup

Have a leisurely lunch at a picnic shelter while watching an essential element of Ohio River shipping — the locks-and-dam system, which is essentially an elevator for watercraft. It allows boats to pass through from one level of water to another by raising or lowering the amount of water inside the lock, a rectangular concrete chamber. The process is fascinating, especially if you've never seen it. There's also a boat ramp for public use.

Camden Park
Route 60, Huntington, W. Va.
• (304) 429-4321

Compared with amusement megaparks like Paramount's Kings Island, Camden Park may not seem like much. It's a bit old-fashioned, yes, but it still packs a punch for this writer, who grew up eagerly awaiting the annual summer outing to the West Virginia park. It's a great way to spend a nostalgic but thrill-filled day with the family.

The original wooden roller coaster, the Big Dipper, is among the 25 rides for adults and children. There's also a looping coaster, a haunted house and various other rides that will take you up and down, around and around and, occasionally, inside out.

Admission is $1, but ride tickets are extra. Your best option is the $12.50 hand stamp, which allows you to ride all day. The summer season also features concerts by nationally known country artists.

Nearby State Parks

Greenbo Lake State Resort Park
Ky. Hwy. 1, Greenup • (606) 473-7324

This 3,300-acre park, 17 miles west of Ashland, is set in a wooded area that adds to the lake's scenic beauty. The 181-acre Greenbo Lake, built in 1955, is popular with pleasure boaters, swimmers and anglers, especially those seeking rainbow trout or channel catfish. Hikers can follow the 25-mile Michael Tygart Trail, which connects the park with the Jenny Wiley National Recreational Trail. The Jesse Stuart Lodge has a library and reading room with Stuart's works and personal mementos, as well as a fine restaurant. The park also offers a boat dock, launching ramp, campgrounds, miniature golf and picnic area with shelters.

Grayson Lake State Park
Ky. Hwy. 7, Grayson • (606) 474-9727

Grayson Lake, which lies in both Carter and Elliott counties, is a common fishing, boating and swimming destination for Eastern Kentuckians. The 1,500-acre lake was created by a 1968 impoundment of the Little Sandy River. A marina, picnic shelters, handicap-accessible nature

trail, campground with showers, beach and several launching ramps are among the features.

Carter Caves State Resort Park
Ky. 182, Olive Hill • (606) 286-4411

Like caves? Carter Caves State Resort Park's 1,350 acres, in nearby Carter County, contain more than 20 of them, many of which remain unchartered. Cave tours are available, or you can explore on your own (in some cases).

For more information on cave tours see our Parks and Recreation chapter. Even if you don't like dark, damp places, you can have fun playing golf or fishing. Accommodations include a 28-room lodge with pool, cottages and camping sites.

Jenny Wiley State Resort Park
39 Jenny Wiley Rd., Prestonsburg
• (606) 886-2711

This beautiful eastern Kentucky park offers a wealth of outdoor activities, including fishing, boating, golf, camping, hiking, swimming, softball, basketball and tennis. Discover a magnificent view from the top of a bluff accessible by sky lift. See a play performed in the acclaimed outdoor theater, one of the oldest outdoor summer musical theaters in the country. (For more information see our Arts chapter.) Other amenities include a picnic area and a convention center. The park, which also contains a historic one-room schoolhouse, is named in honor of Jenny Wiley, a Kentucky pioneer who was kidnapped by American Indians but escaped.

Annual Events

July

Summer Motion / Regattafest
Riverfront and Central Park, Ashland
• (800) 377-6249

The Ashland area celebrates Independence Day in a big way, with a festival that runs for several days. Music by nationally known and local country, rock and bluegrass artists; a boat race and other competitions; and other activities for children and adults literally keep things in motion. Hometown boy

Billy Ray Cyrus was grand marshal of the 1997 festivities.

September

Poage Landing Days
Downtown and Central Park, Ashland
• **(606) 377-6249**

Music, storytelling and arts and crafts are making this three-day event in mid-September an increasingly popular one. Poage Landing, or Poage Settlement, was the original name for Ashland, given to it by the Poage family from Virginia when they settled in the area in the 1780s.

Jesse Stuart Weekend
**Greenbo Lake State Resort Park,
Greenup • (606) 473-7324**

The Jesse Stuart Weekend honors the life and work of Jesse Stuart, author of *Taps for Private Tussie*, *The Thread that Runs So True*, *God's Oddling*, *The Beatinest Boy*, *A Penny's Worth of Character* and other works of fiction, nonfiction, and poetry for adults and children. Stuart, who was born in Greenup County and made his longtime home there, devoted much of his life to realistic writings that celebrated the Kentucky mountain region and its people. He has been called "The American Robert Burns."

November-December

Christmas in Ashland
Ashland is a bright and colorful place to spend the holidays, with several events and a ton of lights. **The Festival of Trees**, which runs for the last week or so of November at the Paramount Arts Center, features some of the most creative Christmas trees you'll ever see, designed and donated by local individuals and businesses; if you see one you like, you can make a bid on it. The annual **Christmas Parade**, held during Thanksgiving Week, is highlighted by local marching bands, an-

tique cars, clowns and a visit from Santa Claus. **Winter Wonderland of Lights**, which starts Thanksgiving week and runs through January 1, turns Central Park into a blinking, multicolored extravaganza of toy soldiers, skaters, elves, animals and much more. If you're an ice skater, you can also enjoy Central Park's outdoor rink, which opens in late November.

Restaurants

Alexander's at Ashland Plaza Hotel
1 Ashland Plaza, Ashland
• **(606) 329-0055**

Alexander's, in the Ashland Plaza Hotel at 15th an Winchester avenues, serves pasta, steak, seafood and homemade desserts, and the restaurant has a full bar. Try the Sunday brunch.

Bluegrass Grill
3505 Winchester Ave., Ashland
• **(606) 324-3923**

Remember "Happy Days"? That's the feeling you're likely to get when you visit the Bluegrass Grill, long an Ashland tradition, especially on summer nights when the young and young at heart "cruise" the parking lot to meet friends and make new ones. The food — burgers, fries and rings, shakes, fried chicken and terrific strawberry and coconut cream pies — is great, but that's just part of the appeal. You can eat inside, or make use of the old-fashioned carhop service. Hey, all that cruising is bound to make you hungry.

C.R. Thomas' Old Place Restaurant
1612 Greenup Ave., Ashland
• **(606) 325-8500**

This downtown restaurant, which has a sister in Barboursville, West Virginia, features steak, seafood, sandwiches, salads and appetizers, including excellent fried mushrooms.

INSIDERS' TIP

One of the best places to have breakfast — and rub elbows with thoroughbred trainers and jockeys — is at Keeneland's Track Kitchen.

The first circular horse racing track was laid at the William Whitley House in Lincoln County in 1785.

Columbia Steak House
1290 Montgomery Ave., Ashland
• (606) 329-1012

Like its counterparts in Lexington, Frankfort and Berea, this steakhouse has long been a favorite among beef lovers. The tenderloin special, marinated in garlic butter, and the Diego salad are sure to please. (See our Restaurants chapter.)

J J Restaurant
5260 13th St. (U.S. 60), Ashland
• (606) 325-3816

One down-home way to describe the fare served at this family-owned restaurant is "food that sticks to your ribs." If you grew up in the country, you know what we mean. Specialties include pan-fried pork chops, pan-fried chicken breast, liver and onions and brown beans with cornbread.

Bardstown

Bardstown-Nelson County Tourist Commission
501 E. Stephen Foster Ave., Bardstown
• (502) 348-4877, (800) 638-4877

Known as the "Bourbon Capital of the World" and home of My Old Kentucky Home, the state park which inspired the famous Stephen Foster song, Bardstown has a rich and colorful history.

Originally known as Salem, the area that is now Bardstown was formed by William Bard in the 1780s from a land grant of 1,000 acres issued by the Virginia General Assembly. Bardstown is the seat of Nelson County, formed in 1784 by the Virginia General Assembly as Kentucky's fourth county.

Bardstown is the site of the original Kentucky Court of Appeals, and it became a distillery center because its water has an abundance of lime, a necessary ingredient for making bourbon (see our Distilleries and Breweries chapter).

About an hour's drive southwest of Lexington on the Bluegrass Parkway, Bardstown is home to many historic sites, as well as the popular outdoor musical Stephen Foster — The Musical, featuring more than 50 songs by one of America's most beloved composers. See our Arts chapter for more information.

Bardstown's old houses and pretty downtown, with many antique and speciality shops, will make you want to stay. Some of its most famous attractions are described below.

Talbott Tavern
107 W. Stephen Foster Ave., Bardstown
• **(502) 348-3494**
America's oldest stagecoach stop and inn, Talbott Tavern has hosted some of the nation's most colorful historical figures, including Daniel Boone, Andrew Jackson, Jesse James, Abraham Lincoln and Gen. George Patton. You can't get a bucket of oats for your horse at the inn anymore, but you can still spend the night in one of the inn's spacious rooms. Talbott Tavern is open daily for lunch and dinner.

St. Joseph Proto-Cathedral
310 W. Stephen Foster Ave., Bardstown
• **(502) 348-3126**
Completed in 1816, St. Joseph's was the first Catholic cathedral west of the Alleghenies. It now contains a valuable collection of 17th-century European paintings. Guided tours are offered Monday through Friday from 9 AM until 5 PM, Saturday 9 AM to 3 PM and Sunday 1 to 5 PM. Admission is free.

My Old Kentucky Home State Park
501 E. Stephen Foster Ave., Bardstown
• **(502) 348-3502**
Made famous throughout the country by the Stephen Foster song immortalizing it, My Old Kentucky Home is a beautiful park surrounding the southern mansion, Federal Hill, which was the inspiration for the song. Federal Hill is open from 8:30 AM to 6:30 PM daily June through August, and 9 AM to 5 PM the rest of the year. The legendary play, Stephen Foster — The Musical is performed here.

Admission to the house is $4 for adults, $2 for kids and $3.50 per person for groups and senior citizens.

Wickland
U.S. Hwy. 62, Bardstown
• **(502) 348-5428**
The Smithsonian called this historic home, built in 1817, the most perfect example of Georgian architecture in the country. The interior is furnished with unusual antiques, and the double parlors with matching mirrors are a focal point.

It is open for tours by appointment. Admission is $4 for adults, $1.50 for kids and $2 per person for groups. It's a half-mile east of Court Square.

My Old Kentucky Dinner Train
602 N. Third St., Bardstown.
• **(502) 348-7300**
This unique dinner excursion allows you to enjoy an elegant four-course meal during a two-hour round trip run from Bardstown to Limestone Springs. The dinner train is made up of 1940s vintage railroad cars.

Excursions are available Tuesday through Saturday at noon and 5 PM. Lunch is $36.95; dinner is $59.95.

America's Miniature Soldier Museum
804 N. Third St., Bardstown
• **(502) 348-4879**
The kids won't believe it! This unusual museum displays more than 10,000 toy soldiers from around the world. It's open May through December, Tuesday through Saturday from 10 AM to 5 PM. Admission to the museum is

$2 for adults, $1 for kids and $1 per person for groups.

The Doll Cottage Museum
213 E. Stephen Foster Ave., Bardstown
• (502)348-8210

More than 700 dolls, from Barbie to G.I. Joe to Shirley Temple, are on display at the Doll Cottage. The museum is open daily in the summer from 10 AM to 5 PM. Winter hours vary. Call for information. Admission is $1.50 for adults and $1 for kids 12 and younger.

Danville and Perryville

Danville-Boyle County Tourist Commission
304 S. Fourth St., Danville
• (606) 236-7794

The site of one of the most desperate battles of the Civil War, the location of the filming of the epic motion picture *Raintree County* starring Elizabeth Taylor and the home of the Great American Brass Band Festival, the Danville/Perryville area offers a wide variety of daytrip activities to enjoy.

Your daytrip to Danville and Perryville, about 45 minutes southwest of Lexington (take U.S. 27 to Ky. 34), should definitely include a visit to historic Centre College, established in 1819. Its famous alumni include U.S. vice presidents Adlai Stevenson and John Breckinridge and U.S. Supreme Court justices John Marshall Harlan and Fred M. Vinson. The college is on W. Walnut Street.

Other areas of interest include the Perryville battle site, a 500-acre wildlife refuge on Battlefield Road, the Kentucky School for the Deaf (202 S. Second Street) and Pioneer Playhouse outdoor dinner theater (see our Arts chapter for more about Pioneer Playhouse).

Danville is the site of the framing of Kentucky's first constitution in 1792 and of the first post office west of the Alleghenies, which still stands today in Constitution Square. In fact, Constitu-

tion Square is probably a good spot to start your tour of the Danville/Perryville area.

All attractions detailed below are in Danville unless otherwise noted.

Constitution Square State Historic Site
105 E. Walnut St., Danville
• (606) 236-5089

Called the birthplace of Kentucky's statehood, 10 constitutional conventions took place here before the final Kentucky Constitution was finally drafted. Today, this historic site features the oldest original post office west of the Alleghenies and replicas of the meetinghouse, jail and courthouse that were around at the time of Kentucky's statehood. A park, gift shop and picnic areas are open year round, and a museum and art gallery are open April through October. These attractions are free and open daily 9 AM to 5 PM.

McDowell House & Apothecary Shop
125 S. Second St., Danville
• (606) 236-2804

Visit this turn-of-the-century Georgian-style home of Dr. Ephraim McDowell, the Kentucky surgeon who performed the first successful removal of an ovarian tumor in 1809. The apothecary shop with all its beautiful old medicine bottles is a real highlight. The site is open Monday through Saturday 10 AM to noon and 1 to 4 PM and Sunday 2 to 4 PM (closed Monday November through February). Admission to the McDowell House is $5 for adults, $2 for ages 13 through 21, $1 for those 12 and younger and $3 for ages 62 and older. Group rates are available for 10 or more.

Jacobs Hall
202 S. Second St., Danville
• (606) 236-5132

This 1855 Italianate building is home to the offices of the Kentucky School for the Deaf, the first state-supported school for the deaf in

---

INSIDERS' TIP

Fayette is one of three original Kentucky counties created in 1780, 12 years before Kentucky gained statehood.

Photo: James Archambeault, courtesy of the Lexington Convention and Visitors Bureau

You'll need a full day to explore the 2,700 acres at Shaker Village of Pleasant Hill.

the United States. The school was founded in 1823. The museum, free and open Monday through Friday 8 AM until 4:30 PM, has artifacts and photos of the school's history, as well as period furnishings on display.

Perryville Battlefield State Historic Site
Battlefield Rd., Perryville
• (606) 332-8631

On October 8, 1862, Kentucky's greatest Civil War battle was waged at Perryville. It was the South's last serious attempt to gain control of Kentucky. Today, this battle is reenacted annually on the weekend closest to the actual battle date. It is unique among many such reenact-

ments because it is staged on the actual site of the battle. This 100-acre park also features a Civil War museum open April through October, picnic shelter, playground and gift shop. It is open free throughout the year.

William Whitley House State Historic Site
U.S. Hwy.150, Crab Orchard
• (606) 355-2881

This beautifully preserved Flemish Bond brick house and its Colonial furnishings are well worth the drive, which is a little off the beaten path. Aside from its historic value as a 1780s home used as a refuge by Kentucky frontiersmen, the William Whitley House is perhaps

INSIDERS' TIP

Pack a lunch and find a scenic Bluegrass spot to have a tailgate picnic.

best known for its significance to American horse racing.

In 1785, Col. Whitley laid the country's first circular horse racing track here, and to defy the British he raced his horses counterclockwise around the track, setting a precedent for all future American racetracks.

The house is open from 9 AM to 5 PM daily from Memorial Day to Labor Day. A $3.50 admission fee is charged for adults, $2 for children. It's between Stanford and Crab Orchard.

Renfro Valley

Rockcastle Tourist Commission
U.S. Hwy. 25, Renfro Valley
• **(800) 252-6685**

A visit to "The Valley Where Time Stands Still" is indeed a trip back in time. Renfro Valley is home of the nationally famous Saturday Night Barn Dance, started by John Lair in 1939. Featuring such famous country musicians as Red Foley and Lily May Ledford and the Coon Creek Girls, the Barn Dance was broadcast on WGN from Chicago for many years. The "Sunday Morning Gatherin'," still being broadcast today, is the second-oldest radio broadcast in America. You can attend the "Gatherin'" Sunday mornings at 8:30.

Renfro Valley is about an hour south of Lexington on I-75, near Mount Vernon (Exit 62). This is more of a late day and evening trip, because you'll want to be sure to take in one of the great country-western music variety shows offered several evenings a week — the Barn Dance, the Gospel Jubilee and the Jamboree. Special shows, headliner concerts and festivals are also scheduled throughout the year. These shows feature some of the region's best performers, from singers and a left-handed fiddler to cloggers and comedians — "Bun" Wilson is a longtime Renfro Valley favorite, along with Old Joe Clark, Betty Lou York and Pete Stamper. The shows run a little longer than an hour, and they're worth every cent of the $12 admission for adults. Call (800) 765-SING for a schedule of show times or for more information.

The shows staged in the Old Barn are a unique treat: When the crowd really gets into the music, the wood plank floor vibrates with the stomping of hundreds of feet, and you feel like you truly are in an old-fashioned barn dance. The New Barn, on the other hand, is a grand auditorium with a state-of-the-art sound system. Shows in both barns are perfect for the entire family. The casual, down-home atmosphere, with lots of folks joining in singing, tapping their feet and clapping with the music, is accommodating to fidgety kids.

You'll probably want to start your trip to Renfro Valley in the afternoon so you can visit Renfro Village, a replica of an old-time small Southern town. It features gift and candy shops and craft stores displaying and selling the fine handiwork of many local artists and craftspeople. All this activity is bound to work up an appetite, and there are two restaurants in the village.

There are several motels in the area, as well as a new campground behind the parking lot. Call the Rockcastle Tourist Commission for more information on lodging.

Shaker Village of Pleasant Hill

3501 Lexington Rd., Harrodsburg
• **(606) 734-5411**

Comprising 33 19th-century buildings on 2,700 acres of beautiful Bluegrass farmland, Pleasant Hill is the largest of all restored Shaker villages. This quaint, peaceful settlement 7 miles east of Harrodsburg and 25 miles southwest of Lexington on U.S. Highway 60 was established in 1805 by a group of the United Society of Believers in Christ's Second Coming. This religious sect was better known by the name "Shakers" because of the energetic dances that played a big role in their religious ceremonies.

The Shakers were the largest and most well-known of the communal societies in 19th-century America. The Pleasant Hill settlement was an attempt to establish a utopic community whose residents could pursue their religious beliefs and simple lifestyle in peace. An interesting aspect of Shaker life was that they believed in celibacy. Men and women worked, worshipped and slept in segregated quarters, and the only way they added to the population of the village was by adopting children into the community.

Practical and innovative, the Shakers are still known today for their economy, beauty and simplicity of style. They invented many time-saving devices, including the flat broom. The Shakers believed in equality of race and sex and freedom from prejudice.

By the middle of the 1800s, the Pleasant Hill community had grown to some 500 residents and 4,000 acres. Nationally, there were some 6,000 Shakers in the eastern United States, from Maine to Kentucky.

Due partially to the fact that the Shakers practiced celibacy, the society dwindled during the last part of the 19th century, and the village at Pleasant Hill closed in 1910. The village sat unused for 50 years until restoration efforts began in 1961.

Today the Pleasant Hill community is open for tours throughout the year. While it takes about two hours to complete your self-guided tour of the village, to take in the whole village, from the working furniture, weaving, candlemaking and broom-making studios to the riverboat excursion on the sternwheeler Dixie Belle, you should set aside the better part of a day.

Shaker Village of Pleasant Hill is open year round, except Christmas Eve and Christmas Day, 9 AM to 6 PM April 1 through October 31. While the village is open throughout the rest of the year, some of the exhibition buildings are closed November through March. From November through March, some buildings are open from 9 AM to 5 PM. After 5 PM, you can still drive through. Admission to the village is $9.50 for adults, $5 for ages 12 through 17 and $3 for ages 6 through 11. Families are admitted for $25. For the combination riverboat excursion and village admission, the cost is $13.50 for adults, $7 or youth and $4 for kids. Families pay $35. Kids younger than 6 are admitted free with parents.

Below you'll find some detailed information about your stay at this beautiful and interesting piece of Kentucky.

Group Reservations

With reservations, groups of 20 or more receive a special rate for entrance to the village. For group reservation information call (800) 734-5611 Monday through Friday 9 AM to 5 PM.

Riverboat Excursions

A picturesque and relaxing addition to your visit to Pleasant Hill is a one-hour Kentucky River excursion on the sternwheeler Dixie Belle. Excursions leave from Shaker Landing on the Kentucky River at 10 AM, noon, 2, 4 and 6 PM April 28 through October 31. Special cruises are offered in the spring and fall, and the Dixie Belle is also available for charters.

All departure times are subject to weather conditions, special cruises and previous charters. Rates for the cruise only (excluding admission to the village) are $6 for adults, $4 for ages 12 through 17 and $3 for kids ages 6 through 11.

Dining

Traditional Kentucky country cuisine is served at three meals daily in the Trustee's Office by servers in Shaker costumes. Reservations are necessary for lunch and dinner, and there is a no-tipping policy. A children's menu is available.

Call (800) 734-5611 for reservations.

Lodging

Lodging on the grounds of Pleasant Hill is available in 15 restored buildings. For reservations, call (800) 734-5611 Monday through Friday 8 AM to 6 PM and Saturday 8 AM to 4 PM.

Rates are $56 to $115 for a single, $66 to $125 double, January through March, and kids younger than 17 stay free with parents. Rates drop about $10 January 1 through March 31. A house is also available for $150 to $190 for two people.

Winter Activities

Shaker Village offers several special activities and packages during the winter months (November to spring). Call the general reservation number for a calender of special events.

Winter Weekend Packages include lodging Friday and Saturday night, five meals, in-depth guided tours, seminars and special music presentations.

Winter Weekday Packages are available

Sunday through Thursday night and include one night's lodging, dinner and breakfast.

Big South Fork

• **(615) 879-3625**

Big South Fork Recreation Area and National Park Service covers a big chunk of southeast Kentucky and north-central Tennessee. The recreation area traces the waters of Big South Fork, which is a branch of the river, for more than 80 miles and covers some 125,000 acres of protected wildlands on the Cumberland Plateau.

With an area this immense, you could spend weeks enjoying the dozens of outdoor recreational activities available — from swimming, canoeing and whitewater rafting to hunting, hiking and horseback riding.

We suggest you decide on one or two activities you'd most enjoy, then pick the most favorable spots to do them. The Kentucky areas of Big South Fork Recreation Area are mostly within two to three hours' drive from Lexington. The Tennessee portions of the park can be a six- to seven-hour drive, depending on where you're headed.

We've described several activities you might enjoy.

Big South Fork Scenic Railway
U.S. Hwy. 27 N., Stearns
• **(800) 462-5664**

Hopping on the Big South Fork Scenic Railway will give you an exciting trip to another time and another culture as you "ride the rails" to the Blue Heron Outdoor Historical Museum of coal-mining and logging life in the isolated regions of the Big South Fork river basin.

This unique museum includes frame structures you can visit; inside, you'll hear taped oral histories of families who lived in the immediate area where the museum now sits. Other displays describe the conditions of men who worked underground coal mines and other varied aspects of mountain life.

The train ride itself is a beautiful three-hour trip through some of eastern Kentucky's lushest forests and mountain areas, so you'll want to be sure to bring your camera. The museum has a gift shop and snack bar.

Train fare is $10 for adults, $9.50 for seniors and $5 for kids younger than 12; kids 3 and younger are admitted free. The scenic railway operates May through October, with two daily trips on Saturday and Sunday and one trip Wednesday through Friday. Call for more detailed departure information.

Hiking

Big South Fork has more than 150 miles of marked hiking trails, ranging in length from a mile to 50 miles, suitable for day hikes or backpacking trips.

Hunting and Fishing

Both hunting and fishing are allowed within the recreation area and are subject to all state and federal regulations and licensing procedures. Because the recreation area covers parts of two states, make sure you hold valid licenses for each state in which you want to hunt or fish.

Camping

Primitive camping is allowed throughout most of the backcountry, except within marked safety zones, directly on the trail or within 200 feet of paved roads and developed areas.

The Blue Heron Campground on Kentucky's side of the Big South Fork has 50 improved sites with water and a restroom/shower house. Call (606) 376-3787 for more information.

Water Sports

Sheltowee Trace Outfitters
Ky. Hwy. 90, Whitley City
• **(800) 541-RAFT**

Call Sheltowee Trace Outfitters if you're interested in rafting, beginner and family canoe trips or whitewater raft or canoe trips in the Big South Fork area. Rates for these trips range from $20 to $65 per person. Reservations are strongly suggested.

Lexington has a variety
of neighborhoods to suit
your lifestyle, aesthetic
preferences and budget.

Neighborhoods and Real Estate

Once you've found a place to live in Lexington, there's a little game you should try. (If you haven't found a place, bear with us, we'll discuss your situation presently.) First you need to find a longtime resident. It could be one of your new neighbors, or someone you meet at church or the grocery. Who the person is doesn't matter as much as whether he or she has lived in Lexington long enough to remember the "good ol' days." Casually steer the conversation toward the subject of your new neighborhood. Then wait to find out whether your new friend says, "I remember when it used to be out in the boonies."

Unless you live downtown, there's a fairly good chance that you will get such a response. ("Boonies" is a Kentucky colloquialism meaning "where Daniel Boone once walked." Just kidding!) In recent years Lexington has grown quickly, spreading subdivisions and shopping centers into the once-virgin countryside. And the entire metropolitan area has grown with it.

Understandably, many of us get concerned about the pace of growth. The Bluegrass is a place widely known for its countryside, not for its subdivisions and shopping centers, although some of those are very nice. The challenge is finding a balance: nice home, nice stores and restaurants, nice view. In recent years, the powers-that-be have allocated millions of dollars in federal, state and local money to maintain scenic and historic sites, including the picturesque horse farms so closely associated with the state. In 1993, a $1 million grant was announced to help preserve what Gov. Brereton Jones referred to as "the rich cultural heritage" of the Lexington area.

Which brings us back to the underlying theme of this book: Lexington is a great place to live. The fact that you're reading this book would seem to indicate that you 1) live in Lexington, 2) are thinking about living in Lexington or 3) are visiting Lexington.

Lexington has a variety of neighborhoods to suit your lifestyle, aesthetic preferences and budget. We have established, "old money" areas with elegant 19th-century homes on shady, tree-lined streets; luxurious condominiums with a wealth of amenities; "starter home" neighborhoods filled with young families; a number of well-landscaped new "executive" communities characterized by large estate homes; and more.

Obviously, we can't come close to mentioning every Lexington neighborhood. What we have tried to do is come up with a cross-section that is representative in terms of location, style, age and price of home. In trying to come up with a representative sampling, we have sought the opinions of local Realtors and other experts.

According to data from the Lexington-Bluegrass Association of Realtors, in 1998, the average price for a three bedroom house sold in Lexington was $106,127.

In looking for a home, you may come across the phrase "urban service area." Fayette County's urban service area is, in a nutshell, land that is developable, meaning it has access to sanitary sewers. The concept of the urban service area was designed to help preserve horse farms and other rural areas. Other factors that enter into the equation are topography, watersheds and such. If you really want to know the minute details, you can contact the Division of Planning at 258-3160.

When the city and county governments merged in 1974, those areas that received certain urban services such as sewer service, garbage collection, street sweeping and streetlights kept those services. Fayette County neighborhoods are taxed at varying rates depending on the level of services they receive. All new developments are required to be connected to sanitary sewers and to have streetlights and city garbage collection. Some older areas do not have all these services; for example, residents of certain neighborhoods have to contract with a private company for garbage collection.

To reach a different level of service, which means an increase in the tax on the district, a neighborhood must go through a petition process and obtain a certain percentage of signatures. Realtors should be able to provide service information about any neighborhoods you're considering, or you can call Public Works at 258-3400.

Lexington has nearly 150 active neighborhood associations. If you visit the Division of Planning at the Lexington-Fayette Urban County Government building, on the 10th floor at 200 E. Main Street, you can pick up a directory of neighborhood associations as well as a 34-by-42-inch neighborhood associations map. Call them at 258-3160 first, however, to make sure these items are still available.

Numerous houses and other buildings in Lexington's downtown areas fall under the auspices of local zoning laws designed to protect the area's historic districts. Properties in historic zones require approval by a design review board before any exterior changes can be made. For more information, call the His-

toric Preservation Office at 258-3265. The Blue Grass Trust for Historic Preservation is a society with a similar goal: preserving and protecting the area's cultural history and monuments. Buildings designated by the trust are distinguished by the "BGT" plaques that grace their fronts.

FYI

If no area code is given, it's a local call from Lexington-Fayette County. If an area code is given, whether it's 606 or 502, it's a long-distance call: dial 1, the area code and the number. See the How To Use This Book chapter for detailed information on calling.

Neighborhoods

A cautionary note: If you want a house sitting on a big lot, you'll have to either buy an older house or pay a lot of money. Because land today is costing developers more, they are compensating by putting more houses on the same amount of space.

Of course, buying an older house isn't necessarily a bad thing, by any means. Greater Lexington has thousands of older houses that are elegant, fascinating and beautiful. Tradition can be a wonderful thing.

During most parts of the year — with the general exception of the Thanksgiving-to-New-Year's season when available real estate agents and properties can be hard to find — you can find whatever type of property you want. Buy now before the interest rates go up. We'd love to have you as a neighbor.

Downtown and Central Lexington

Gratz Park

Gratz Park is tiny, with only about 15 residences. But this downtown neighborhood might well contain more history per square foot than any other area in Lexington. Its development dates to 1793, when it became home to the forerunner of Transylvania University; it

---

INSIDERS' TIP

A good way to find a house in the country is to drive the back roads. Some people prefer selling their property themselves instead of listing with a Realtor.

became Gratz Park in 1884. In 1955 it became the first organized historic district in Lexington when citizens who were determined to save the Hunt-Morgan House banded together and formed a society that later grew into the Blue Grass Trust for Historic Preservation.

The park is named for Benjamin Gratz, a lawyer, hemp manufacturer and Transy trustee who played an important role in Lexington's 19th-century development. Throughout the 1800s some of the city's most influential doctors, lawyers, educators, publishers, generals and statesmen lived in this area of just larger than an acre. Today it retains much of its historic flavor with the Hunt-Morgan House, the Bodley-Bullock House, the Carnegie Center for Literacy and Learning (former site of the Lexington Public Library) and other landmarks. The wide variety of architectural styles — including neoclassical, Greek Revival, Italianate, Queen Anne and Federal — makes it possible for students of architecture to trace the development of the city.

In the mid-'80s, residents of homes around the park sold bricks for 50¢ each and raised $28,000 to put brick walkways in the park. Strangely enough, in recent years there has been a fair amount of turnover, which has been a source of some consternation to those who have lived in Gratz Park for 30 years or more. Because the park represents many periods of architecture, the prices of these homes, when available, may vary from $250,000 or less to more than $750,000. Obviously, not everyone will get a chance to buy one. If you ever do, you'll truly own a piece of Lexington's history.

Chevy Chase

We're not talking about the comedian or the D.C. suburb. Lexington's Chevy Chase is its own entity, a prestigious one that seems to evoke something of a mystique. It's a large but relatively stable neighborhood — even considering the fair amount of rental property lying within its borders — that was started in the 1940s. Before that, it was farmland, but it was close enough to town that the Ringling Brothers and Barnum & Bailey Circus would pitch a tent in the area each year to put on the greatest show on earth for Lexingtonians.

Today Chevy Chase is blessed with access to many restaurants and any number of specialty shops, as well as to downtown and the University of Kentucky. Tates Creek Road, Euclid Avenue/Fontaine Road, Chinoe Road and Cooper Drive are the approximate boundaries. The residential areas reflect a diversity of styles, from charming brick and fieldstone houses to four-plexes. Always middle- to upper-middle-class, in the last decade or so Chevy Chase has steadily acquired more of a yuppie sheen.

Difficult as the neighborhood's character might be to define, Chevy Chasers are determined to preserve it. The neighborhood association showed it could unite with some clout when it challenged the developers of Chevy Chase Plaza on Euclid Avenue, claiming the planned nine-story restaurant, retail and office development would irrevocably damage the area's character. Ultimately the plaza was built at five stories, with the upper ones recessed from the road. Everyone seems to be at least reasonably happy with the result.

Ashland Park

The Ashland Park neighborhood was developed around the turn of the century from the original Woodland Horse Farm, which was then on the outskirts of town. With houses built between 1880 and 1910, it has been placed on the National Register of Historic Places. The neighborhood provides a splendid array of Colonial Revival, Tudor Revival, American Foursquare and Victorian residential architecture among large trees, green lawns and medians. These houses, which generally start at $150,000, have traditionally provided homes for community business and government leaders, professionals and educators from the University of Kentucky.

The nearby Ashland neighborhood, which includes the estate of Henry Clay, was designed by the architectural firm of Frederick Law Olmsted, which also designed New York's Central Park and many Louisville parks in the early 20th century. Both of these neighborhoods, while conducive to gracious and quiet residential living, are close to downtown, UK, major transportation routes and neighborhood specialty shops and services.

West and Southwest Lexington

Gardenside and Garden Springs

These two neighborhoods, once on the edge of town, now have the convenience of being near (within easy walking distance for most people) Turfland Mall, two major groceries and various shops and neighborhood parks. The elementary, middle and high schools that serve Gardenside and Garden Springs are widely considered to be among the best in town.

This author must admit a positive bias toward these two neighborhoods, because he has lived in one or the other since moving to Lexington in 1983.

Gardenside, developed in the early to middle '50s, contains a variety of ranch, story-and-a-half and two-story homes, mostly brick or stone, selling for $65,000 to $100,000 and more. Unlike most newer neighborhoods, these homes are distinguished by comfortably sized lots. Garden Springs, about 15 years younger than neighboring Gardenside, was built on land that was once part of a horse farm. Its streets are named after trees or flowering plants — Azalea, Larkspur, Honeysuckle and Pinebloom, for example. Houses average around $80,000. Both of these neighborhoods are home to primarily middle-class families with lots of children, dogs and cats.

Firebrook

Firebrook, a little more than a mile south of Man o' War Boulevard off Harrodsburg Road, not far from the Jessamine County line, is one of Lexington's newest and most prestigious neighborhoods. Although the neighborhood is only about three years old, its history can be traced back to its original land grant in 1793. An elegant mansion and guest house from those early days are still standing.

At present there are about 150 occupied homes in Firebrook; 400 are projected. These houses, all custom-built by some of the top developers in the city, range from $170,000 to $300,000, with most falling in the $200,000 to $300,000 range. Amenities include tennis courts, a swimming pool and cabana, a jogging trail, clubhouse with fitness room and kitchen, and two stocked lakes.

Harrods Hill

Development of Harrods Hill began in the late '70s, and the neighborhood now comprises a variety of ranch, two-story, brick traditional and contemporary houses, priced from $100,000 to more than $200,000. It is also well-landscaped with nice lots. But Harrods Hill, while containing some beautiful homes, may be even more notable for its "neighborly" aspects. The neighborhood association is active and publishes an annual directory to foster interaction among its residents. There is a city park with a soccer field, playground and basketball court; residents can also become members of a neighborhood recreational complex that has tennis courts, a pool and sundeck.

The population of the neighborhood is diverse, with retired people, singles, executives and families with teens and younger children. A nearby shopping center, with several restaurants, a large grocery and various other shops, has added greatly to the convenience of Harrods Hill.

Stonewall Community

Stonewall Community, built in about four phases in the '60s, is a quiet, largely working-class neighborhood characterized by huge lots (many of which are a half-acre or larger), a variety of styles and a lot of shared neighborhood pride. The primary developer was Stoll

---

INSIDERS' TIP

When the Chevy Chase area was still farmland, the circus often set up there.

Meyers, which also developed the Dixie subdivision in northeast Lexington's Eastland Parkway neighborhood (see subsequent listing). Houses range from $90,000 to $175,000.

Stonewall, like many of Lexington's well-established neighborhoods, is a place filled with retirees who have spent most of their lives in the same house. But it's also a place where many children grow up, leave and then return to live with their own families. The pride that residents take in their neighborhood is evident in the $10,000 they raised, spurred by a promise of matching funds from the city, to develop a nature park on a 7-acre wooded area that was left undeveloped. Stonewallers will also tell you it's a great walking neighborhood.

Dogwood Trace, Copperfield and Clemens Heights

These three contiguous neighborhoods near the Jessamine County line are primarily professional, upper-middle-class. Dogwood Trace, built in the mid-'80s, consists mainly of two-story houses, with a few larger one-stories, selling for $130,000 to $220,000. A large field separates Dogwood Trace from nearby Copperfield, a similar development that is several years younger and a little less expensive. Clemens Heights, which also lies partially between Dogwood Trace and Copperfield, is distinguished by attractive split-foyer homes and Mark Twain-inspired street names.

South Lexington

Belleau Wood and Walden Grove

Many families who have been moved to Lexington because of corporate transfers settle initially in the Belleau Wood/Walden Grove area, which is composed mainly of modern-style homes ranging from $65,000 to $110,000 in Belleau Wood and up to $150,000 in Walden Grove, which lies on the opposite side of Wilson Downing Road. The relocation aspect has lent a certain "transient" flavor to the neighborhood, as many people live here for three to five years before moving to another part of town. The population consists largely of young professionals in their early 30s to mid-40s, many with young children. Prime selling points of the neighborhood are its relatively affordable homes, its convenience to Fayette Mall and Tates Creek Centre, a park with a city-run recreation program and a neighborhood association that holds an annual Easter egg hunt and family picnic.

Hartland

Hartland, a fully planned, all-residential community, is 500 acres of single-family homes (about 1,000 in all) ranging from $150,000 to more than $500,000. It is characterized by beautifully landscaped boulevards, decorative streetlights and grand entryways.

A private membership amenity package provides access to a junior Olympic-size swimming pool, six tennis courts and a clubhouse building. Two areas within Hartland, the estate and executive areas, are contained within the main sections and offer varying levels of additional amenities.

North and Northwest Lexington

There's a fairly widespread perception that all the good places to live are on the south side of Lexington. Boy, does this ever tee northsiders off! They point out, correctly, that there's simply more available land on the south side for new developments. Then they add that not that much old real estate is available because "people in this area don't move . . . so if you want to buy a classy old house on the north end, you may have to wait for someone to die." Talk to several longtime residents of the north side, and you're likely to encounter a rather fierce sense of pride in what this part of Lexington has to offer.

Meadowthorpe

Meadowthorpe, a subdivision planned in 1949 on property owned by distillery owner James E. Pepper, is an old-fashioned neighborhood filled with traditional homes and plenty of history. For example, the land once

contained an airport known as Halley Field; Charles Lindbergh landed here in 1928 and stayed in the "old mansion" nearby. Today there are about 500 single-family homes in Meadowthorpe, with the average house priced at $80,000 to $87,000. These homes don't often come on the market, however, because people are inclined to stay there. Many residents have lived in their homes for 30 to 40 years, and in recent years numbers of young people who grew up in the neighborhood are moving back to raise their families.

Elkhorn Park and Deepwood

These neighborhoods, which were "county" before the merger in 1974, lie on opposite sides of North Broadway. Elkhorn Park is a traditional neighborhood that was developed slowly around the middle of the century; as such, it exhibits much individuality. Houses, if you can find an available one, generally range from $80,000 to $135,000. Mature trees line the streets, and the area has six triangular traffic islands. In 1993 the neighborhood got a city grant to beautify the islands and went about the task with vigor. Deepwood is smaller, more elite and more expensive. Both are among that category of neighborhoods where young people return to raise their families. And two fine new groceries in the vicinity — a Randall's and a Kroger — have made things even better.

East Lexington

Eastland Parkway

Eastland Parkway is a road that leads northeast from New Circle Road toward I-75, then makes a U-turn and heads back southwest until it hits Winchester Road. Eastland Parkway is also a neighborhood that comprises two subdivisions, Dixie and Eastland, where development began 30 to 35 years ago. Eastland Parkway, the road, is the main feeder street for the neighborhood. Dixie came first; though a few families bought lots and then had homes built on them, most of the homes were already built, then put up for sale under the slogan "Dixie in '60."

Most of the residences are brick or partly brick single-family. There is a mix of people, from young professionals to retirees, and there is a range of homes and prices suitable for first-time buyers on up. The neighborhood also contains duplexes and apartment complexes.

The Eastland subdivision, which has some larger and higher-priced homes, is split from Dixie by a little creek. It was developed by Stoll Meyers, the company that did Stonewall Community (see previous listing). Eastland was built when IBM was expanding rapidly, and many IBM people bought homes here. Prices in this diverse neighborhood range from $60,000 up to much more for the finer, custom-built homes.

Idle Hour

Idle Hour is bounded by Richmond Road, New Circle Road, a small industrial warehousing area and the Idle Hour Country Club. Lexington Mall and an assortment of Richmond Road restaurants are within spitting distance. Most of the streets are named for saints: St. Margaret, St. Ann, Sts. Michael and Mathilda and so on. It's a largely middle-class neighborhood built during the '50s — one of the city's last big new neighborhoods before Eastland Parkway came along — and it's aging gracefully. Most of the houses are ranches or Cape Cods of brick or fieldstone, and they generally sell for between $60,000 and $80,000.

Andover

Andover Golf & Country Club is a focal point of this fast-growing, upscale subdivision, which was started around 1990. Todds Road divides the golf course (there's an access tunnel beneath the road) and splits the neighborhood into two sections: Andover Hills and Andover Forest. Both sections have a healthy supply of doctors, lawyers and other professionals. Most of the 400 or so homes, many of which line the golf course, are custom-built, two-story, brick traditional homes with prices ranging as high as $500,000. Exceptions are Andover Park, a new area within Andover Hills built by Cutter Homes with houses starting around $120,000, and Golf Villas, a small section of about 30 condominiums occupied primarily by retirees.

New Construction

Meanwhile, Lexington continues to grow, with new developments springing up so fast that any attempt to list the latest ones would probably be outdated by the time the book came out. If you're looking for a brand-new home, contact your real estate agent — or just take a leisurely drive around Lexington and its outlying areas — and you're likely to find something that suits your needs.

Real Estate Agents

Real estate agents are seemingly everywhere, in case you haven't noticed. But that fact shouldn't keep you from looking for one. Although there are plenty of agents out there, not all of them are right for you. So you should take steps to ensure that you and your agent are a good match. Start by asking someone you know and trust for a referral.

If you're coming from another area and you have a home to sell in that particular area, then you probably have a real estate agent there. Find out if that agent has a contact with any companies in this area. Realtors do a lot of networking at national conventions, handing out cards and saying things like, "If you ever have anybody coming this way, call us."

The first step in a Realtor search is to make a phone contact, talk to the person and try to get a feel for whether you would like to work with him or her. Give your impressions to your Realtor. "We often get calls from Realtors in other towns saying, 'Jane and John are moving to Lexington,'" said Carolyn Edwards, a RE/MAX Creative associate who is a past president of the Lexington-Bluegrass Association of Realtors. "I give them a call immediately and tell them: 'We got this information from your Realtor there. Can I send you a packet of what I can do for you, or a homes magazine or corporation relocation packet?'"

Regardless of your impression of your first contact, it's a good idea to interview at least two or three other Realtors from different companies. Ultimately, you need to choose whoever makes you feel most comfortable. "This is the largest investment you're going to make," Edwards said. "You need to be represented. You need someone you feel comfortable with, someone you can share your innermost thoughts with, someone you can tell, 'Hey, you're way off track. This isn't what we want at all.'"

In a similar vein, if you are the seller, you should keep in mind that you are selling what very well may be your most prized possession. So you want someone who is going to work hard to market your property, someone who will stay in touch with you and keep you informed of any progress.

In general, the real estate firms listed in this chapter are the ones with the biggest market shares. Keep in mind, howovor, that bigger doesn't necessarily mean better. You have specific needs, and only you can accurately determine who can best fulfill those needs. There are numerous one- and two-person firms in the area, and you may well find someone at one of those companies who does the job for you. On the other hand, there is often a clear cause-and-effect relationship between those agents and companies that are most successful and the level of service they provide. Those listed here have developed good reputations over the years. If you'd like information about other companies in the area, call the Lexington Board of Realtors at 276-3503.

Rector-Hayden Realtors
2100 Nicholasville Rd. • 276-4811, (800) 228-9025
260 Crossfield Dr., Versailles • 873-1299
118 E. Main St., Georgetown • 278-0005

With 100 full-time sales associates, locally owned Rector-Hayden is the Lexington area's No. 1 real estate company. The firm, which has been serving the Bluegrass since 1969, provides services in all areas of residential real estate for Greater Lexington and surrounding areas such as Lawrenceburg, Cynthiana and Owenton. Through The Relocation Center, a specialized department within the company, Rector-Hayden helps make relocation less of a hassle for corporations as well as for transferring employees and their families.

Paul Semonin Realtors
3358 Tates Creek Rd. • 269-7331
3580 Lyon Dr. • 224-0707
Semonin Hotline • 224-4663,
(800) 548-1650 relocation division

Louisville-based Paul Semonin Realtors, the largest real estate company in Kentucky, has more than 100 agents serving the Bluegrass area from its Lexington office. The company offers both residential and commercial properties.

The "Semonin Home Show," a half-hour paid advertisement that airs each Sunday at 11:30 AM on WLEX (channel 18), features up to 40 homes for sale.

RE/MAX All Star Realty
2 Paragon Centre • 224-7711, (800) 859-8788 relocation
RE/MAX Creative Realty
230 Lexington Green Circle, Suite 100 • 273-7653, (800) 860-7468 relocation

Lexington has two full-service RE/MAX franchises dealing in residential, farm and commercial properties. The older, Creative, has some of Lexington's top producers and a large number of certified relocation professionals among its 40-plus associates. Broker/owner T.L. Wise has been in business in Lexington for 20 years. RE/MAX All Star Realty, which opened in October 1992, now has 16 associates. In addition to residential properties, RE/MAX offers buyer representation, property management, executive leases, help in securing optimum financing, new construction, historical properties and help in securing optimum leasing.

Turf Town Properties Inc.
800 East High Street • 268-4663

Turf Town Properties maintains a high profile despite its size — three partners and about 20 associate agents. This locally owned company, established in 1978, provides a full range of services, with residential properties ranging from $40,000 starter homes to fine Bluegrass

Photo: James Archambeault, courtesy of the Lexington Convention and Visitors Bureau

Lexington's wide neighborhood streets and rural roads are
great for long bike rides or leisurely strolls.

estates. Its agents are known for their experience, market knowledge and high production. Turf Town is also a member of RELO relocation service.

Century 21 Dampier Real Estate
1910 Harrodsburg Rd. • 278-2322, (800) 442-8909

Century 21 Dampier Real Estate is a full-service company founded in 1978. It provides expert relocation services for both incoming and outgoing residents. The company has 45 agents and deals in residential, farm and commercial properties and investments. Century 21 Dampier Real Estate also has a property management department and its own auction company.

Smith Realty Group
Tates Creek Centre, 4071 Tates Creek Rd., Ste. 101 • 271-2000
134 E. Main St., Georgetown • 863-1733

With two Bluegrass offices and more than 30 associates, Smith Realty serves the entire Greater Lexington area. Since Doug Smith founded the agency in 1971, it has grown into a full-service company. Services include sale of residential, farm, commercial and multi-family properties; a relocation program; property management and maintenance; auctions; and new construction. Smith works out of the Georgetown office; Carol Bryant is the managing broker for Lexington.

Prudential A.S. de Movellan Real Estate
620 Perimeter Dr. • 266-0451, (800) 928-0451

Prudential A.S. de Movellan, founded in 1967, has been a Prudential franchise since 1989. The Prudential affiliation gives the agency the ability to enter 5,000 markets all over the United States as well as in Canada and Europe. The agency, which has 45 full-time associates, deals in residential, farm and commercial properties and also has a strong relocation department for incoming corporate transferees.

Justice Real Estate
518 E. Main St. • 255-3657, (800) 455-5580

Coldwell Banker Justice Real Estate
518 E. Main St. • 255-6600, (800) 455-5580

Bill Justice, a veteran of the Lexington real estate market, founded his own agency in 1980. Today the company has two divisions. The residential division, Coldwell Banker Justice Real Estate, is part of the country's largest real estate franchise. The farm division, Justice Real Estate, specializes in horse farms and other rural properties. According to Justice, this division has sold more farm property than any other company in the region in the last decade.

Realty World — Mays & Associates Inc.
296 Southland Dr. • 278-7501

Realty World's Lexington franchise is a medium-size, primarily residential company that has been in business since 1984. The 25 associates' commitment to quality rather than quantity is reflected in an annual list-to-sale ratio that has exceeded 90 percent since 1990. Bonnie Mays, a native Kentuckian and University of Kentucky graduate, is the principal broker.

Kay Ledbetter & Associates
3138 Custer Dr. • 273-2825

This small company, which maintains an average of about 10 agents, specializes in horse farms and estates. Kay Ledbetter, who has been involved in the sale of a number of prominent horse farms, is the exclusive Kentucky member of the Estates Club and Club Immobilier, which produces magazines that are distributed nationally and internationally. These memberships extend Ledbetter & Associates' coverage to Europe, South America, the Far East and Canada. The company also handles residential and commercial properties.

Peacock Realty Group
116 S. Keeneland Dr., Ste. 1, Richmond • (606) 623-7554

Peacock Realty has served Madison County for more than 10 years and has experience in single-family residential marketing, construction, subdivision development and commercial property sales. Broker-owner Mark Peacock has been in the business for more than 12 years and holds two of the real estate industry's highest educational designations. He and his staff are also equipped to provide assistance in surrounding counties.

Temporary Housing

StudioPLUS
2750 Gribbin Dr. • 266-4800
3575 Tates Creek Rd. • 271-6160

Studio Plus leases new, furnished efficiency apartments with flexible terms. Rates run from $39 to $59 a night, depending on the length of stay. Amenities include all utilities, free TV, microwave, pool, exercise room and laundry facility. The Gribbin Drive apartments have 60 units; Tates Creek has 72.

Extended Stay America
2650 Wilhite Drive • 278-9600

Lexington's link in the Extended Stay America chain offers 126 efficiency rooms — a dozen with two twin-size beds, the rest with the standard queen-size bed. Rooms include recliner; nine-channel satellite TV with remote; kitchenette with two full-size burners, full-size refrigerator-freezer, microwave, dishware, glassware and utensils for two people; and bathroom. The guest laundry facility has four washers and six dryers. Rates for one person are $39 a night and $199 a week. An extra person is $5 to $10 more a night.

Hotels

Several Lexington hotels offer executive suites with short and extended terms available for corporate relocations and other temporary housing needs. Hotels with executive suites include the Campbell House, 255-4281, 1375 Harrodsburg Road; Courtyard by Marriott, 253-4646, 775 Newtown Court; and Hilton Suites of Lexington Green, 271-4000, 3195 Nicholasville Road. (See our Hotels and Motels chapter.)

Apartment Complexes and Condominiums

There are several criteria to consider when

searching for an apartment or condominium to rent. The weight you lend to each one depends upon your personal preferences, lifestyle and budget. For some people, price will be the dominant factor. Others might choose a property based on factors such as style, amenities, location, convenience or security. Most complexes have laundry facilities and an outdoor pool. Among the other amenities available are indoor pools, tennis and volleyball courts, whirlpools or saunas, fireplaces, washer and dryer connections, individual alarm systems, exercise and weight rooms, garages or covered parking and clubhouses for private parties. Some properties even have restaurants and bars on the premises.

At some complexes, the renter pays all utilities. Other properties include all or most of the utility charges in the flat monthly rate. If you hate paying bills, it may be worth your trouble to find a place where everything is included. All prices listed in this chapter are from 1997 and are subject to change.

We have selected a cross-section of properties from the many available in Lexington. It may seem as if we have focused more on the south end than the north, but that's simply because more property tends to be available on the south end. If you need additional help, call the property managers at the numbers listed below, pick up one of the free guides available all over town or call one of the location and referral services (see below). Only you know which characteristics matter most to you. It may seem a cliche to say Lexington has something for everyone, but it's essentially true. Although, in general, most properties maintain a low vacancy rate, with a little persistence you can find what you're looking for.

Biscayne Apartments (north)
150 Northland Dr. • 254-4502

These secluded apartments off North Broadway range from $345 for one bedroom to $395 to $425 for two bedrooms, including all utilities except electric. Washer and dryer hookups are available in the two-bedroom floor plans. The complex has a pool and laundry facilities.

Brandywine Apartments (south)
1550 Trent Blvd. • 272-7226

Prices range from $449 to $469 for one bedroom to $570 to $600 for two bedrooms at this attractive complex featuring an elegant clubhouse and pools with sun decks. Many apartments come with fireplaces.

Breckinridge Court (south)
420 Redding Rd. • 271-1655

Rent is $435 to $525 for one bedroom (six styles available) and $590 to $625 for two at this apartment complex with fireplaces, vaulted ceilings and private patios and balconies. Breckinridge Court also has a pool, hot tub, tennis courts and volleyball.

Cloisters on the Green (south)
3501 Pimlico Pkwy. • 272-4561

These spacious apartments back up to Tates Creek Golf Course, and some have views of the course. The complex also has two outdoor pools, a lighted tennis court, volleyball, basketball and a clubhouse. One bedrooms go for $465 to $490, two bedrooms for $550 to $640 and three bedrooms for $785 to $825.

The Gate House (east)
1825 Liberty Rd. • 252-4489

All utilities are included with rental, which start at $399 for one bedroom and $499 for two. Apartments include large walk-in closets. A laundry facility and 24-hour maintenance are available. The heated indoor pool is surrounded by tropical plants.

The Greenhouse (south)
3543 Tates Creek Rd. • 272-7686

One-bedroom apartments start at $550 plus electric, and two bedrooms started at $750

INSIDERS' TIP

Some of the prettiest front yard gardens can be seen at the bungalow-style houses on Richmond and Victory avenues off East Main Street.

"Postlethwait's Phoenix":
A Memorable Two Centuries at One Corner

Call it Postlethwait's Phoenix. From tavern to hotel to (at least twice) smoking ruins and back to hotel and finally to its current incarnation as a public library, high-rise apartment building and park — the corner where John Postlethwait once served libations to thirsty travelers has played a significant role in Lexington history.

John Postlethwait's Tavern became a popular watering hole almost instantly when it opened in 1797 on the southeast corner of today's Main and Limestone streets. In its first year, it witnessed the organization of Kentucky's first Jockey Club. (The American Jockey Club, a national, nonprofit group dedicated to the betterment of thoroughbred racing, was founded nearly a century later, in 1894). The site grew into a 38-room inn popular with stagecoach travelers. Visitors included several U.S. Presidents: Monroe, Jackson, Grant, Arthur, Eisenhower and Kennedy, as well as Mexican Gen. Santa Anna.

The Phoenix in one of its previous incarnations.

Fire destroyed the building in 1820, but it was rebuilt, and in 1833 (possibly after a second fire) it was renamed the Phoenix Hotel in honor of the mythical Greek bird that burned itself every 500 years and then was reborn from its ashes. In just 59 years, however, this Phoenix again burned. The final Phoenix Hotel was built in 1914 and remained open until 1974. It reopened under new ownership in 1975 before closing for what proved to be the last time in April 1977.

During its peak years, the Phoenix earned a national reputation for its outstanding food, drinks and service. It played host to grand balls, political rallies and other gala events. Later it became known for its pool room, where some of the best players in the country gathered during the spring meet at Keeneland. Toby Kavanaugh taught the game of pool to Walter Tevis, who went on to write *The Hustler* and *The Color of Money*, both novels were turned into hit movies. Kavanaugh, who was murdered in 1994, spoke of Tevis and the Phoenix during a 1993 interview: "In the flyleaf of my copy of *The Hustler*, he [Tevis] wrote, 'Many thanks for a profitably misspent youth.' ... He and I liked to slip off and go down to the Phoenix Hotel poolroom and play pool instead of being in class. ... The hustlers came through and played too. During the Keeneland meets, especially in the spring, they all came here from Hot Springs. The Derby weekend was the hustlers' big weekend; there was a lot of loose money." Kavanaugh added: "Back during the Depression, the poolroom was the only thing that turned a profit in the whole Phoenix. The rooms and the bar and the dining room and everything were losing money, but the poolroom was making money." The Phoenix's 1977 closing was followed by years of talk about a possible renovation, but it never happened.

The city razed the building in 1982. Today the site is home to the main branch of the Lexington Public Library as well as Park Plaza Apartments and a small park. The $9.4 million library, completed in April 1989, is a visually arresting postmodern structure made largely of granite and glass. Its five stories contain more than 110,000 square feet, with an impressive atrium extending from the first-floor lobby to the top of the building. The library also houses a theater, a changing art gallery, a Kentucky Room with extensive books and files of state history, numerous computers and conference rooms. The park, built in 1985, was initially a temporary measure to camouflage the ugly pit left by the destruction of the hotel. For five years it existed with the fairly accurate but unimaginative name of Central Park. But public support grew for a name that would reflect the site's history: In May 1990 it was rededicated as Phoenix Park.

Today the park is the site of the Lexington-Fayette County Vietnam Veterans Memorial, a three-panel black granite slab with names engraved in gold. The memorial sits on an "island" landscaped with rocks and trees and surrounded on three sides by a tiered pool with waterfalls, fountains and two concrete bridges. Near the front of the park, facing Main Street, two flags — U.S. and Kentucky — mark a plaque honoring veterans of World War II. A memorial to slain peace officers is also planned. With picnic tables, seven trees ringed by chairs and a popular deli on the ground floor of the apartment complex, the park is an attractive place for downtown workers to meet for lunch. The library, of course, brings additional visitors. Occasionally bands set up and play in front of the Vietnam memorial. In other words, there's still plenty of action at this corner. Wonder what John Postlethwait would think?

---

plus electric. This attractive complex overlooks a well-stocked fishing lake and features two lighted tennis courts, covered parking, exercise room and large pool with sun deck. Apartments come with washer and dryer as well as private garden patio-entry.

The Heritage Apartments I (southeast)
2150 Richmond Rd. • 266-4011

These roomy apartments, minutes from UK and downtown, start at $399 for one bedroom, $459 for two and $609 for three. Small pets

are permitted. Spacious closets and a large swimming pool are among the amenities.

Jamestown Apartments (southeast)
2200 Richmond Rd. • 266-0777

Jamestown features large two-bedroom, townhome-design apartments with 1½ bathrooms. Amenities include ceiling fans, private patios, a swimming pool, picnic area, volleyball court, horseshoe pit and a free video library. Pets are welcome. Rent starts at $541 plus electric.

Kirklevington Hills (south)
3050 Kirklevington Dr. • 273-1717

Kirklevington Hills' one-bedroom apartments and two-bedroom townhomes feature oversized sun decks. Other amenities include a barbecue pit, swimming pool, clubhouse with wide-screen TV, free video library and 24-hour laundry facilities. Rental starts at $480 for one bedroom and $710 for two-bedroom townhomes, which come with washer and dryer hookups. Small pets are welcome.

Kirklevington North (south)
857 Malabu Dr. • 269-4302

One-bedroom apartments as well as two- and three-bedroom townhouses, all with private patios or balconies, are available at Kirklevington North. The complex has two pools and an exercise room. Prices start at $470 for one bedroom, $660 for two and $820 for three. All utilities are paid. Pets are welcome.

Lake Shore Apartments (southeast)
209 Lake Shore Dr. • 266-0801

Lake Shore Apartments has spacious one- and two-bedroom accommodations with prices starting at $420 and $550, respectively. The complex has a swimming pool and five laundries. Features include fireplaces, garages and hardwood floors. Pets are welcome.

The Landings (southeast)
2414 Richmond Road • 268-4334

These apartments with a peaceful lakeside setting are just minutes from downtown. They have ceiling fans, private patios or balconies, washer and dryer connections and generous closet space. On the grounds you'll find a swimming pool, tennis court and sand volleyball. Swimming, fishing and boating are available on the lake, and there's a neighborhood golf course and park. Prices range from $509 for one bedroom and one bath to $809 for three bedrooms and two baths.

Merrick Place (south)
3380 Tates Creek Rd. • 266-0714

These spacious one- to three-bedroom apartments and townhouses with fireplaces share grounds with the classy Merrick Inn restaurant. Prices range from $485 to $1,275 at the complex, which has two swimming pools and lighted tennis courts. Residents who sign a new one-year lease receive a free membership to nearby Lexington Tennis Club.

Park Place Apartments (south)
4030 Tates Creek Rd. • 273-7464

Luxuries abound at Park Place, located on 28 landscaped acres at the corner of Tates Creek Road and Man o' War Boulevard. One-bedroom apartments start at $719 and 1,098 square feet; two bedrooms start at $919 and 1,450 square feet. Downstairs apartments feature screened-in porches and 9-foot ceilings. Upstairs you'll find cathedral ceilings and covered balconies. All apartments have marble, wood-burning fireplaces, marble baths, utility rooms, wallpaper, washer and dryer hookups and alarm systems. Some have Jacuzzis. An extended cable-TV package is just $15 a month. Other amenities include a swimming pool with outdoor Jacuzzi, dry sauna and tanning bed, lighted tennis courts, racquetball courts, fitness center and garages.

Park Plaza Apartments (downtown)
120 E. Main St. • 252-5559

This convenient downtown location by the Central Library offers a range of options, from efficiencies to penthouses. The price range is: efficiencies $465 to $585; one-bedroom apartments $560 to $720; and two bedrooms $680 to $925. All utilities and basic cable are provided, along with washer and dryer connections. The health club includes sauna, indoor pool, spa and fitness center. There's a rooftop sun deck, and covered parking is available. Meeting rooms are available for residents, there's a doorperson to greet you 24 hours a day, and the ground floor also houses the Park Plaza Deli.

Patchen Place Apartments (southeast)
200 Patchen Dr. • 269-4913

Attractive natural landscaping immediately distinguishes these townhouses and garden apartments behind Patchen Village. Fireplaces, ceiling fans and patio or balcony are among the features. The property includes a clubhouse, swimming pool, laundry facilities and lighted tennis courts. Heat is included in the rent, which ranges from $519 for a one-bed-

Photo: Ken Colebank

Henry Clay's former estate is located in the Ashland neighborhood.

room townhouse to $789 for a three-bedroom garden apartment.

The Racquet Club (south)
3900 Crosby Dr. • 271-2582

The Racquet Club proudly touts its "exclusive country-club atmosphere" with restaurant and bar, racquetball and volleyball, indoor and outdoor pools, indoor Jacuzzi, marble fireplaces and fitness center. Rent ranges from $475 to $615 for one bedroom and $700 to $800 for two. Washer and dryer connections are provided.

Saddlebrook Apartments (southeast)
151 Todds Rd. • 266-1191

One-bedroom apartments start at $402; two-bedroom $443; and three-bedroom $567. Apartments include ceiling fans and miniblinds. The facilities include two pools, tennis and volleyball courts and a weight room.

Shillito Park Apartments (south)
3500 Beaver Place Rd. • 223-9891

Fireplaces, balconies or screened patios, large walk-in closets, ceiling fans and a variety of outdoor athletic opportunities are available here for prices starting at $510 for one bedroom and $625 for two. Shillito Park, which has a pool, baseball fields, basketball and tennis courts, soccer fields, volleyball courts, jogging trail and picnic shelters, adjoins the complex.

Stoney Brooke Apartments (south)
175 N. Mount Tabor Rd. • 268-0962

Stoney Brooke Apartments, available with one or two bedrooms, feature wood-burning fireplaces in some units, built-in microwaves and reserved covered parking. You can also make use of heated indoor and outdoor swimming pools, lighted tennis courts, a fitness center that offers free step-aerobics classes, a Jacuzzi and sauna and a clubhouse. Prices start at $515 for one bedroom and $600 for two bedrooms.

Stoney Falls (south)
2020 Armstrong Mill Rd. • 273-7500

Stoney Falls, at Man o' War Boulevard and Armstrong Mill, has spacious one-bedroom apartments priced from $455 to $495 and two-bedroom apartments from $545 to $600. Amenities include private patios or balconies,

Lexington is more than a great place to visit. It's a great place to live.

washer and dryer hookups, ceiling fans, fitness center, pool with deck, lighted tennis courts, wood-burning fireplaces and clubhouse. Some apartments have vaulted ceilings.

Tates Creek Village (south)
3051 Kirklevington Dr. • 272-3481

All utilities are paid at Tates Creek Village, where apartments have generous closets, washer and dryer connections, and oversized patios and balconies. On-site amenities include 24-hour exercise room, saunas and laundry, two tennis courts, sand volleyball, two swimming pools and free tanning facilities. The clubhouse has a fireplace, billiards and wide-screen TV, and there's a free video library. Rent ranges from $538 for one bedroom to $958 for a townhouse with three bedrooms and 2½ baths.

Turfland Apartments (southwest)
2070 Garden Springs Dr. • 278-6056

A one-bedroom is $415, two bedrooms $500, including utilities, with an indoor pool open year round as well as an outdoor pool.

West Chase Apartments
1346 Village Dr. • 231-8112

West Chase, a landscaped courtyard community just minutes from the University of Kentucky campus and Historic Keeneland racetrack, features spacious two-bedroom apartments with abundant closets, ceiling fans and mini blinds. All utilities are included in the rent price. Amenities include free video library, pool, playground and laundry facilities in each building. Pets are welcome.

Rental Assistance

These location and referral services are free to the users. The companies are paid out of the advertising budgets of the property owners.

Lexington Residential & Apartment Referral Service Inc.
155 Prosperous Place, Ste. 2-B • 263-3740

This company, a member of the Lexington Apartment Association, the National Apartment Association and the Greater Lexington Chamber of Commerce, offers same-day referrals and corporate relocation among its services. Housing choices include furnished and unfurnished apartments, houses, condominiums, duplexes and four-plexes, townhouses, studios and efficiencies.

Double A Referral Service
• 271-0701

Double A, owned an operated by Amy Copas, offers exclusive prearranged discounts at area communities, relocation specialists, corporate housing moving advice and more.

Bluegrass Apartment Connection
• 278-3733

More than 40 properties are available through Dan Chapman, a licensed real estate agent who specializes in apartments.

Lexington is responding to the relatively new population of seniors through a variety of activities, work and volunteer programs, healthcare services and social-service programs targeted specifically at Lexingtonians older than 55.

Retirement

As the number of people in the 55-and-older category grows daily, Lexington is working hard to meet the needs and wishes of this expanding segment of our population. New challenges and opportunities are being created to keep older adults a viable part of the Lexington community.

As one elderly Lexingtonian said of the retirement community where he lives, "It's fascinating to observe the entirely new social structure that is developing where large groups of retired and older people are living, working and socializing together."

Lexington is responding to this relatively new population through a variety of activities, work and volunteer programs, healthcare services and social-service programs targeted specifically at Lexingtonians older than 55. Education and special interest classes and workshops are offered through the Elderhostel Program and the Donovan Scholars Program at the University of Kentucky. Recreational activities, trips, classes and volunteer opportunities are provided by a number of agencies and organizations, ranging from the Lexington Senior Citizens Center to the American Red Cross. This means that older adults have opportunities to do things they might have wanted to do when they were younger, but never had the time or opportunity. There is everything from line dancing classes to fiction writing workshops to art classes, drama groups and piano lessons. There are bridge groups out there just looking for a fourth hand. These days, older really is better!

But Lexington programs are not limited to services provided to or for older adults. This is by no means a segment of the Lexington community that needs to be "taken care of." Retirement does not mean an end to one's effectual contribution to society. Many Lexington organizations and programs focus on what older adults can do for Lexington. The Service Corps of Retired Executives (SCORE), for in-stance, works through the Small Business Administration to use the expertise of retired business people to help local people starting or operating small businesses. There are also programs that encourage local businesses to hire retired and older people.

What is listed in this chapter is an overview of services and programs for older and retired Lexingtonians, plus suggestions for finding other resources. Areas of focus include programs and organizations for older adults, services (medical/nutritional, advocacy and government assistance) and residences (retirement communities and apartments). You will also find a section dealing with education, job placement and volunteer opportunities.

Programs and Organizations

Senior Centers

Bell House Senior Citizens Center
545 Sayre Ave. • 233-0986

The Division of Parks and Recreation operates this senior citizens activity center in Bell Mansion. The wide range of cultural, recreational and social activities offers something for everyone. Activities include ceramics, oil painting, crafts, aerobics, bowling, square dancing, piano lessons, water exercise, trimnastics, bingo, Card Day, and day and overnight trips.

The center, located near a bus line, is open 9 AM to 5 PM and is handicapped accessible. Programs are open to anyone 60 years old or older, and a lifetime membership costs only $2!

You can get more information on two other senior citizen activities centers through the Bell House. These are the Lafayette Center, Lafayette Christian Church, 1836 Clays Mill

Rd.; and the Connie Griffith Manor and Ballard Place, 540 W. Second St. Both of these centers offer activities and trips. Contact Bell House or Lexington Senior Citizens Center for information.

Lexington Senior Citizens Center
1530 Nicholasville Rd. • 278-6072

This is by far the most important place seniors need to know about, not only because it's one of the most cheerful, upbeat places with all kinds of creative things going on, but also because the facility serves as a clearinghouse for information on services for older adults. Among the services offered are information, referral, recreational, social and some health services to any Fayette County resident over 60 years old. The center operates Monday through Friday 8 AM to 5 PM. Senior citizens groups can schedule meeting space during the day, and the center is available in the evenings and on weekends for rental. There's also an adult day-care program.

The Division of Parks and Recreation runs a recreation and education program at the center, which includes activities such as exercise, day trips, arts and crafts, square dancing, bridge and area history classes. Two free publications, available at the Senior Citizens Center, include information on dozens of services, activities and programs: the *Parks and Recreation Fun Guide*, and *Information for Older Adults* published by the Lexington-Fayette Urban County Government mayor's office and Central Baptist Hospital.

The following programs are in the center (but not necessarily part of the center).

• **Bluegrass Community Services**, also known as the Elder Nutrition Program, provides daily noon meals and nutritional education for older people, as well as transportation

FYI

If no area code is given, it's a local call from Lexington-Fayette County. If an area code is given, whether it's 606 or 502, it's a long-distance call: dial 1, the area code and the number. See the How To Use This Book chapter for detailed information on calling.

to and from the Nutrition Center and limited essential trips, such as grocery shopping. Family-style meals are served Monday through Friday at three Lexington locations — the Senior Citizens Center; Black and Williams Cultural Center, 498 Georgetown Street; Dunbar Center, 545 N. Upper Street. Call 277-6141 for more information.

• **Bluegrass Long-term Care Ombudsman Program**, 278-6072, ext. 322, is staffed by folks who can answer questions about the quality of care and information about nursing homes, as well as working to solve problems through ombudsmen in local nursing homes.

• **Retired Senior Volunteer Program**, 277-1100, is for people 55 and older who want to volunteer their time and abilities to help other Central Kentuckians. Transportation is provided to RSVP volunteers to and from the location where they are offering their services and they are covered by insurance at no cost.

• **Meals on Wheels** provides a hot noon meal, breakfast cereal, milk, juice and a supper snack to homebound people in Fayette County. Meals are delivered between 11:30 AM to 12:30 PM Monday through Friday. Alternative meals are available for those on special diets. There is a weekly sliding scale cost for the meals, and the maximum cost per week is $18 or $19, or $21.25 for special diets. Call 276-5391 Monday through Friday 8:30 AM to 12:30 PM for more information.

Manchester Center
1026 Manchester St. • 255-1047

The center's activities are open to those 55 and older, or disabled without need of special care other than assistance with mobility, at no cost (fees are charged only for special events and field trips). The center operates

---

INSIDERS' TIP

Adults 65 and older can further their education through the University of Kentucky's free Donovan Scholars Program.

Tuesday through Friday 10 AM to 2 PM, and transportation is available for folks living in any area within 4 miles of the Manchester Center.

Adult Day Care Centers

Center for Creative Living
1530 Nicholasville Rd. • 278-6072

This center offers social activities, medical care, counseling and therapy for about 30 people each day. To be eligible, a person must be a Fayette County resident, 60 or older, and must have a need for mental, physical or social health care during the day. The cost is on a sliding scale and there may be a waiting list.

Central Adult Day Center
219 E. Short St. • 254-5300

For people over 60 who need assistance with daily living activities, Central Adult Day Center provides mentally and physically stimulating activities and a hot lunch Monday through Friday. People of any age who have memory disorders are also accepted into this program. Fees are based on a sliding scale based on income.

Caretenders
2432 Regency Rd. • 278-1958

This personal care facility recently started a day-care program which includes day trips, a hair salon, a light breakfast and a hot lunch, social activities, transportation to outside appointments, and also transportation to and from the center for seniors who need help with daily living activities. It's open Monday through Saturday. Cost depends on services used.

Helping Hand
460 E. Main St. • 252-6282

As part of the Alzheimer's Association, Helping Hand offers respite care for people with Alzheimer's Disease and other nontreatable memory disorders. The program features activities specifically planned to stimulate people with memory disorders. A highlight is that each participant is paired with a trained volunteer who provides one-to-one companionship for several hours each week. An in-home respite program is also available. It operates in the Second Presbyterian Church Monday through Saturday.

Groups

American Association of Retired Persons (AARP)
2265 Stone Garden Ln. • 223-0676

The Lexington AARP chapter meets once a month at the Senior Citizens Center, 1530 Nicholasville Rd. Nationally, AARP is a lobbying organization to influence legislation dealing with issues of specific concern to retired people and senior citizens. Anyone older than

Photo: Norman Drake

Fertile land has provided Kentucky with its best-known exports: horses, burley tobacco and bourbon whiskey.

50 can join, and annual dues are $8 national and $5 local.

Bluegrass Retired Teachers Association
271 Burke Rd. • 252-7872

This is part of a state and national organization of retired educators. Members meet monthly and participate in group activities. Members are also eligible for such benefits as insurance, pharmaceutical, travel and educational programs. Local dues are $5 per year, state dues are $15 per year, and national dues are $5 per year.

Eldercraftsmen
Black and Williams Center,
498 Georgetown St. • 252-1288

Open 10 AM to 2 PM Monday through Thursday, the Eldercraftsmen program schedules a variety of activities for senior citizens, from crafts and ceramics to special interest courses, line dancing and "fun days." Anyone 55 or older is eligible to join, and the fee is $1 a month.

Golden K Kiwanis Clubs
540 Merrimac Dr. • 223-7918
580 Greenfield Dr. • 273-2231

There are two local chapters of this national community service organization, which is open to people of retirement age. Anyone is eligible to join, and there are annual and program dues, depending on the club.

Service Corps of Retired Executives (SCORE)
Lexington Civic Center, 410 W. Vine St.
• 231-9902

Members of this organization volunteer their time and expertise in the business field by advising and helping people running or starting a small business in the area. Sponsored by the Small Business Administration, SCORE is open to any retired executive. There is no cost to join, and the office is open Monday through Friday 9 AM to noon.

Discount Programs

Lexington's older adults are eligible for a number of special discounts to everything from performances by local school children to taxi and bus rides. Following are some of the discounted and free programs available. In addition to these, most local attractions and arts organizations offer senior citizen discounts of 10 percent to 50 percent off regular admission.

Gold Cards for Seniors
• 281-0108

This card entitles those 65 and older to free admission to programs of the Fayette County Public Schools.

Older Kentuckians Discount Card
Lexington Senior Citizens Center
• Contact: outreach worker 278-6072

If you are a Kentucky resident age 60 or older or disabled, you are eligible for this card, which entitles you to special discounts from participating merchants and other organizations.

Transportation

LexTran
• 253-4636

If you are 65 or older, you can get a special ID card from the Lexington Transit Authority public bus system that entitles you to 50 percent to 60 percent discount off bus and trolley rides. There are also special transportation options available for seniors and those with permanent disabilities. See the Getting Around chapter for more detailed information on these services.

INSIDERS' TIP

A good way to exercise and socialize at the same time is to join the Lexington Striders walking club, which meets at Turfland Mall on Harrodsburg Road. To sign up or for information, call 278-6072.

Photo: Berea College Crafts

There's no dearth of arts and crafts opportunities in the area.

Taxis
• 233-4890

United Transportation Inc., which operates the Lexington taxi services, offers coupon booklets for 20 percent discounts off taxi rides for senior citizens.

Services

Better Business Bureau of Central & Eastern Kentucky Inc.
410 W. Vine St., Ste. 280 • 259-1008, (800) 866-6668

While this group serves the population as a whole, older residents are often targeted by unscrupulous sales and service people. If you're looking for information on the reliability of local and national businesses or other consumer topics, the Better Business Bureau is the place to turn. Office hours are 8:30 AM to 5 PM and phone hours are 9:30 AM to 4 PM, Monday through Friday. The Bureau has a 24-hour automated phone system.

Department for Social Services
710 W. High St. • 246-2276

This agency investigates reports of abuse, neglect or exploitation. It also offers information about and referral help with nursing home placement.

Kentucky Medical Assistance Program
1175 Winburn Dr. • 246-2085

Based on financial need, which is determined by state and federal guidelines, you may be eligible for KMAP's services These include medical assistance to the elderly, blind or disabled. This office is also responsible for Medicaid.

Lexington-Fayette Urban County Human Rights Commission
162 E. Main St., Ste. 226 • 252-4931

If you are between the ages of 40 and 70, you are covered by the age discrimination law of Kentucky, as well as that of the federal government. This agency deals with cases of discrimination because of age in employment, housing and public accommodation.

Social Security Administration
1460 Newtown Pike • 259-3419, (800) 772-1213

This office administers several monthly income programs including Social Security Retirement Benefits, Supplemental Security Income, and Medicare. There are specific age, income and status requirements for these programs, so call the office for more detailed information.

Eyeglasses

Lexington-Fayette County Health Department
650 Newtown Pike • 252-2371, ext. 314

For those who are medically indigent, the Health Department works with the Lions Club to provide free eye exams and glasses. Applications are available at the Health Department.

Elderly Health Maintenance Clinics

Lexington-Fayette County Health Department
650 Newtown Pike • 288-2319

Fayette County residents 60 and older are eligible to participate in these nurse-conducted health clinics held at various times each month throughout the community. Check the newspaper for specific times and locations. Medical services provided include blood pressure monitoring, evaluation, help with diet and prescriptions, and referrals to physicians and other health services. There is no charge for the clinic, but contributions are welcome.

Residences

People of retirement age have a number of housing options in Lexington. Listed in this section you will find apartment complexes and retirement communities. There is also information about services available to those older adults who live in their own homes but need assistance from time to time.

Apartment Complexes

The following rent-subsidized apartment complexes are open to people older than 50 who are able to live independently, as well as to disabled people. Cost is figured on a sliding scale based on your income. The apartment units are unfurnished, but each kitchen is equipped with a stove and refrigerator. Each complex has programs and activities for its residents. Most of the complexes have waiting lists for admission, so call as far ahead as possible to get your name on the list.

Briarwood Apartments
1349 Centre Pkwy. • 272-3421

Christ Church Apartments
137 Rose St. • 254-7762

Christian Towers Apartments
1511 Versailles Rd. • 253-3625

Emerson Center
2050 Garden Springs Rd. • 278-0526

Malabu Manor Apartments
145 Malabu Dr. • 278-5111

Ballard Place
635 Ballard Pl. • 281-5060
Hearing impaired • 281-5054

Connie Griffith Manor
540 W. Second St. • 281-5060
Hearing impaired • 281-5054

Sayre Christian Village
3816 Camelot Dr. • 273-1845

Main Street Baptist Church Manor
428 Darby Creek Rd. • 263-5153

**Central Christian
Church Apartments**
249 E. Short St. • 252-3671

Retirement Communities

Lexington has several community living options for people who are able to live independently but want the comfort and socialization of living in a small community setting.

These retirement communities are quite luxurious, and in many cases quite costly. However, they offer all the creature comforts and conveniences of a small, self-contained community, with everything from hair salons and medical-care stations to full-service white-tablecloth restaurants, golf, craft and art studios, libraries and exercise rooms.

Lafayette Retirement Community
690 Mason Headley Rd. • 259-1331

Lafayette Retirement Community, opened in 1985, is made up of three types of living arrangements for senior citizens and retirees. The independent living section is designed for those people who do not need assistance, but who want to live in a secure and friendly community setting. The Ambassador Club members receive some assistance in the performance of daily living activities, but they are still able to live independently for the most part in their own apartments. The health care facility has 111 skilled nursing beds, and it is designed for those people who need supervised health care and are unable to live independently.

The retirement community has 100 apartments. Monthly rents are $1,550 for a studio unit, $1895 to $1925 for a one-bedroom unit, and $2,300 for a two-bedroom unit. Included in this monthly rate are all utilities (except cable

TV and telephone), two meals a day, transportation anywhere within Fayette County, weekly housekeeping and linen service.

Lafayette organizes programs, parties, trips and entertainment for residents throughout the year. Other amenities include 24-hour doorman security services, an exercise room and 10 free days in the health center each year.

Richmond Place
3051 Rio Dosa Rd. • 269-6308

Located in southern Lexington far enough away from the "main drag" to be serene and picturesque yet close enough to be convenient, Richmond Place offers its residents full-scale retirement living including a comprehensive health-care plan.

Apartment options range from studios (480 square feet) to two-bedrooms (1,064 square feet), and these are priced from $1,460 to $2,585 per month. The monthly rent price includes one meal per day, weekly housekeeping, utilities, maintenance, security and use of the fitness center, heated pool, library, putting green, tennis court, walking and jogging paths and woodworking shop. Garden spaces are also available.

The on-site wellness program offers a range of health-care services, from optical and podiatry care to pharmaceutical and emotional well-being services, There is also a convenience store and beauty salon/barber shop at the facility. Richmond Place also operates an in-house home health agency. In early 1999, two more buildings were under construction with 60 homes personal care apartments for those with memory impairments.

Mayfair Village
3310 Tates Creek Rd. • 266-2129

Conveniently located just across the street from a branch of the public library, restaurants, banks, doctor and dental offices, specialty shops and boutiques, Mayfair Village offers many of the amenities you'd look for in a retirement community, such as 24-hour security, weekly housekeeping, nutritious meals, transportation and a full calendar of planned activities.

Mayfair Village has 16 floor plans, ranging from a studio to a luxurious penthouse. Independent-living apartments include all utilities, maintenance and upkeep, transportation, weekly housekeeping and a meal allowance. Monthly rates range from $1,635 for a single studio apartment to $2,897 for a double-occupancy penthouse. Apartments come equipped with a solarium or terrace, individually governed heat and air conditioning and kitchen appliances.

Ashland Terrace Retirement Home
475 S. Ashland Ave. • 266-2581

For women 65 and older who are ambulatory and able to take care of themselves, Ashland Terrace offers a homey community living option. The $600-per-month rent includes three meals a day, planned activities, and weekly linen and housekeeping services. This nonprofit facility has 22 units.

Friendship Towers
580 Greenfield Dr. • 271-9000

Part of the Sayre Christian Village Complex, Friendship Towers offers moderately priced apartments equipped with electric heat, air conditioners, carpet, window coverings, electric range, refrigerator and cable TV hookup. To be eligible, you must be 55 or older and live independently. There are no income requirements.

Assistance Programs

If you choose to stay in your own home, but sometimes feel the need for a little added security or perhaps medical assistance, Lexington has several programs that offer everything from home health care to someone to

---

INSIDERS' TIP

Pack a lunch and join the Bluegrass Senior Citizens Club at noon every Monday at the Bell House, 545 Sayre Avenue. For information call 233-0986.

talk to if you're feeling lonely or just want to pass the time of day. Some of these programs are described below.

American Red Cross
1450 Newtown Pike • 253-1331

The Bluegrass Area Chapter of the American Red Cross offers several free programs for older adults. The Carrier Alert program, coordinated through the U.S. Postal Service, arranges for your postal carrier to alert the Red Cross if you are not picking up your mail. This service is available to people living alone. The Hello Daily Line, for the elderly and disabled who are homebound, arranges for someone who shares your interests to call you at scheduled times throughout the week to chat. This is a good volunteer opportunity as well. Additionally, because the calls are scheduled, if you do not answer the phone at the agreed-upon time, the Hello Daily volunteer will alert the Red Cross.

Senior Companion Program
3445A Versailles Rd., Frankfort
• (800) 456-6571

This program is great both for those folks who need a companion and helper for daily living activities and for those who want to spend some time each week helping the homebound elderly. To be eligible to get a companion, you must be older than 60 and live alone. To be a companion (for which you are paid a small hourly stipend for about 20 hours a week), you must be older than 60 and have a limited income. Companions provide such services as personal care, meal preparation, errand and escorting services. There is no charge for this program.

Emergency Signaling Devices
Life Line of Central Baptist Hospital
• 275-6100
Link to Life of Grogans Healthcare Supply
• 254-6661
Perfect Companion of the Humana Seniors Program • 268-3753

These organizations provide emergency signaling devices that operate through your telephone to alert a monitoring station when you are in trouble at home. The devices, which

can be worn or carried with you, are available for rent for $15 to $50 per month.

Volunteer, Education and Other Activities

From updating your driving skills to starting a new career, Lexington has quite a few opportunities for older adults to go to college, volunteer their time and skills or just get together and have fun doing something they enjoy. In this section, a few of these opportunities are described.

Defensive Driving Classes
AAA Safety Foundation, Bluegrass Automobile Club, 155 N. Martin Luther King Blvd. • 233-1111, (800) 568-5222

Whether you want to tune up your driving skills or qualify for an "after 55" insurance discount, AAA provides an eight-hour classroom course that covers everything from knowing what prescription drugs affect driving ability to how to avoid being involved in rear-end collisions. There are no tests, and the course costs $20 for AAA members, $30 for nonmembers.

Careers After Sixty
Lexington Senior Citizens Center
1530 Nicholasville Rd. • 278-6072, ext. 320

If you are older than 60 and would like help finding a full- or part-time job, call the Careers After Sixty office between 9 AM and noon on weekdays.

Hire Older Workers
1530 Nicholasville Rd. • 278-6072, ext. 323

To be eligible for this program, you must be a Fayette County resident 55 or older with a limited income (specific guidelines apply). This program offers job referral and placement, workshops, occupational training, assessment and testing.

Book Buddies
Lexington Public Library, 140 E. Main St.
• 231-5592

This program pairs volunteers and homebound people older than 50 who have chronic disabilities. Homebound participants receive two visits a month from their Book Buddies, who bring books, records or tapes from the public library. Volunteers must go through a training program and submit to a police check.

Donovan Scholars Program
**Ligon House, University of Kentucky
• 257-2656**

The Donovan Scholars Program is a great way for folks older than 65 to go to college. The program provides tuition-free education at the University of Kentucky for people older than 65. Other special noncredit course are offered, including the Forum on Tuesday and Thursday afternoons, Great Discussions book groups, writing workshops and a radio drama

group. The only expenses that might be incurred are for textbooks, special materials for classes and travel.

Kentucky Elderhostel
643 Maxwelton Court • 257-5234

For people 60 and older or those whose participating spouse or companion is 60 or older, Kentucky Elderhostel offers a broad range of exciting and interesting classes and programs throughout the state in cooperation with universities, community colleges, education agencies, state resort parks and environmental centers. These weeklong residential education programs cost an average of $275 per week, which includes the course, lodging, recreation and food. Scholarships are available.

People in Lexington like to get involved in their community, whether it's sitting on a school council, selling hot dogs at a soccer game, teaching someone how to read or donating blood.

Volunteering: Neighbors Helping Neighbors

One of the nicest things about Lexington is that it has a lot of the characteristics of a big city — a strong cultural element, public transportation, major universities and even, unfortunately, traffic — but it still maintains the feeling of a small town. Folks know their neighbors and their neighbors' granddaddies, and everyone went to school with everyone else and played football and/or basketball together. There is a strong sense of community, and because of that there is an equally strong sense of responsibility for the common good of the community.

Which is a roundabout way of saying that people in Lexington like to get involved in their community, whether it's sitting on a school council, selling hot dogs at a soccer game, teaching someone how to read or donating blood. There are hundreds of clubs, groups and organizations that represent thousands of opportunities for Lexingtonians to get involved and volunteer their time and expertise for the betterment of the community.

There is a strong commitment here to the idea of neighbors helping neighbors. And the evidence of this commitment can be seen every day and in virtually every circumstance.

Folks getting together, for instance, to build creative playgrounds at city parks for local youngsters. Or a couple dozen people turning up early on a cold Saturday morning to construct a home for Habitat for Humanity. Or members of the local 4-Wheelers Club transporting medical and emergency personnel to work in the midst of a winter storm.

If you're trying to figure out how to get involved, there are a few questions you might ask yourself. What needs do I see in my immediate neighborhood, my kids' school, my church? What do I enjoy doing? What skills do I have to offer? How much free time do I have?

Once you identify a need you are interested in helping to fill, and you have determined what skills, time and other resources you have that will help you fill that need, you're well on your way to community involvement. It is at this point, however, that you'll probably come up against a barrier. How do you go about doing what you see needs to be done?

One of the main answers to this question is that there is likely to be a group in Lexington that is either (1) addressing the need in some other area or some other way or (2) is interested in doing so and is just waiting for someone like you to come along with the extra excitement and energy to make the project fly.

So how do you get in touch with these groups?

We suggest starting with a couple of larger umbrella agencies, such as the Volunteer Center of the Bluegrass, your local school council or the Ask Us referral line and the publications it offers about hundreds of groups and organizations.

This chapter details some of the information and referral services offered by these umbrella groups as well as gives some specific information on a cross-section of groups and volunteer opportunities in the area. It is by no means a comprehensive listing. Rather, the listing is designed to give newcomers to the area an idea of the variety of projects and activities in which they can get involved. Chances are, no matter how unusual your interest, there's a group out there with the same interest!

Referral Services

Ask Us
201 Burley Ave. • 255-2374

When in doubt, start with Ask Us. This program provides an invaluable service to Central Kentuckians in its role as an information and referral clearinghouse for hundreds of community groups and organizations, whether you need some kind of special assistance or are just looking for a fun or stimulating group to join. Ask Us is open weekdays and links 22,000 callers to social and community services each year.

The program was started in 1972 as part of the Suburban Woman's Club to help fill the big need in the community to link people with the services they need. It's independent now, and Ask Us also publishes a comprehensive community services directory every few years that is an invaluable resource for people dealing with social and community service organizations.

Volunteer Center of the Bluegrass
2029 Bellefonte Dr. • 278-6258

The Volunteer Center of the Bluegrass is the heart of Lexington's volunteer connection and referral efforts. The center keeps files on the volunteer needs of hundreds of area agencies and organizations. People who are looking for ways to become volunteers call the center, and staff members there work to match

---

FYI

If no area code is given, it's a local call from Lexington-Fayette County. If an area code is given, whether it's 606 or 502, it's a long-distance call: dial 1, the area code and the number. See the How To Use This Book chapter for detailed information on calling.

---

up the volunteer's skills and interests with the needs it has on file.

Special volunteer placement programs include the Retired Senior Volunteer Program and the University of Kentucky Student Volunteer Center. The Volunteer Center of the Bluegrass also provides training sessions and sponsors annual awards for volunteer efforts in the community.

Organizations

There is no reasonable way to present or even attempt a comprehensive list of community organizations in which you might want to become involved, but described below is a sampling of some of the Lexington organizations you may want to join. Not all are community service organizations — some are social, some are trade and some are just for fun. But what they all have in common is that they provide the space in which Lexingtonians from diverse backgrounds and experiences can join together with their neighbors and experience the true spirit of community.

AIDS Volunteers of Lexington
152 W. Zandale Dr., Suite 201 • 278-7494

As the number of people affected by HIV and AIDS continues to grow in our country and in our community, so does the need for caring.

AIDS Volunteers of Lexington, or AVOL, was started in 1987 to serve the needs of people in Lexington and Central and Eastern Kentucky. AVOL offers a wide range of services, from education about the disease to emotional support. Some of the confidential support groups AVOL offers include HIV+ Individuals, Partners of HIV+ Individuals, Caregivers of AIDS Patients and Family and Friends Support Group.

If you have a few spare hours a week, you can help AVOL provide these vital services to the community. Volunteer hours are flexible, and training and support are provided. Volunteer opportunities include providing office, telephone and clerical support, assisting with transportation of clients, serving as Buddies for HIV/AIDS clients, presenting community education programs and offering telephone support and help with hospital visits.

EarthSave
P.O. Box 8414, Lexington KY • 293-8966

This is a nonprofit health and environmental organization that educates and supports people who want to shift toward a plant-based diet. It's a local affiliate of EarthSave International. Monthly meetings on the second Sunday of each month feature a speaker, but the best part is that you get a chance to sample all kinds of delicious vegetarian dishes because each person is asked to bring one along. (How do vegetarian sushi, red lentil pâté and couscous cake with blueberry sauce sound?) The meeting and meal is free for EarthSave members, $3 for nonmembers and $5 if you want to eat but don't bring a dish. Call for meeting locations or more information.

Gay and Lesbian Services Organization
P.O. Box 11471, Lexington, KY 40575 • 255-2374

From funding, planning and sponsoring events during Gay Pride Week each year to offering programs that educate the public about issues related to gay and lesbian people, the Gay and Lesbian Services Organization is dedicated to providing information, emotional support and referral services to Lexingtonians.

Started in 1977, GLSO is the oldest continually operating gay and lesbian services organization in Kentucky. There are many ways to get involved, whether you're looking for ways to volunteer in the community or to participate in social and recreational activities. Membership is $10 for individuals and $15 for couples. For information call the Ask Us number above.

Habitat for Humanity
219 E. Short St. • 252-2224

What more basic need can you help provide than a clean, new, affordable place to live? The Lexington chapter of Habitat for Humanity does just that — helps families build modest homes with volunteer labor and donated construction materials from the community.

Many area churches and service organizations have a continuing commitment to the work of Habitat for Humanity, but there is always a need for more volunteers. If you can heft a hammer, wire a house, paint or tote two-by-fours, Habitat for Humanity can use you. Check local media announcements for house building projects or call the office for more information.

Kentucky Women's Leadership Network
251 W. Second St. • 252-5258

The KWLN was established by the Kentucky Commission on Women in 1993 to help improve the personal, professional, economic and public status of women in Kentucky through a series of workshops led by recognized experts, leaders and newsmakers from Kentucky and from the nation. The organization strives to bring together Kentucky women with diverse geographic, ethnic, cultural and professional backgrounds to attend these workshops. Participants are selected on the basis of their achievements, as well as their desire to assume a greater leadership role.

Kiwanis Club
Various locations • 255-2374

Each of the eight clubs in Lexington, part of Kiwanis International, generates money for community needs with projects such as Soup and Chili Day in December or maintaining the University of Kentucky Children's Hospital teddy bear program. Much of the proceeds go toward helping needy children. There are clubs in various areas of town, as well as for retirees. For information about a specific club, call the Ask Us number above.

Lexington Creative Camera Club
1900 Richmond Rd., Shriners' Hospital • 223-8037, 299-9333

Whether you're really into photography or you're just looking for a creative and interesting hobby the whole family can enjoy, the Lexington Creative Camera Club might be what you've been searching for. The group began about 15 years ago and today has close to 75 members. Meetings are held the third Thursday of the month at the Shriners' Hospital from 7 to 10 PM. Meetings include a presentation on a specific area of photography, such as portraiture, weddings or commercial work.

Additionally the club sponsors competitions monthly, and members display their work at the club's annual print show, which is usually held at the Central Kentucky Blood Center on Waller Avenue in November. Weekend workshops provide hands-on work with a variety of subjects and are usually held at various outdoor locations in the region.

Members also volunteer their time to photograph the Special Olympics in Lexington each year.

Membership in the club costs $22 a year for individuals and $28 a year for families.

Lexington Jaycees
222 S. Limestone St. • 245-9003

Also known as the Junior Chamber of Commerce, the Lexington Jaycees is a group of 275 men and women between the ages of 21 and 39 who are dedicated to leadership training through community service. The Jaycees are best known for their annual Halloween Haunted House, which raises money for more than 100 annual projects. Each member is taught a 10-step planning process that can be applied to all areas of their lives, both business and personal. Members also participate in seminars — on topics that range from time management to how to plan a party — and then they apply these skills to worthwhile community projects.

Lexington Philharmonic Women's Club
161 N. Mill St. • 268-1510

This group, an arm of the Lexington Philharmonic Society, is for women interested in volunteering to help strengthen the financial base of the Philharmonic Orchestra. It raises funds through community projects and social functions.

Lexington Rape Crisis Center
P.O. Box 1603, Lexington KY 40592
• 253-2615, 253-2511 crisis hotline

Providing emotional, legal and medical support for victims of sexual assault and their families, the Lexington Rape Crisis Center has a number of volunteer needs that range from staffing a 24-hour crisis hotline to counseling victims of sexual abuse and assault.

The center holds volunteer training sessions throughout the year and needs people to volunteer for a number of areas, including accompanying people to court or meeting victims at hospitals and providing follow-up services and referrals to other agencies.

Among the services provided by the Lexington Rape Crisis Center are crisis intervention counseling, support groups for women recovering from rape and child sexual abuse, advocacy services for victims of abuse and a therapy and individual counseling program.

Lions Club
809 Glendover Rd. • 266-8727

Started in 1921, the Lexington Lions Club (175 members strong) is the city's original Lions Club. Today, however, there are a total of five clubs in town. To find out the meeting times of the club that best suits your schedule, call Jim Alcorn at the number listed above. Lexington Lions and Lionesses are involved with numerous fund-raising events to generate money to support a wide range of charities, from the eyesight conservation program (to date the club has purchased more than 700 pairs of eyeglasses for people who need them but can't afford them), to youth camps for blind children and kids with diabetes.

The Lexington Lions Club's primary fund-raising event of the year is the Lions Blue-

www.insiders.com
See this and many other
Insiders' Guide®
destinations online.
Visit us today!

INSIDERS' TIP

If you know someone who needs emergency or professional help, see the greybox of emergency numbers in our Healthcare chapter. For a complete list of referral numbers call Ask Us, 255-2374; they can either look a number up for you or send you a complete list.

grass Fair, held each June at Masterson Station Park. (See our Annual Events chapter.)

Operation Read Inc.
251 W. Second St. • 254-9964

Giving someone the gift of literacy is one of the most rewarding and exciting examples of neighbors helping neighbors. This nonprofit organization, with headquarters in the Carnegie Center for Literacy and Learning, was started by a group of concerned citizens in 1979 as an outgrowth of the Lexington Public Library.

The services provided by Operation Read serve a great need both locally and across the state. Some 340,000 Kentuckians cannot read a newspaper, job application or the warning label on an aspirin bottle. In Lexington alone an estimated 31,000 adults cannot read above a sixth-grade level. The mission of Operation Read is to help those 31,000 neighbors achieve a level of functional literacy that is the first step toward an enriched life.

Operation Read has volunteer needs that range from serving as a reading tutor to helping with fund-raising and publicity or donating money for operating costs. Last year Operation Read served 339 students, trained 128 new tutors and recorded more than 12,000 volunteer hours.

Optimist Club
Various locations • 255-2374

The seven Lexington clubs are part of Optimist Clubs International, a group of business and professional men devoted to civic improvement, friendship and projects to help youth. Activities include programs that award teen volunteers; essay and public-speaking contests; and assisting Cub Scouts in their annual Pinewood Derby. For information about clubs in various parts of Lexington, call the Ask Us number above.

Women's Clubs

The Kentucky Federation of Women's Clubs is the blanket organization for four clubs in Lexington. The focus of these groups is to improve the general life of the community through assistance to recognized charities, involvement in various service and leadership projects and participation in educational forums. Membership is open to women who have the time and interest to dedicate to the club's particular focus. Call the club you think you might be interested in for a membership application.

Bluegrass Junior Woman's Club
• 272-9642

This club is especially for younger women between the ages of 18 and 40. It sponsors a yearly Casino Night with proceeds going to charities for children. Members also volunteer at various places throughout the community.

Lexington Woman's Club
• 269-1642

Since 1948 the club has run a clothing center that has helped dress thousands of elementary school children. "Bids for Kids," a charity auction and raffle, is this club's major fund-raiser, and proceeds go to kid-oriented charities. This club has departments of interest that include gardening, creative arts, public and international affairs, education and women's issues.

Metropolitan Woman's Club
• 266-0008

The Miss Lexington Scholarship Pageant, the club's main fund-raiser, provides a cash scholarship plus a nontraditional scholarship for young women each year.

Suburban Woman's Club
• 269-1456.

The main fund-raiser of this club is the popular Open Horse Farm Tour in June. (See our Horse Country chapter for more information about this tour.) The club has donated more than $300,000 to local charities with proceeds from this tour.

Lexington is the site of many pioneering medical efforts in the state, the nation and the world.

Healthcare

It may sound morbid to say this, but Lexington is a good place to get sick.

With five general hospitals, five special-service hospitals and a dozen walk-in immediate-care clinics prepared to deal with everything from the flu to broken legs to newborn babies to major heart surgery to drug addiction, Lexington is fortunate to have a wide variety of healthcare options available. Growth and competition in our area have made medicine a big business, so it's no wonder we have more than a dozen clinics devoted to specialties such as plastic and reconstructive surgery, kidney stone treatment, infertility — even a clinic where patients can get a "non-claustrophobic" Magnetic Resonance Image or MRI.

Lexington is the site of many pioneering medical efforts in the state, the nation and the world. The state's only bone-marrow transplant program can be found at the University of Kentucky's Chandler Medical Center, which is part of the University of Kentucky Hospital, as can the first nonprototype MRI diagnostic system in the world. Lexington's Shriners Hospital for Crippled Children is one of only 19 Shriners orthopedic hospitals in the world.

The listings in this chapter detail some of the services offered by local hospitals and clinics and by the Fayette County Health Department. Though alternative-medicine practitioners in Kentucky aren't protected by legislation as they are in some other states, local interest is growing rapidly, so we have included some resources. For more information on individual physicians by specialty, check the Yellow Pages of the phone book.

Medical Centers and Hospitals

Lexington-Fayette County Health Department
650 Newtown Pike • 252-2371

Governed by the Board of Health, which meets monthly, the Lexington-Fayette County Health Department provides a wide array of health services to Lexingtonians, including general outpatient clinical care, dentistry, X-ray, social services, school health and health and nutritional education and counseling. Additionally, the department is responsible for restaurant and hotel regulations and inspections. See the grey box at the end of this write-up for phone numbers of services you might need from the Health Department.

The Health Department's Primary Care Center, licensed in 1980, combines traditional health services with nontraditional comprehensive healthcare service such as home health, health education, and adult day care. And the center combines preventive healthcare with the diagnosis and treatment of acute and chronic diseases. You can get more information about any of these programs by calling the Primary Care Center.

Payment for services is on a sliding-scale basis, but no one is refused services because they can't pay. Clinics are open Monday through Friday (except Wednesday) 8 AM to 4:30 PM and Wednesday 12:30 to 7 PM. Appointments are necessary for all services.

INSIDERS' TIP

Kentucky is known as a state that is somewhat hostile toward alternative medicine, but because of growing interest, a citizens organization called the Patients Rights Advocacy Group (PRAG) is pushing for state legislation that would protect a practitioner's use of alternative treatments.

Among services available in the Primary Care Center is the General Medical Clinic offering preventive and maintenance care for adults 18 and older, including physical examinations, diagnoses and treatment of acute and chronic health problems. The Child Health Program offers healthcare services to children up to the age of 17, including vision and hearing testing, physical exams, developmental testing and counseling and sickle cell and tuberculosis skin tests.

Other Primary Care programs and services include the Family Planning Program for women ages 20 to 44 who are at or below 150 percent poverty level; a maternity program offering both medical and educational services; breast and cervical cancer screening and education program; a healthcare program for the homeless; and the Bluegrass District Commission for Children with Special Health Care Needs.

FYI

If no area code is given, it's a local call from Lexington-Fayette County. If an area code is given, whether it's 606 or 502, it's a long-distance call: dial 1, the area code and the number. See the How To Use This Book chapter for detailed information on calling.

In addition, the Primary Care Center has a communicable disease clinic that tests for, treats and monitors a variety of diseases including tuberculosis; sexually transmitted diseases; and AIDS/HIV.

The Health Department's Division of Community Nursing encompasses a broad range of home- and school-based healthcare programs, as well as field-testing programs for such things as tuberculosis and communicable diseases. This division is also responsible for many of the department's services to the elderly, including the Center for Creative Living Adult Day Health Care Center (for more information, see our Retirement chapter) and the Elderly Health Maintenance clinics held monthly at different locations in the community for people 60 and older.

The Division of Nutrition and Health Education is responsible for many of the educational services offered by the Health Department. Among the programs in this division are the Diabetes Control Program, 288-2310; the Child Car Seat Program, which lends car seats (required by law for children up to 40 inches tall) to Lexingtonians; and the Teen Initiative Center, an after-school drop-in center for youngsters in the Bluegrass-Aspendale Housing District.

And if you have problems with anything from unsanitary public restrooms or pest infestations to sewage backup, the Division of Environmental Health is the place to turn. Also covered under this division are such things as vending company licenses and mobile homes, public and private swimming pools, hotels, motels, restaurants and school inspections for code violations.

Central Baptist Hospital
1740 Nicholasville Rd. • 275-6100

Since opening in 1954, Central Baptist Hospital has remained dedicated to the tenets of its vision statement, which emphasize the hospital's role in creating quality care in a compassionate, family-oriented environment — what the hospital calls The Healing Force.

Health Department Phone Numbers

Primary Care Center information and main number, 252-2371
Appointments, 288-2307
Aids/HIV program services, 288-2437
Bluegrass Commission for Children with Special Health Care Needs, 276-5563
Cancer screening, 288-2431
Car Seat Program, 288-2333
Communicable Disease Clinic, 288-2461
Dental Clinic, 288-2417
Diabetes Control Program, 288-2310
Division of Community Nursing, 283-2338
Environmental Health, 231-9791
Family planning services, 288-2436
Immunization information, 288-2483
Sexually transmitted diseases information, 288-2461
SIDS, 288-2469
Teen Center, 254-4633

As one of four acute-care hospitals in the Baptist Healthcare System, Central Baptist Hospital provides numerous health and educational services, ranging from state-of-the-art radiology services to one of the finest obstetric and pediatric departments in the region. More Lexington babies are born at Central Baptist than at any other local hospital.

The 383-bed hospital has grown a great deal over the past 43 years. The most recent addition to the hospital complex is a six-story office building and an expanded parking garage to accommodate the more than 50 physicians' offices.

In addition to the "regular" services, the hospital's features include cardiac services with close to 1,400 open-heart procedures performed each year, cancer care and stroke services and a subacute care unit. Central Baptist also operates many special programs, such as home health services, community outreach programs and continuing education programs for doctors and nurses, as well as community education programs.

One of the best-known Central Baptist programs is Women's and Children's Services, which includes a 16-bed neonatal intensive care unit, a perinatal diagnostic center, a lactation center to help new mothers learn more about breastfeeding, gynecology services, a mammography center, and an assisted reproduction program to help infertile couples. Along with their complete pediatric services is an after-hours clinic for sick and injured children called Kids Central.

Samaritan Hospital
310 S. Limestone St. • 252-6612

This 336-bed acute care facility offers a broad spectrum of medical and surgical services, including outpatient surgery, a pain-care center, wound-care center and sleep-apnea center. Obstetric services include a newborn unit and infertility services.

A specialty of the hospital is the Center for Behavioral Health, which unites mental health services in seven counties. Services include both inpatient and outpatient treatment for mental health and chemical dependency needs. Additional outpatient programs focus on the Brain Injury Recovery Program, psychological testing and a variety of support groups. There's also an Attention Deficit Disorder Clinic.

Columbia's emergency department — called ERgency — guarantees that patients will be seen and evaluated by an emergency physician within 30 minutes of completing the registration process. If you don't see a doctor within 30 minutes, you may request a credit for the emergency room fee and physician's charges.

Saint Joseph Hospital
1 St. Joseph Dr.
• 278-3436

The largest private not-for-profit hospital in Central and eastern Kentucky, Saint Joseph Hospital traces its roots back to 1877 when the Sisters of Charity of Nazareth arrived in Lexington to staff the city's first hospital.

In 1959 the first open heart surgery in Central Kentucky was performed at Saint Joseph, and the Saint Joseph Heart Institute remains one of the cornerstones of the hospital's service areas. Specially equipped surgical suites for patients, a cardiothoracic unit, a coronary care unit and two telemetry units provide care of the highest quality for the more than 3,500 patients who undergo cardiac catheterization, angioplasty or other interventional procedures at Saint Joseph each year.

Other special programs at Saint Joseph include the Cancer Center, which addresses a wide range of needs of cancer patients and their families, from the latest in diagnostic services to psychological and spiritual support. Saint Joseph's Brain and Spine Institute is the largest provider of neurological care in eastern Kentucky. The Saint Joseph Sleep Disorders Center, Central Kentucky's first nationally accredited full-service sleep center, provides diagnosis and treatment of sleep disorders including insomnia and sleep apnea.

Other programs include the Chemical Recovery Center and the Care Flight air medics service, which provides helicopter transport services to patients throughout eastern Kentucky.

Saint Joseph East
150 N. Eagle Creek Dr. • 268-4800

Though it has continued to stay operating as Lexington's only major medical facility in the growing southeast part of town, this hospital continues to undergo management changes. In March of 1995 Jewish Hospital HealthCare Services assumed management of this former Humana Hospital and changed its name to Lexington Hospital. In the fall of 1997, the hospital was sold to Jewish Hospital, and in 1998 underwent another name change.

As it stands, St. Joseph East Hospital is a general acute-care facility located on a 36-acre medical campus with over 500 staff members. Services include a critical care and cardiovascular unit; a 28-bed telemetry division where a patient's cardiac data can be constantly monitored; maternity and pediatric departments; a cardiopulmonary department; and radiology and surgical sections. There's also a 24-hour pharmacy for inpatients, as well as free programs for expectant parents. The Golden Opportunities program is a hospital-based organization designed for people over 50 which helps them do tasks like filing insurance claims, and helps get them involved in social events, traveling and dining out, as well as participating in health screenings.

University of Kentucky Hospital (A.B. Chandler Medical Center)
800 Rose St. • 257-1000

During the past three decades, the University of Kentucky Hospital has evolved into a nationally recognized patient-care, education and research facility. The College of Medicine is recognized as one of the top 10 medical schools for primary-care training in the country. The UK Hospital and its affiliated clinics provide healthcare to residents of all 120 Kentucky counties, nearby states and even foreign countries.

The 473-bed hospital is staffed by more than 600 faculty physicians and dentists, 500 resident physicians and 3,100 other health professionals. UK Hospital offers specialty services in cancer, cardiology and neurosciences, as well as comprehensive care for women and children.

UK Hospital's 250,000-square-foot critical-care center includes an emergency department that treats over 34,000 patient visits yearly and supports central and eastern Kentucky's only Level 1 trauma center.

The UK Children's Hospital, a 64,000 square-foot facility adjoining the main hospital, consolidates over 20 pediatric specialties.

It includes a pediatric intensive care unit, a Level III neonatal intensive care unit, a short-stay service, private rooms and overnight accommodations for parents.

Lexington Clinic
1221 S. Broadway • 255-6841
Lexington Clinic East
100 N. Eagle Creek Dr. • 258-4000

On July 1, 1920 a team of Lexington surgeons established a "partnership for the practice of surgery" which was modeled after Minnesota's renowned Mayo Clinic. They named it Lexington Clinic.

Through the 1920s the clinic expanded into Kentucky's first multispecialty group medical practice by inviting only the best physicians with specific specialties to join the staff. The clinic became a forerunner with the addition of cardiology, otolaryngology and the first pathology and radiology departments in Lexington.

By the early 1950s the staff had grown to 21 physicians and had expanded its departments with the addition of neurosurgery, ophthalmology and pediatrics. By 1958 the clinic had outgrown its downtown location and moved to a 11.6-acre site on South Broadway into a spacious new three-story building. The clinic added eight more specialties, including the Family Practice department, along with construction of a second major facility, Lexington Clinic East, which made services more accessible to Lexington residents. At the same time, the clinic added Jessamine Medical Center, a primary care satellite, in Nicholasville.

Today Lexington Clinic has more than 150 physicians representing over 30 specialties. Those physicians practice at 24 branch locations in 11 different communities in Kentucky. These satellite locations include several primary care clinics, a radiation clinic (in Corbin) and optometric centers in Georgetown, Nicholasville and Lexington.

Physician Referral Services for Local Hospitals and Clinics

Central Baptist Hospital	275-6433
Samaritan Hospital	(800) 265-8624
Lexington Clinic	281-2273
University of Kentucky Chandler Medical Center	257-1000
University of Kentucky emergency dental care	323-5850 days
	323-5321 evenings

Walk-In Clinics

Most walk-in clinics accept a variety of insurance and most are open daily, but call first to make sure.

FirstChoice	
3061 Fieldstone Way in Beaumont Centre	296-9900
1221 S. Broadway	258-4000
MedFirst	
450 New Circle Rd. N.E.	253-9791
Medwalk	
3735 Harrodsburg Rd. in Palomar Centre	296-9472
QuickCare	
3050 Harrodsburg Rd.	367-6000
Urgent Treatment Centers	
1055 Dove Run Rd.	269-4668
3174 Custer Dr.	272-4882
1498 Boardwalk Rd.	254-5520
4001 Nicolasville Rd.	245-4882
100 Eastside Dr.; Georgetown	868-7500
976 N. Main St.; Nicholasville	885-2882
1230 U.S. Highwas 127 South; Frankfort	(502) 227-4882

Health Dimensions:
A Healthy Dose of Information

It's happened to most of us. We visit a doctor or go to an appointment with a family member. We receive a diagnosis, along with some basic information about what's wrong, and leave with prescription in hand — then, on the way home, we think of five questions about that diagnosis we didn't ask.

Enter Health Dimensions, a user-friendly health-information facility in Lexington's Fayette Mall sponsored by Central Baptist and St. Joseph as a community service.

Many people feel intimidated about asking a lot of questions in a clinical setting, and many of us just don't know what questions to ask, explains Health Dimensions manager Karen Blakeman. "Part of the anxiety of an illness is not knowing," she says. "We try to make health information accessible in a non-intimidating setting and help people get over that white coat syndrome."

Accessible is a bit of an understatement. The facility provides more than 1,000 pamphlets, 150 videos (childbirth is the most popular) and hundreds of books that can be checked out, dozens of magazines and a five-CD-ROM data base that is updated every month, all free. In addition, Health Dimensions is online.

There's also a classroom with regularly scheduled programs on everything from healthy cooking to looking good while undergoing cancer treatment. Outside clinicians come in on a regular basis to provide cholesterol and glucose screenings, as well as health risk assessments and hearing tests. Most screenings are free or require a very small fee for laboratory costs. A number of support groups have their monthly meetings here. They also run fun

A young visitor reads about nutrition at Health Dimensions, a health information resource center.

Photo: Elizabeth Hench

safety programs for kids and help for the woebegone parent of a teen about to get a driver's license with a program called Safe Driving for Teens.

Another service is free blood pressure checks that can be done anytime the facility is open. "We found about 3 people in the past year with blood pressure so high we advised them to go to an emergency room immediately," says Blakeman.

The extra-friendly staff includes a medical librarian and a dietician (no white coats!), and health educators who help you track down what you're looking for.

Don't think you have to be sick to use Health Dimensions though. "One of the topics people ask about most is nutrition," says Blakeman. (The second most-asked-about subject is the newfound and somewhat-controversial disease, fibromyalgia, a form of muscular rheumatism characterized by tenderness, soreness, pain, muscle spasms and fatigue.) "People are really getting more educated and want to be in charge of their own good health." More than 22,000 people visited the facility in its first year of operation (it opened in the summer of 1996). According to user-response cards, 38 percent of the visitors dropped in while on a shopping trip: "We get a lot of husbands waiting for their wives to shop," said Blakeman. "And a lot of students doing reports have found us." Physicians also refer patients to Health Dimensions.

Health Dimensions is open from 10 AM to 9 PM Monday through Saturday, from noon to 6 PM Sunday. It's in the south end of the mall (the McAlpins end), across from Talbots. Phone 272-6099 for information or a program schedule.

Pattie A. Clay Hospital
801 Eastern Bypass, Richmond
• (606) 623-3131

Because Pattie Amelia Clay spent so much of her time caring for the sick and unfortunate during the 1800s, after the death of her husband, Brutus Clay, son of famous abolitionist Cassius Marcellus Clay, she donated a brick cottage and its surrounding grounds to the women of Richmond to be used as the town's first hospital. It was dedicated to her memory in 1892.

A new Pattie A. Clay Hospital was built in 1970 on the more accessible Eastern Bypass; a $4.2 million addition was completed in 1980.

In 1993 the hospital became affiliated with Jewish Hospital HealthCare Network in Louisville, making it part of a large network of hospitals throughout Kentucky and southern Indiana.

This 105-bed hospital has a medical staff of more than 40 physicians who offer care in more than 20 medical specialties. Special patient services include cardiac catheterization, a sleep disorders lab, nurse-midwife services, EmployCare care occupational medicine services, cardiac and pulmonary rehabilitation and same-day surgery.

Markey Cancer Center
800 Rose St. • 257-4500

The Markey Cancer Center, opened in January 1996, is a comprehensive center with a national reputation that continues to grow as a result of its research, patient care, community outreach and educational programs.

Markey Cancer Center patient care facilities include 56 beds, a bone marrow transplant unit, and a 7,000-square-foot outpatient-care section, all integrated with the major services of the University of Kentucky Medical Center. The cancer center treats approximately 1,000 new cancer cases per year, offering about 150 treatment options, a number of which are the result of research conducted by physicians and researchers associated with the cancer center.

Markey Cancer Center Director Dr. Kenneth Foon is a national leader in research on the development of vaccines to treat different types of cancer.

Cardinal Hill Rehabilitation Hospital
2050 Versailles Rd. • 254-5701

For nearly a half-century, Lexington's Cardinal Hill Rehabilitation Hospital has been providing specialized services for kids and adults in Kentucky and the surrounding region. This not-for-profit, comprehensive rehabilitation center is licensed for 100 inpatients and is the largest physical rehabilitation center in Kentucky.

The hospital has made a name for itself by providing, as its mission statement says, "benchmark patient and customer services in physical rehabilitation."

An interdisciplinary team of physicians, nurses, occupational and physical therapists, teachers and case managers addresses the wide range of needs of people dealing with orthopedic and neurological problems, whether congenital or from illness or injury. Disabilities treated include: stroke, spinal cord injury, brain injury, orthopedic injury, amputation, joint replacement, multiple sclerosis, arthritis, chronic pain and developmental delays.

Inpatient and outpatient programs have different requirements. But to be admitted to Cardinal Hill, a person must have an identified problem which causes physical and/or cognitive disability, along with a strong desire for treatment and the backup of family or friends to help with the rehabilitation process and the transition back into an independent-living situation. Anyone can make a referral and evaluations are done in one of Cardinal Hill's outpatient clinics.

Charter Ridge Hospital
3050 Rio Dosa Dr. • 269-2325

As the only freestanding Central Kentucky facility specializing in the treatment of psychiatric illnesses and addictive disease, Charter Ridge Hospital has been offering psychiatric and medical care to Central Kentuckians since 1982.

A variety of inpatient, partial hospitalization and outpatient services are designed to deal with emotional and behavioral difficulties ranging from addiction to drugs and/or alcohol to childhood and adolescent behavioral or emotional disorders.

Free confidential screening is available to help people determine what level of care would best suit them or the person about whom they are concerned. Call 268-6400 or (800) 753-HOPE, ext. 400, for more information about the screening program.

The Steps to Recovery Program is a six-week-long intensive outpatient chemical dependency program that includes mandatory weeknight and Saturday morning sessions designed to help people recover from an addictive disease.

Photo: Wilson Francis, Natural Bridge State Resort Park

You won't have to go far to find beauty in this region.

Partial hospitalization programs include the Young Champions program for emotionally troubled teens and the Voyages, an addictive-disease day program for chemically dependent adults. These programs, scheduled for weekdays 8 AM to 4 PM, provide intensive structured activities and therapy sessions as a more inexpensive alternative to inpatient services.

Another unique Charter Ridge program is Wings, which ministers to the spirit, soul and body using the spiritual resources of the Christian faith in conjunction with medical and psychiatric services. (Charter Ridge is nonsecular. Only Wings is religion based.)

Eastern State Hospital
627 W. Fourth St. • 255-1431

The second-oldest state psychiatric hospital in the country, Eastern State Hospital opened in Lexington on May 1, 1824. The hospital provides psychiatric and medical services to adults from 74 counties in Central and eastern Kentucky.

People dealing with emotional problems are usually referred to Eastern State from other state or community agencies, private physicians, individuals and families. Many patients are first evaluated by local comprehensive-care centers (see the listing for Bluegrass East Comprehensive Care Center in this chapter).

The hospital provides treatment regardless of an individual's ability to pay for services. If Medicare, Medicaid or private insurance is not available to pay for hospitalization, fees are charged on a sliding scale.

Eastern State Hospital's services are concentrated in three main treatment programs. The Intensive Treatment Service emphasizes very focused short-term therapy with a quick return to the community — usually in about 30 days. For longer-term stays, patients may be placed in the Psychiatric Rehabilitation Service, which uses such therapy techniques as milieu therapy, group therapy and community involvement. Finally, the Medical and Extended Care Service is designed for those patients — typically geriatric patients — who require close supervision and medical attention while being hospitalized for psychiatric illness.

About 60 percent of those people discharged from Eastern State are able to live in their own homes or the home of a family member. Others are placed in halfway houses or other institutions. Eastern State employs about 500 full- and part-time staff members.

Veterans Affairs Medical Center
2250 Leestown Rd. • 233-4511
Cooper Dr. • 233-4511

The Veterans Affairs Medical Center provides inpatient and outpatient care to U.S. veterans from the area. This modern tertiary-care facility comprises two divisions — the Leestown Road and Cooper Drive complexes — with a total of 720 hospital beds. The medical center also has a 100-bed nursing home.

Special patient care programs include substance-abuse treatment, open-heart surgery, hospital-based home care, geriatric evaluation and rehabilitation, prosthetics, kidney dialysis, audio and speech pathology, nuclear medicine and women's health services, including mammography.

The more than 1,800 employees of the medical center are dedicated to providing quality healthcare to 132,000 outpatient visitors and 8,500 inpatients each year. The medical center serves the needs of veterans in Central and eastern Kentucky as well as portions of Ohio, West Virginia and Tennessee.

Research is an integral part of the medical center's activities. An annual budget of $3.5 million supports more than 300 medical research projects, allowing the VA Medical Center to recruit and retain some of the region's most outstanding physicians and medical personnel.

Shriners Hospital for Children — Lexington
1900 Richmond Rd. • 266-2101

One of 19 such orthopedic hospitals operated worldwide by the Shriners, an international fraternity, the Lexington Shriners Hospital for Crippled Children provides treatment for a variety of orthopedic problems free of charge to children up to the age of 18.

The hospital works with orthopedic problems such as scoliosis (curvature of the spine), orthopedic complications of cerebral palsy, limb deficiencies and growth problems, spina bifida with myelodysplasia (paralysis of arms and legs caused by congenital

Numbers to Call

Emergency Medical Service, police or fire department	911
Abuse Hotline	(800) 752-6200
Alcoholics Anonymous	276-2917
Ask-A-Nurse, St. Joseph Hospital's 24-hour confidential information and referral service	278-3444
Crisis Intervention	233-0444 or (800) 928-8000
Hospice of the Bluegrass	276-5344
Kentucky AIDS Hotline	(800) 654-AIDS
Kentucky Council on Child Abuse	276-1299
Kids Central after hours medical treatment at Central Baptist Hospital, by appointment only	275-6433
Poison Control	(800) 722-5725
Rape Crisis Center	253-2511
University of Kentucky Twilight Children's Clinic, by appointment only	257-6370

misdevelopment of the spine and spinal nerves), club foot and dislocated hip, rickets and leg-length discrepancies. The hospital also treats children with orthopedic problems that are the result of scarring and deformity from severe burns.

The Shriners Hospital emphasizes a family-centered treatment approach that focuses on both the healing of the body through medicine and the healing of the mind and spirit.

Bluegrass East Comprehensive Care Center
201 Mechanic St. • 233-0444

As the only full-service mental-health center in Lexington, Comprehensive Care serves people of all ages and income levels. It treats a wide range of mental health problems.

Mental health services offered by Comprehensive Care include prevention and education programs, outpatient counseling and residential treatment programs. Services provided by the center are located in schools, the criminal justice system, businesses, industries, churches and homes. The center operates Monday through Friday 8 AM to 5 PM and evenings by appointment. Appointments are necessary for those seeking service from the center. Comprehensive Care's staff of trained professionals includes psychologists, psychiatrists and physicians, social workers and nurses.

Individual, family and group counseling is available, as are psychiatric evaluation services, specialized programs for teens and support groups.

Comprehensive Care also operates a 24-hour-a-day crisis intervention hotline: 233-0444, or (800) 928-8000 outside the Lexington service area. More than 28,000 callers use this service each year.

Comprehensive Care facilitates and works with a number of other special programs in Lexington, ranging from drug and alcohol programs to intensive programs for children with long-term serious emotional problems. Call for a brochure detailing the services available. Treatment fees may be adjusted according to family size and income level.

Hospice of the Bluegrass
2312 Alexandria Dr. • 276-5344

Providing compassionate care for terminally ill patients and their families and providing a way for people to die at home with dignity, love and care is the Hospice of the Bluegrass's mission. In-home care for terminally ill people is provided through a multidisciplinary team of volunteers, physicians, nurses, social workers, home-care aides and clergy members who attend to the spiritual, emotional and physical needs of patients. A number of support groups for family members and caregivers complement Hospice's efforts to offer services to the whole family. Hospice of the Bluegrass and its satellite programs serve 20 counties.

A special facility called the Hospice Care

Urgent Treatment Centers

Fayette Place ....(606) 245-4882
4001 Nicholasville Road
8 a.m.-8 p.m. Mon.-Fri.; 8 a.m.-6 p.m. Sat.

Lansdowne ....(606) 269-4668
1055 Dove Run Road
8 a.m.-10 p.m. Mon.-Sun.

North Park ....(606) 254-5520
1498 Boardwalk
8 a.m.-8p.m. Mon.-Fri.; 8 a.m.-6p.m. Sat.

Park Hills ....(606) 272-4882
3174 Custer Drive
8a.m.-8p.m. Mon.-Fri.; 8 a.m.-6 p.m. Sat.

Frankfort ....(502) 227-4882
1230 U.S. 127 South
8 a.m.-8p.m. Mon.-Fri.; 8 a.m.-6 p.m. Sat.;
12:30-5:30 p.m. Sun.

Georgetown ....(502) 868-7500
100 Eastside Drive, Suite 2
8 a.m.-8 p.m. Mon.-Fri.; 8 a.m.-6 p.m, Sat.

Nicholasville ....(606) 885-2882
976 N. Main Street
8 a.m.-8 p.m. Mon.-Fri.; 9 a.m.-5p.m, Sat.
Occupational Medicine, Mobile Services,
Administrative Offices ....(606) 273-8882

UTC
Urgent Treatment Centers *A UK HealthCare Affiliate*

Center is a 12-bed unit in St. Joseph Hospital which provides acute care for Hospice patients for symptom control so that the patient doesn't have to be admitted to the main hospital. The Hospice Care Center is decorated more like a home — with pullout couches and a family kitchen. Pets are even allowed to visit.

Urgent Treatment Centers

Most of us are familiar with the scenario. You twist an ankle and it swells up double-size, cut a finger deeply enough that you're sure it needs stitches - or one of the kids develops a painful earache. It's 5:30 PM and your regular doctor's office has just closed. Or it's Saturday and there's no chance of seeing your doctor.

Enter Urgent Treatment Centers, walk-in medical emergency treatment facilities which are located around the Lexington area, as well as in Nicholasville, Georgetown and Frankfort

Since 1982, UTC's have operated with one goal in mind: To provide access to affordable, convenient health care services with extended hours.

UTC's are equipped to handle most minor emergencies (with the exception of heart attack or stroke victims who should call 911 or go to the nearest hospital emergency room). They also offer physical examinations for school or sports programs, and can even serve as a patient's primary care provider. In addition, UTC's provide industrial and occupational medical services to the more than 2,000 companies throughout central Kentucky.

Call the UTC nearest you for specific hours.

Alternative Healthcare

Lexington Wellness Center
2891 Richmond Rd., Ste. 202 • 269-7456

The Lexington Wellness Center provides activities and educational programs which promote healthy lifestyles, wellness and self-care — with stress management being high on the list of requests. A rundown of classes includes yoga, tai chi and chi gong, reiki, massage, vegetarian cooking and introductory classes to acupuncture, homeopathy and naturopathy. Call for a class schedule and newsletter.

Bluegrass Holistic Health Network
2312 Alexandria Dr. (meeting place)
• 278-2097

Started by two nurses and now merged with the Alternative Practitioners Group, this organization meets the second Tuesday of each month with a featured speaker. Call for information or to subscribe to their newsletter.

Several large employers, such as Toyota Manufacturing in Georgetown and the University of Kentucky, have highly rated on-site child-care facilities.

Schools and Day Care

The schools in Greater Lexington are generally among the top academic performers in a state that, as a whole, is seeking ways to provide a better, more rounded education for everyone. Most public schools in the region, and many private ones, are accredited by the Southern Association of Colleges and Schools.

This chapter looks at educational options in Fayette County and in the surrounding counties of Madison, Jessamine, Woodford, Franklin, Scott, Bourbon and Clark. We'll also give you an idea of where to look for day care for preschool children.

Before you enroll your child in school in the Lexington area, or anywhere else in Kentucky, you should know a little about the Kentucky Education Reform Act, or KERA. The Kentucky Supreme Court declared the state public school system unconsitutional in 1989 because of inequities in financial resources between districts such as Lexington and Louisville, which have a broad economic base from which to draw operating money, and smaller rural districts that do not.

KERA, passed by the Kentucky General Assembly in 1990, primarily establishes performance outcomes for all students and requires schools to ensure that all students successfully meet these outcomes. Major provisions of the reform act include school-based decision-making councils that allow parents and teachers to become more actively involved in determining how individual schools are run. A newly established Primary Program replaces kindergarten through grade 3 with ungraded primary school, a structure that allows students to progress at individual rates.

Other KERA provisions include incorporating technology and family resource and youth services centers into the school setting. In addition, the law requires school districts to raise property or other taxes to a minimum rate to pay for better schools.

The reason you should be familiar with KERA is that it not only significantly affects your child's educational experience, both structurally and philosophically, but it is also being looked at nationally as a model for school reform. Plus, everyone's always talking about it. Change almost always brings controversy, and KERA is definitely about change.

Enrollment

Children who are 4 years old before October 1 of the year they are entering school are eligible for the preschool program, as are children ages 3 through 5 with special needs who would benefit from an early intervention program. School attendance is compulsory in Kentucky for students ages 6 through 16. Children must be 5 years old on or before October 1 of the year they enroll to be eligible for the Primary Program. Any child who becomes 6 years old on or before October 1 must enroll for that school year.

Immunizations and Medical Exams

All children entering school are required by Kentucky state law to present a valid immunization certificate upon registration. Students must be immunized against polio, diphtheria, tetanus, rubella (German measles), and rubeola (red measles).

All students entering the 6th grade are required to have a second measles/mumps/rubella vaccination before the beginning of school. Additionally, each child enrolling for the first time must be tested for tuberculosis within one year before registration. All first-time enrollees (including transfer students) must have a medical examination within six months prior to or one month following admission. Students entering the 6th grade must have another examination before the start of school.

Fayette County

Fayette County Public Schools
701 E. Main St. • 281-0100

About 32,500 students were enrolled in the Fayette County Public Schools for the 1997-98 school year. The school system, formed by the merger of the county and city districts in 1967, includes 34 elementary schools (including the two newest, Rosa Parks Elementary and Veterans Park Elementary, which opened in the fall of 1997), 11 middle schools for grades 6 through 8, 5 high schools, 17 magnet schools or programs and 3 alternative schools.

About 2,200 teachers and 1,400 other personnel were employed in the system during the 1997-98 school year. Nearly 1,600 of the teachers had earned their master's degrees, and about one-third that many had their Rank I, which is 30 graduate hours beyond the master's degree. Sixteen had earned their doctorates.

Fayette County public school students consistently score above state and national averages on the SAT and ACT, and more than 72 percent of high school graduates continue on to college. An average of 34 students qualify each year as National Merit Semifinalists. All schools in the system feature a wide range of academic offerings, with a variety of extracurricular activities including athletics. Fayette

FYI

If no area code is given, it's a local call from Lexington-Fayette County. If an area code is given, whether it's 606 or 502, it's a long-distance call: dial 1, the area code and the number. See the How To Use This Book chapter for detailed information on calling.

schools have long been noted for their academic and athletic excellence. To graduate from high school in Fayette County Public Schools, students must complete a minimum of 20 units in grades 9 through 12. Twelve units must be completed in required subjects including language arts, mathematics, biological and physical sciences, social studies, health and physical education; while eight units must be completed in elective subjects.

A systemwide partnership program pairs more than 56 businesses with Fayette schools, allowing business representatives to share their knowledge with students.

The Fayette County Public Schools system is governed by a five-member board of education. School board members are elected to four-year terms. The school year ordinarily runs from the end of August to the end of May

Grading Periods

The Fayette County public elementary school year is divided into four nine-week grading periods, with reports sent home at the end of each period. Middle school students get interim reports every 4½ weeks and regular report cards every nine weeks. High school students get a report card at the end of each of two semesters; interim reports are sent on either a six- or a nine-week basis, depending on the school.

A Continuous Progress Report is sent home when the academic performance of a student falls by one letter grade or more or begins at an unacceptable level (D or F).

Special Schools and Programs

In addition to regular programs, Fayette County has 20 magnet schools and programs that focus on students with special abilities and interests: visual and creative arts, foreign language, math and other subjects. Most

Photo: YWCA

The YWCA of Lexington sponsors all kinds of programs for kids.

students who get accepted in the programs perform well. However, some parents, staff and school board members question whether magnet programs are serving students equitably.

Entrance to a magnet program - which has a limited number of slots - is attained by application in the fall, and students are usually selected on the basis of grades, abilities and an interview. High standards of conduct, performance and adherence to dress codes are upheld, and most students can expect to have up to three hours of homework nightly. There have also been complaints concerning students who live in a neighborhood close to a magnet school, but don't have the qualifications for acceptance - or simply don't desire to attend a magnet program.

In November of 1998, the Fayette County Board of Education approved a controversial measure that dropped admission requirements for sixth grade students who live near one of the oldest magnet programs, Lexington Traditional Magnet School. Of course, those students must maintain a C grade average, adhere to the dress code and exhibit good behavior to stay in the school. A measure was

also approved to bus children who live in an magnet school's attendance area to an optional school out of their neighborhood. Strict evaluations of magnet programs are expected to continue for the next few years. For information about the magnet programs call 281-0123. There are also schools for students with special interests or needs.

Eastside Center for Applied Technology
2208 Liberty Rd. • 252-4464
Southside Center for Applied Technology
1784 Harrodsburg Rd. • 278-0470

The Eastside Center for Applied Technology and the Southside Center for Applied Technology provide vocational and technical training for high school students in Fayette, Jessamine, Scott and Woodford counties. Students attend the technology center for half the day and their home school for the other half. Program areas include applied communications, applied mathematics, applied physics, auto-body repair, auto mechanics, aviation, carpentry, electricity, electronics, health services, heating and air conditioning, horticulture, machine tool technology, masonry, plumbing and welding.

Central Alternative School
120 Walton Ave. • 281-0322

The Central Alternative School, adjacent to the Central Office building, the main administrative building for Fayette County Public Schools serves middle and high school students who cannot function at the best of their ability in a regular school program and would benefit from individualized instruction. Central Alternative is set up for education and assessment of a diverse population, with 11 self-contained classrooms usually divided by age group and class level. The school emphasizes basic academic skills, and students who meet the criteria have the opportunity to attend one of the applied technology schools.

The Fayette School
301 W. Fourth St. • 233-7718

The Fayette School is designed to serve middle and high school students with severe emotional or behavior problems. The school emphasizes the development of appropriate social skills while providing individualized and small-group academic instruction. When students have made significant progress, they may return to their home school.

Fayette County High School
400 Lafayette Pkwy. • 281-0350

Fayette County High School is dedicated to providing nontraditional educational opportunities for students with special needs. The flexibility of the instructional program supports the school's philosophy that all students are entitled to a high-quality education and an opportunity to receive a standard high school diploma. The school offers after-school tutoring, Saturday school and year-round school. To gain admission, a student must be promoted to the 9th grade or have passed the 8th-grade equivalency test. He or she must also have dropped out of school, be documented as a potential dropout or be on academic probation.

Private and Parochial Schools in Fayette County

While there are many excellent educational opportunities available in the public school system, many parents choose to send their children to private or parochial schools, which offer special programs or special emphases, such as Bible study or performing arts. Fayette County's 13 private and parochial schools enroll more than 4,000 students. We have included information about several of Lexington's bigger private schools.

The Lexington School
1050 Lane Allen Rd. • 278-0501

The Lexington school, founded in 1959, is a private coed school for preschool through 9th grade. The school stresses a traditional curriculum with a fine-arts and performing-arts component. Small, self-contained classes and a 13,000-volume automated library are among the strong points of the school. The Lexington School fields interscholastic soccer, basketball and tennis teams, and the athletic program has a no-cut policy, which means everybody gets the chance to play. In the upper school (grades 7 through 9) the course of study is high school and college preparatory, with lab-based science courses and sequential courses in art, music and drama. The school enrolls about 485 students, and testing is required for admission.

Bluegrass Baptist School
1330 Red River Dr. • 272-1217

About 190 students attend Bluegrass Baptist, which was established in 1969 for preschool through 12th grade education. The school offers a traditional curriculum with a Christian emphasis. An interview is usually required prior to admission.

Lexington Catholic High School
2250 Clays Mill Rd. • 277-7183

With an enrollment of 580 students, Lexington Catholic ranks as the largest of Lexington's private and parochial schools.

Sayre School

Established 1854

"Education of the widest range and highest order"

Independent • Co-educational • College Preparatory

Grades Preschool through Twelve

❏ Small Class Size

❏ Athletic Teams

❏ College Placement

❏ SAT/ACT Scores above National/State Averages

194 North Limestone Street
Lexington, Kentucky 40507

(606) 254-1361
Fax: (606) 231-0508

Open to students in grades 9 through 12, the school stresses a precollege curriculum. Freshmen are required to take a placement test. Interscholastic sports, such as basketball and soccer, and other extracurricular activities play a big role in students' lives. The school was established in 1951.

Mary Queen of the Holy Rosary
2501 Clays Mill Rd. • 277-3030

Established in the early 1960s, Mary Queen of the Holy Rosary serves students in kindergarten through the 8th grade. Nearly 500 students are enrolled, mainly from parish families.

The Lexington Christian Academy
570 Delzan Place. • 223-8502

Lexington Christian Academy stresses a strong academic curriculum combined with a spiritual perspective. Bible-based principles are incorporated into the entire academic experience for students in preschool through 12th grade. As for extracurricular activities, students can participate in basketball, baseball, soccer, tennis, golf and swimming. Students attend a weekly chapel service and follow a strict dress code. Lexington Christian Academy's high school students moved into a new $10 million building in early 1999. Other students attend classes at different locations in the Lexington area.

Trinity Christian Academy
3900 Rapid Run Rd. • 271-0079

Trinity Christian Academy, established in 1988, offers students in kindergarten through the 8th grade a Bible-based Christian education. An interview and testing are required for admission. The school has a basketball team for boys in grades 5 through 8.

Sayre School
194 N. Limestone St. • 254-1361

Established in Lexington in 1854, Sayre School is one of the oldest schools in the Southeast. Since its inception, Sayre has continued to cement its reputation as one of the finest coeducational college preparatory

INSIDERS' TIP

The first public schools in Lexington opened in the 1830s. Lexington's newest elementary schools, opened in the fall of 1997, are Rosa Parks Elementary, off Harrodsburg Road, and Veterans Park Elementary, off Tates Creek Road.

schools in the area. About 600 students attend Sayre in programs from pre-school (age three) to senior high.

Sayre students receive a well-rounded education that emphasizes college preparation but also includes athletics, fine arts and community service. Students are actively involved in community service projects at the middle and upper school levels.

Small class size, Honors and Advanced Placement classes, individual attention and an open athletic policy that ensures all children can participate in athletics are just a few of the things that make Sayre special.

Sayre School has a selective admissions policy. Appointments for screenings are arranged after an application is received.

Madison County

Madison County
Board of Education
550 South Keeneland Dr., Richmond
• **(606) 624-4500**

The Madison County School System, which serves 8,000 students from kindergarten through grade 12, plus about 240 in the Early Childhood Program, has gained a reputation for progressiveness in placing technology in its schools. The district has one of the largest computer inventories in the state, based on enrollment, and hopes to provide one computer for every six students by the end of the 1997-98 school year. The school system is made up of eight elementary schools, three middle schools and two high schools, and it employs nearly 600 teachers and administrators and 400 classified employees.

Students in kindergarten through grade 5 are provided with a broad foundation in reading, language arts, arithmetic, social studies and science. Each school has a full-time guidance counselor, librarian, music teacher and physical education teacher. Itinerant teachers in art, gifted/talented, band and speech also

serve each school. A half-day early childhood program is available for 4 year olds who qualified under the free-lunch program or are handicapped. Other offerings include special education classes, a Title I instructional program, a migrant education program and intramural sports.

Middle school students take courses in science, social studies, mathematics, language arts, reading, physical education, art, computer science, technology education, home economics, Spanish and music. Other activities include choral music, band, intramural and interscholastic sports, drama, applied arts, academic competition and various clubs. High school students, grades 9 through 12, can choose from a wide range of courses, including more than 75 elective classes, and vocational and career offerings. Requirements include language arts, science, social studies, mathematics, health and physical education. Many extracurricular activities are also available.

Jessamine County

Jessamine County School System
501 East Maple St., Nicholasville
• **885-4179**

Enrollment growth has been rapid for the Jessamine County School System, with an average increase of 100 students a year during the last 25 years. As a result, the district has made significant expansions and renovations to a number of schools, opened a new middle school and, in September 1995, started construction on a second high school (still unfinished at this writing). When that school is completed, there will be five elementary, two middle and two high schools, as well as an alternative high school. More than 6,000 students were enrolled in the district for the 1996-97 school year, with 413 teachers and administrators and 420 classified personnel. More than three-quarters of the faculty have a master's

INSIDERS' TIP

Children love feeding breadcrumbs to the ducks and geese that live in front of Lexington Mall on Richmond Road.

degree, and more than a quarter have completed at least 30 hours of additional study. School staff have captured 18 state professional awards since 1980.

Curriculum-resource teachers work in every school to provide ongoing training and daily support to teachers and administrators. Training has focused on effective teaching strategies and standards-based instruction. One of the district's goals for professional development is to provide opportunities for teachers to become experts in areas of interest and to share expertise with other teachers. Each elementary school has a full-time guidance counselor, art, music and physical education teacher as well as its own academic competition team. Both middle schools offer state-of-the-art technology programs and use technology as a learning tool. Accelerated classes are offered in language arts, social studies, math and sciences. The high school program offers advanced placement courses in English, biology, U.S. history, calculus, Spanish and French. Vocational programs include power mechanics, graphic arts, business, agriculture and home economics.

The Independent High School, opened in January 1989, offers an alternative setting to reduce the dropout rate and to offer an opportunity for previous dropouts to complete their education. A child-care program provides parenthood instruction and a nursery for teenage mothers who wish to complete their education.

Woodford County

Woodford County Board of Education
131 Maple St., Versailles • 873-4701

The Woodford County School System, with four elementary schools, a middle school and a high school, served 3,825 students during the 1996-97 school year. As with many school systems in Central Kentucky, Woodford is putting a great emphasis on technology and computers, with one computer per classroom at all schools, CD-ROM resources at all schools and Internet access at the high school. Special programs include English as a Second Language, head start/preschool, gifted education services and a school-to-work program designed to prepare all students for the workforce.

Woodford County High School's programs include a conventional college preparatory program with advanced placement courses and a gifted and talented program. The Tech Prep program focuses upon child care, health careers, business and office, vocational studies and others. Electives include band, chorus, media, home economics, art, vocational education and agriculture.

Franklin County

There are two public school systems in Franklin County: the Franklin County Public School System and Frankfort Independent Schools.

Franklin County Board of Education
916 East Main St., Frankfort
• (502) 695-6700

About 6,200 students were enrolled during 1996-97 in the Franklin County Public School System's six elementary schools, two middle schools and two high schools. The district also includes a vocational/technical school for high school students, a comprehensive community education program, a magnet school for gifted and talented students, a family resource center, an alternative education school and an extensive adult education program. The elementary schools have classes ranging from traditional, structured settings to open-space classrooms. Teachers are assisted by specialized instructors in such disciplines as art, music and physical education. The two middle schools parallel the elementary schools in classroom structure and services. The two secondary schools provide wide and varied curricula to prepare each student for adult life, whether he or she plans to attend college or immediately enter the work force after graduation. The district employs 425 professionals, including a psychologist, educational diagnostician, computer coordinator and writing program coordinator.

Frankfort Independent School System
315 Steele St., Frankfort • (502) 875-8661

The Frankfort Independent School System, with about 125 employees, serves 900 students at three schools. The Second Street School, for early childhood through eighth grade, offers enclosed classrooms, a fully automated media center and a networked computer lab. In addition to traditional subjects, the curriculum includes extensive instruction in the fine arts. Frankfort High, which serves grades 9 through 12, has a teaching staff of about 20 and also has visiting educators. It offers advanced placement classes and networked technology in every classroom. Two out of three graduating seniors go on to post-secondary education, and the school offers tens of thousands of dollars in scholarships each year.

Scott County

Scott County Schools
2168 Frankfort Pk., Georgetown
• 863-3663

Scott County schools continue to make great strides toward improving the quality of educational opportunities in their community. Enrollment during the 1995-96 school year was 5,076 students at six elementary schools, two middle schools and one high school. These students were served by 372 teachers and administrators — for an impressive professional-staff/student ratio of 14 to 1 — and 368 other support personnel. Scott County High

School was formed during the 1950s by the merger of five smaller community high schools. During the 1970s, the Georgetown City School System merged with the county school system, combining Georgetown High School into Scott County High School and adding an elementary and a middle school.

A new $17 million, geothermally heated and cooled high school building was completed for the 1996-97 school year. The new facility has interactive video teleconferencing capability throughout the building, allowing the school to link up with any other site that has similar technology. New academic programs have also been added in medical services, construction trades and manufacturing and communications, augmenting a curriculum that includes 11 advanced placement classes, five foreign languages, group piano lessons, music theory and agri-science.

When the new high school was completed, Scott County Middle School moved into the old high school building and the old middle school building became a 9th grade high school next to the new high school. Preschool programs are available at four locations in the county. The district also has gained attention for its Community/Adult Education Program, voted the state's best in 1993-94.

Bourbon County

There are two public school systems in Bourbon County: the Bourbon County School system and the Paris Independent School District.

Bourbon County Board of Education
3343 Lexington Rd., Paris • (606) 987-2180

The history of the Bourbon County school system as been one of constant evolution and adaptation to the changing educational needs of the community it serves. From one- and two-room schools in the 1850s, through numerous expansions, relocations and

---

INSIDERS' TIP

For a lunchtime treat with kids, pack a lunch and eat in front of the fountain at Triangle Park downtown. The Lexington Children's Museum is just across the street.

consolidations, the system has grown into its present situation with four elementary schools, one middle school and one high school. About 2,700 students were enrolled during the 1996-97 school year in the district, which enjoys pupil/teacher ratios ranging from 16-1 to 18-1. Each elementary school offers a full curriculum including basic core subjects, art and humanities, music, physical education, a library program, gifted programs, computer technology classes, an intramural sports and academics program and extended school services. These schools also have innovative, hands-on science and math programs.

Bourbon County Middle School, which underwent extensive renovation in 1995, has a new computerized media center and science labs. The middle school's core curriculum includes accelerated classes in reading, math and science; classes also are offered in industrial arts, music, band, choir, health and physical education, family living, visual arts, Spanish and computer science. All students participate in advisory classes dealing with topics such as conflict resolution, peer pressure, study skills and self-esteem.

Bourbon County High School offers advanced placement courses in math, social studies, English, biology and Spanish. Gifted and talented students have extensive opportunities to excel in their areas of talent throughout the school year and during summer break. A technology education label allows for hands-on exploration of technology careers, and a co-op program with local businesses places business students in an exploratory career setting. Multimedia and vocational agriculture programs are also available.

Paris City Board of Education
301 West Seventh St., Paris
• **(606) 987-2160**

The Paris Independent School District is small, with fewer than 1,000 students, but it can point with pride at a number of champion-

ship academic and athletic teams, including three undefeated state football championship seasons. Today, all three schools use instructional strategies such as cooperative learning, thematic and collaborative teaching and curriculum integration. Opportunities include advanced placement and gifted programs; Latin, French and Spanish courses; interdisciplinary middle school instruction; computer programming instruction; programs for handicapped and at-risk children; extensive vocational programs; and numerous extracurricular activities.

Clark County

Clark County Board of Education
1600 West Lexington Ave., Winchester
• **(606) 744-4545**

The Clark County School System, with eight elementary schools, two middle schools and one high school, consists of about 5,400 students. The Clark County Vocational Extension Center serves students from the high school, and an alternative school program is available for middle school and senior high students. About 370 teachers and administrators and 360 support personnel are employed by the district, and more than two-thirds of the teachers have advanced degrees. The system has a number of programs for students in all areas of special education, including itinerant teachers, resource rooms and special classes for the disabled.

Education Services

Stanley H. Kaplan Educational Center Ltd.
2201 Regency Rd. • **276-5419**

The oldest and largest standardized test and licensure preparation service in the United States, Kaplan Educational can help you get ready to score well on a wide range of standard

---

INSIDERS' TIP

To help parents find good child care, the Better Business Bureau of Central Kentucky suggests picking out a facility, then interviewing the parents of three children who attend that center.

admission tests, from the ACT and SAT to the MCAT (medical school) and GRE (graduate school). Kaplan Educational can also help students prepare for the NCLEX (RN board review), LSAT (law school admission test) and GMAT (business school admission test).

Kaplan offers both live and videotaped classes.

College and School Planning Services
628 North Broadway • 258-9168

Owner Rose M. Lucas and Dr. Garland Niquette, a licensed psychologist, offer a PSAT/ACT/SAT preparation course limited to 12 people per class. Niquette also offers assessment and analysis of educational needs on an individual basis. Lucas also offers planning for college, preparatory school, graduate school and alternative education placement.

Child Care

The good news is, Lexington has about 139 licensed day-care centers, 49 certified family child-care homes and 10 licensed child-care homes. The bad news is, many of the most popular and well-established facilities have waiting lists, and it's always more difficult to find care for an infant. But many new national child-care franchises have opened their doors in Lexington, and a spot-check in April of 1997 showed some vacancies. Check the Yellow Pages in the phone book for a complete listing.

Kentucky recognizes four basic categories of day-care services. Nonregulated-care facilities are usually private homes that care for three or fewer unrelated children. Certified family day-care homes are for one to six children. Type 2 facilities are licensed family day-care homes that can accommodate seven to 12 children, and Type 1 licensed family day-care facilities are for 12 or more children.

On-site employer-sponsored day care is not as widespread in Lexington as it is in many other cities, but several large employers, such as Toyota Manufacturing in Georgetown and the University of Kentucky, have highly rated on-site facilities.

A number of Lexington churches, and several local hospitals including Saint Joseph and Central Baptist, have state-of-the-art day-care centers. Additionally, the YMCA of Central Kentucky holds after-school programs in area schools for older children.

The Child Care Council of Kentucky
880 Sparta Ct. • 254-9176

The Child Care Council of Kentucky, a non-profit agency, can help refer parents to the child-care facilities that best suit them and their situation. Carolyn Covington, director of the Child Care Council, said her agency answers 3,000 information calls per year. The majority of people who contact the council are new parents, parents of preschool-age children, and people who are just moving into the area.

When parents call the council for help, staff members ask them for information about their geographic location, their work location, and the ages of their children. The council staff then searches through a database that contains all the licensed and certified facilities in a 17-county area and gives the parents a list of facilities that matches their needs.

Covington added, however, that the Child Care Council does not make recommendations or referrals: It simply tries to help parents meet their day-care needs. If you want to check out a particular day-care center, you can call the Division of Licensing in Frankfort and they'll tell you if any complaints have been made about that center. For information about a licensed family day-care home call (502) 564-2890. For information about any other type of center call (800) 421-1903.

The Child Care Council is also an excellent resource for child-care providers. Each year, it provides training and technical assistance to 2,000 caregivers in Central Kentucky. A resource library at the council which contains many of the most up-to-date child-care books and resources is available for use by the public.

The Council is open Monday through Friday, from 8 AM to 5 PM.

Public After-School Programs

Nearly all Fayette County Schools have enrichment programs or a Creative Activities Program (CAPS) that costs about $5 per day for children in kindergarten through fifth grade. Parents who need time to get to work can drop off children up to an hour before school starts and the programs last from after school until 6 PM. Information is available at each school.

Sick and Respite Care

Caretenders
2432 Regency Rd. • 276-5656

Daycare centers do not allow sick children to attend. If working parents have an urgent need for care for a sick child, Caretenders, a highly respected personal care center for adults and children, can provide a babysitter or nursing care. Expect to pay about $10 an hour, more for nursing care. Call and ask for the personal care department.

Mothers Morning Out Programs

Maxwell Street Presbyterian Church
180 E. Maxwell St. • 225-9578
Porter Memorial Baptist Church
4300 Nicholasville Rd. • 272-3441
Immanuel Baptist Church
3100 Tates Creek Rd. • 266-3174
Chapel Hill Presbyterian Church
3534 Tates Creek Rd. • 272-2311

There are several Mothers Morning Out programs operating at churches in the area. There might be a waiting list, and Maxwell Street Presbyterian Church is the only one that reserves spaces for drop-ins each day. Prices and hours vary, as do sign-up procedures. Keep in mind that, in most cases, church members have first priority. Call for specific information.

Of course dads (or grandparents or anyone else responsible for child care) can participate. This program has been available in Lexington for more than 15 years, so the name is a little behind the times!

Nanny and Au Pair Services

Nanny and Au Pair services will cost more, but think of the luxury of having full-time child care in your home.

Sullivan College Professional Nanny Program
2659 Regency Rd., Office of Graduate Employment • 276-4357

Sullivan College in Lexington has a nanny program and you can get in touch with young women who have completed the Professional Nanny Program.

Au Pair In America
1002 Greenwich Ave., Greenwich, Conn. • (800) 928-7247

The young, foreign women and men who participate in the program are part of a cultural exchange program with varying degrees of experience in child care. Their ages range from 18 to 26. They are allowed to work 45 hours weekly and can take classes at a local college or university (up to six credit hours per year). Their social activities are arranged by a community counselor who lives in the Lexington area.

Babysitting

Lexington Newcomers
Catherine Nalli • 263-3556

Most parents look for someone nearby who has been recommended by a neighbor or friend to meet their child-care needs. But an option for child care — and a way to meet a lot of new people as well — is to join the Lexington Newcomers organization which includes a babysitting exchange as part of its activities. Members earn points by caring for other parents' kids and redeem those points when they need child care. If you have lived in Lexington for two years or less, you're eligible to join.

Caretenders
2432 Regency Rd. • 276-5656

If you're staying in a Lexington hotel and need a sitter, many of the larger chain hotels recommend Caretenders. They can make the arrangements for you or you can call directly. Expect to pay about $10 an hour.

Today the state's small colleges such as Berea, Centre and Transylvania University are continually ranked among the top small liberal arts schools in the nation. And the bigger universities have developed programs and areas of specialization that place them on the cutting edge of research and development.

Colleges and Universities

Insiders know that Kentucky is a great place to get a college education. Both your authors have degrees from the state (one from the University of Kentucky and the other from Eastern Kentucky University) — and just look at how much we know! Okay, we're just kidding, but one thing we have learned is that Lexington and the region are top notch in the field of higher education. Our larger universities have developed programs and areas of specialization that place them on the cutting edge of research and development. And our small colleges such as Centre and Berea College and Transylvania University are continually rated as the top liberal arts schools in the nation.

In addition, Lexington and the Bluegrass area are good places to live while going to college. We have pretty, tree-filled campuses that give students a homey feeling of being in a small town, yet there are plenty of arts and cultural and sports (boy, do we have sports!) activities going on. And don't forget we have horses, too. A surprising number of students choose UK or Midway College just so they can continue — or start — horseback riding.

Area colleges and universities are major contributors to the local economy, both through the influx of students to the area each year and through the numbers of people they draw to the Bluegrass area through special events.

There's sure to be something going on at one of our schools that will perk your interest — whether you're looking for continuing education, full-time undergraduate study, a cultural event or a team to cheer for. See for yourself . . .

Lexington Universities and Colleges

Universities

University of Kentucky
500 S. Limestone St. • 257-9000

Started in 1865 as part of Kentucky University, a land-grant institution, the University of Kentucky today has close to 70,000 students enrolled in classes at the main Lexington campus and the 14 community college campuses around the state. UK employs 1,800 full-time academic staff members, 98 percent of whom hold the highest degrees in their discipline.

UK's main campus comprises 16 colleges and schools: agriculture, allied health, architecture, arts and sciences, business and economics, communications and information studies, dentistry, education, engineering, fine arts, human and environmental sciences, law, library and information science, medicine, nursing, social work and the graduate school. Academic degrees at all levels are offered in dozens of majors.

The $58 million William T. Young Library was completed in 1998. The six-floor facility has more than 350,000 square feet and seating for 4,000 people.

UK receives national attention not only in its many fields of study but on the playing field as well. Student athletes compete in 22 sports on the national level.

The UK Wildcat basketball team, under the

direction of former Coach Rick Pitino, rarely dropped out of the Associated Press ranking of the top 10 teams across the nation. Over the years, UK has won five NCAA championships and consistently takes championship honors in Southeastern Conference competition (see our chapter on Big Blue Basketball and Other Spectator Sports).

The Wildcat teams are near and dear to the hearts of Lexingtonians, and UK fans are some of the best in the country. On game days, don't be surprised if Lexington appears to be swathed in a royal blue haze. Actually, it's Kentucky Blue, and it adorns people, cars and anything else it can be attached to, draped over or prominently displayed on. Big Blue (as the UK sports program is affectionately known) paraphernalia is hot stuff from the retail point of view.

The number of National Merit Scholars entering UK consistently ranks it among the top ten public universities in the country academically. The university presently educates about 39 percent of all the students in private and public colleges in Kentucky.

In the field of research UK maintains 23 centers which conduct applied research in areas as diverse as tobacco and health, aging, cancer, toxicology, equine health, mineral production, manufacturing systems and public policy.

All work and no play is not part of the curriculum at UK; there are 250 campus organizations students can participate in, as well as 17 sororities and 22 fraternities.

Three types of financial aid are offered at UK: aid based on financial need; unsubsidized loans not based on financial need; and aid offered on academic merit which is awarded by certain academic departments and colleges.

FYI

If no area code is given, it's a local call from Lexington-Fayette County. If an area code is given, whether it's 606 or 502, it's a long-distance call: dial 1, the area code and the number. See the How To Use This Book chapter for detailed information on calling.

Transylvania University
300 N. Broadway • 233-8242, (800) 872-6798

The oldest college west of the Alleghenies and the 16th-oldest in the country, Transylvania University consistently ranks among the best institutions of higher learning in the nation. In 1989 and 1993, *U.S. News & World Report* ranked Transylvania as the best regional liberal arts college in the South.

About 1,000 students attend Transylvania (called "Transy" by Lexingtonians), an independent liberal arts college that's associated with the Christian Church (Disciples of Christ). Among Transy's alumni are two U.S. vice presidents, 50 U.S. senators, 100 U.S. representatives, 36 governors and 34 ambassadors. Jefferson Davis (president of the Confederacy during the Civil War), noted abolitionist Cassius Marcellus Clay and Stephen F. Austin, a founder of Texas, all attended Transy.

Established in 1780 as Transylvania Seminary, the school became home to the first law and medical schools in the West in 1799. At one time, Henry Clay served as a law professor here.

Today Transy offers bachelor of arts degrees in 23 majors: art, biology, business administration, chemistry, computer science, drama, economics, education, English, French, history, human movement, mathematics, music, philosophy, physical education, physics, political science, psychology, religion, sociology, sociology/anthropology and Spanish. Students can also design their own majors with assistance from an adviser and the dean of the college they wish to study in. Advising and undergraduate preparation are available for careers in dentistry, engineering,

INSIDERS' TIP

Even if you're really a big fan of another college team, you never root for any team but the University of Kentucky Wildcats during basketball season. Go, Big Blue!

Club sports offered at Transylvania University include women's cross-country.

law, medicine, pharmacy, physical therapy and veterinary medicine. An extensive study-abroad program is also available and many students spend an academic term abroad.

Transy provides opportunities for its students to participate in a number of extracurricular activities. Transy competes nationally in the National Association of Intercollegiate Athletics (NAIA). Men's varsity sports include baseball, basketball, cross country, golf, soccer, swimming and tennis. Women's varsity sports include basketball, cross country, fast-pitch softball, field hockey, golf, soccer, swimming and tennis. About 80 percent of students participate in some form of athletics, including 20 intramural sports for men and women.

The college has more than 50 student organizations, including student government, speech and debate teams, a radio station, print publications and four national fraternities and four sororities.

A number of financial aid options are available to students, including grants, loans, work-study programs and merit scholarships.

Students come from 31 states and 10 foreign countries. The student to faculty ration is 14 to 1.

Colleges

In addition to the major institutions of higher learning, there are several business and junior colleges offering associate degree programs in everything from fashion merchandising and travel to accounting and computer programming.

Sullivan College
2659 Regency Rd. • 276-4357

With diploma and associate degree programs in accounting, computer programming, secretarial/word processing, legal secretary, paralegal, management, marketing and sales, travel and tourism and professional nanny services, Sullivan College offers Lexingtonians a convenient, quick way to work toward a better career or to improve their position in their chosen career. Newly added bachelor degree programs are offered in business management with a concentration in accounting, computers, management and marketing, along with a bachelor's degree in paralegal studies.

Among Sullivan's "perks" for students are the four-day week of classes (Friday is optional attendance and is used for catching up or more in-depth study) and a student apartment complex near campus for those students living beyond commuting distance.

The Louisville campus of Sullivan College is accredited to offer four-year bachelor's degree programs, making Sullivan the first private career college in the South to move from two-year to four-year accredited status. A master's degree in business administration has been added recently.

Kentucky College of Business
628 E. Main St. • 253-0621

An accredited junior college of business, Kentucky College of Business was founded in 1941. Today, in its efforts to prepare students for positions in a variety of business and technical careers, Kentucky College of Business offers 12 diploma and associate degree programs.

www.insiders.com
See this and many other **Insiders' Guide®** destinations online.
Visit us today!

The following programs are available: accounting, business management, fashion merchandising management, business administration, management information systems, data processing, word processing specialist, executive secretarial, legal secretarial, administrative office specialist, medical secretarial, receptionist, medical records technician, medical administrative assistant and travel and tourism specialist.

The six campuses of the Kentucky College of Business system are in Lexington, Florence, Richmond, Danville, Louisville and Pikeville.

Classes are offered on a quarterly basis, and there are a number of scholarships and financial aid options available to students to help cover tuition and other expenses.

Fugazzi College
406 Lafayette Ave. • 266-0401

Serving Lexington since 1915, Fugazzi College names small class size, coupled with a good variety of associate degree and diploma programs, among its most desirable characteristics for students.

Degree and diploma programs are offered in medical assisting, radio and television broadcasting, management, accounting, travel and tourism, medical transcription, business administration and computer application.

Fugazzi also offers students career counseling and training upon graduation and throughout their course of study. Day and evening classes are offered, and financial aid is available for those who qualify.

Other Institutions

Lexington Theological Seminary
631 S. Limestone St. • 252-0361

Originally known as the College of the Bible, Lexington Theological seminary is the oldest ministerial school of the Christian Church (Disciples of Christ). It was founded in 1865 as one of the colleges of Kentucky University.

In 1950 the College of the Bible moved to its current South Limestone Street location, and in 1965 the school changed the name it had carried for a century to Lexington Theological Seminary.

Today the school offers a number of divinity and ministry degrees and programs, including a joint divinity and social work program with the University of Kentucky. The school also offers master of divinity and master of arts degrees as well as a doctor of ministry degree. About two-thirds of the students who attend Lexington Theological Seminary are from the Christian Church (Disciples of Christ) denomination.

Lexington Theological Seminary is a member of the ecumenical Theological Education Association of Mid-America and the Appalachian Ministries Education Resources Center.

Regional Colleges and Universities

Lexington has not cornered the Central Kentucky higher education market. There are a number of nationally recognized and rated private schools and state universities located in the immediate Lexington vicinity. With the exception of Centre College in Danville, all the colleges and universities listed in the following section are located in the counties highlighted in our chapter on Lexington's Neighbors. Danville is highlighted in our Daytrips chapter.

In the early years of our country, Kentucky was a national leader in higher education, establishing many of the first colleges and universities on the western frontier. However, that reputation declined in the 20th century, and in recent years the state has struggled to reestablish its reputation for academic excellence.

The struggle has paid off. Kentucky is once again coming into its own as a national higher education leader, and the schools listed below are playing a crucial role in that effort.

Asbury College
1 Macklem Dr., Wilmore • 858-3511

Named for the famous circuit-riding preacher Francis Asbury, who became the country's first Methodist bishop, Asbury College was established in 1890.

The school is governed by a 30-member board of trustees who operate Asbury according to the principles of "entire sanctification" and "scriptural holiness" taught by the Rev. John Wesley Hughes, who established the college. Although the college is predominantly Methodist in its enrollment, it is officially nondenominational and receives neither denominational nor government support for its programs.

This private, four-year, coed liberal arts college has an undergraduate enrollment of about 1,100 students. Asbury College offers a wide range of undergraduate majors from Christian ministries and ancient languages to biology, nursing and art.

Berea College
201 N. Main St., Berea • (606) 986-9341

"Anti-slavery, anti-caste, anti-rum and anti-sin, giving an education to all colors, classes, cheap and thorough."

This was the vision the Rev. John G. Fee

had of an ideal academic institution when he founded Berea College in 1855. The famous Madison County abolitionist and politician, Cassius Marcellus Clay (cousin of Lexington lawyer Henry Clay), donated the land on which Fee built the college.

However, Fee's dream of an interracial school didn't go over too well in the tense months leading up to the start of the Civil War. He and the first Berea teachers were driven from the state just before the war began. But they were not defeated. They returned after the war and opened the Berea Literary Institute, which enrolled 96 blacks and 91 whites its first term.

Fee's vision was again stymied in 1904 when Kentucky passed the Day Law forbidding the education of whites and blacks together. This law was not amended to allow integration until 1950.

Even during the years of forced segregation, however, Berea College never stopped in its pursuit of Fee's vision. In 1904, the college founded and supported the Lincoln Institute, a separate school for blacks, near Louisville. At home, the college turned its attention to the Appalachian region, focusing its efforts on making a quality education available to needy students from the region who lacked access to such education opportunities.

Today Berea College consistently ranks among the nation's top small liberal arts colleges. Eighty percent of Berea's 1,500 students are from the southern Appalachian region, and the remaining 20 percent come from across the country and around the world.

The mission of the college — to provide a low-cost, high-quality liberal arts education within the context of the Christian faith and ethic — remains the guiding principle for the administration of the school. To be admitted, students must demonstrate financial need, and they pay no tuition. The costs for room and board are paid in large part by the money students earn in the unique college labor program, which teaches them trades and crafts-

---

INSIDERS' TIP

During the Civil War, Transylvania's buildings were taken over by the Union army and used as a hospital.

manship while allowing them to earn money to pay for the nontuition aspects of school.

Centre College
600 W. Walnut St., Danville
• **(606) 238-5350**

Nationally acclaimed Centre College in Danville has much to be proud of in its current list of alumni that includes U.S. vice presidents, chief justices of the Supreme Court, congressmen, governors and business leaders.

In fact, Woodrow Wilson once said of the school in a speech at Princeton University, "There is a little college down in Kentucky which in 60 years graduated more men who have acquired prominence and fame than has Princeton in her 150 years." It was probably not a comment that made him popular at Princeton, but it does illustrate the significant role this small Central Kentucky college has played in national higher education.

Founded in 1819, the college was named (as you might guess) for its central location in the state. Since that time, Centre has earned a national reputation for educational leadership, consistently ranking in independent surveys among the country's very best liberal arts colleges.

The Presbyterian denomination has maintained control of the school since 1824. In 1830 a new college president began a 27-year tenure that would play a decisive role in the future of the struggling school. During his presidency, John C. Young expanded the student body from just 30 students to 225.

As with most other efforts in Kentucky, however, the Civil War drastically diverted the positive expansion of the school. Enrollments sig-

Photo: Lee Thomas, Transylvania University

Computer-related courses are popular choices for students at major institutions as well as business and junior colleges.

nificantly dropped, and campus buildings were used by Confederate soldiers before the famous nearby Battle of Perryville in October 1862 and by Union soldiers after that battle.

But the college, like the state and the nation, recouped its losses in the years following the Civil War and slowly rebuilt its student body, gaining greater recognition for its academic excellence and its role as a training ground for many of the nation's future political leaders.

In October 1921, Centre gained national recognition on the athletic field when its football team defeated Harvard 6-0 in Cambridge, Massachusetts. Fifty years later, *The New York Times* called the game the football upset of the century.

Centre College became coed in 1926.

Today, the private, four-year liberal arts college enrolls about 300 new first-year students each year who enter a wide range of undergraduate programs, ranging from biochemistry and molecular biology to psychobiology, education, religion, and foreign languages. Within six months of graduation (on average), 98 percent of Centre students will either be employed or engaged in advanced study.

Centre College has grown to about 1,000 students and has further enhanced its reputation as a national educational leader. During the last decade, Centre has established national records for the percentage of alumni who make a financial contribution to the school and the college leads all state schools in terms of alumni support per student. Among the results of this recognition and support: More than 85 percent of entering students at Centre ranked in the top 20 percent of their classes. After they arrive at Centre, more than half of the students will get the opportunity to study abroad at one of the college's two international study programs in London, England, or Strasbourg, France. At the Norton Center for the Arts, located on the Danville campus, students have access to world-class art, plays, musicals, symphonies, and ballet; such events are also popular with the local community.

Eastern Kentucky University
Lancaster Ave., Richmond
• **(606) 622-1000**

Eastern Kentucky University traces its beginnings back to the normal school movement in the first years of the 20th century (a "normal school" is focused on the training of teachers and educators). In 1906, the Kentucky General Assembly passed a bill establishing the Eastern State Normal School. The school's exclusive focus on the training of teachers continued into the 1920s when it began offering four-year degrees. By the mid-1920s, enrollment had reached well over 1,000 students, and the school was renamed Eastern State Teachers College in 1930.

World War II saw Eastern's enrollment drop to a fraction of its normal number, and the campus was used for a Women's Auxiliary Army Corps training school.

However, the postwar boom years of the 1950s and 1960s saw enrollment triple, and new buildings sprang up across the campus. In 1966 the school was again renamed Eastern Kentucky University. Today EKU's enrollment comprises about 15,000 students in 150 programs offered on the Richmond campus, at three off-campus centers and throughout the state. Many EKU programs are designed to meet specific local, regional and national needs including law enforcement, allied health and nursing and education, among others.

Georgetown College
400 E. College St., Georgetown
• **(502) 863-8000, (800) 788-9985**

Georgetown College traces its history back more than 150 years to its cutting-edge position in forming the backbone of the western frontier higher education community. In 1827 Georgetown College became the first Baptist

---

INSIDERS' TIP

Some of the top football coaches in collegiate and NFL history, including Paul "Bear" Bryant, Don Shula, Howard Schnellenberger, Chuck Knox and Bill Arnsparger, were once coaches with the University of Kentucky program.

Photo: Jennifer Smith, Transylvania University

Kentucky's temperate climate makes outdoor class sessions possible.

college west of the Alleghenies and the sixth Baptist college organized in the United States.

The college flourished under the leadership of Howard Malcom of Philadelphia, who became president in 1840. He was forced to resign in 1860 because of his opposition to slavery. His successor, Duncan Campbell, presided over the school's largest graduating class in the 19th century. However, the Civil War brought a sharp end to that period of rapid growth, as the school closed shortly after the war broke out.

The small faculty struggled to reopen the school and rebuild the academic program after the war, and the school's successes, both in the classroom and on the playing field (the school football and basketball teams are among the most successful in the National Association of Intercollegiate Athletics, or NAIA), stand as a tribute to their efforts.

The 2,000-member student body at this private, four-year, coed Southern Baptist liberal arts college is drawn from around the world. The school offers 27 major programs ranging from information systems and medical technology to political science, music education and environmental science.

Kentucky State University
400 E. Main St., Frankfort
• **(502) 227-6813, (800) 325-1716**

Established in 1886 by a vote of the Kentucky legislature at the urging of the Colored Teachers State Association, Kentucky State University officially opened in 1887 as the State Normal School for Colored Persons.

In 1890 the federal government began providing for the development of land grant colleges for people of color, and the State Normal School for Colored Persons began instruction in agriculture and mechanics in order to qualify for federal money. The school changed its name in 1902 to Kentucky Normal and Industrial Institute to reflect this new diversity in its academic programs.

Because of its location in Frankfort, the state capital, and because of the governor's right to appoint the school's board of trustees who in turn appoints the college president, that position quickly became a highly political matter; the leadership of the school proved mercurial at best until the early 20th century. At that time the school's sixth president, Rufus Atwood, withdrew from the tempestuous arena of partisan politics and concentrated on forging the position of college president into a professionally legitimate office.

The school changed names again in 1926 to Kentucky State Industrial College for Negroes. During this time the school's academic standards fell to an all-time low, and the college went into debt. Atwood strove to improve the school's accreditation level, and in 1939 (after again changing its name to Kentucky State College for Negroes) it was recognized as a class A college by the Southern Association Committee on Approval of Negro Schools.

By the time Atwood retired in 1960, Kentucky State had become Kentucky's preeminent black institution of higher learning. The phrase "for Negroes" was removed from the name of the school by a vote of the state legislature in 1952, and in 1972 the Kentucky General Assembly passed legislation officially establishing Kentucky State University.

Today Kentucky State University has about 1,700 full-time undergraduate students who study a wide range of majors, from art education and criminal justice to biology and business administration.

Midway College
512 E. Stephens St., Midway • 846-5346, (800) 755-0031

As Kentucky's only college for women, Midway College was founded in Woodford County in 1847 with the express purpose of preparing financially disadvantaged women for teaching careers. It was formerly known as the Kentucky Female Orphan School.

Today equine studies and interests play a key role in the programs Midway College offers its students. The hallmark of this interest is the college's Keeneland Equine Education Center with indoor and outdoor riding facilities, along with 50 acres for cross-country riding. Midway also offers associate degrees in equine management and equine office administration.

Other associate (two-year) degrees are available in computer information systems, business administration, early childhood education, equine management, general studies (science), in-home child care, nursing, paralegal studies and physical therapist assistance.

In 1989 Midway began offering four-year bachelor of arts and bachelor of science degrees in several fields including biology, business administration, early childhood education, English, nursing, paralegal studies, psychology and teacher education. An equine studies degree is offered with a concentration in equine management or equitation instruction, along with a business administration degree with a concentration in equine business.

Midway is a private liberal arts school affiliated with the Christian Church (Disciples of Christ), and the student body comprises about 600 full-time and 350 part-time students. About 87 percent of students receive financial aid.

The morning *Herald-Leader*, which got its start in 1870 as the *Lexington Daily Press*, is the second-largest newspaper in Kentucky, covering most of the state, with a daily circulation of about 120,000 and a Sunday circulation of 162,000.

Media

Lexington's history as a communications leader dates to 1787, when John Bradford began publishing the weekly *Kentucke Gazette*, recognized as the first newspaper west of the Alleghenies. Although Bradford's background was in land surveying and he had no printing experience, he was nonetheless awarded the task of keeping the region's frontier dwellers informed as they made plans to separate from Virginia and form a new state. Ultimately the Kentuckians were successful, of course, and so was the *Gazette*, which soon learned how to spell Kentucky correctly. It continued to publish through the end of 1848.

The pioneer tradition continued with radio and television. The University of Kentucky, in conjunction with Louisville radio station WHAS, received national attention in 1929 when it began educational broadcasts from the Lexington campus to remote areas of the state. In 1940, UK started WBKY (now WUKY), the oldest university-owned, noncommercial FM station in the country. And the Lexington-based Kentucky Educational Television network, nationally recognized for its excellence, began broadcasting in 1968.

Metro Area Newspapers

Lexington Herald-Leader
100 Midland Ave., Lexington • 231-3100

The morning *Herald-Leader*, which got its start in 1870 as the *Lexington Daily Press*, is the second-largest newspaper in Kentucky, covering most of the state, with a daily circulation of about 120,000 and a Sunday circulation of 162,000. It has been Lexington's only daily newspaper since 1983, when the morning *Herald* merged with the afternoon Leader.

Although there have been periodic rumblings about starting a rival newspaper — usually following such perceived slights as an unsatisfactory report about the beloved UK Wildcats or an inflammatory Joel Pett editorial cartoon or because of the paper's "liberal" editorial policy in general — none has materialized.

Before the merger, the *Democratic Herald* and the *Republican Leader* had been owned by the same company since 1937. Since 1973 the *Herald-Leader* has been owned by Miami-based Knight-Ridder Inc., whose other papers include *The Philadelphia Inquirer*, *the Detroit Free Press* and *The Miami Herald*.

The *Herald-Leader*, which has regional bureaus throughout central and eastern Kentucky and a bureau in Washington, D.C., has won two Pulitzer Prizes. In 1985 it earned one for investigative reporting — along with the wrath of thousands of Kentucky Wildcat basketball fans — with its series detailing improper payments to UK players. Editorial writer Maria Henson received another Pulitzer in 1992 for her series of editorials on battered women. Columnists include the often controversial Merlene Davis on the lifestyles beat, Don Edwards and Dick Burdette on the metro desk, Chuck Culpepper and Billy Reed in sports and Kevin Nance on the arts.

An extensive revamping of the newspaper's format and appearance was completed in 1993, making the *Herald-Leader* more reader-friendly and giving it a special tabloid section for each day of the week. Another format update was made again in September 1997. Now, Sunday covers "Technology and Your Money"; Monday brings "Business Monday"; Tuesday has "Living Well," with a focus on health, fitness and nutrition; Wednesday is "Bluegrass Communities" day, with features on what your neighbors in Fayette and surrounding counties are doing; Thursday has "YOU," devoted to a variety of women's issues; Friday's "Weekender" gives you the information you need to make plans for your blessed days off; and Saturday's "Home and Garden" section looks at decorating, gardening and home improvement.

The Kentucky Kernel
University of Kentucky, Journalism Bldg., Lexington • 257-2871

The Kernel, the student-run newspaper of the University of Kentucky, marked its 100th anniversary in 1994 with an extensive redesign. Free copies are available in racks around campus and in selected businesses nearby. *The Kernel*, which has seen a number of its alumni go on to distinguished journalism careers, is published Monday through Friday during the regular school year and on Thursdays during the eight-week summer session.

The Richmond Register
380 Big Hill Ave., Richmond • (606) 623-1669

The Register, published daily, covers Madison County. It also includes some state, national and international news.

The Berea Citizen
711 Chestnut St., Berea • (606) 986-0959

This weekly paper, delivered by mail every Thursday, features news of Berea and other parts of Madison County.

The Jessamine Journal
507 N. Main St., Nicholasville • 885-5381

This newspaper covers Jessamine County, including Nicholasville and Wilmore and is delivered by mail every Thursday.

The Woodford Sun
184 S. Main St., Versailles • 873-4131

Established in 1869, this weekly can claim the distinction of being the oldest newspaper still being published in the Lexington metropolitan area. The paper, which covers Versailles, Midway and the rest of Woodford County, is delivered by mail every Thursday. The late Gov. A.B. "Happy" Chandler was a former president of the *Sun*.

The State Journal
1216 Wilkinson Blvd., Frankfort • (502) 227-4556

The State Journal, which comes out around noon each day except Saturday, covers local, state and national news.

The Kentucky Gazette
101 E. Main St., Frankfort • 875-8325

The Kentucky Gazette, mailed to subscribers every other Tuesday, covers state and national government, politics and business.

The Georgetown News Graphic
P.O. Box 461, Georgetown, 40324 • 863-1111

This thrice-weekly (Wednesday, Friday and Sunday) evening newspaper is the result of the merger of two weeklies. It focuses on Scott County, including Georgetown, Sadieville and Stamping Ground.

The Bourbon County Citizen-Advertiser
123 W. Eighth St., Paris • (606) 987-1870

We actually have two county newspapers here: the *Citizen*, published on Wednesday, and the *Advertiser*, published on Monday. The *Citizen* is a paid subscription newspaper delivered by mail; the *advertiser* is more ad-oriented and is mailed free to all county households.

The Winchester Sun
20 Wall St., Winchester • (606) 744-3123

This source for Winchester-Clark County news is published Monday through Saturday afternoons.

Other Publications

ACE Magazine
263 N. Limestone St., Lexington • 225-4889

"ACE" is an acronym for "Arts, Commentary and Entertainment," and that's what this twice-monthly newsprint tabloid covers, frequently with style and wit. Publisher Susan Yeary, along with two now-departed partners, bought the magazine in 1994 from founding editor Jennie Leavell. *ACE* showcases a group

---

FYI

If no area code is given, it's a local call from Lexington-Fayette County. If an area code is given, whether it's 606 or 502, it's a long-distance call: dial 1, the area code and the number. See the How To Use This Book chapter for detailed information on calling.

of local contributing writers as well as syndicated features that take a sometimes irreverent, sometimes serious look at life in the Bluegrass and elsewhere. You can pick up *ACE Magazine* for free at numerous locations around town.

The Blood-Horse
1736 Alexandria Dr., Lexington
• 278-2361

The Blood-Horse, published weekly by the Thoroughbred Owners and Breeders Association, is a slick magazine offering news, features statistics and commentary on thoroughbred breeding and racing. *The Horse*, published monthly, is devoted strictly to equine health care. Both magazines are sold at Joseph-Beth Booksellers, the Kentucky Horse Park, airport shops and various newsstands.

The Cats' Pause
2691 Regency Rd., Lexington • 278-3474

For the die-hard University of Kentucky sports fan, *The Cats' Pause* offers game recaps, recruiting news, analyses, statistics and opinions regarding UK and the Southeastern Conference. The publisher is Landmark Community Newspapers, a Shelbyville company that bought *The Cats' Pause* from Oscar Combs in 1997. Subscribers get 35 tabloid issues a year: weekly from September through March and monthly from April through August. It is sold at various newsstands throughout the state.

Central Kentucky Golf
466 Woodlake Way, Lexington
• 330-3846

Central Kentucky Golf is a tabloid with a variety of features, departments and tips for area duffers. It is published monthly from March through August, for a total of six issues a year. You can pick it up free at the public library and various courses, driving ranges and golf retail stores around town, or get a free

subscription by mailing your name and address to the publisher's office.

Community Voice Newsjournal
629 N. Broadway, Lexington • 281-1111

Community Voice, started in 1987 to provide news and commentary to the African-American Community, added a separate Hispanic-language edition in February 1997. The paper, delivered by mail to paid subscribers, can be found free at Kinko's and other selected locations around town.

Horseman & Fair World
1910 Harrodsburg Rd., Lexington
• 276-4026

This glossy weekly publication is devoted to the sport of harness racing. It is sold at the R.E. Fennell Co. tack shop on Red Mile Road.

The Kentucky Manufacturer
1084 Wellington Way, Lexington
• 223-6703

This monthly tabloid profiles successful manufacturing operations in the state, offers informative articles written by industry insiders and provides news of plant openings and expansions. The publisher, The Manufacturers Group, also puts out similar monthly publications for Ohio, Indiana and Tennessee. *The Kentucky Manufacturer* is sold at various area newsstands.

The Lane Report
269 W. Main St., Lexington • 244-3522

The Lane Report, a monthly publication subtitled "The Business & Economic News Magazine for Central Kentucky," offers analyses of relevant issues, interviews with business and political leaders, business updates, financial advice and profiles of area companies, entrepreneurs and women in business. It is sold at various bookstores and newsstands.

INSIDERS' TIP

Noah Adams, host of National Public Radio's *All Things Considered*, is a native of Ashland, Kentucky, about two hours northeast of Lexington.

Radio Free Lexington

The signal for Radio Free Lexington, a student-operated, commercial-free 250-watt station on the University of Kentucky campus, doesn't carry far beyond Fayette County. But what it lacks in broadcasting range it makes up for in musical range.

Mislabeled by some as strictly a "college" or "alternative" rock station, WRFL 88.1 FM actually offers a smorgasbord of programs catering to tastes that include blues, jazz, rap, rockabilly, folk, Celtic, reggae, world beat, metal, women's and Christian. Pick up a "Rifle Comix" program guide at assorted on-campus sites or at Cut Corner Records and other stores near campus.

You probably won't care for all the programming on WRFL, but you may find yourself planning your schedule around the programs you do like. The disc jockeys aren't professional — after all, they're volunteers — but it's the music that matters. And much of this music you're simply not going to hear on a commercial radio station.

One of Radio Free Lexington's most popular shows is *The Hot Burrito Show*, which runs Sunday from noon to 3 PM. Hosts Bobby and Rob play a wide variety of so-called alternative country, traditional country and roots music featuring artists including Steve Earle, Wilco, Buck Owens, Gram Parsons, Shaver, Dale Watson, Junior Brown, Emmylou Harris and much more.

Though there are a number of genre-specific pro-

Pat Procissi is the host of "The Hard Travelin' Revue," a folk-music show on WRFL.

grams, at other times WRFL has an open format, and the volunteer DJs are generally open to requests. In fact, you're unlikely to find any other station around here that's as likely to play your request as soon after you request it — it's often literally just a matter of minutes. See and hear for yourself by calling the station at 257-WRFL.

Lexington Kids
3529 Cornwall Dr., Lexington • 223-1765

Lexington Kids, a free, monthly, general-interest parenting magazine, includes a sports section called "Champs: Lexington's Youth Sports Report," which features game coverage and features. It is distributed to all schools and library branches in the area as well as many retail establishments around town.

The Thoroughbred Times
496 Southland Dr., Lexington
• 260-9800

The Thoroughbred Times, like *The Blood-Horse*, is a weekly publication for thoroughbred owners and breeders. As such, it has plenty of statistics on stakes races, sires and the like. It is sold at various newsstands in Lexington.

Real Estate Publications

Harmon Homes Magazine
2250 Regency Rd. • 277-9067

The Bluegrass-area edition of this free national magazine is published every two weeks and can be found near the entrances of many groceries, drugstores and shopping centers.

Lexington Apartment Guide
P.O. Box 4207, Lexington, KY, 40544
• 223-4085

Bob Culp founded this free publication, the largest apartment guide in the Bluegrass, more than 10 years ago. It consists of paid advertising by apartment communities and is available at hundreds of locations throughout a six-county area.

The Real Estate Book of Lexington
114 Dantzler Ct. • 276-3263

This free publication is available at numerous locations around town.

Television

In addition to the stations listed below, cable subscribers receive such basic channels as CNN and CNN Headline News, ESPN and ESPN2 sports programming, C-SPAN, The Discovery Channel, The Learning Channel, Arts & Entertainment, MTV, WTBS (Atlanta), WGN (Chicago), American Movie Classics, The Nashville Network, Country Music Television, Lifetime, The Family Channel, Animal Planet, Nickelodeon, The Weather Channel, The Travel Channel and The Cartoon Network.

Premium cable channels, available for an additional fee, include Home Box Office, Showtime, Cinemax, The Movie Channel, The Disney Channel, Starz and Encore. TCI, 268-1134, the local cable provider, also offers a selection of pay-per-view programs.

A note about channel designations: Cable subscribers will notice that the cable numbers assigned to channels usually do not match the channel numbers. For example, WLEX is Channel 18, but it's number 8 on cable. A channel guide is included in the *Lexington Herald-Leader* each day, and you'll also get one when you subscribe to cable.

WLEX-TV (Channel 18)
NBC affiliate

WKYT-TV (Channel 27)
CBS affiliate

WTVQ-TV (Channel 36)
ABC affiliate

www.insiders.com

See this and many other
Insiders' Guide®
destinations online.

Visit us today!

INSIDERS' TIP

ACE Magazine **is a good source of thought-provoking commentary and information about the arts and entertainment. You can pick it up for free at locations all around town.**

Photo: Lexington Herald-Ledger

WRFL-FM (88.1) is a student-operated, commercial-free station on the University of Kentucky campus that plays a wide range of music.

WDKY-TV (Channel 56)
Fox affiliate

WKLE (Channel 46)
Kentucky Educational Television/Public Broadcasting System

Radio

In most cases, radio station phone numbers listed are for request lines. Please keep in mind that radio formats do change from time to time. Note also that not all stations cover the entire Greater Lexington area.

Adult Contemporary
WMXL 94.5 FM
WGKS 96.9 FM
WKYL 102.1 FM
WKED 103.7 FM
WHAS 840 FM
WEKY 1340 AM

Country
WVLK 92.9 FM

National Public Radio
WEKU 88.9 FM (classical)
WRVG 89.9 FM (classical)
WUKY 91.3/92.1 FM (jazz, blues)

Religious
WVRB 95.3 FM (adult contemporary)
WJMM 106.3 FM (adult contemporary)
WCGW 770 AM (Southern gospel)
WCBR 1110 AM (Southern gospel)
WUGR 1250 AM (urban contemporary gospel)
WLNT 1380 AM (Christian country)
WYGH 1440 AM (Southern gospel)

Pop/Rock
WRFL 88.1 FM (modern, eclectic)
WKQQ 100.1 FM (classic and new)
WLRO 101.5 FM (classic)
WLTO 102.5 FM (oldies)
WXZZ 103.3 FM (modern)
WLKT 104.5 FM (contemporary hits)
WKYW 104.9 FM (classic)
WFKY 1490 AM (oldies)
WTKT 1580 AM (urban contemporary)

News/Talk
WLW 550/700 AM
WVLK 590 AM
WLAP 630 AM
WLXG 1300 AM

To this day, religion
plays a big role in the
lives of Lexingtonians,
who live in the "Bible
Belt" of the South.

Worship

You probably couldn't tell it from the grand old churches that highlight many of Lexington's streets and neighborhoods, but the early years of Christianity in the area were far from grandiose. Many of what are today large and prominent congregations in Lexington began in the 1700s in log cabins, makeshift buildings and even people's homes.

Lexington was part of the western frontier, and pioneer life was never a bed of roses. In fact, Kentucky's first sermon was preached in 1775 by an Episcopal priest under an elm tree at Fort Boonesborough, just south of Lexington.

Even when groups of people from the various denominations did begin to gather, they often found themselves without a "real" minister. The few preachers and priests in the region often served numerous small congregations on their "circuits." But despite the hardships, fledgling congregations under the leadership of such men as Lewis Craig, Adam Rankin, Bishop Francis Asbury, James Moore and Peter "Old Captain" Duerett clung to their beliefs and their mission to establish the churches of the future. (For more information about these influential early men of God, keep on reading.)

To this day, religion plays a big role in the lives of Lexingtonians, who live in the "Bible Belt" of the South. Baptists form the biggest group in Lexington, but they're far from the only ones. There are about 250 churches and synagogues in Fayette County, representing some 50 denominations and religious groups, from Southern Baptist, Catholic and Methodist to Baha'i, Islamic, Mennonite, Mormon and Quaker. There are churches targeted at Chinese Christians and Spanish Jehovah's Witnesses as well as a number of interdenominational and nondenominational congregations.

To find out more about specific churches and denominations, look in the phone book, check out the worship section of Saturday's *Lexington Herald-Leader* or contact the Chamber of Commerce at 254-4447.

Spiritual Pioneers

Daniel Boone might be the best-known pioneer associated with Kentucky, but his brother Squire was a pretty respected frontiersman in his own right. And you could probably call Squire Boone a spiritual pioneer as well. As a Baptist minister, he is credited not only with preaching the first sermon in what is now Louisville but also with performing the first Kentucky marriage; the wedding took place August 7, 1776, at Boonesborough.

Elder Lewis Craig, a fiery Baptist preacher from Virginia, organized one of the earliest Baptist congregations in the Bluegrass on South Elkhorn Creek in the early 1780s. He and his brother Elijah Craig were leaders of a movement of several hundred independent Baptists who fled Virginia after being persecuted for their beliefs, which ran contrary to the established Anglican church there. (Elijah Craig, incidentally, is credited by many with the invention of bourbon whiskey; both Craig brothers later became distillers.)

While we're still on the subject of Baptists, let's talk about Peter Duerett, popularly known as "Captain." Duerett, a slave who moved to Kentucky with his owners in the 1780s, organized a small Separate Baptist Church in 1785 just outside Lexington near what is now Richmond Road. A few years later he hired himself and his wife out from their owner and moved into town. In 1790, Lexingtonian John Maxwell allowed Captain some space on his land to build a cabin, and it was there, at Lexington and Euclid avenues, that the former slave established African Baptist Church, the first black Baptist church west of the Alleghenies. That church grew into Historic Pleasant Green Missionary Baptist Church, which is now at 540 West Maxwell Street.

Adam Rankin of Virginia was called to lead one of Kentucky's first Presbyterian congregations near today's Versailles. Rankin also led another Presbyterian congregation during this time, in a small log church that members built on his land.

Methodism was relatively slow to take root in Kentucky, in part because of the denomination's opposition to slavery. But Bishop Francis Asbury, leader of the movement in America, helped it spread through a system of circuit preachers who rode from settlement to settlement. He came to Lexington for a two-day conference at Kentucky's first Methodist church in 1790 and became a regular visitor to the state. Asbury College in Wilmore is named for him.

James Moore, a Virginia native, was the leader of a small group of Episcopalians who began holding services in 1796 in a makeshift frame building on the corner of what is now Market and Church streets in Lexington. He went on to become the first president of Transylvania University.

Reaching Out

Today Lexington's churches are actively involved in ministering to their community through a variety of programs. In addition to an assortment of missionary programs, common beneficiaries include Habitat for Humanity, the annual Lexington Clergy Campaign for the Homeless, Meals on Wheels and blood drives. In other outreach programs: Calvary Baptist, 150 East High Street, in cooperation

> **FYI**
>
> If no area code is given, it's a local call from Lexington-Fayette County. If an area code is given, whether it's 606 or 502, it's a long-distance call: dial 1, the area code and the number. See the How To Use This Book chapter for detailed information on calling.

with First United Methodist Church, 214 West High Street, runs the High Street Neighborhood Center, a child-care program for low-income families. First United Methodist Church supports Nathaniel Mission, which offers not only worship opportunities but also a medical and dental clinic, veterinary clinic and clothing bank for people who need these types of services but are unable to get them elsewhere.

Central Christian Church (Disciples of Christ), 205 East Short Street, sponsors a variety of service programs including the Central Church Apartments, a child-care center and an adult day-care center for senior citizens who need assistance in everyday living. First Presbyterian Church, 171 Market Street, is active in its support of the HOPE Center homeless shelter, and it also runs the Children's Learning Center, a child-care facility for inner-city kids.

Historic Pleasant Green Missionary Baptist Church, 540 West Maxwell, supports such causes as Black Achievers, Community Action and the Black Coalition. Porter Memorial Baptist Church, 4300 Nicholasville Road, provides special ministries to the handicapped and the deaf and also ministers to nursing home residents and the homeless.

Immanuel Baptist Church has sign language classes and trained interpreters that allow the church to minister to the deaf, and a Japanese worship service is offered each Sunday morning. Southern Hills United Methodist Church, 2356 Harrodsburg Road, supports Nathaniel Mission and God's Pantry, collects clothing and toys for Appalachian youngsters, and "adopts" families at Christmas.

Temple Adath Israel, 124 North Ashland Avenue, holds a huge nonperishable foods drive each fall as just one of its many efforts for social justice.

INSIDERS' TIP

The Rev. Martin Luther King Jr. spoke in Frankfort, the state capital, during a civil-rights march in March 1964.

Racial Healing

The Rev. Martin Luther King Jr. has been quoted as saying that the most segregated hour of the week is 11 o'clock Sunday morning, when people are in church. Lexington's churches are not all that different from those elsewhere in the United States, in that they are largely segregated. But more and more of them are making efforts to get together on a regular basis, if not every Sunday. Worship exchanges, interracial dialogue groups and other programs, both formal and informal, allow members of black and white churches to share faith, music, dialogue and prayers for much-needed racial and cultural understanding.

One notable exception to the segregation "rule" is Family Worship Center, a charismatic church at 3412 Clays Mill Road. It's known as one of Lexington's most integrated congregations, with its 250 or so members equally divided among blacks and whites.

Eleven downtown churches formed the Downtown Unity Task Force in 1991. The task force organizes annual congregational worship exchanges, organizes racial dialogue groups and holds an annual Martin Luther King Worship Service.

East Second Street Christian Church, a mostly black congregation at 146 Constitution Avenue, and Central Christian Church, a mostly white congregation at 205 East Short Street, have also joined for a community-wide annual celebration of King's birthday. Members of the Elkhorn Baptist Association, a group of mostly white Southern Baptist churches and missions, helped build the mostly black Morning Star Baptist Church.

Lexington's three downtown Catholic churches — mostly black St. Peter Claver and mostly white St. Peter and St. Paul — get together several times a year to share music programs. After the shooting of a black teenager by a white police officer touched off riots in 1994, about 400 people from across the city turned out when the congregations of Christ the King and St. Peter Claver invited ministers and congregations from across the city to come together and pray for understanding.

Some churches are crossing denominational "boundaries" as well. In August 1996, for example, Immanuel Baptist Church, Centenary United Methodist Church and Tates Creek Christian Church — three neighboring churches on Tates Creek Road — got together for a shared summer picnic. It was a small gesture aimed at finding the common ground rather than emphasizing the differences in doctrine and ritual.

A Joyful Noise

Music-loving churchgoers will be happy to know that Lexington's churches have a tradition of fine choirs and singing groups.

For close to 40 years, the Jimtown Male Choir — from Jimtown First Baptist Church, 2231 Jimtown Lane — has been singing traditional spirituals and hymns for audiences around the city and the region. Calvary Baptist Church, 150 East High Street, has a Sanctuary Choir that has gained regional recognition throughout the South. The choir at Immanuel Baptist Church, 3100 Tates Creek Road, performed in a presentation of Handel's Messiah at Carnegie Hall in 1988.

Christ Church Cathedral, 166 Market Street, is noted for its fine Choir of Men and Boys and its Girls' Choir, both of which are maintained in the English tradition in affiliation with the Royal School of Church Music. Southland Christian Church, 5001 Harrodsburg Road, has a music ministry that has become legendary in the area, and the church's two main special annual musical events — the Easter musical drama and the

Photo: Kentucky Department of Parks

Fort Boonesborough was the setting for Kentucky's first sermon.

Living Christmas Tree — draw standing-room only crowds.

Sin and Salvation

Many people have found ironic the fact that Lexington and the rest of Kentucky, in the middle of the Bible Belt, contribute so heavily to the liquor, tobacco and horse-racing industries. But maybe it's not so ironic after all — isn't it only natural that sin and salvation exist side by side? It's hard to have one without the other. We'll close this chapter with one particular tale of atonement.

Until the summer of 1998 the senior minister at Lexington's First Presbyterian Church was none other than Jeb Stuart Magruder. You might remember him from his previous life, during the Nixon administration. As deputy director of the Committee to Re-elect the Presi-dent, he was involved in Watergate, the 1972 scandal (a break-in at Democratic National Committee headquarters) that eventually resulted in Nixon's resignation. In 1973, Magruder pleaded guilty to conspiring to obstruct justice — by destroying records and committing perjury — in the Watergate cover-up.

After doing time in prison, the convicted felon found religion and turned his life around. He attended Princeton Theological Seminary and was ordained as a Presbyterian minister in 1981. He served as an assistant minister at a church in Columbus, Ohio, before accepting the call in 1990 to become senior minister at Lexington's First Presbyterian Church. Magruder led a resurgence at the church, increasing membership and attendance, adding a second Sunday morning service, hiring additional ministers and building a new chapel.

Index of Advertisers

Index